Indian Economy in the Globalised World

(in 2 volumes)

Indian Economy in the Globalised World

(in 2 volumes)

Edited by
M. Sarngadharan
S. Rajitha Kumar

Volume I

New Century Publications
New Delhi, India

NEW CENTURY PUBLICATIONS
4800/24, Bharat Ram Road,
Ansari Road, Daryaganj,
New Delhi-110 002
Tel.: 23247798, 65396605
Telefax: 011-41017798
E-mail: indiatax@vsnl.com
www.newcenturypublications.com

Editorial office:
34, Gujranwala Town, Part-2,
Delhi - 110 009
Tel.: 27247805, 27464774

First Published 2006

ISBN: 81-7708-126-8 (Set)
81-7708-127-6 (Volume I)
81-7708-128-4 (Volume II)

Published by New Century Publications and printed at Singhal Print Media, New Delhi -110 005

PRINTED IN INDIA

About the book

Business environment in India is changing fast, bringing new opportunities as well as posing challenges. Economic liberalisation and globalisation have created keen interest in foreign investors, resulting in comfortable foreign currency reserves, stability of Indian Rupee, vibrant stock market and expanding financial and services sector. However, the operations of multinational corporations and policies of WTO pose threats to some sectors of the Indian economy, especially to small and medium industries and agriculture.

The present work in two volumes contains articles on issues crucial to the contemporary business and economy in India. The book in two volumes contains 25 articles which have been organised into seven theme titles. Each theme title consists of papers contributed by scholars in their respective fields of specialisation. These articles replicate, verify and comprehend the procedures and results of investigations carried out by the contributors on issues of common interest.

The book highlights the challenges posed by globalisation to the agricultural sector and rural development efforts and the consequent impact on rural poverty, food security and employment opportunities. Macro and micro level observations on the above issues made in this book will give valuable insight into current issues and problems related to rural economy of India. The work is of topical interest as it covers major areas of concern with regard to globalisation and its impact on agriculture, rural industries and employment. The editors have made sincere efforts to bring out a comprehensive volume to highlight latent issues for debate among policy makers and academicians

Editors' Profile

Dr. M. Sarngadharan is Professor and Head of the Department of Commerce, University of Kerala since 1994. He secured his M.Com. degree with first class first rank from the University of Kerala (1975) and Ph. D. in Commerce from the University of Calicut (1986). He has been teaching at the post-graduate level for the past 30 years and carrying out research activities for the last 25 years. He has served as Administrator of the SNDS Trust, Sivagiri with the full powers of the Trust Board taken over by the Government of Kerala for management for two years (1997–99). He has authored 14 books and 469 articles. He has also served as Dean, Faculty of Commerce, University of Kerala and Member Senate, Cochin University of Science and Technology. Presently, he is a Member, Senate and Academic Council and Chairman, P.G. Board of Studies in Commerce, University of Kerala and Member, Curriculum Committee, VHSE, Government of Kerala under the Chairmanship of State Minister for Education. He has participated in several International Conferences and visited Spain, UK, Singapore, Malaysia and Nepal. He is the Chief Editor of *Journal of Business Studies* published from Trivandrum. He has successfully guided 26 candidates for Ph.D. degree and 102 candidates for M. Phil degree.

Dr. S. Rajitha Kumar is Lecturer in the School of Management Studies, Cochin University of Science and Technology, Kochi, Kerala. He secured his M. Com., M. Phil., and Ph. D. Degrees from the University of Kerala. He is an approved research guide in the Faculty of Social Science of Cochin University of Science and Technology. He has served as Lecturer in the Institute of Cooperative Management, Dehra Dun and Regional Institute of Cooperative Management, Bangalore. He has teaching experience of more than 8 years at the post-graduate level. He has participated and presented papers at the national and international conferences and seminars. He has published 12 research papers in leading journals.

Note on the Book by the Editors

Globalisation refers to widening and deepening of international flow of trade, capital, labour, technology, information and services. It involves liberalisation of national and global markets in the belief that it will result in higher growth rate and human welfare. Globalisation is not an end point, but a beginning for an enlarged process. It warrants liberalisation and privatisation of native economies. India too has adopted the path of liberalisation and consequently both positive and negative impacts of globalisation on the economy have been felt. It has been persistently a debatable issue over the losses and gains of globalisation on Indian economy.

Business environment in India is changing fast, bringing new opportunities as well as posing challenges. Economic liberalization and globalization have created keen interest in foreign investors resulting in comfortable foreign currency reserves, stability of Indian Rupee, vibrant stock market and expanding financial and services sector. However, the operations of multinational corporations (MNCs) and policies of (WTO) pose threats to some sectors of the Indian economy, especially to small and medium industries and agriculture.

The present work in two volumes contains articles on issues crucial to the contemporary business and economy in India. The book contains 25 articles which have been organised into seven theme headings. Each theme heading consists of papers contributed by scholars in their respective fields of specialisation. Thanks are due to all of them for their contributions and co-operation. Brief notes on each of the articles included in the present book are given in the following paragraphs.

The wood based industrial units are divided into large, medium and small on the basis of size of investments and employment. Gwalior Rayons (Grasim Ltd.) and Western India Plywood Company Ltd. are the two large sized units in the private sector and the Hindustan Newsprint Ltd., in the public sector that utilise wood as the major raw material. Travancore Plywood

Industries Ltd., and Forest Industries Travancore Ltd., are the other wood based industries operating in Kerala. Sibila Pius has attempted to evaluate the forest industrial products of the Forest Industries Travancore Ltd., the sole public secotr unit located in the state. Being a unique enterprise with exceptional raw material requirement depending on the natural resources of the forest, the management of different functional areas like marketing, production, personnel and finance of Forest Industries Travancore Ltd. is critically examined in the work. The study focuses on the working of the company and its impact on the buying attitude of the different categories of consumers of wooden furniture such as individuals, private enterprises, public enterprises and Government departments.

The electrical equipment industry in India has been going through a crucial period during the past several years, with lower production levels, few orders, delayed payments and diminishing profit margins. The demand for electrical equipment is a derived demand dependent on the growth of the power sector, industrial requirements, and urban and rural demands. The power projects envisaged in the Eighth Plan did not materialise as expected, and hence requirement of electrical requirement was far below expectation. The slump in demand is forcing the manufacturers to accept orders at priced that could be unremunerative. Fall in demand is, therefore, the main issue of concern for the public sector electrical equipment industry in Kerala. The public sector electrical equipment industry in Kerala has also been facing fierce competition in the domestic market from other public sector and private sector undertakings in the country. The major competitors in the field are multi-product companies who have active technical collaboration with parties outside India and are profit-making companies. With liberalisation, foreign companies have also entered the market. The net outcome of the problems is the low rate of return on capital invested and negative net worth. This has led to a situation where neither technological developments nor new investments have become feasible. This, in turn, resulted in huge losses and made them less competitive as commercial concerns. Anandan D. evaluates the working of public sector electrical equipment industrial units highlighting the crucial problems faced by them.

The cotton textile industry is the first major industry to develop among the modern Indian industries. It is the base on which the pyramid of the industrial sector of the country has been built. What started largely as a spinning enterprise a century ago has now gradually developed into a mature composite industry. It provides employment to around 11.5 lakh workers, accounting for 18 per cent of all factory labour. There were three spinning mills closed in Kerala during 2000 due to sickness, with an installed capacity of 76 thousand spindles and 2873 workers. There were 6 mills registered with the Board for Industrial and Financial Reconstruction in 2000. The various factors, which led the cotton mills to the present predicament, require attention. The important problems, which affected the mills in the state adversely, include low capacity utilisation of installed spindles and looms in the mills led to lower machine productivity and lesser profit. Backlog of modernisation due to non-availability of adequate funds; and to inadequate cash generation from the operations in the earlier years, is treated as one of the problems of the mills in the State. Many of the mills have low profitability on account of increased cost of production and lower sales prices. The major elements which have increased the cost of production are low labour productivity and higher interest cost for borrowings and debts. The increase in power cost coupled with poor quality of power, usually affects the economical working of the mills. The mills in the State depend on market outside the State for their raw material requirements and also for sale of finished products. The article on textile industry in the public sector prepared by Manilal M.K. and included in the book requires special attention against this background.

Developing countries, many of which attained independence after World War II, were under strong pressure to bring about rapid economic progress. These countries lacked the necessary conditions under which private enterprises could be expected to attain rapid economic progress. The economies of such countries were characterised by unfavourable factors such as low level of savings and investment, limited technical, managerial and entrepreneurial talents, under developed economic infrastructure and basic industries and non-existence of capital market. Such being the case, the Governments of these countries were left with no alternative but to participate directly in the economic process, which was mainly promotional and entrepreneurial in nature. Faced with the problem of raising the standard of living of people in the shortest possible time, the developing countries had before them two models of economic planning and public enterprises, and the Western Model of development through private enterprises. Since the Soviet Union (as it existed earlier) had attained within five decades a measure of economic and technological development, which the western democracies had taken two centuries to achieve, the Russian Model was an obvious choice. In spite of the rapid increase in investment and dominant role of the public sector in the economy, there has been considerable criticism about the public enterprises in India. While the Government has been pushing ahead with more and more public sector undertakings, there has been considerable criticism about the poor performance, and in some cases the utter failure of Government undertakings in the country. The article on Financial Management of Public Sector Undertakings prepared by Anil Prasad V. contains a detailed analysis of the issues related to procurement and channelisation of funds.

Tourism, in its broadest, generic sense, can do more to develop understanding among people, provide jobs, create foreign exchange and raise living standards than any other economic force known. Tourism is the second largest industry in the world, first being the oil industry. In the nearer future, this industry would become the biggest industry in the world. Kerala, popularly known as 'God's Own Country' in the tourism world has wide potential in the tourism industry, keeping pace with the alarming growth of the tourism industry in the global arena. Considering the socio-economic significance of tourism, Kerala Tourism

Development Corporation Limited owned by the State Government, is expected to promote tourism industry at large through many developmental schemes and projects involving huge investments. Objective evaluation of the role of the Kerala Tourism Development Corporation Limited in promoting tourism in the light of its past performance and expected future prospects becomes imperative, particularly in the context of large scale investments, added social responsibility and in the context of tourism industry being processed to become the biggest industry of the world by the turn of this century. It is against this backdrop, the study results evaluating the role of Kerala Tourism Development Corporation Limited in the promotion of tourism carried out by Joseph Antony G. finds prominence in the edited volume.

Cashew processing has been an export-oriented traditional industry in India. It is of great significance to the national economy on account of the fact that it earns more than Rs. 300 crore annually by way of foreign exchange. The year 1990-91 witnessed an all-time record in terms of export value of cashew products (Rs. 446.52 crore) with a net foreign exchange earning of Rs. 411.51 crore. The state of Kerala enjoyed monopoly of cashew industry and trade till the mid 1960s. Of the total 273 processing factories in India in 1966, 211 were located in Kerala. Despite the loss of monopoly in the subsequent years, the State still had 252 factories, which accounted for about 50 per cent of the total processing factories in the country as on 31st March 1991. The credit for about 80 per cent of the export of cashew production in India goes to Kerala. The processing industry is significant also to the economy of the State in as much as it provides employment to more than one lakh workers, mostly women. The re-introduction of the scheme in 1988 landed the Industry in another crisis. Most of the private processors refused to open their factories and lift the nuts procured by the government agency, as a measure of protest against the monopoly procurement scheme. In this predicament, the Corporation was obliged to play a more responsible role. Dayanandan M.N. has gone in deep into the problems faced by the Cashew Development Corporation and the findings of the study are incorporated in this volume.

The paper by Jayakumari. S deals with the promotional measures for export trade of traditional items such as cashew, marine products, spices and coir. Following the policy initiatives taken by the government there was a perceptible improvement in India's export performance, both at the overall level and across commodities. The commodity composition of India's export basket changed in favour of technology intensive industrial products such as engineering goods, high value agricultural products etc. Most of India's export promotion measures aim at fostering non-traditional exports. As a result of all these measures and the industrial development taking place in the country, the prominence of traditional items began to decrease in the export basket. India has potential for significantly increasing the exports of many of these traditional items. But India failed to exploit the potential satisfactorily. Though the other developing countries advanced so much in the field of export of such commodities, there exists a lot of scope for substantially increasing the exports of many of these products. A primary analysis showed that the structure of India's export trade has changed a lot. The non-traditional export item gained prominence, after the reform process and the traditional items loses its prime position in the export basket. This change in the composition of items brought certain far reaching implications in the economy of Kerala, as Kerala is a major contributor of traditional items. This study is concentrated on the export trade of four such traditional items of Kerala namely cashew, marine products, spices and coir for a period from 1991-92 to 2001-02. This study has tried to analyse the problems faced by the exporters of traditional items of Kerala after the liberalisation movement in the country.

The marketing problems of SSI sector have been widely debated in the present context because of a number of reasons. First, the competition from large scale units is fast increasing and becoming more and more intensified. Many small units find it difficult to compete with the large manufacturers who are far better equipped with modern methods of marketing. Secondly, because of the growing number of small units spread over different parts of the country, there is at present inter-unit competition within the SSI sector itself. Thirdly, with the production of a varied variety of products both by the small and large scale units, market for many products has shifted from 'sellers' to 'buyers' market. Fourthly, lack of government assistance in the form of large purchases from the small scale producers. Fifthly, unorganised sales due to lack of co-operative marketing organisations. Sixthly, absence of market researches either by the small entrepreneurs or by government. Effective marketing has, therefore, become a vital necessity for the small scale sector to meet the new challenges in the market. The research study results presented by Rajitha Kumar S. are highly beneficial to the researchers, planners, policy makers, administrators and entrepreneurs.

All governmental efforts have been made since 1950s for the upliftment of the village industries sector. In spite of all the organised attempts Khadi and Village Industries have not succeeded remarkably in raising the income of the rural folk. There are criticism levelled against KVIC and KVIB that they have failed in identifying and encouraging potential entrepreneurial talents in the rural sector. This has resulted in the unutilisation, underutilisation and misutilisation of the indigenous natural resources available throughout the rural areas in the country. Development of indigenous technology for tapping such resources also stands as a myth. Problems such as ineffective marketing, inadequacy of finance, non-availability of raw materials, poor managerial and technical knowledge remain as major banes for the village industries to grow. The results of research study carried out by Thomas P.C. present a vivid picture of the state of affairs prevailing in the village industrial units in Kerala.

The role of small-scale industries is vital in a situation where the primary sector is virtually stagnating for the reasons that it is failing to respond to increasing investments. The significance of SSI sector becomes crucial when many of the large-scale industries, which are mostly in the public sector, are chronically in the red. The importance of small-scale industries lies in the fact that they create immediate and permanent employment on a large-scale at relatively low costs, meet a substantial part of the demand for consumer goods, facilitate mobilisation of resources of capital at various levels, which might otherwise remain unutilised, and bring about integration of the industries with the rural economy on the one hand and the large-scale industrial sector on the other. Besides the large number of village and small-scale industries, the industrial sector of Kerala consists of a few large and medium units, mainly in the public sector. The village and small-scale industrial sector consists of traditional industries like handloom, coir and cashew and modern industries like printing, wood, metal products and chemicals. Considering the growing population and the rising unemployment, it is essential to develop the industrial sector of Kerala, mainly through the development of small-scale industries. Thus, for greater prosperity, a campaign of wide industrialisation through the popularisation of small-scale industrial units is very essential. However, mere establishment of a number of small-scale units does not ensure efficient economic activity. To achieve this, effective evaluation of the operational influence of government policies and of the working of the small-scale units is essential. The article by Ambili Kumar on the working of SSI units in Kerala gains special attention against the background.

Since July 1991, a series of reforms in industrial policy, the external sector, financial and fiscal areas have been executed in the economy. These reforms have ushered in a new phase in the industrial development of India. However, there have been sharp differences of opinion on the rationale for the reforms and more importantly, their impact on the productivity of the industrial economy. While the supporters of the reforms expect greater growth, competitiveness and productivity, the critics are skeptical both about the possibilities of growth as well as nature of growth it would lead to. In particular, it is pointed out that the enjoying liberalisation is without regard to the needs of the traditional sector industries in terms of long-term objectives. Earlier, because of industrial licensing and other promotional and regulatory policies and because of the greater role accorded to the public sector it was possible for the government to direct substantial investment to backward sectors and areas. But as a result of liberalisation, which resulted in the de-licensing of industries and removal of subsidies, government is unable to direct investment to specific sectors or areas where it feels it is most efficient. This will further aggravate the fate of traditional industries, which are already at their weakest point. The article by Sarngadharan M. and Raju G. presents a brief account of the research findings on the traditional industries in Kerala. It is hoped that the social scientists would benefit a lot out of it.

As the society moves through the beginning of the 21st century the marketing concepts are fast changing. The traditional marketing concepts were focusing on satisfying consumer needs and wants. The changing marketing concepts now focus on a third consideration, that is, welfare of society. Emphasis is now being placed on how marketing affects the society as a whole, in an era of scarce resources, environmental degradation and worldwide competition. This social orientation demands classification whether satisfying customer needs serve the long-term interest of society. Thus, the new concept referred to as the social marketing concept has become a management philosophy that blends the welfare of society as well as the interest of the firm and its customers. It is a fact that no two classes of customers are alike. Every customer, who approaches the bank, has entirely different expectations and intentions. A middle-income man on the verge of retirement needs an additional source of income to supplement his pension. So his focus is on a monthly income deposit scheme. The investor cannot be wooed with anything less than the best market rate for his funds, for him the reinvestment scheme earning interest has to be designed and delivered. This is equally true for loaning and subsidiary services as well. Since it would not be flexible to expand business to cover all segments under a branch, some segments should be single out for special coverage. These segments and their potential value would constantly undergo changes and the banker must ensure that no viable worthwhile business slips through his hands due to his indifference. Muraleedharan K. in his paper titled Marketing of Bank Services narrates the changing scenario with the support of data collected from customers, bank officials and experts in the field.

The history of man's transition from primitive life to civilised life throws light on three facets of phenomenal changes in his attitude, such as consciousness about nutritious food, desire for convenient dwelling place, and passion for comfortable clothing. All human activities are driven by these facets of attitude and hence food, shelter and clothing have been universally accepted as the Basic Human Necessities (BHN). Though clothing is ranked the third factor in BHN, in Kerala, it often appears as the 'prime factor' taking priority among the needs to be satisfied. The Keralites are overwhelmingly interested, it is observed, in dressing up impressively. Understanding the consumers more closely and precisely is the 'panacea' for the problem of the dynamic behaviour of the market. This is seen to be result fetching, as the purchase decision of the consumers determines the fate of a product in the market. A behavioural approach in designing marketing strategies seems to be indispensable to fortify the existing market share applicable to each retailer. Such an approach must be in the line of a meaningful analysis of the purchase behaviour of prospective consumers, because 'profit is made from people not product'. The paper titled Consumer Behaviour in Retail Marketing of Textiles by Jacob Thomas assumes significance against this backdrop.

Housing problem is essentially a problem of poorer and weaker sections of the community. Though the last few decades have shown significant institutional development in the field of housing finance, they cater mainly to the requirements of affluent sections of the population. Most of the Housing Financing

Companies being profit making institutions, have a portfolio of 70 per cent salaried class, and out of balance are professionals such as doctors, engineers, lawyers and the rest are from the affluent business and agricultural segment. Economically Weaker Section and Low Income Groups because of their poor repaying capacity are generally outside the purview of such institutions. It is pertinent that more than 72 per cent of the loans advanced by housing co-operatives belong to such vulnerable sections. Competition is heating up in the housing finance market and there has been apprehension about the survival of Housing Co-operatives. Significant research studies have not been conducted in the field of housing co-operatives both at national and state levels. In Kerala, there are more than 30 Housing Finance Institutions engaged in financing housing. When the demand for housing finance in the state contracted due to steep decline in the housing shortage, the supply considerably increased owing to the entry of existing and newer institutions into the arena of housing. The primary housing co-operatives in Kerala have very limited sources of funds and are working mainly with the financial and managerial assistance from the apex – Kerala State Co-operative Housing Federation Ltd. The housing co-operatives in the state are confronted with a number of structural and operational issues. Gireeshkumar G. S. presents his findings on the operation of primary housing co-operative societies in Kerala. The findings are well backed by empirical analysis of the data collected from authentic sources.

Indian economy is able to tap the global market by exporting natural rubber and rubber products, which would ensure maximum prices to the growers. This is an attractive and favourable situation especially for Kerala, which is the main producer of natural rubber in the country. But, in the changing scenario, it is imperative to become competitive both in natural rubber production and in rubber goods manufacture. Quality is the essential qualification of rubber products for export, which cannot be achieved through the present conventional methods of production to enable the rubber industry to achieve better quality, it is necessary that all the processing factories should adopt the quality assurance system suggested by the International Organisation for Standardisation in processing and marketing activities. Moreover, a strict delivery schedule should be followed in foreign trade. There is a growing demand for rubber products like tyres, tubes, automobile parts, foam rubber, sports goods, footwear, rubber bands, toy balloons, rubber hoses, tread rubber, coir foam, household and industrial gloves, surgical gloves, battery container, contraceptives, 'V' belts and fan belts, conveyor belts, 'O' rings, radiator hose, rubber-insulated cables, rubber rised canvas hose, rubber rised clothes, moulded rubber goods, oil seals, block rubber, rubber compounds, hot water bags, erasers, micro cellular rubber sheet for foot wear, etc. India produces nearly 35000 different rubber products. But rubber-based industries in Kerala produce only very limited items like rubber bands, tread rubber, tyres and tubes, manufactured by the three major units. The article titled Problems and Prospects of Rubber-based Industries described special treatment against this background.

Entrepreneurship development is a process, and the entrepreneur as an individual is a significant element in the process. It may be highly useful to understand how the social set-up has been instrumental to the emergence of entrepreneurs from among the womenfolk. This may also be helpful in planning educational investment to enable them to think and grow as entrepreneurs in their society. Owing to certain cultural considerations and value systems, there are restrictions on the potential women to be fully functional. Therefore, a clear understanding of the values can facilitate the process of change, either by increasing and strengthening the promoters or by decreasing and weakening the inhibitors. The task of integrating women in development requires simultaneous efforts to improve their working conditions from both economic and social angles. This is so because women's multiple roles put them in a position to be influenced by, and to influence, the social and economic processes. Broadly, women's participation in economic development calls for arrangements that would lighten their domestic workload in order to realise them for other economic and socially productive work. This calls for an identification of opportunities for women with more avenues for self-employment, and a conscious effort towards the development of women entrepreneurship. Resia Beegam S. presents problems and prospects of women entrepreneurs with her rich experience as a social scientist specialised in this area.

Prospective entrepreneurs have grievances over the insufficiency of infrastructure and encouragements to make use of their abilities. The existing industrialists are gripped with the problems of marketing, inadequacy of finance, scarcity of raw materials and poor managerial and technical know-how. This takes back the State to attain the desired industrial development. The success of non-banking financial institutions depend upon balanced industrial development of the economy, entrepreneur motivation, initiative for starting new enterprises, provision of infrastructure facilities for industrial development, rural development, services to industrial units for marketing finished products, procurement of raw-material, technical advice and guidance to industrialists. Thomas Koshy has attempted to evaluate the role of prominent non-banking financial institutions in Kerala (KFC and KSIDC) in the industrial development of the State.

In India, the early 1970s witnessed an extensive debate on the 'trickle down' hypothesis, the nexus between unemployment and poverty, and the need for special measures to alleviate the conditions of the poor and the unemployed who are by-passed by growth (Vaidyanathan A., 2000-01). There were near general agreement in the country, as also from international bodies including the World Bank, that growth alone would not suffice to eliminate poverty and that special programmes designed to directly augment income and employment of the poor were essential. In operational terms, these programmes are of three basic types such as the programmes for generating self-employment opportunities among the poor through asset development or asset transfer combined with technology and skill upgradation; the programmes for generating wage-employment among the poor; and the minimum needs programmes for improving the living environment of the poor through better housing, health, sanitation, drinking water and education. These schemes are known as promotional social security schemes operating in India for the unorganised sector. The paper titled Employment Security Measures in Unorgansied Sector – An Evaluation Study by Yohannan Varghese has attempted to evaluate the security measures particularly self-employment and wage-employment schemes implemented by the government.

India has one of the finest textile traditions in the world. The compelling magic about India's textile traditions can be back to Harappa and Mohenjodaro in the Indus Valley of some 5000 years ago. Indian textile design has its root in the philosophical and social aspects of Indian traditional ways of living. The quiet sensitivity of the weaver rooted in customers, rituals and his religious fervour created a relationship between him and the cloth that he wove. The cosmos, the ordered universe itself was considered to be one continuous fabric with its grid pattern of warp and woof over which is painted life in all its cycles with all its illusions and dreams. The Atharva Veda, in one of its passages, personifies day and night as two sisters weaving with the warp of darkness and the woof of light of day. Human resources play a crucial role in the textile industry mainly on account of the large involvement of human force directly. It has the objective of moulding the people into a dynamic organisation that can attain its objectives and also sustain a high degree of morale of employees. All mangers are personnel managers, and all management is essentially human resonance management. Human beings as a resource do not demean or belittle their self-respect or dignity. It does not imply that people are equated to other resources such as machines or materials. On the other hand, it endows them with an importance and significance, hitherto denied to them viz., that people are so very important and in fact, far more important than every other resource required for the industry. Nandakumar Damodara Prasad presents a vivid picture of the state of affairs of the textile industry in respect of human resource management.

The role of trade union leaders in developing the unions in their present form has to be viewed with proper care and seriousness. In any organisation, the effectiveness of unions depends upon the quality of their leaders. The union movement in the beginning stages was guided by some able and selfless leaders. But in recent times, the activities of the politically motivated leaders, it is alleged, have diluted many of the divine principles of unionism, which were achieved by the former leaders by sacrificing their flesh and blood. The existing union leadership has been facing severe criticism for all the undue tendencies prevailing in the trade union front in the State. All these characteristics of unionism and union leadership in the State render the study on the topic challenging and interesting. Moreover, a trade union is a symbol of a voluntary organisation, and one of its professed objectives is to promote democratic practices. Perhaps, it would be useful to have an occasional critical look on their working, so as to make others aware about the viability of such voluntary organisations, and to identify the gap between their internal practices and their professed objectives. Availability of necessary information is a pre-requisite for the effective presentation of matters connected with trade unions before the Government or the employer, or in seminars, national or international. The research work carried out by Sajeev S. is an attempt to study and highlight the nature and working of trade unions in Kerala. The efficiency of trade unionism, as already stated, is closely related with the leadership it is endowed with, and much emphasis has been given to such basic concepts in this study.

India has over 300 major tea companies, and has over 12000 large tea estates and 1300 tea factories. In India, tea is cultivated mainly in the northern region, which includes Assam, West Bengal, Bihar, and Tripura. In South India, tea is grown in Tamil Nadu and Kerala. Kerala has a long tradition in tea production, dating back to colonial times. The production of tea in Kerala is concentrated in the two high range districts of Idukki and Wynad. The tea plantations are located in isolated and remote areas in the high altitudes of the Western Ghats. Substantial parts of the estates are on Government lands, on long-term lease. The unit cost of production of tea in Kerala is higher than in other States. It is partly because of higher wages in Kerala in comparison with other competing States, and partly due to low productivity per unit of land put under tea. The situation in tea plantations in the State has been deteriorating steadily over the past few years. Due to mounting financial burden, 22 large tea plantations in Peerumedu, the main tea pocket in Kerala, have either been closed or abandoned and about 18 processing factories have closed shutters. At the current price level the industry apprehends closure of many more estates and factories. In the marketing field, the tea industry in Kerala has been facing problems both in primary marketing and secondary marketing. This situation calls for the intervention of social scientists to enquire into the issues in depth. The paper on Tea industry: problems in production and marketing by Noushad P.M. attempts to spell out the issues.

Plantation means an agricultural undertaking regularly employing hired workers and is situated in the tropical or sub-tropical regions. It is mainly concerned with the cultivation or production for commercial purposes of coffee, tea, sugarcane, rubber, bananas, cocoa, coconuts, groundnuts, cotton, tobacco, fibers, citrus, palm oil, cinchona and pineapples. This concept is applicable in India, largely to four major crops - Tea, Coffee, Rubber and Cardamom. It does not include family or small-scale holdings producing for local consumption and not regularly employing hired workers. A plantation is large enough to apply commercial farms practices to maximise the net farms return. In India, large plantations operate in commercial scale for the above four crops along with the small farms owned and operated by small and marginal farmers. Thus, the crop concept of considering the above four crops as plantation crops can be interpreted as a policy decision to widen the concepts of agri-business orientation, technology upgradations, value addition, direct producer marketing, introduction of the changing management concepts and also to achieve a wider coverage of the credit needs of the producers through motivational credit agencies. The article on this issue written by Unuskutty K.K. focuses on the role of plantation crops in the development of the states economy, the institutional arrangements for extending long-term credit facilities for the development of plantation crops in Kerala and the role played by the State Land Development Bank in catering to these credit needs.

Since the linguistic reorganisation of Indian States in 1956, Kerala has become the largest plantation state in India as per the Report of the Committee for the Plantations Industry Wages and Bonus, 1960, and the Minimum Wages Committee for Rubber Products Industry, Kerala. The major plantation crops of Kerala are rubber, cardamom, coffee and tea and naturally too many studies can be expected on each of them or on all of them taken together. But only very few studies on individual aspects of each of these crops have so far been produced. And most of them are in the form of dissertations at the University level. Studies on the different aspects of particular plantation industries in Kerala are profuse, while an analytical study comprehensing the common problems and prospects of the major plantation industries taken together namely Rubber, Cardamom, Coffee and Tea is rare. Manoharan Nair K. has attempted to fill in this lacuna and the findings of his study are presented in the article problems and prospects of plantation industries

Information and communication has always been an important and integral element of the growth of any civilisation. Rapid technological advancement in this field reinforces the fact. With the advent of digital age, information has become the primary source for economic development. Information Technology has also the potential of double-edged impact on the process of social development. The IT policies of the Centre and States seem to hold unanimously that if any technology can create new opportunities to bridge the gap between the haves and have-nots in society in the present times, it is IT. It aids the process of development by sharing knowledge, increasing productivity, overcoming geographical boundaries and procedural openness. It also has the potential to promote rural income generation. The Government of Kerala has been trying its level best to promote e-governance in rural self-governmental set up in the thrust areas like education, health care, poverty eradication and in providing public utilities. On account of its core competence in near universal literacy, high awareness levels of its densely networked communities, superior telecom connectivity, propensity for quick technology absorption, there is much scope for e-governance in the State, for ensuring effective and efficient rural self-governmental administration. Minimol M.C. has studied on E-governance and rural self-government against this backdrop.

Panchayats play an important role as local government units in the rural areas. They have an enlarged sphere of obligatory activities, but it is often heard that there has not been any significant improvement in their resource position to discharge their obligatory functions. The fundamental problem of panchayat finance may now be stated quite simply. It is how to provide the money necessary to meet the cost of the services carried out without imposing an intolerable burden upon the tax payers and without the local bodies becoming unduly dependent upon assistance from the state government. Such being the situation, making the best use of the available resources and channelling them into proper fields of expenditure is an important task. When the resources are strictly limited, and the needs know no bounds, it becomes a matter of the utmost importance to exploit fully the resources and avoid all waste due to laxity, lack of prudence, or administrative inefficiency. Gopi V.K. presents an analysis of the problems involved in the better exploitation and utilisation of the available resources of the panchayats in Kerala.

We present this edited volume with a view to replicating, verifying and even comprehending the procedures and results of investigations carried out by social scientists on issues related to common interest. The research work of all the papers included in this book was carried out under the guidance of M. Sarngadharan, Professor and Head, Department of Commerce, University of Kerala.

The Editors place on record their immense gratitude to the management and staff of New Century Publications, New Delhi for improving and standardising the texts of papers included in this work. This edited book is presented to the social scientists with an appeal to critically evaluate the contents and to bring the shortcomings to the attention of the editors.

Thiruvananthapuram, Kerala
September 5, 2006

M. Sarngadharan
S.Rajitha Kumar

Contributors

Dr. P. O. Abraham
Reader and Head, St. Gregarious College, Kottarakkara, Kollam, Kerala.

Dr. V. Ambili Kumar
Assistant Professor, College of Fisheries, Kerala Agricultural University, Panangad, Kochi, Kerala.

Dr. D. Anandan
Reader, Department of Commerce, Sree Narayana College, Kollam, Kerala.

Dr. V. Anil Prasad
Lecturer (Senior Grade), Government College, Manjeswaram, Kasargod, Kerala.

Dr. M. N. Dayanandan
Reader, Department of Commerce, T.K.M. College of Arts and Science, Karikkode, Kollam, Kerala.

Dr. G. S. Gireesh Kumar
Lecturer (Senior Grade), Newman's College, Thodupuzha, Idukki, Kerala.

Dr. V. K. Gopi
Reader, Department of Commerce, Sree Narayana College, Natika, Thrissur, Kerala.

Dr. Jacob Thomas
Reader, Department of Commerce, C. M. S. College, Kottayam, Kerala.

Dr. S. Jayakumari
Reader, Department of Commerce, N. S. S. Hindu College,

Changanassery Kottayam, Kerala.

Dr. G. Joseph Antony
Reader and Head, Department of Commerce, Christian College, Kattakkada, Thiruvananthapuram, Kerala.

Dr. M. K. Manilal
Reader, Department of Commerce, Sree Narayana College, Chempazhanthi, Thiruvananthapuram, Kerala.

Dr. K. Manoharan Nair
Reader, Department of Commerce, V. T. M. N. S. S. College, Dhanuvachapuram, Thiruvananthapuram, Kerala.

Dr. M. C. Minimol
Lecturer, Department of Commerce, St. Joseph's College for Women, Alappuzha, Kerala.

Dr. K. K. Muraleedharan
Reader, Department of Commerce, Government College, Madappally, Vadakara, Kozhikkode, Kerala.

Dr. Nandakumar Damodara Prasad
Reader and Head, Department of Commerce, Sree Narayana College, Sivagiri, Varkala, Thiruvananthapuram, Kerala.

Mr. P. M. Noushad
Lecturer (Senior Grade), Department of Commerce, Government College, Manimalakkunnu, Kottayam, Kerala.

Dr. S. Rajitha Kumar
Lecturer, School of Management Studies, Cochin University of Science and Technology, Kochi, Kerala.

Dr. G. Raju
Reader, Department of Commerce, University of Kerala,

Thiruvananthapuram, Kerala.

Dr. S. Resia Beegam
Reader, Department of Commerce, University of Kerala, Thiruvananthapuram, Kerala.

Dr. S. Sajeev
Assistant Professor, Institute of Management in Government, Thiruvananthapuram, Kerala.

Dr. M. Sarngadharan
Professor and Head, Department of Commerce, University of Kerala, Thiruvananthapuram, Kerala.

Dr. Sibila Pius
Reader, Department of Commerce, St. Xavier's College, Aluva, Ernakulam, Kerala.

Dr. Thomas Koshy
Reader and Head, Department of Commerce, Mar Ivanious College, Thiruvananthapuram, Kerala.

Dr. P. C. Thomas
Reader and Head, Department of Commerce, F. M. N. College, Kollam, Kerala.

Dr. K. K. Unuskutty
Pro-Vice Chancellor, Mahatma Gandhi University, Kottayam, Kerala.

Dr. Yohannan Varghese
Reader, Department of Commerce, St. Gregarious College, Kottarakkara, Kollam, Kerala.

Contents

Volume I

Theme Title 1: Public Sector in the Emerging Scenario

Theme Title 2: Small and Traditional Industries

Theme Title 3: Marketing Strategies

Volume II

Theme Title 4: Industry and Enterprise

Theme Title 5: Human Resources and Employment

Theme Title 6: Plantation Industries

Theme Title 1
Public Sector in the Emerging Scenario

1

Forest Industrial Products in the Public Sector

Sibila Pius

Forest is a natural resource which forms the main body of the terrestrial ecological system. It is a complete natural resource base, a stock of asset, serving as sources of scarce inputs that can yield utility through production or provision of goods and services. Natural resources are a necessary ingredient of all economic activity. They can be of three types – non-renewable, reproducible and non-expendable. Forests fall under the second and third type. Forest can be naturally or artificially re-established. Forest resource has certain special characteristics such as: it is not possible to clearly distinguish or separate the forest capital and the products to be derives there form, therefore, the likelihood of over-exploitation of forest leading to harmful effects; and forest have high level of externalities which are social benefits or costs, outside the market mechanism. The inter-related and multiple roles of forests, covering the whole spectrum of environmental conservation and rational utilisation of forest resource are vital for human welfare and sustainable socio-economic development.

Forests can be defined as a plant association, predominantly of trees and other woody vegetation (Society of American Forests, Forest Terminology, Washington, 1958). Considering their nature the value of the contribution of forest resources can be end use values which include direct contribution in terms of goods and services and direct contribution to soil formation, watershed conservation, recreation carbon sink capacity and water yield augmentation. Non-use values are of option value which cover the potential future by later generations or by themselves. and existence value which is the positive attitude that people place on an asset or resource independent of any use in the present or in the future, like ecological health. Forest resources provide considerable externalities. They have many ecological and amenity functions such as safe-guarding and productivity, maintaining water quality, facilitating a self sustaining process of nutrient recycling, positive influence on climate and whether patterns, conserving biological and landscape diversity and supporting overall environmental stability.

Contribution of forest can generally be classified as goods and services. Goods are physical objects over which ownership rights can be established. Services are not separate entities over which ownership rights can be established and they cannot be treated separately from their source of production. Forest goods are tangible product and fall under two categories – wood products as timber, industrial wood and fuel wood, and non-wood products as gums, rexines, edible products, medicinal plant flavours, fragrances and so on. Services are broadly of two types – environmental and recreational. Benefits in the form of wood product are derived through cutting down of trees and can be obtained only once in the life cycle of a tree. Other benefits that are non-wood and service benefit can be derived uninterrupted as long as resources maintained.

The forest dwellers of the different tribal communities depend primarily on the mirror forest products for their sustenance, while the forest based industries depend on the commercially valuable wood. Besides, to the forest dwellers of the trial population forest is one of the main sources of sustenance. They collect food from the forest, use timber to construct their houses or make different other types of implements, collect fuel wood for cooking and different other objects from the forest required by them for a variety of purpose.

The forest is a large area supporting not only continuous cover of tree but forms a complex association of shrubs, plants and other forms of animals, etc. All of these do not occur accidentally but depend on one another for their existence. Forest has a major role in the overall ecological pattern of nature. They protect soil against forces of erosion and provide home for distinctive forms of animal life. Forests are the results of many natural factors as well as imposed by humans. Climate is the most important factor, which has direct effect on plants and indirect effect on development of soil by weathering of parent material. Natural resources determine the course of development and constitute the challenge, which may or may not be accepted by the human mind. Forest wealth constitutes an essential ingredient of progress. The contribution of trees to the healthy development of living beings is immeasurable. In ancient time forest were considered sacred and sustained all life-Humans, Wild Life, Birds, Bees and Butterflies and the destruction of forest meant death knell to the life around.

There had been a wide recognition of the vital role that forest play in the struggle to sustain the world's growing population. Since the end of World War II there has been a wide spread recognition of the degree to which man has devastated the face of this earth. This had led to considerable improved forestry practice in many countries and a serious reexamination of conventional attitudes concerning the use of forests by native people. Many of the problems of modern forestry particularly in tropical and sub tropical countries are related to the effects of primitive people's activities on the forest echo systems of the world. An area of rehabilitation of degraded forestland has been vitiated and forest conservation has achieved in the public consciousness that they have not had previously. Forests are increasingly regarded as a renewable resource with multiple uses, rather than as a single use resource. There is greater acceptance of the view that well managed forests on the periphery of great urban areas have a very high socio genetic value.

Natural resources constitute a key factor in the economic development of a country. They are potential wealth and if they are fully exploited and properly utilised, economic development of a country can be accelerated. The connection between the economic development of a country and its natural resources is an important factor in its economic growth. Forests constitute one of our principal natural resources. They are essential in maintaining environmental stability. They provide raw materials to a number of important industries that contribute to the evolution of sound national economies. Above all forests provide the poorer half of mankind with some of the essentials for survival, fuel for cooking, building materials for shelter, fodder for their livestock and protection for their food crops. The contribution of forestry to development can only be fully realised, however, when forests are effectively managed. A social dimension must be added to the traditional production and protection orientations of forestry activities. Correct perception of the potential and benefits of forests is necessary to device the right frame for its development. For this one has to begin with the elaboration of the picture of its cultural use and potential at present. A better use and a large potential of forests can be realised within the framework of the existing ownership pattern of forest.

The conservation and economic exploitation of the exhaustible resources and the fuller utilisation of the renewable resources are essential for accelerating the economic growth of a country. Wood is needed for paper, pulp, newsprint, rayon, furniture, matches, etc. Wood for construction, plywood and other panels for furniture making, paper board for packing and paper for printing and meeting all source of the basic commodities required in modern life. The industries that manufacture these products form an important part of the world's industrial base. The industries, which are mainly concerned with timber, are heavily concentrated in industrialised countries. It has been emphasised that forestry represents long term investment possibly attractive to corporations, governments or other long lived institutions, but not to the individual.

The extraction of the forest product is potentially economic operation. Ideally the forest is given minimal subsequent care and clear-cut simple machines. From a single passage once the ground the harvest begins with the safely stored fruits of several years' growth. The long run capacity of one-forest lands to produce wood is limited. A limit is set by competing uses of forests and other lands, space, recreation, farming rights, urban and sub-urban development and so on. Timber values are interpreted by the market place even though the timber market is subject to major imperfections. Again a very high degree of uncertainty is attached to any estimate of future values as a guide to current production decisions. The typical forestry enterprise produces more than one product among the major forest based industries are pulps, paper, newsprint, rayon, saw milling, wood panel products, matches, resins and medicinal herbs. These products and forest based industries play an important role in the life and economy of the forest folk who are completely dependent on them. Forests also play some part in earning the foreign exchange for the country. The main export items are teak, rosewood, paper and paperboard, etc. In addition to the benefit to the country of foreign exchange there is also the revenue to the government in the form of royalty from the bases of forest products like bamboos or wood to forest based industries. Besides it also provides employment.

The use of industrial wood in tropics is far out weighed by the use of fuel wood by a factor of more than five. Three quarters of the people in developing country rely on wood for cooking and heating, using more than 1500 million cubic meters of wood each year. The extraction of wood for industrial purpose is annually increasing by almost four percent for the world as a whole. But more than 80 per cent of the wood still comes from the developed countries. In contrast 80 per cent of the wood produced in the developing world is used as a source of energy. Sawn wood which is used in construction, furniture making and packaging is the most common processed wood product. The second largest category is wood pulp. The third major industrial use is in the production of wood based panels including plywood, fibreboard, particleboard and veneer. Forest products other than wood, sometimes, referred to as minor forest products are extremely numerous and varied. They include fibres, rubber and resins, waxes, pharmaceutical and cosmetic products and ornamental plants. The commonly used structural timbers can be grouped on the basis of their strength, characteristics and their natural durability into several classes in terms of their suitability for small (3-6) medium (6-12) and large spans and for permanent and temporary structures. There is a significant relation between forestry and rural development as about 80 per cent of our people live in rural areas. There is no doubt that development of forest can go a long way in raising the level of living of the poor and vulnerable sections of the country.

Of the various components of natural systems, forests and soil are crucial in ecological security. Of these components, forests are a facet of the ecosystem very much interfered with and susceptible to rapid degradation. Forests have several uses or functions which often compete with each other. Forests are scarce and are becoming increasingly scarce in the face of pressure on them. The situation apparently fits neatly with in the framework of the economic problem. Forests have a modulatory role in tempering local climate regulating the hydrological cycle and in generating and protecting soils, apart from many poorly understood roles in atmosphere and biogeochemical cycles. This is in addition to meeting the requirement of a wide range of bio-resources for the rural people such as fodder, fuels small timber and a lot of other materials for daily use. They support many known and unknown organisms and wild life. Forests help in maintaining a balanced environment. Among the interested parties there are the locals, that is, those who live in forest region and depend on the forest for their sustenance. Apart from fuel wood, fodder, raw material like bamboo for artisans, and minor produce like honey, local use of forests can take the form of clearance of forests either for shifting settled cultivation. Even if not cleared for cultivation, forests support local agriculture by providing green manure and fodder, preventing soil erosion and maintaining ground water recharge.

Commercial and industrial interests of the larger economy also find the forest resources immensely useful. Hardwood or timber is needed for construction, furniture, the railways and the like, while softwood is required for paper and pulp mills and for packaging they try to dominate the use of forests both through influencing the government and through settling their own agents in the forest regions. Their interests arise from the determine in the process of commercialisation of the forests, which is but a part of the transformation of both the regional and the national economy from a pre-capitalist to a market oriented mode of production. This process also involves integration of the forests with the larger national economy and fundamental technical changes in low forest resources are treated and exploited.

The state or its concrete form – the government – is the third interested party in forest use. Presumably, it is interested in the welfare of all citizens. Since promoting economic growth makes available a large amount of resources to it with which it can govern, and since such growth is also basic to improving the levels of living of its people, the modern state is always concerned about maximising the rate of economic growth. But modern economic growth takes place through commercialization and capitalist development, involving exploitation of natural resources and integration of regional economies into the national economy.

The Government becomes one of the three main actors in the struggle for the use of forest resources, responding to pressures of other actors and also to technical changes in the larger economy. The character of the state as well as its ideology regarding forest use and management undergo a change from time to time. The changes not only alter the conditions affecting the demand for and supply of forest resources. They also alter the relative status of different interest groups demand in future can be predicted taking in to account factors such as general economic development of the country, rate of anticipated industrial growth, literacy, urbanization, availability of alternatives to wood and cultural traditions.

The forest product markets, which have not received the attention of researchers so far, may have a great influence in shaping demand. To the extent markets integrate producers with consumers, they facilitate commodity production as producers allocate their resources on the basis of signals they receive from markets. Thus the demand is communicated to the producers (and gathers) through the medium of markets, and may have little relevance in a market economy. If market conditions are changed, demand for the product will change, even if other conditions remain undisturbed. Thus demand and even supply is influenced by the nature of markets and quantification of demand cannot be done in isolation to market factors. The demand for wood is increasing day by day and when the Government is proceeding to privatise public sector undertakings, Forest Industries (Travancore) Ltd. [FIT] the only Government unit producing furniture and joineries need to be protected.

Review of Literature

Several studies have been undertaken on the performance of public sector undertakings. Studies have also been done on the forest management. When contribution of trees to the healthy development of living beings is significant, studies relating to wood based industries are meagre. An attempt is made here to present a brief review of such studies.

A study (1972) carried out by the National Council of Education Research and Training emphasised that the optimal functioning of an economic system is depended upon the even matching of the capability and efficiency level attained by its productive and distributive system. The study also suggested that the marketing was probably the least developed aspects of the Indian economy and that there have been very little systematic attempt to study its problem in India. This confirms with the observation of Peter F. Drucker (1978) that marketing was generally the most neglected area in the economic life of developing countries. The significance of marketing was brought out (1979) by Paul Hoffman, former Administrator of the United Nation Industrial Organisation, as it was illusory to think that a country could be industrialised by building factories – industrialisation means building markets.

Peer Muhammed S. (1981) in his paper, 'The Status of Government Owned Industries in Kerala' stated that the policy objectives for industrialisation must be periodically renewed and well defined and the highest decision making layer at the Government level, must be modernised making it technically competent, efficient in evaluating performance and energetic in administrating corrective changes. He also emphasised that if a selective approach is not followed, the total efforts in industry will continue to be distracted by the necessity to tend continuously a growing stream of sick industries. Modi K. N. (1981) former President FICCI, while discussing the possibilities and problems of industrial development in Kerala, said, Kerala has virtually everything needed for rapid industrialisation, and pleads the businessman to re-assess the industrial potentiality of Kerala and explore possibilities of investing in the state. At the same time, Modi, urged that the State Government must on its part do some introspection and adopt a pragmatic approach to the problems and help initiate.

Smt. Indira Gandhi (1982) late Prime Minister of India observed that the public sector could claim no virtue, unless it functions effectively as an instrument of production and development and as a creator of new wealth. The final test lies in profitability, service and growth. If the public sector cannot pass these tests, then there is no meaning in it. Pranab Mukherjee, in his inaugural address at the second conference of Chief Executives of Public Enterprises held on 30th May 1983 said sufficient return must come out of the investment made, surplus generation is essential for further growth and development. Man Mohan Singh (1986) in a lecture on Planning and Markets held at Indian Institute of Science, Bangalore stated that a stage has been reached that unless resource generation capability of public enterprises improves substantially, the development process itself will in jeopardy. He went on to warn thus, indeed, if the present unsatisfactory trend in resource generation persists, the presence of privatisation is bound to grow. In an interview with Blitz, Vasanth Sathe (1986) said an inefficient public sector is a drain on public resources and ultimately results in depriving the poor, because it is the programmes for the poor that are curtailed for want of funds.

Mohanan Pillai P. (1991) in a paper Reforms in Kerala's Industrial Sector since Liberalisation, stated that the new economic reforms in operation since July 1991 have ushered a new phase in the industrial development of the country and the responses of the state Government to the new phase has not been uniform. Raveendran T. M. carried out a study (1993) on the socio-economic aspects of the problems of timber and wood based industries in Malabar. The study aimed at locating the problems confronted in running the unit and came to a conclusion that the growth of wood based industrial sector is impeded by the decline of the forest land which is being converted for non-forest purposes, thus the prospect can be ensured only with the support of the Government and the public in general. Sharma K. C. (1997) in a paper on Industrial Policy in India pointed out that the industrial sector was to play a key role in the achievement of the socio-economic changes and public enterprise was seen as harbinger of this transformation.

Udayalakshmi V. (1998) in a paper on forest resources management stated that advanced technological tools like Remote Sensing and Geographic Information Sensing could call for optimal and efficient management of forest resources. Narendra Prasad S. (1998) in a paper revealed that Geographic Information Sensing habitat changes which is crucial for understanding dynamics of vegetation, assessment of impact on the changes on patterns and process of the ecosystem and for evolving rational and sustainable forestry policies. Murali K.S. (1998) in a paper suggested that any classificatory process of forest vegetation should consider the spatial dynamics of all the three layers namely, tree, shrub and herb. The existing methods of classification of forest vegetation with little information derived from other layers, so an attempt has been made to offer on objective method of classifying the vegetation using Geographic Information Sensing. Udayalakshmi V. and Dutt C.B.S. (1998) carried out a study on the Micro level planning and sustainable forestry programmes implemented through micro level planning have been gaining momentum showing a transition from traditional forest management to people's participatory programmes, to ensure perpetual supply of forest produce in meeting the growing demand of the local people, primarily for fuel, wood, and fodder, a careful planning is essential. Sarachachandra Lele, Rajashekhar G., Venkatarama Hegde R., Prevish Kumar G. and Saravana Kumar P. (1998) in their study suggested that a micro scale inter disciplinary field studies are essential for understanding the complex process leading to the social use and misuse of forests. Chandra Choodan Nair B. (2000) in his article pointed out that wood is one of the versatile materials which find very wide application in every day life. So the key challenge to the industry is to keep the sector responsive to the changing needs without any compromise on environmental factors.

On a thorough review of the available literature mentioned above it is noted that the performance of the Forest Industries Travancore Limited, a major public sector enterprise in the state has not attracted the minds of the social scientists and hence the present study.

Statement of the Problem

The wood based industries may be divided in to large, medium and small on the basis of size. Gwalior Rayons (Grasim Ltd.) and Western India Plywood Company Ltd. are the two large sized units in the private sector and the Hindustan Newsprint Ltd., Kottayam in the public sector that utilise wood as the major raw material. Travancore Plywood Industries Ltd., and Forest Industries Travancore Ltd., are the other wood based industries operating in the state. The study of all these units is outside the scope of the present study. The study concentrates on the Forest Industries Travancore Ltd., and their larger socio-economic implications. Being a unique enterprise with exceptional raw material requirement depending on the natural resources of the forest of Kerala the management of different functional areas like marketing, production, personnel and finance of Forest Industries Travancore Ltd. is taken for a critical evaluation in the present study.

The present study was undertaken on the background that no scientific study has so far been made on the working of Forest Industries Travancore Limited, despite that the establishment of the company was a landmark in the history of forest industry in the state. The study focuses on the working of the company and its impact on the buying attitude of the different categories of consumers of wooden furniture like individuals, private enterprises, public enterprises and Government Departments.

Objectives of the Study

The objectives of the present study are:

- to determine the performance of Forest Industries Travancore Ltd., in relation to the procurement of timber and the processing;
- to evaluate the working results of the corporation in relation to the management of funds; and
- to assess the satisfaction of varied categories of consumers such as individuals, Government Department, public enterprises and private enterprises on the products of Forest Industries Travancore Limited.

Data relating to the performance of the Forest Industries Travancore Ltd. were collected both from primary and secondary sources. Primary data were collected from two sources consumers and employees. Consumers of different items of furniture manufactured by the company are located throughout the state. Consumers include individuals, Government departments, Private enterprises and Public enterprises. However, the company is mainly targeting Government offices in the state followed by the other three categories. Such being the case, on the basis of a pilot study carried out. Stratified random sampling was used for collection of primary data from the consumers. Data were collected from 700 Government offices, 100 private enterprises, 100 public enterprises and 100 individuals from the Northern,

Central and Southern districts of the state. Data were also collected from 80 employees – supervisors – 15, workers – 25 and others – 40 associated with the Forest Industries Travancore Ltd. Thus 1000 consumers and 80 employees were the sample for the study.

Primary data relating to the performance of the company in relation to the procurement of inputs and the processing were collected from the employees using a questionnaire for the study. In addition to the primary data collected from the employees, secondary data collected from the company, Government publications and various periodicals and the reports were used to determine the performance of the company. In order to assess the satisfaction of the consumers, primary data collected from consumers were relied upon. The data from the consumers were collected by using a pre-tested interview schedule. Consumers were interviewed in their respective offices and resident visits were highly useful in making personal observation and assessment of the quality. The responses of the consumers were by and large encouraged.

However a few workers and consumers were reluctant to respond freely in the initial stage and they co-operated only after being convinced they would not be personally identified. In addition to collecting responses of the consumers and employees discussions were held with experts in the field and leaders of trade unions. The study covers a period of 10 years commencing from 1991-92 to 2000-01. However data related to the employees pertaining to the year 2002-03. In order to determine the performance of the company tools like averages, ratios and percentages were used through out the report. With a view to measuring the level of significance, chi-square tests were employed.

Data related to the performance of the company were collected from the office records and there was no mechanism available for counter verifying the reliability. It is against this situation that primary data, were collected from the employees for an in depth analysis. In many cases responses were furnished by the employees from their memories. This sort of a limitation was again noticed on the responses of the consumers in relation to their satisfaction on the products of the company. However in almost all cases, on the spot observation was helpful to make the data from both the sources more accurate.

Findings

The wood based industry experience a set back. However, Forest Industries Travancore Ltd., today continues to occupy a prominent place being the only Government owned wood industry supplying furniture and joineries. The major findings of the present study are summarised below.

Timber: The data brought about the fact that FIT was purchasing timber through public auction, where they had to compete with the private parties, who too participated in the auction. Thus high price has to be paid for purchasing the required material. Since high price is paid for timber it leads to an increase in the cost of production thereby leading to a high selling price. The data collected for the present study revealed that the quality of timber purchased was high. FIT purchases only high quality timber so as to give the customers the best quality products which suit their needs and to avoid waste of timber to a certain extent. High price was the most prominent problem. FIT had to pay high price to get best quality timber and the customer had to pay high price to get the best quality products. The analysis led to the conclusion that fine quality timber was purchased in order to reduce the waste of timber to a certain extent. Though waste in the form of sawdust is an inherent nature of raw material, it can be reduced if fine quality is used for production. The glittering appearance of the finished product can be obtained only if it is made out of fine quality timber. The data collected for the present study brought out of the fact that there were sufficient facilities for the storage of timber and they were satisfied with the way it was been stored.

Labour and other inputs: To analyse this issue the factors relating to skilled and unskilled labour and its efficiency was studied. It was felt that there was sufficient labour both skilled and unskilled on FIT, but their efficiency has to be made more sharp. On the problems related to the availability of other inputs it was responded that all other inputs except power was sufficient. Power cut declared in the state is a threat to their effective working.

Extent of damage of finished goods: The data clearly indicated that the damage of furnished goods is very low. As already noted that the labourers were skilled enough to make best furnished product, the damage caused to it is low. Moreover, when goods are produced from best quality timber the damage will be very low.

Wages/salaries and other facilities: It is worth mentioning in this regard that the views of the employees belonging to different categories were different. When the view of the employees whose income falls below Rs. 2,000 was taken, it was noted that 60 per cent of them were very much happy and stated that the wages received was good. When 4 per cent of the employees belonging to the group Rs. 2,000-4,000 and Rs. 4,000-6,000 stated that the salaries they get is only medium. Forty per cent of the group above Rs. 6,000 said that what they get was poor. The data indicated that the employees were not satisfied with the welfare schemes available. They said that the facilities were insufficient to safeguard the interest of the workers. It was noted in this connection that 71 per cent of the employees were of the opinion that welfare facilities were insufficient.

The data related to the views of the respondents on the social security measures available in FIT showed that 62 per cent of them was of the opinion that it was insufficient. Analysis of the welfare facilities also gave a similar picture and it was against this observation the views regarding social security measures were also collected. Both the data revealed that FIT has to take measures for introducing various schemes. Safety measures in the factory are another area where again FIT has to make necessary steps for providing safety measures to the workers. 58 per cent of the respondents state that the measures are insufficient. In an attempt to ascertain the views of the employees regarding the over all working atmosphere it was observed that 56 per cent of the employees were satisfied, 15 per cent opined as good and only 9 per cent were of the opinion that it was poor. It is quite interesting to note that all benefits available to the employees were quite insufficient. Studies had already revealed that the respondents were not satisfied with the facilities available in FIT. Again another 62 per cent is of the opined that there existed a very poor promotion policy in FIT. It is note worthy that the respondents are satisfied with the non-monetary measures provided to them. Fifty per cent of the respondents have this opinion.

When enquired about the commitment of management towards the workers, it is learned that their commitment motivate the workers a greater efficiency, 59 per cent of the respondents was satisfied with it saying that it is only medium and more emphasis has to be given to this area. The respondents were also asked to give their views regarding the organisation culture for which 55 per cent of them found that there existed a very favourable atmosphere. This led to increase in the efficiency of the work.

Sales promotion measures: The data collected with a view to ascertaining the sales promotion measures available to the unit, it was felt that the employees were satisfied with the measures available. In an attempt to ascertain the views of the employees regarding the price quoted it was found that they feel the prices to be of medium only, but the views of customers collected tell that the prices of the products are high. Though there were many distribution channels, FIT had only the direct selling agency directly from the manufacturing unit to the customers more than 50 per cent of the respondents stated that this system is good, they are satisfied with the present way of selling out the products. It was noted that even though there is not much effort from the side of FIT to canvassing orders, since government is the principal buyer the method does not adversely affect to get sufficient orders. Studies reveal that though the method of canvassing is insufficient, there is sufficient number of orders, because

Government is the principal buyer of FIT products. An attempt was made in the present study to ascertain the views of the respondents regarding the advertisement policy of FIT. Majority of the respondents were of the opinion that FIT had to spend more on advertisement. Since furniture and joineries are the products of FIT, it normally does not require away after sales service, still they are always ready to provide services if necessary.

Availability of funds: The analysis on the availability of funds has led to the conclusion that there are sufficient funds for the smooth functioning of FIT. Sixty per cent of the respondents are of this opinion. As already observed FIT is using more long-term funds for financing the needs of the unit for which high rate of interest becomes payable, which adversely affects the rate of return on investment. Here again the analysis reveals that FIT has sufficient sources of working capital. Fifty eight per cent of the respondents viewed that there is sufficient amount of working capital for the working of the unit.

Capacity utilization: The capacity of a firm is measured in terms of production, 50 per cent of the respondents are of the opinion that FIT is working at the optimum capacity while the other 50 per cent is of different opinion but 32.50 per cent viewed as under utilised and thus the reason for it was also collected. The respondents were asked to mark the prominent problems faced for under utilisation in order of priority. High price was marked to be the most prominent problem followed by high cost of production and high competition.

Need for modernisation in production: Sixty per cent of the respondents state the insufficiency of the tools and machines in FIT. Technology has been changing rapidly accordingly FIT should install the most modern tools and equipment. The analysis reveals that 63 per cent of the respondents are of the opinion that modernisation is needed in FIT. At the dawn of the new millennium the world around us is changing fast. To sustain and accelerate the growth of economy, policies must combine with the rapid economic reforms wherever necessary. The data collected with a view to ascertain the opinion of the respondents regarding the prosperity of the organization revealed that FIT has a bright future.

Training facilities and communication methods: The Indian market has been undergoing a significant metamorphosis due to the globalisation. Tapping the potential market would be the critical challenge of FIT in the coming years, for which employees have to be given proper training to equip with the technological developments and improvements. The respondents have opined that sufficient training is imparted. The analysis on communication methods led to the conclusion that FIT has sufficient communication methods and the employees are quite satisfied with the present system. Sixty eight per cent of the employees stated that the method is sufficient.

Views of Consumers

To analyse the performance of FIT views of the consumers of FIT were also collected and the findings thus obtained are presented below.

Frequency of purchase made: Forty-six per cent of the respondents belonging to the Government departments make purchases regularly, while 29 per cent make occasionally and another 25 per cent only rarely. Views regarding the public enterprises were quite different, only 10 per cent make purchase regularly, while 50 per cent occasional and 40 per cent only rarely. Private enterprises claimed that 70 per cent of them make purchases regularly, 10 per cent occasional and 20 per cent rarely. Of the 100 individuals of the sample, 42 per cent make purchases regularly, 26 per cent make purchases occasional and another 32 per cent make purchases only rarely. An analysis was made to know how the customers had made contacts with FIT and it was found that 84 per cent of the customers had established contacts directly, 7 per cent through intermediaries and 9 per cent through the employees.

Quality of the product: An attempt was made here to analyse the quality of the products of FIT and it was found that the customers were very much satisfied with the quality. When 4 per cent of the respondents judged the products to be very good 28 per cent judged as good, and 17 per cent as satisfactory. Thus it reveals that quality timber was purchased for producing quality products to satisfy the needs of the customers. It was stated by majority of the respondents that the goods are of durable nature. It is quite interesting to note that a majority (86 per cent) of the respondents were happy with the durability of the products. When 50 per cent claimed to be very good, 21 per cent stated to be good and another 15 per cent judged to be satisfactory. It is noteworthy that a majority (86 per cent) of respondents had judged the quality of the products as good. Since timber is the raw material and fine quality is being purchased the products made out of that also will be highly durable. Finish of the products is highly favoured as a success strategy for the manufacturing units. On an analysis with the consumers covered under the sample it was made known by the majority (72 per cent) that they viewed the finish appearance of the product as good, 10 per cent viewed as very good and 11 per cent opined as satisfactory.

Artistic beauty is highly favoured as a success strategy for the manufacturing units. The customers are attracted towards the products by its exquisite glittering appearance. On an enquiry with the consumers covered under the sample it was made known by the majority (60 per cent) that they viewed the artistic beauty of the furniture made to be satisfactory. This states that it is essential for FIT to be able to taste the essence of what is happening around all the time, not merely to survive, but to thrive. Another important factor by which the customers are brought nearer to the product is by inculcating the changing fashions. The underlying rule of fashion in suit yourself, here furniture should suit in the right place and at the right time. The right type can mask the weakness and high light the positive. Appropriateness is the key to a good style. Studies have revealed that 59 per cent respondents are satisfied with the fashion, 2 per cent feel it to be very good, 16 per cent says to be good and 23 per cent judges that the fashion is poor. FIT should try to change the fashions by observing the surroundings.

Price of the products: Analysis with regard to the price of the timber purchased has already revealed that high price has to be paid to purchase best quality through public auction. Thereby it will lead to an increase in the cost of production and the price will also be made higher. 78 per cent of the customers revealed that very high price has to be paid for the products of FIT.

Approach of the employees: Ninety nine per cent of the respondents were satisfied with the approach of the employees. When 61 per cent of the customers opined to be very good 31 per cent stated as good and another 7 per cent viewed as satisfactory. This itself makes the respondents make further visits to FIT.

Terms and conditions: The respondents were asked to indicate their views on the terms and conditions of sale offered by FIT. It was quite noteworthy that only 2 per cent viewed as poor while a majority of 98 per cent was satisfied with terms. When 9 per cent viewed as very good, 72 per cent viewed as good and 11 per cent were quite satisfied. Analysis has already stated that the approach of the employees was also good. A majority of 99 per cent of the respondents was of this opinion.

Execution of orders: Studies reveal that the part played by the employees of FIT is good. They are always rendering good service to the customers. Analysis reveals that all orders are executed at the earliest without much delay. It was observed that 11 per cent of the customers viewed as very good, 70 per cent as good and other 11 per cent as satisfactory. An analysis was made to find out the effectiveness taken by the employees in executing the orders, and it was found that 70 per cent of the respondents claim that the punctuality is good, and 9 per cent claims to be very good, 11 per cent states as satisfactory and only a small figure (10 per cent) states that the punctuality on the part of the employees is poor.

After sales service: The data related to the views of the respondents on the after sales service indicates that when 5 per cent viewed it very good, 59 per cent viewed it good and 19 per cent viewed it satisfactory. Since the products are furniture and joineries it will not need much after sales service.

Sales promotion measures: An attempt was made in the present study to ascertain the views of the respondents regarding the sales promotion measures and it was found that 59 per cent of the respondents was satisfied with the measures available in FIT. Seasonal discounts were one of the major sales promotion measures. Another 7 per cent of the employees stated as good and 2 per cent was of the opinion that it was very good and only 32 per cent opined as poor. Customers are always influenced by advertisement. Views of the employees have indicated that much amount is not spent in advertisement because Government is the principal buyer of the products. Here the customer's views also tell us that 3 per cent viewed as very good, 17 per cent as good and 62 per cent as satisfactory and 18 per cent as poor. This reveals that in a state like Kerala where there is 100 per cent literacy advertisement can bring in fruitful results. The data collected for the present study brought out the fact that FIT has adopted only a single distribution channel, that is directly from producer to consumer and 75 per cent of the respondents claimed that this system is good, 5 per cent viewed as very good, 18 per cent were satisfied with it and only 2 per cent opined as poor. This brings into light the fact that FIT had been successful in dealing with the consumers directly.

Accuracy in specification: Studies reveal that only 7 per cent of the respondents have viewed the accuracy in specification as poor, all others viewed as good, very good and satisfactory. This brings to light the commitment of the employees and their skill marking specifications for various designs of furniture and joineries.

From the foregoing analysis on the basis of the views of the employees in FIT and consumers and also on the basis of the observation made at the time of collection of primary data it can be concluded that FIT has been largely depending on the long term funds, the prices of the products are much higher as opined by all the respondents, the products though paid higher are of best quality which no one can ever deny as opined by the respondents and inadequate sales promotion measures and delay in modernisation has adversely affected the working results of FIT. Every business operation is adorned with changes and flexibility. Similarly the operation of a public sector undertaking inspite of its inherent limitation and constraints, attempts to keep its business policy dynamic and flexible. And this aspect in fact brings to light the development mechanism of a public sector undertaking. Resources both internal and external play a crucial role in every development effort of the unit. Under the concept of public sector undertaking the main sources of finance are from equity and loans from the Government, internal resources, loans from public financial institutions and arrangements for working capital with the nationalised commercial banks.

In public sector units however the decision about the capital structure rests with the Government, which emphasises uniformity, without taking into account the special nature of different enterprises. It transpires from the details of the capital structure, that FIT has been using long term funds to a great extent, thus brining down the return on investment. Further it may be mentioned that from the long term financial analysis it is found that long term borrowings are a major source of finance for the unit. The interest to be paid becomes higher than the corresponding return on investment.

Analysis of the short term financial position has also been made. It reveals that much of the working capital is in the form of debtors, which has not yet been fully realised. Since Government is the principal consumer debt has also increased which has to be realised. Total working capital increased gradually from year to year, but the return on such funds did not record a corresponding rise. It is pertinent to note that with the increase in working capital, the percentage return on it reveals a gradual decline. This implies that the induction of additional funds employed could not be utilised fruitfully to yield sufficient return on it. Analysis of profitability is inevitable for a public sector undertaking. Measuring profitability is the analysis of futurity of net wealth creation which is necessary to measure the commercial success of the unit. This will enlighten on the success of the unit as a commercial identity. The profitability of the unit has been found to be increasing since 1995-96, despite the fact that the unit had to pay interest on the long term borrowings. There was a gradual increase in the amount of profit. Efficient management of the unit would increase the profitability of the concern.

Recommendations

Based on the findings of the present study it is proposed to recommend the following measures.

If Forest Industries Travancore Ltd. is to meet the emerging challenges ahead especially those around the turn of the century and beyond, a review of existing systems and their streamlining must be done now. Instead of looking ahead of what is need in the next ten years, and if feasible, providing the systems, procedures and technology for it, that are still tangled with the number of vouchers, norms, etc., so to extend computer facilities in the unit. It may be thought of laterally and innovatively to include as many areas as possible for introducing constructive changes in systems and procedures which paves the way for efficiency.

The market which was largely controlled by the private sector due to increased price offered by Government sector has to face stiff competition. Forest Industries Travancore Ltd. has to think of customers differently. Focus on retail business will help them in increasing their spread to large co-operates. It would also give them an opportunity to build a low cost base. Retail business presents a huge untapped potential, if FIT can offer on a low cost basis for which changes in the Government regulation is necessary. Stringent measures should be taken at the Government level for the strict execution of the price preference scheme for Government purchases. Markets have become truly global and it is recognised that there is a need to have a global regulator. Export potential is to be ascertained through active involvement and encouragement of the Government. The product of FIT must attract international market. In this era of globalisation FIT should wake up and the products should go across the country. There should be a regulator to maintain price index.

Apart from the traditional products they have to take steps to build themselves into a shop where all wooden products would be available. They have to cater to the needs of customers. FIT will be forced to cross sell there products through different channel. From product enhancement point of view one of the biggest challenges is to identify a variety of products of the latest fashion and design. Technology has become an important medium of not only attracting new customers but also in retaining them. The new private sector industries have made a strong presence in the most lucrative business areas in the country because of technology upgradation. Private sector has taken a lead introducing new variety. Only if value added products are offered by FIT it will result in clients migrating from private sector to Government sector. Thus FIT has to virtually create an exist barrier by broadening their product range and effectively cross selling them with the latest available technology. FIT on the hand is not lagging behind, but technology improvement has to be launched.

Specialisation has to be developed. Initially there may be sum resistance but an objective placements policy on the basis of professional qualification, previous experience would be appreciated in the long run. This should also be considered for promotion. New skills may be required because of automation. Training shall help the employees to develop broader view of work and their own role in the organisation. Many of the employees have to be trained well in routine work who lack professional expertise for facing new challenges. In the changing scenario re-training, re-educating the employees is a must for survival. Strategies for motivating the employees for facing the challenges also need to be evolved.

Quality of work force matters much in this industry so a systematic long-range manpower plan is needed. New skills may be required to cope with the competitive environment. For which training senders have a major role to play in imparting these skill. Emotional needs are more apparent during mid-carrier phase and training shall health the employees to develop broader view of work and there on role in the organisation career counseling programmes could be organised. A systematic long-range manpower development plan is the need of the hour in FIT. Equipping the work force to adapt to changing environment should be the foremost priority in the unit.

Absence of dynamic and proactive management, lack of autonomy for restructuring operations, poor wage structure is dampening their growth prospects. The more efficient and proactive players would be able to take a lead. Some market participants are tough about credit stability. As competition in the market place increases the likely effect will be for the dealers and as FIT is a Government undertaking credit facility can be offered to Government employees from whom credit can be realised easily. A reliable base for such credit transaction should be created. The achievement of exemplary credit quality requires an unconditional commitment from the top management boards and everyone involved in the credit process.

In a competitive industry like FIT customer has to be understood has a product. The greatest challenge facing today is therefore the development of manpower resources to meet the new and infinitely more competitive circumstances of tomorrow. History is full of examples of organisations that have succeeded or failed on account of the quality of the people they employ. As a commercial organisation FIT has to earn profits. From this angle FIT has to reduce the cost by a simplified tax structure. Timely collection of dues is one of the most important measures to be implemented. With the creation of new products and product variant depending upon consumer needs and behaviour pattern a wider market can be achieved. Profits are earned when people buy things, for that you have to do more than just create a customer, so quality products have to be produced and sold at an average price. The traditional sales culture focuses on short term transaction, making it nearly impossible to build lasting client relationship that lead to greater profits.

It is clear from the analysis that FIT can change its industrial landscape. It has to initiate to build up a modern, efficient and customer friendly system. Technology will help to grab market share with superior quality product offered at medium price. Thus it leads to improvement in productivity. FIT needs to be vigilant in the years to come, for market opportunities particularly with the competition envisaged in the field. In 2002 and beyond the key element is that it should strive to achieve significant increase in their productivity, efficiency and profitability. Towards this end the basic objective should be survive, survive with growth, and grow with profit. Towards this FIT will be forced to develop only quality products with cost reduction. Offering the right product at the right cost would lead to success.

References

Albert C, *Worrell Principles of Forest Policy*, M.C. Graw Hill Book Company.

Budhadeb Chaudhari, Ashok Kumar, Mittal M.C., *Forest and Forest Development in India*, Inter India Public Publication.

Chandrasekharan C., *Wood Use in Kerala and Its Implications on Forest Land Use and Development*, Kerala Forest Research Institute, Trivandrum.

Chandrasekharan C., *Forest Resources of Kerala, - A Quantitative Assessment*, Kerala Forest Development, Trivandrum.

Eckholm, Erck, *Planning for the Future Forestry for Human Needs*, World Watch

Joshi Gapa, *Forest Policy and Tribal Development – Problems of Implementation, Ecology and Exploitation*, Social Action.

Karunakaran C.K., *Keralathinte Vanasampathu*, State institute of Languages, Trivandrum.

Karunakaran C.K., *Keralathinte Vanangali Noottandukaliloote*, State Institute of Languages, Trivandrum.

Kulkarni Sharad, *Encroachment on Forest - Government Versus People*, Economic and Political Weekly.

Sagreiya K.P., *Forest and Forestry*, National Book Trust of India, New Delhi.

Sharma D., *Forest Tribal Economy and Regional Development*, Ministry of Home Affairs, Government of India, New Delhi.

2

Electrical Equipment Industry in the Public Sector

D. Anandan

The level of advancement in technological culture primarily depends on the development of energy sources for the needs of man among the different one. The use of electricity over the last one hundred years has brought an industrial revolution and has given a tremendous impetus to the development of society. An electrical equipment industrial unit can be defined as an establishment which is engaged in the manufacture of machinery, apparatus and supplies, for use directly in the generation, storage, transmission of electric energy. It covers the production of thousands of essential articles. The electrical equipment industry is distinct from plants and distributing the power so generated. The electrical equipment industry manufactures, among countless things, machinery and apparatus that serve to equip these plants for generation of power and its transmission. The electrical equipment industry includes both consumer goods and capital goods producing or using such as a paper mill or steel mill and also the equipments necessary for the generation, transmission and distribution of electrical power. The electrical machinery group has six major divisions, termed 'sub-industries', namely, electrical power machinery and switch-gear, equipment for distributing electrical equipment, electrical equipment for medical purpose, and other electrical equipment, such as electrical lamps.

Capital goods in the industry include those used for generation, transmission, and distribution of electricity, as well as electric motors and furnaces in industrial installation to make final products. For electricity production and distribution, the principal equipment includes turbines, generators, power distribution transformers, switch–gear and rectifiers. Turbines for electrical generation may be powered by water of steam. A system of transformers either step up current for transmission at higher voltages (it is economical to transmit power over long distance at higher voltages) or steps down the current for use at lower voltage in industry and home. Electrical motors complete the system by converting electrical power into mechanical power.

In most cases, heavy equipment must be custom-designed. It is not susceptible to assembly line production with substantial economies of scale. For example, transformers must convert different currents, and electrical drives serve special purpose in particular plants. However, a 'batch flow' production technique can be applied to very large orders of identical machines. Production requires high investments in testing facilities, machines, tools and skilled personnel. Engineers must be able to design large machinery, working with particular alloys, small tolerances and special raw-materials. The major producers of capital goods are among the largest electrical equipment companies, such as BHEL (India), GEC (UK), Siemens (Germany), and Hitachi (Japan).

Consumer products are less complicated and are relatively new to the industry's product lines. Light bulbs are the industry's oldest consumer products, which provided the initial strength to the industry. Another familiar appliance is the electric fan. But modern consumer products such as refrigerators, air conditioners, washing machines, water heaters, hair dryers, etc., come to be marketed on a massy scale, only after the Second World War. Unlike capital goods, consumer products are sold through distributors directly to consumers. With a few expectations, the final consumers are not professional buyers, and so advertising and other techniques permit considerable product differentiation. Marketing of products to the public is the most important element of non-price competition. Also, unlike capital goods, most consumer goods are subject to considerable production economies of scale as well as to advertising economies. Phillips, Godrej, Whirlpool, BPL and Anchor are the leaders in this field.

Development

Inventors in the industrialising world laid the technological foundation for the electrical industry during the nineteenth century. Oested, Faraday and others made discoveries in electromagnetism that led to the development of the telegraph. The first line was established between Baltimore and New York in 1846. Faraday had invented dynamos in 1831 and Sprague had designed an electric motor in 1844, although their commercial application waited technological break through in transmission. When Edison and Swann demonstrated their incandescent bulbs in 1879, the commercial possibilities for an electrical industry became suddenly bright. Bulbs provided the consumers; a complete system of electric generation, transmission and distribution was needed. Garland and Gibbs in 1883 divided an alternating current system with transformers. Problems of generation were overcome when Sweden's Carl Gustavo de Laval invented the steam turbine in 1882 and England's Charles parsons connected his reaction-type steam turbine to a generator.

In the twentieth century, the electrical industry all over the world grew explosively. Inventions made in the ninetieth century were constantly improved and adapted and the industry became increasingly diversified. The electrical equipment industry developed rapidly in India where the large market provided the fertile soil for its development. The industry grew with the successful inventions by Edison, Houston, etc. This means that from its birth, the industry was connected in the hands of a few firms legally empowered to sell most electrical equipment. The companies made arrangements for pricing and production in their own interest. In the early years of the industry, the Commonwealth countries were primarily the domain of Philips, GEC and the British manufacturers.

In 1938, Philips, GEC, AEI (now GEC) and Crompton Parkinson incorporated the Electric Lamp Manufacturers Private Limited (ELM) of India. This joint venture was to produce lamps for its owners, to be marketed under their brand names. Indeed price competition was virtually eliminated. The four sellers of lamps quoted identical rated for their products. The Registrar of Restrictive Trade Practices stated that in the open market the prices of their brands were almost identical, resulting from clandestine understanding between them as to the common fixation of prices of their goods. The Registrar concluded that distorted competition brought about manipulation of prices and imposed on consumers unjustified costs. Thus the major international producers exercised control of product supply and production technology, through ELM. In the case of capital goods also, large international firms controlled the production and supply of the products.

Before the Second World War, electrical industries in India concerned themselves with the manufacture of fans, lamps, wires and cables. India planned large growth in electric power generation in the post-independence periods. Initially, all the necessary items of equipment for power generation; transmission and distribution were imported into the country, which naturally meant a drain on India's foreign exchange. In order to meet the growing demand for electrical equipment, through indigenous sources, it was decided to setup an electrical equipment factory in the country. For this purpose, the Heavy Electrical Equipment Project Enquiry Committee was set up in 1954. On the recommendations of the Committee, Heavy Electrical Limited was incorporated as a Government Company, in 1956, with the objective of manufacturing transformers, switch-gears, motors, generators, hydraulic turbines, etc. Besides meeting the internal demand, the company has so far exported its equipment items to over 30 countries in South East Asia and the Middle East.

In India, the electrical industry has developed through joint ventures, technical collaborations, and indigenous research and development. At present, the installed capacity of the electrical industry is considers adequate to meet the domestic demand as well as the amount of exports. Most of these industrial and commercial activities are in the public sector like BHEL and TELK has the largest capacity. Under the new industrial policy, the industry has been diligence. Many of the electrical items like electric motors, JFTC, optic fiber cables and pumping sets also quality for 51 per cent foreign equity and automatic foreign collaboration under the new industrial policy.

Role of the Public Sector

The industrial revolution gave rise to many bitter social evils. It also gave birth to private capitalism. Consumers and workers were exploited and, therefore, there arose the need of the state intervention in the industrial field, which led to the evolution of public sector undertakings. Khera takes 'public sector undertakings' to mean the industrial, commercial and economic activities carried on by the Central Government or by the state Government, in each case either solely or in association with private enterprise, so long as it is managed by a self-contained management.

The evolution of the public sector in India is recent. Prior to 1947, there was virtually no public sector, barring the field of transport and communication. Railways, Posts and Telegraphs, etc, have been managed by the Central Government since the pre-independence period. During the post-independence period, the growth and development of industries in India has been largely governed by the industrial policy announced by the Government in 1948, which placed the responsibility for the economic welfare of the people on the State. In pursuance of this policy, Government decided to enter the industrial field, and define the scope of activities for the public and private sectors. The Industrial Policy Statement, 1948, needed to be modified to suit new challenges and changing conditions. As a result, Government of India issued Industrial Policy Statements in 1956, 1973, 1977, 1980 and 1991. In each of these documents, the role of the public sector in India in the process of industrialization has been clearly spelt out.

The public sector has an important role to play in the developing economies, especially in those, which have adopted a system of development planning. It also has to play role-providing revenue to government treasury. They serve the purpose of bringing down social and ethnic imbalances and bringing about a more equitable distribution of income. Many public enterprises have operated as disguised instruments of social security for certain groups of persons or regions. Closely related to the economic development is the objective of establishing public enterprises for the purpose of providing employment and fuller use of human and others resources. Many public sector undertakings are often required to keep their manpower in employment even if they are running at a loss. In the public sector's recruitment policies, scheduled castes and schedules tribes are given reservations. Another important objective is to achieve self-reliance and improvement of the balance of payment situation through import substitution and export promotion. This is no less evident in the electrical industry. Encouraging local talent and depending on local equipment, on the public sector has fostered national self-reliance in electrical equipment.

A key social function said to be performed by the public sector is that of regional development through the establishment of its plants in economically backward areas of the country. That certainly is true of the electrical equipment plants, which are located in less developed areas of the State of Kerala. The Government of India announced the New Industrial Policy in 1991, which contain provisions for encouraging private participation. Even though the new policy does encourage private enterprise, it does not neglect the role of the public sector in the economy. But it has redefined the role of the public sector and clearly defined the approach to the existing public sector enterprises and the priority areas of growth of public enterprises in future.

Public Sector in Kerala

Public sector enterprises were started in Kerala even before the formation of the State through the unification of the princely states of Travancore and Cochin, with Malabar (Malabar was a part of the Madras Presidency). Out of these three units, Travancore was the only region that registered considerable industrialisation. It was, in fact, the first State to nationalize trade in commercial crops in 1750 itself. In 1904, the railway route from Quilon to Thirunelveli was opened by the princely State of Travancore, and by 1935 Cochin Government acquired the rights over Cochin Port. The Travancore Government nationalised the Electricity Department, and setup the Rubber Factory at Trivandrum in 1929 and 1935 respectively. The transport system in Travancore was nationalised in 1937. In the beginning of the twentieth centaury certain other public sector companies were started by the State of Travancore and Cochin. They include the Land Mortgage Bank, Kerala Soaps and Oils Ltd., etc. A real growth of the public sector in Kerala was achieved only after the formation of the State in November 1956. The State Government had introduced a more systematic policy of industrial development and started public sector companies like Kerala Government Ceramics and Kerala Cycles Ltd. A considerable push to the public sector in Kerala came after 1970 and a number of public sector units and promotional institution were set up as part of an organised effort for the promotion of industrial growth.

According to the review of public enterprises in Kerala for the year 1999-2000 (published by Bureau of Public Enterprises, Kerala) there were 111 public sector enterprises in the State, which included five units in various steps of liquidation. The State fully owns 76 of the 111 enterprises. The total investment in public enterprises in the State was Rs. 13,770 crore in the year 2000, providing employment for 1,25,814 persons. The total turnover of these enterprises during 1999-00 was Rs. 5703.60 cores. While 45 enterprises together registered profits amounting to Rs. 285.44 crore, other incurred losses totaling Rs. 331.66 crore.

At present, there are four major electrical equipment industrial undertakings in the public sector in Kerala, viz., Kerala Electrical and Allied Engineering Company Limited (KEL), United Electrical Industries Limited (UEI), Traco Cable Company Limited (TRACO) and Electrical Kerala Limited (TELK). Of these, KEL is wholly owned by the Government of Kerala and

UEI and TRACO are under the joint ownership of government of Kerala, KSIDC and private partners. The ownership of TELK is vested in the Government of Kerala, Financial institutions, public, and Hitachi, Japan. In terms of capital invested in the State level public enterprises, TELK occupies very prominent place among the public enterprise in India. The electrical equipment sector as a whole provides only 3.30 per cent of the total employment in the public sector, for which 1.30 per cent of the total investment was made. The public sector electrical equipment enterprises in Kerala produce both capital goods such as transformers, alternators, meters and switchgears, and consumer goods such as electric wires and cables, fuse units, cutouts and switches.

Statement of the Problem

The electrical equipment industry in India has been going through a crucial period during the past several years, with lower production levels, few orders, delayed payments and diminishing profit margins. The demand for electrical equipment is a derived demand dependent on the growth of the power sector, industrial requirements, and urban and rural demands. The power projects envisaged in the Eighth Plan did not materialise as expected; and hence requirement of electrical requirement was far below expectation. The slump in demand is forcing the manufacturers to accept orders at priced that could be unremunarative. Fall in demand is, therefore, the main issue of concern for the public sector electrical equipment industry in Kerala.

The public sector electrical equipment industry in Kerala is also facing fierce competition in the domestic market from other public sector and private sector undertakings in the country. The major competitors in the field are multi-product companies who have active technical collaboration with parties outside India and are profit-making companies. With liberalisation, foreign companies have also entered the market. The net outcome of the problems is the low rate of return on capital invested and negative net worth. This has led to a situation where neither technological developments nor new investments have become feasible. This, in turn, resulted in huge losses and made them less competitive as commercial concerns.

The main customers of the public sector electrical undertakings in Kerala are Indian Railways, KSEB and other State Electricity Boards and other public sector undertakings. These undertakings are also in a difficult financial situation, as a result to which procurement is at lower levels and payments for procured equipment are delayed. Lack of financial discipline is another reason for the poor performance of public sector electrical undertakings. The modern techniques of excellent utilisation of funds have remained out of reach for these undertakings.

Review of Literature

A thorough review of available literature reveals the fact that an in-depth study on the overall performance of electrical equipment industry in the public sector in the State yet to be undertaken. However, a brief review of the available literature on the related topics is attempted here.

Jules Backman reviewed the working of electrical machinery industry in the USA, covering the classification of electrical machinery, pricing of products, marketing, and profit margin, in the context of the US economy. Richard Newfarmer outlined the origin and growth of the electrical industry in Brazil. He also pointed out the problems associated with the development of the electrical equipment industry in India. In the early years of the industry the markets of the developing countries were comparatively inconsequential. Often, they were considers territories of one or two American or British manufacturers. He concluded that the major international technology in developing countries.

Sreevalsan criticised the present field set-up of Kerala State Electricity Board on function basis, and stated that it was most infective and caused avoidable financial strain to the Board. He pointed out that poor purchasing policy, inefficient works management, and excess staff strength were problems faced by the Board. In order to judge the managerial set up and administrative problems in the State level public sector undertakings in Kerala, Gangadharan Pillai conducted a study on the Kerala State Road Transport Corporation, Kerala State Electricity Board, Trivandrum Rubber Works Limited, and Kerala State Industrial Development Corporation. He concluded that political interference, inefficiency of management, defective recruitment system, lack of funds, and indiscipline among workers were the major problems faced by these public sector undertakings.

A study on the functioning of the workshops in the capital goods sector of the Indian Electrical Engineering Industry was carried out by Bharat Bhushan with emphasis on the division of labour on the shop floor. He commented that there could be no universal definitions of technology; and that technology and technical change needed to be defined in relation to workers, to specify production processes. He argued that skill was not a homogeneous category and that technical change could have different impact on the different attributes of skill. Bhasi outlined the slow progress of the electrical motor industry in the State and the hardships faced by the railways in the process of indegenisation of machinery. He suggested various ways for improvement of the performance of the industry, such as diversification of products, proper advertisement, and good after sale services.

Roy discussed the problem of control over public sector undertakings in Orissa with particular reference to the problems of personnel. After stating the rational underlying such control, the author referred to different models of control. The principal among them are legislative control, government control and the control wielded through the bureaucracy. Hemalatha Rao criticized the functioning of Karnataka State Electricity Board and pointed out that it could not generate enough internal resources to finance further power development programmes in the State. The study revealed that defective planning, high cost of manpower, excessive dependence on borrowed funds, wasteful energy consumption, etc. were some of the problems faced by the Board.

Ushakumary noted that the electrical machinery industry in Kerala had failed to generate adequate forward and backward linkages with the local economy. This lack of linkages has developed certain structural bottlenecks in the industrialisation in the State.

In a study on the performance evaluation of the United Electrical Industries Limited, Thampi concluded that the overall performance of the company was not satisfactory. Due to inefficiency, the production cost had increased. The capital structure of the company was also not sound. Syamala discussed the inventory management techniques followed by Kerala Electrical and Allied Engineering Company and suggested the employment of computers for production, design, inventory management, quality control and cost accounting. Chandra Bose made an assessment of saving inventories of public sector electrical equipment companies due to inventory management. He suggested that the total activity of the materials department in the public sector electrical equipment companies in Kerala had to be integrated under one senior manager with the same status as other departmental heads. This would help to obtain economy, efficiency and savings from the martial organisation. In a study on the financial performance of public sector enterprise in Kerala, Nataraja Iyer analysed the productivity performance, profitability performance and financial solvency of he State enterprises in Kerala, and the contribution made by them. Wilson evaluated existing system of financial planning and control and its role in reducing losses and increasing profits, in his study entitled 'Social Planning and Control in Public Sector Undertakings in Kerala'.

Remesh stressed the existence of a potential market for co-axial cables in Kerala. He suggested that in the present context Traco Cable Company, which had been looking for diversification in related fields with low investment, should plan to go for manufacturing such cables. In the study conducted by Nishanth regarding the transformer industry in Kerala, with special reference to Transformers and Electricals Kerala Limited, he identified the export strategies recommended by the management, such as multilateral aided projects, bilateral the counter trade, pricing strategy and appointment of agents. He suggested the need to improve the Research and Development Department for product improvement and innovation of new products.

A close observation of the available literature in the area reveals the fact that an evaluative study of the overall performance of the public sector electrical equipment industry is yet to be made, and hence the present study.

Objectives

The present study aims at the following objectives:

- To ascertain the operational efficiency of the public sector electrical equipment industrial units in Kerala in relation to production and marketing.
- To assess the measures taken by the units for the management of human resources.
- To evaluate the effectiveness of the management of funds in relation to liquidity, profitability and assets backing.

The study covers the four major public sector electrical equipment industrial units in Kerala, viz., Kerala Electrical and Allied Engineering Company Limited (KEL), United Electrical Industries Limited (UEI), Traco Cable Company Limited (TRACO) and Transformers and Electrical Kerala Limited (TELK). As on the date of collection of data, there were 4009 employees working in these undertakings. They included 451 executives, 508 supervisors and 3050 workers. The sample for the study consisted of 90 executives, 102 supervisors and 611 workers (20 per cent of the totals), selected on a random basis from the lists made available by these companies. The sample frame is given in Table 2.1.

The study was based upon both primary and secondary data. The primary data were collected from the executives, supervisors and workers of the undertakings. For this purpose, a questionnaire was developed. The questionnaire was finalised after holding discussions with officers at different levels and conducting a pilot study among 50 respondents. The relevant secondary data for the

Table 2.1: Population and Sample

Company	Executives		Supervisors		Workers		Total	
	Total	Sample	Total	Sample	Total	Sample	Total	Sample
KEL	262	52	169	34	943	189	1374	275
UEI	46	9	35	7	298	60	379	76
TRACO	28	6	49	10	646	429	723	145
TELK	115	23	255	51	1163	233	1533	307
Total	451	90	508	102	3050	611	4009	803

study were collected from the office records of these companies and various published documents of State Planning Board, Bureau of Public Enterprises, Reports of the Comptroller and Auditor General of India, Reports of the Committee on Public Undertakings, and Public Enterprises Survey of the Central Bureau of Public Enterprises. The data collected for the study were tabulated and analysed by employing mathematical and statistical tools like percentages, ratios, index numbers and Z-test. A ten-year period from the financial year 1990-91 to 1999-2000 was chosen for the analysis of secondary data. However, data for the year 2000-2001 were also included, whenever found appropriate.

The present study is an exploratory one, carried out by primarily depending upon the responses of employees and upon published financial statements. It was noted that accounts of two companies were not up-to-date and audit of accounts were pending. So, provisional figures were depended upon in some cases. It was also noted that, in some cases, responses were provided extempore. The quantitative tools used for analysis such as ratios and index numbers were also not free from limitations. However, sufficient care was taken to make the analysis logical and the study meaningful.

Findings

For diversification, KEL had proposed the setting up of three new projects, requiring an estimated investment outlay of Rs. 6,537 lakh including State Government equity of Rs. 2,264 lakh The company received Rs. 1,085 lakh from the Government and invested Rs. 735 lakh in these projects. It is doubtful whether the project would be commercially viable in view of the time and cost overruns and the changed market conditions. UEI was the first factory in India to manufacture electricity supply meters. For diversification, the company started manufacturing several products. But these diversification programmes became a failure due to stiff competition. At present, the demand for electro-mechanical meters has declined and the replacement of it with electronic meters requires only lesser manpower. This is a major threat on the labour front, faced by UEI. In the Report of the Task Force on Public Sector Industries (1997), it was stated that the company has required upgrading its basic technology, in order to survive in the market. However, no attempt has been made so far by company in this direction. During the ten-year period under review, TRACO started diversification of production several times to face the competition in the market, and most of them became successful. At present the company has also proposed diversification into manufacture of XLPE cables. Due to demand recession in the electrical industry throughout the country, as well as heavy competition, TELK fell into difficulties. Since the net worth was negative, TELK was referred to BIFR in 1996.

Production

The production indices of the principal product of KEL (i.e., alternators TL) were satisfactory during the period, even though it showed a fluctuating trend. The production indices of alternators (GP) showed an increasing trend during this period, but its capacity utilization was very low. The production of HRC fuses also showed satisfactory position. However, the production indices of other products showed a declining trend during this period. In UEI the production indices of the principal product (i.e., KWH Meters) showed a satisfactory position, especially in the last three years under review. However, the production indices of Motor Control Gears registered a fluctuating and decreasing trend this period. Of the four products manufactured by TRACO, the production indices of two products recorded a better position and those of the other two products showed a declining trend. The management of the company stated that stiff competition from other manufacturers reduced the market and therefore the company was compelled to reduce its production. In TELK, the production of the principal product (i.e., Power Transformers) and CT/PT decreased during the period under study. However, the production of GCBs and others increased at same time. All the four public sector electrical companies in Kerala operate by make-to-order process in respect of their principal products. The CAG, in his reports, notices several instances of failure on the part of these companies to deliver goods in time, which resulted in huge loss to these companies.

Capacity utilisation

The managements of all the four major electrical companies were of the opinion that demand recession in the electrical industry throughout the country and heavy competition from home and abroad were the causes of low production in the industry. But in KEL, there was an over-utilisation of capacity for distribution transformers and electrical accessories in all the ten years under review, which ranged from 136.3 per cent to 354.8 per cent. At the same time in the case of the main product (i.e., alternators TL) there was under-utilisation of the capacity in five years and over-utilisation in the remaining five years. The company did not utilize its full installed capacity for other items also. It was because of high competition and low demand for these products. The increase in the capacity by KEL was made by means of overtime, multiple shifts and sub-contracting. The cost effect of this alternate source of capacity beyond normal limits also affected the productivity by excess wear and tear of machinery.

Data on the capacity utilisation in UEI revealed that the company utilised almost its full capacity (and even over-utilised it to a limited extent in certain years) for its principle products i.e., Energy Meters throughout the period under review. In the case of motor control gears, there was poor capacity utilisation in all the ten years. The CAG, in his report identified the reasons for low production in UEI as lack of working capital, low orders, high cost of production due to excess consumption of materials, payment of idle wages delayed execution of orders. However, the position of the company in respect of working capital was far better in the later years under review. Similarly, the execution of orders was also prompt in the later years. The management of UEI viewed that lack demand for of motor control gears was the main problems. The customer has preferred electronic meters to electro-mechanical meters. Replacement of electro-mechanical meters with electronic meters will affect the installed capacity of electro-mechanical meters in the coming years.

In TRACO, the capacity utilisation of JFTC showed a comparatively better position than that of the other products. Capacity utilization of other products was very low in the later years under review. The management of the company said that the stiff competition in the market caused low demand for the products. In the CAG Report (1993) relating to TRACO, it was stated a very high installed capacity than required was one of the reasons for under-utilisation of capacity. In the case of TELK, the overall production in terms of installed capacity was very low. The capacity utilisation of all the products registered a fluctuating trend during the ten-year period under review. The management stated that shortage of working capital and stiff competition were the problems faced the company in the utilisation of its installed capacity in full.

Regarding the process of operations, a good number of respondents from all the four companies opined that the process of operations of the companies was satisfactory. A considerable number of respondents considered it good. The majority of the respondents from the electrical industry conferred to efficiency in the management of operations and production of quality goods by these companies. Shortage of power was not a problem faced by these companies. Interruption of the production process due to non-availability of power was moderate. The interruption of the production due to shortage of spare parts was not a problem in KEL, UEI and TRACO. But it was a major problem in TELK. The interruption of the production process due to non-availability of other inputs, such as water, was not a problem in all these companies.

Research and Development

A good number of employees covered under the study belonging to the categories of executives and supervisors from

KEL, UEI and TRACO had the opinion that the R & D activities are effective. But a considerable number of workers from these three companies held the view that they were ineffective. In TELK, the majority of the respondents from the three categories stated that the R & D activities were effective. As a whole, it can be said that the R & D activities of the electrical industry were effective.

Raw Material Procurement and Control

All the four electrical companies under review followed the limited tender method for purchase of raw materials. Lists of approved suppliers are very essential for purchases through limited tenders. But in these companies, there was no system of registering suppliers for all the items of materials and maintaining an up-to-date list of them. It is also necessary to fix the number of suppliers to whom the limited tender enquiries will be sent based on the value of raw materials. But such a purchase policy was not followed by these public sector undertakings. Several instances of defective purchase procedure in the past were noticed, which resulted in heavy loss to these companies. The CAG Report relating to procurement of raw materials revealed the system deficiencies of the purchase policy followed by these electrical companies.

A good number of respondents from these companies were of the opinion that the existing method of purchase of raw materials was good or satisfactory. The opinion of the respondents did not conform to the mention made in the CAG Reports. During discussion, the managements of these companies stated that they had incorporated a well-defined policy for purchase of raw materials. However, some modifications are inevitable for the efficient operation of the purchase policy of these concerns. The responses provided by different categories of employees revealed that the costs of vital, essential and desirable items of raw materials procured by the electrical companies under review were reasonable. But a considerable number of respondents opined that the costs were high and even very high. Therefore, it can be concluded that some modifications are inevitable in the existing arrangements for the purchase of raw materials.

The electrical undertakings selected for this study had not properly maintained various stock levels such as minimum level, maximum levels for the majority of the items. The system of continuous or periodical physical verification of stock was not adopted by these companies. They valued the stock periodically from various stock records. None of these companies had been applying ABC technique in its true sense for various aspects of materials management. KEL, UEI and TELK had attempted to classify materials as ABC on the basis of the annual consumption value of materials. But this exercise was being done for academic purpose only. As far as application of this technique in various areas of material's management is concerned, it was completely neglected in all the undertakings.

A periodic review of all the items of stores is very essential to reveal the presence of slow-moving and non-moving items of materials, but in practice, this was not done by these companies. Mention was made in the CAG Reports regarding the slow/non-moving items of stores. In the opinion of the managements of these companies, change in design and other technological changes in products and processes of manufacture were the reasons for materials becoming slow moving and non-moving. The majority of the respondents from these companies, especially executives and supervisors, were satisfied with the existing method of stores management. But their opinion did not conform to the observation made in the CAG Reports.

However, a considerable number of respondents, especially workers, were not satisfied with the existing method. These companies had not practically adopted stores control techniques. Hence, it can be concluded that the stores management system and the conditions of stores were not satisfactory. All the issues from the store are made on the basis of properly signed requisition. Pricing of issues is made on the 'weighted average price' method. A good number of respondents from all the four companies were of the view that the stores issue methods prevailing in these companies were satisfactory. The statistical test revealed that the views of respondents in this regard were associated with the general response from the industry, except in the case of TRACO, where slight variations were noted. These companies had not calculated and followed the EOQ for determining the quantum of raw materials purchased at a time. The materials were mainly purchased on the basis of orders received from customers. The materials managers of these companies stated that there was no way to ascertain the procurement cost and inventory carrying cost. These companies had also not followed other systems such as replenishment order system and optional replenishment system.

Procurement of excessive quantity of vital items of materials was a problem faced by TELK. In the case of the other three companies, procurement of insufficient quantity was the problem associated with the vital items of materials. The opinion of a good number of respondents (58.4 per cent) from the electrical industry regarding the quantum of essential items procured was that it was moderate. However, in KEL, UEI and TRACO, a considerable number of the respondents opined that certain essential items of materials procured were insufficient. A considerable number of respondents from TELK opined that certain items of materials procured were excessive and certain other items were insufficient for production. A good number of respondents from all the four companies were of the opinion that the quantum of desirable items of raw materials procured was moderate. However, a considerable number of respondents from KEL, UEI and TRACO opined that procurement of sufficient quantity was a major problem. In KEL, UEI and TRACO, there were instances of stoppage of production and delay in the execution of orders in time due to non-availability of raw materials. But in TELK, a considerable number opined that procurement of excessive quantity was a problem faced by the company.

A good number of respondents from the industry (41.1 per cent) were of the opinion that the deterioration of vital items of raw materials kept in the stores was moderate. In UEI, no respondent considered it either very high or high. None of the respondents from TRACO considered it very high. There were mixed responses from the respondents of KEL and TELK regarding the deterioration of vital items of stores. On the whole, it can be concluded that the deterioration of vital items of stores was moderate in all these companies. The opinions of respondents regarding the deterioration of essential and desirable items of raw materials were similar to that regarding the vital items. It showed the effectiveness of stores control adopted by these companies. The majority of the respondents from KEL (61.3 per cent), UEI (51.3 per cent), TRACO (62.8 per cent) and TELK (62.2 per cent) expressed their view that the wastage of vital items of raw materials in the production process was moderate. None of them opined that wastage was either high or very high. Similarly a good number of respondents from KEL (54.5 per cent), UEI (52.6 per cent), TRACO (62.8 per cent) and TELK (43.3 per cent) opined that the wastage of essential items of raw materials in the production process was moderate. No respondent from the industry opined that the wastage of either vital items or essential items of raw materials was either high or very high. The opinion of respondents regarding the wastage of desirable items of raw materials in the production process was also similar to that in respect of the essential items. It revealed that there existed a satisfactory system for the management of vital, essential and desirable items of raw materials in the production process.

The responses provided by the different categories of employees led to the conclusion that wastage of vital, essential and desirable items of raw materials during processing was moderate or even low. However, excess consumption of materials may be a symptom of abnormal wastage. There were occasions of excess consumption of raw materials by KEL and UEI, which were noted in the CAG Reports. The managements of these companies stated that the excess consumption was for research purposes.

Human Resources

The majority of the respondents (62.7 per cent) from the electrical industry were satisfied with the recruitment of executives. Similarly, the majority of the respondents (72.5 per cent) were satisfied with the recruitment of supervisors and 64.6 per cent were satisfied with the recruitment of workers. However, the remaining respondents opposed the existing policy. They suggested that the recruitment for all categories of employees should be made by the Public Service Commission. They also opined that the Chief Executive must be a senior grade employee of the company promoted from among them.

The level of remuneration to employees of each category in these four companies was more or less the same. A good number of respondents belonging to the three categories were of the view that their remuneration was low or even very low. No respondent had the opinion that the remuneration was very high. However, an interesting point noted was that a considerable number of respondents from each category had the impression that the remuneration to the other categories was moderate or even high. The study led to the conclusion that the majority of the employees from the industry were not satisfied with their remuneration. They opined that their total emoluments were lower than those for similar posts in the other industrial sectors and in government services.

The health and welfare measures provided by all the four companies to their employees were average and satisfying to a majority of the respondents belonging to the three categories. The retirement benefits provided to the three categories of employees from the electrical industry were not satisfactory. None of the respondents considered it as either excellent or good. The majority of the employees from KEL, TRACO and TELK were not satisfied with the job security assured to the three categories of employees. In UEI, the majority of the respondents were satisfied with the job security and they said that it was because of the fact that the company had been working on a profit, continuously. However, no respondent from any of the four companies stated that it was excellent. Even though a good number of employees from all the four companies were satisfied with the safety measures adopted by these companies, a considerable number were not satisfied with it. No respondent had the opinion that it was excellent. KEL, UEI and TRACO were not providing accommodation to its employees, except to the Managing Director and the General Manager. TELK had provided accommodation facility to 168 employees as against 1533 employees working in the company. On the whole, the accommodation facility of the industry was poor.

The majority of the employees covered under the study from all the four companies were satisfied with the relationship of top management with other levels. However, about 40 per cent were not satisfied with it. They opined that the importance of recognition of good workmanship, grievances handling procedures, and freedom of self-expression had not been recognised properly by the management. The opinions of also revealed that the efficiency of all the three categories of employees of the industry was satisfactory. A good number of employees covered under the study from all the four electrical companies under review were of the opinion that the absenteeism in their companies were moderate. However, about 21 per cent of them stated that it was high or very high. They said that inadequate housing, health problems of employees and their family members, and maternity reasons were the causes of absenteeism. The majority of theme from all the four electrical undertakings was of the view that the labour turnover was moderate. None of them considered it either high or very high. Hence, labour turnover was not a problem in these companies.

There were mixed responses from the respondents regarding the information set-up for decision-making. The majority of the respondents from KEL and TELK opined that the information set-up was poor or very poor. But in UEI and TRACO, the majority of the respondents were satisfied with the present set-up for decision making. In the opinion of a good number of respondents belonging to the three categories, the extent of participation of executives in policy formulation and decision making was high. In the case of supervisory staff the extent of participation was moderate and in the case of workers, it was low.

Marketing

In KEL, the sales indices of all the products recorded a fluctuating trend during the ten-year period under review. The sales indices of the principal product of the company (i.e., alternators TL) varied from 24 per cent to 146 per cent during this period. The sale of this product was satisfactory in the last six years. The sale of distribution of transformers recorded a decline in several years. The sale of alternators (GP) and DG sets showed considerable increase during this period. In UEI, sales indices of the main product (i.e., KWH Meters) varied between 93 per cent and 142 per cent, which recorded a satisfactory position. However, the sale of motor control gears registered a fluctuating but decreasing trend. In TRACO, sales indices of JFTC and AAAC recorded a better position. The performance of other products during the period under study was poor. The sales indices of the principal product (i.e., power transformer) of TELK recorded a decreasing trend in the last three years under review. The sale of CT and PT also declined during this period. In the case of GCBs, the sales indices showed a satisfactory position. TELK is the only company in this group, exporting its products abroad. The export declined considerably in 1999-2000. The CAG, in his reports, criticised the sales procedures followed by these companies for appointment of agents, preparation of quotations, etc.

In KEL, 37.1 per cent of the respondents considered the effectiveness of the methods of canvassing order for finished goods to be very poor and 22.9 per cent opined that it was poor. The majority of the respondents from TRACO and TELK also expressed the same opinion. However, in UEI, 39.5 per cent of the respondents considered it satisfactory and 22.4 per cent considered it good. No respondent from the industry had the opinion that it was excellent. The electrical companies selected for this study were not provided any sales promotion methods. The managements of these companies opined that their customers were loyal brand buyers and they did not change their buying patterns as a result of competitive promotion. These companies did not provide any advertisement for their products. The majority of the respondents from these companies were of the view that the after-sale services provided to customers were effective and even highly effective.

All the four companies had followed the cost plus pricing method. However, on some occasions of stiff competition, they were forced to reduce the prices of their products, which were specified in the White Paper published by the Government. In the opinion of the majority of the respondents from these companies, the prices charged by these companies were not high, but moderate and even low or very low.

In the opinion of the majority of the respondents from electrical equipment undertakings, the extent of competition for the products was very high. There was not any market research activity in these companies. The respondents of these companies were of the opinion that market research was highly essential for an effective sales forecast and for analysing the utility and marketability of electrical equipment.

There were mixed responses from the respondents of these companies regarding the extent of stock of finished goods in the godown. A good number of executives from KEL (48.1 per cent) opined that the stock of finished goods in the godown was moderate. However, 47.1 per cent of the supervisors and 46.5 per cent of the workers stated that it was high. A good number of respondents from UEI (57.9 per cent) and TRACO (40.7 per cent) considered the stock to be moderate. In TELK, the stock was considered low by a good number of respondents.

Maintenance and Upkeep of Fixed Assets

Replacement and modernisation of assets helps the company to reduce variable operating costs and thus the total cost of goods produced can be controlled. Regarding the replacement/

modernisation of land and buildings, the majority of the respondents from KEL and UEI expressed the view that replacement was not needed. However, the majority of the respondents from TRACO and TELK opined that replacement of land and buildings was needed. None of the respondents stated that it was highly needed. The opinions of respondents were found significantly different from the general tendency in the industry, and this was confirmed by the Z test.

A good number of respondents from KEL (44 per cent) and TELK (51.1 per cent) were of the opinion that the replacement of plant and machinery was highly needed. In UEI and TRACO, a good number (60.5 per cent and 49 per cent respectively) opined that replacement was needed. It revealed the obsolescence of plant and machinery in all these companies, which required immediate replacement. In the White Paper on Public Enterprises published by the Government of Kerala, it was noted that the machinery of KEL was old and required immediate replacement and modernisation.

A good number of respondents from KEL (49.1 per cent), UEI (61.8 per cent) and TRACO (50.3 per cent) were of the view that replacement of furniture and. fittings was needed and a considerable number said that it was highly needed. In TELK, the majority (57.5 per cent) of the workers opined that replacement was not needed and 60.9 per cent of the executives and 47.1 per cent of the supervisors stated that it was needed. On the whole, the opinions of respondents from the electrical companies revealed the deterioration of furniture and fittings, which required replacement/modernisation. A good number of executives (50 per cent) and workers (59.2 per cent) from KEL opined that replacement of other assets like motor vehicles was not needed. But 52.9 per cent of the supervisors said that it was needed. The majority of the respondents from UEI (75 per cent) and TRACO (51 per cent) said that replacement was needed. In TELK, a good number of executives (60.9 per cent) and supervisors (47.1 per cent) opined that replacement was needed, but the majority of the workers (57.5 per cent) opined that it was not needed. On the whole, the responses revealed the need for replacement of other fixed assets like vehicles.

Proper upkeep and maintenance is an important principle for the management of fixed assets. The opinions of respondents from all the four companies revealed that land and buildings were properly maintained. Their views were found significantly associated with the general tendency in the industry. There were mixed responses from the respondents of all the four companies regarding the upkeep and maintenance of plant and machinery. A considerable number of respondents were of the view that the existing method was not satisfactory. They opined that some modifications were required in the existing method of maintenance of plant and machinery.

There were mixed responses from the respondents regarding the upkeep and maintenance of furniture and fittings and other fixed assets. A good number of respondents from all the four companies considered the existing method of upkeep/maintenance of furniture and fittings and other fixed assets to be satisfactory. However, a considerable number of respondents were not satisfied with this and suggested some modifications.

The total debt to equity ratio of TELK was negative throughout the period of study due to negative value of net worth of the company. KEL had recorded a very high ratio compared to other companies. The creditors of UEI had sufficient cushion of net worth towards their claims, while KEL, TRACO and TELK had insufficient cushion, as their claims were very much higher than the net worth of these companies. The ratio revealed that the solvency position of KEL, TRACO and TELK was not good. The policy of trading on equity adopted by these companies cannot be considered good.

Management of Funds

The ratio of net worth to total assets revealed that creditors provided a greater part of funds for financing of assets than the owners in these companies, excepting UEI in six years. The ratio highlights that the financial structure as well as the long-term solvency of the industry was not sound. The ratio of funded debt to paid-up capital of KEL was above unity in five years and below it in the remaining five years. A ratio below unity provides safety to creditors and hence they prefer a lower ratio. There was no funded debt in UEI in the last five years under review. There seems to be vast scope for the company to raise funds through long-term borrowings. In TRACO and TELK, the proportion of debt was always much higher than the paid-up capital. This situation was not satisfactory. The ratio revealed that creditors' interest was not well protected in three companies. The policy of employing lower proportion of funded debt was desirable because the payment of interest and repayment of principal contractual obligations, which must be met if liquidation is to be avoided. The debt service ratio of KEL revealed that there were no sufficient earnings to cover the fixed charges of the company. Its average coverage was only 0.17 times. The debt service ratio of UEI was abnormally high as a result of very low interest charges. In TRACO, the ratio was more than unity in six years, and in TELK, it was more than unity in eight years under review.

The analysis of debt-equity ratio and interest coverage ratio revealed the worsening financial position of the electrical companies as a whole. The very high debt-equity ratio and a low debt service ratio of KEL showed that the financial position of the company was not satisfactory. In UEI, there was no loan capital in the last five years under study. There is vast scope for the company to raise funds through long-term borrowings. The debt-equity ratio and the debt-service ratio of TRACO revealed an undue debt burden to the company. The debt-equity ratio of TELK was negative throughout the period and the coverage ratio was more than unity in eight out of the ten years under reference. As a whole, it can be concluded that the two ratios reveal the need for correcting the imbalance in the financial structure of these companies.

The fixed assets to long-term funds ratio revealed that the fixed assets, being less than the long-term funds, were highly inadequate in all these companies during the period under reference. The ratio was much lower than the accepted standard norm of 0.67 times in the case of UEI and TELK. However, KEL and TRACO registered relatively higher ratio. The overall trend of the ratio suggested that the fixed assets were fully financed by long-term funds and a part of long-term funds were also used for financing working capital. The analysis also revealed that more than 90 per cent of the long-term funds of UEI and TELK were used for financing working capital, which reflected the unsound financial strength of these companies. The trend of fixed assets to funded debts ratio of these companies kept fluctuating during the ten-year period under review. The ratio of three companies, namely, KEL, TRACO and TELK, were very low when compared to the accepted standard norm. The funded debts of these three companies were not fully secured by the fixed assets. In the case of UEI, due to very small amount of funded debts, debts were fully secured by fixed assets. Financing of fixed assets mainly or partly by borrowed funds was a common practice followed by all the electrical companies selected for this study. The ratio of fixed assets to net worth revealed that three companies, namely, KEL, TRACO and TELK were relying more on borrowed funds to finance fixed assets. In the case of UEI, the net worth exceeded fixed assets, except for one year, which showed that the company had followed a well-managed policy for creating fixed assets.

Current ratio is a measure of the firm's short-term solvency. It was noted that the current ratio of these companies did not reach the norm of 2: 1. In UEI, the mean ratio was 1.96 times and in TRACO, it was 1.83 times, which indicated that the position was more or less satisfactory. However, in KEL and TELK, the mean ratio was 1.35 times and 1.13 times respectively, which indicated that the solvency was not sound. The quick ratio calculated to check the adequacy of quick assets revealed that in KEL and TELK quick assets were not sufficient to meet the short-term obligations. In UEI and TRACO, the ratio was higher than the standard norm, which indicated that the liquid position of these companies was sound, but at the same time it signifies that the management of these companies had failed to utilise its assets optimally.

The ratio of long-term debt to net working capital revealed that the whole of the working capital was financed by long-term borrowings and the remaining part of the long-term debt was used in financing fixed assets in the case of three companies, namely, KEL, TRACO and TELK. The mean ratios of three companies were very high, which showed that due to heavy burden of interest charges, the operating results were likely to become disappointing. The ratio was very low in UEI, which showed that a substantial part of the working capital was financed from equity capital. There were no long-term borrowings in the capital structure of UEI in the last five years under review.

The analysis of working capital turnover ratio indicates that the turnover of UEI and TRACO was moderate. In the case of KEL and TELK, the ratio was relatively high, which indicated lower investment in working capital. However, it may be a sign of over-trading. The cash turnover ratio is an indicator of the efficiency in the circulation and utilisation of cash. The analysis revealed that the ratio of all the four companies recorded a fluctuating trend during the period under review. The ratio reflected that there was no uniform policy in these companies regarding cash management. There were mixed responses from the respondents of all the four companies regarding the existing method of cash management. While a good number of respondents were satisfied with the existing method of cash management, a considerable number were not satisfied with it. Hence, some modifications are required in the existing method of management of cash.

In KEL, TRACO and TELK, trade receivables composed a major part of the working capital. In TELK, it was very high. In UEI, the ratio of trade receivables to working capital was less than unity in five out of the ten years, which showed that there was less investment of working capital in the form of trade receivables. The level of investment in receivables can be determined by expressing accounts receivable as percentage of sales. The ratio reflected that the investment in receivables was the lowest in UEI and the highest in TELK, compared to other companies. On the whole, the ratio revealed that the investment in receivables was high in all the four electrical companies.

The average collection period measures the liquidity of accounts receivable and evaluates the efficiency of receivables management. The average collection period of all the four companies was more than three months. It was 6.87 months in TELK which was the highest compared to other companies. The long collection period of these companies reflected that the collection policy was not effective, which was also stated in the CAG Reports. There were mixed responses from the respondents regarding the method of management of receivables. A good number of respondents from KEL, TRACO and TELK were not satisfied with the existing method. In UEI, 40.8 per cent of the respondents considered it satisfactory. All the four enterprises had extended credit beyond 3.5 months. Asked about their views regarding the extent of credit period allowed, the respondents from all the four companies expressed mixed responses. A good number of respondents from KEL and TELK opined that the credit period allowed was high or even very high. In UEI and TRACO a good number of respondents stated that it was moderate.

The inventory to working capital ratio of two companies, namely, UEI and TRACO, can be described as satisfactory because there was sufficient coverage of working capital towards the value of inventory during the ten-year period under study. However, the ratio of KEL and TELK reflected a weak liquidity position. To keep the company in sound health, it is desirable that the inventory should not exceed the working capital. The inventory turnover ratio of all the four electrical companies registered a fluctuating trend throughout the period under study. The ratio of KEL was very low, which indicated accumulation of excess inventory. The ratios of UEI, TRACO and TELK were comparatively higher, which reflected a satisfactory position.

The percentage of trade creditors to total current liabilities in these companies registered a fluctuating trend during the ten-year period under review. It revealed that there was no precise policy regarding the management of creditors, in these companies. Asked about the method of management of creditors, a good number of respondents from all the four electrical companies opined that the method of management of creditors was satisfactory. However, more than 20 per cent of the respondents from these companies were not satisfied with the existing method. The majority of the respondents from KEL (68 per cent) were not satisfied with the extent of credit period allowed by the suppliers. They opined that it was low or even very low. However, the majority of the respondents from UEI (61.8 per cent), TRACO (62.8 per cent) and TELK (52.8 per cent) stated that the extent of credit period allowed was moderate. In these companies also, the remaining respondents were not satisfied with it. No respondent from any company stated that the credit period was either high or very high.

Borrowings from commercial banks for meeting working capital constituted a considerable portion of current liabilities in the electrical companies, except in the case of UEI. In UEI, bank borrowings for working capital were nil in seven out of the ten years under review. In KEL and TELK, the proportion of bank loan to current liabilities was more than the proportion of trade creditors. The opinions of respondents from these companies revealed that the method of management of bank borrowings to meet working capital was satisfactory only in UEI.

The operating profit ratio of KEL revealed that the company was not able to control operating expenses effectively. The ratio did not symbolised a healthy financial position of the company. The operating profit ratio of UEI was satisfactory during the period, compared to other companies. In TRACO, there were operating losses in three years, which resulted from low operating income and high operating expenses. The ratio was satisfactory in the remaining seven years. In TELK, the ratio was above the industry average in seven out of the ten years under review. The mean ratios of KEL and TELK were less than the industry average and those of UEI and TRACO were above the industry average. The net profit ratio was not satisfactory in the electrical companies under reference except in the case of UEI. The mean ratios were negative in KEL, TRACO and TELK. In UEI, the ratio exhibited the presence of higher non-operating income than non-operating expenses, indicating sufficient surplus. The analysis of contribution to the Central and State exchequer from the electrical industry revealed that it increased from Rs. 2,192.09 lakh in 1990-91 to Rs. 3,331.79 lakh in 1999-2000. TRACO had the highest total contribution during the ten-year period, followed by TELK.

In KEL, the Return on Assets (ROA) was negative in two years due to operating loss. The mean ratio of the company (2.63 per cent) was below the industry mean (5.92 per cent). It can be inferred that the ROA of the company was not satisfactory. In UEI, the mean of the ratio (2.33 per cent) was higher than the industry average. The ratio revealed that the operating assets of the company were utilised in a profitable manner. The ROA of TRACO was negative in three years due to operating loss. The ratio was below the industry mean in four years and above it in six years. In TELK, the ROA was negative in the last two years. It was above the industry average in seven years. The overall trend of this ratio was fluctuating and more or less decreasing, except in the case of UEI. The Return on Capital Employed of KEL and TRACO was below the industry average in nine years under review. The ratio revealed that these companies had not been able to utilise the invested capital in a profitable and effective manner. In UEI, the mean ratio was above the industry average, which revealed that the company normally utilised the invested capital in a profitable and effective manner. In TELK, the ratios were much higher than the industry average in eight years, due to the significant decrease in the invested capital of the company. However, it can be concluded from the ratio that the company had utilised the invested capital effectively and profitably.

The electrical companies under review recorded a negative and poor return on shareholders' investment, except for UEI. The performance of UEI was positive throughout the period and hence satisfactory. The ratio of KEL was negative in nine years due to net loss arising from heavy charge of interest on long-term loans. In TRACO, the ratio was negative in four years due to net loss of the company, and on the whole, the ratio was not satisfactory. The net worth of TELK was negative in all the ten years under review, which revealed that the company had failed to follow a suitable financial policy. Asked about the views regarding the working results, the respondents from KEL and TELK opined that they were very low or low. The majority of the respondents from UEI (77.6 per cent) and TRACO (50.3 per cent) stated that they were moderate. UEI earned profit throughout the period, and TRACO in the last two years.

The opinions of respondents revealed that the majority of the employees from all these companies were against privatisation. They stated that only public sector companies could act as a model employer and ensure job security to them.

Recommendations

Based on the findings of the study mentioned, the following recommendations are made.

Composition of the Board: The Boards of Directors of the public sector companies, like the electrical equipment industrial units of Kerala, are dominated by political leaders and civil servants nominated without considering their qualification or business aptitude. The political leaders when appointed as Directors do not devote adequate time and attention to the affairs of these undertakings. Usually, the civil servants, posted on deputation, have to take more care for the Government than for the welfare of the undertakings. Hence, the practice of excessive representation of civil servants and political leaders on the Board should be given up. Care should be taken to see that the Board is well balanced and cohesive. The official representation should be limited to 50 per cent. In addition, at least 50 per cent of the directors should be experienced professionals in the field concerned.

The Managing Director of the company should be either an experienced employee of the company or at least an experienced professional. In order to ensure professionalism in management, a pool of suitable personnel should be identified, from private or other, State/Central public sector undertakings for managing the top posts. The help of Bureau of Public Enterprises can be sought in this regard. Whenever they are appointed, they must be asked to opt for permanent absorption in the company as a measure to avoid frequent change in the top position.

Production Organisation: It is necessary that the electrical equipment undertakings must review their production organisation set-up on a continuous basis and plug the loopholes that may appear from time to time. They should, in particular, examine their existing production organisation in the light of factors such as changes in market standard and quality, production diversification and product development. It is also necessary that highly sophisticated plant and machinery should replace the obsolete and outmoded plants used at present. Wherever possible, computers should be used for production planning and control.

Capacity utilization: The optimum utilisation of capacity is of great significance in any enterprise. Of the four major electrical undertakings selected for this study, KEL and UEI .vorked with an over-utilisation of installed capacity for their main products. Therefore, the installed capacity in respect of these products must be immediately increased by these companies. For this purpose, the urgent attention of the Government is required, and the management should take necessary steps to attain this objective. In the case of the other two companies and other products of KEL and UEI, they were blamed for under-utilisation of capacity. Therefore, there is urgent necessity of optimum utilisation of capacity for all the products of these companies.

In the opinion of the respondent from these companies, the main factors affecting under utilisation are inadequacy of demand and inadequacy of raw materials, especially imported items. The

Government should streamline procedures for import of raw materials and components, and encourage modernisation and diversification schemes as well as export of electrical equipment. The electrical companies should take all steps to upgrade their technology, develop operational skills by training, improve industrial relations, diversify the product mix, and so on. The Bureau of Public Enterprises should be entrusted with the task of conducting an in-depth study to identify the reasons for low capacity utilisation and to suggest steps to improve the situation.

Maintenance: A considerable number of respondents from the electrical industry were not satisfied with the existing method of maintenance of plant. So, the managements should define clearly and carefully the objectives of plant maintenance and the responsibility of persons engaged in it, and the cost that may be incurred for this purpose. The scheme of maintenance should be such as to have the right degree of preventive and breakdown maintenance, so that the costs are at the optimal level. It must be noted that such calculations change with time and this optimality has to be checked from time to time. Schedules of maintenance of plant and machinery must be obtained from the manufacturers and followed throughout the life of the plant. A systematic recording of faults will help better preventive maintenance. Planned maintenance lends itself to the application of modem techniques like CPM and PERT. Systematic work-study including method study and work measurement can be undertaken, based on recorded experience, for reducing the time of scheduled maintenance.

Purchase of materials: All the four electrical companies selected for this study are following the limited tender method for the purpose of purchase of raw materials. There should be a list of approved and registered suppliers for each category and type of materials. It is also necessary to fix the number of suppliers to whom the limited tender enquiries will be sent, based on the value of the purchase order. The register should be kept complete and up-to-date by including the names of new suppliers approved for the purpose and by elimination of existing suppliers who have not proved their efficiency and reliability by past conduct. It was also noted by the CAG that the rates offered by the regular suppliers of these electrical companies were very high compared to other suppliers. Hence, it is advisable to invite open tenders for regular items of stores required by the company. Single tender or direct purchases should be exceptional steps to be taken only in emergent circumstances, where the procurement of stores is of immediate necessity for uninterrupted production, repairs of plant and machinery, or any other production crisis.

It is also necessary to fix the time limit for each stage of purchase, viz., issue of enquiry, receipt and consideration of quotations, issue of purchase order, etc. The time taken to release the purchase orders during a particular period, and the pending indents, should be reviewed periodically with a view to examining the reasons for delay in placing orders and taking remedial measures. A purchase committee for scrutinising purchase proposals can also be appointed to obviate avoidable delays. Similarly, to avoid unnecessary reference to finance, certain financial limits should be laid down. Again, a regular and standard follow-up procedure should be an absolute requirement in the materials flow system. Purchases should be made in ideal quantities. The economic order quantity should be decided with reference to the ordering cost of purchases and the carrying cost of inventory. Purchases should be made after determining various stock levels to all items of stores, such as minimum level, maximum level and safety stock. Ideal and optimum discount terms should be arranged with the suppliers. Through continuous market research and value analysis, substitutes should be purchased when they are more economical, but consistent with quality and service. For imported materials, continuous search should be made to find out alternative acceptable indigenous materials. There should also be a strict and standard system of inspection for incoming materials.

Storage of materials: The study revealed that there was no well-defined policy in these companies regarding the quantities to be stocked, those to be ordered, and when to order them. Even the routine procedures for receiving, storing and issuing of materials were very primitive and unsuitable. Control systems were practically absent. The top management should recognise that materials management requires specialised knowledge, and that the efficiency of the department will depend upon the qualification and experience of the personnel appointed therein. The entire documentation system should be computerised to make an efficient system of stores control. A system of continuous stock verification on cyclic basis should be adopted to cover all materials at least once a year. Discrepancies noticed as a result of such verification should be reconciled promptly and all shortages which come to light must be investigated.

The technique of ABC analysis should be practically applied for inventory control. Careful attention should be paid to estimate the requirements, purchase scheduling, safety stock, prompt receipt and inspection of 'A' items. Their deliveries should also be arranged carefully. This would help in keeping down the investment in inventories. These companies should also adopt techniques like PERT and CPM, to reduce a high level of inventories. The various stock levels such as minimum level, maximum level, and reorder level should be determined for each item of raw material. Disposal management of obsolete, surplus and scrap materials must be given its due importance by the management. Further, it would be useful if proper accounts of these items are maintained. Non-moving items in stores should be identified regularly and decisions must be taken whether to retain them or dispose of them. Wastage in storage should be avoided by careful storing and periodic inspection of materials. Wastage in consumption either due to negligence or to over-consumption should be controlled by fixing norms of consumption at different stages of the production process. Studies should be conducted by the industrial engineers to reduce scrap and wastage in the production process.

Manpower: The excess manpower in all categories of employees has been a heavy burden to these electrical enterprises. This situation necessitates a scientific approach to human resource management in these undertakings. The manpower requirement was fixed by these companies in anticipation of full capacity utilisation. Political interference in the recruitment process also led to this phenomenon. The excess manpower should be wiped off through the implementation of suitable schemes, such as Voluntary Retirement Scheme (VRS) or deputing excess personnel to other suitable positions. In order to eliminate political interference, the recruitment should be entrusted with the Public Service Commission (PSC).

There are wide variations between the pay levels of employees of electrical companies and those of the KSEB and government services. Attempts should be made by the management and government to minimise such difference in the pay levels. It helps to give a sense of equity to the employees. The top management of these companies should pay proper attention to maintain good relations with other levels. They should be aware about the significance of good relations and should identify and rectify the factors which adversely affect their relations with employees. Proper working and safety conditions should be provided to the employees. It is necessary to arrange facilities to maintain employees in good health and safety conditions, which would help to establish good industrial relations. Economic factors are also important determinants in the management-employee relations. The employees should be properly, fairly an equitably compensated and proper welfare services and facilities should be provided by the management of these electrical companies.

The management should understand the significance which the employees attach to their promotion and advancement. Therefore, a proper and fair promotion policy which provides proper opportunities for advancement to different categories of employees should be framed and implemented. Proper attention should be given to the handling of employees' grievances. The management should take necessary steps to create a sense of mutual trust, confidence, and co-operation with the employees. The management should recognise the importance of proper channels of communications with the employees, to foster understanding. Absenteeism creates various problems and it affects production, cost, efficiency and discipline. The company should maintain proper records about the nature, duration and extent of absenteeism. The management should identify those employees who are more prone to absenteeism. The reasons for their absenteeism must be discussed with them and even with the trade unions. If any of the reasons related to the company exists, it should be rectified.

Industrial housing: Although proper industrial housing has a great influence on the employees' health and efficiency to work, it is rather unfortunate that little has been done by the public sector electrical equipment industry in Kerala in this regard. Only TELK has implemented the housing scheme, and that too constitutes only a very small percentage of the total requirement. There is an urgent need of housing schemes meant for the benefits of the employees of these electrical undertakings, especially those coming under low income groups. It is absolutely necessary that instead of shifting the responsibilities from one another, the government, the employers and the trade unions must act in co-operation to tackle this menacing problem of industrial housing.

The housing facilities may be in the form of providing quarters, granting housing loans by the employers themselves, arranging housing loans by the employers from housing societies, banks or housing companies, or reimbursement of house rent by the employer to the employees. But, in the present study, the main reason given by the employers for not providing residential accommodation was financial limitations. Hence these companies can arrange housing loans from the Housing Board or other house building companies and can disburse them through the Employees' Co-operative Societies functioning in these companies. It is necessary to realise that the accommodation programme must be one which the companies can undoubtedly afford. Industrial housing must be given top priority to avoid the problem of dislocation of families of employees, which may lead to high rates of labour absenteeism and turnover.

Marketing: The public sector electrical equipment undertakings in Kerala have a long way to go to improve the efficiency and effectiveness of their marketing systems. The various interfaces between production, marketing and accounts should be improved as a whole for the overall improvement of these undertakings. This can be achieved by market orientation. There was no market research activity in these companies. So, the function of market research should be carried out regularly on a scientific basis. Opportunity scanning studies are suggested to be taken up periodically to identify new growth areas, both in products and markets. Based on the market studies, long-range forecasts should be drawn up. Product modifications and improvements should be carried out, based on market feedback. A detailed study should also be carried out to assess the potential for the current product range and also to identify new products. All these companies should make efforts to shift from dependence on one or a few customers by exploring new markets. For this, new products should be identified and developed by them. These companies should make serious efforts to export their products. In view of the increasing activity of industrialisation in developing countries, as well as the globalisation and liberalisation policy, it would be possible for these companies to establish in the international market. All these companies should adopt advertising and sales promotion techniques to explore new markets and retain the existing market. The marketing departments of these companies should be manned by professionally qualified and experienced personnel. They can help the organisation in becoming market-oriented.

Balanced capital structure: The study revealed that there was no balanced capital structure in these undertakings. The State Government should decide a proper debt-equity ratio for these companies and ask them to follow it strictly. Even though the primary responsibility for fixing the debt-equity ratio depends on the government, these companies should also strive hard to generate more and more internal resources for meeting their financial requirements by improving their profitability and performance.

Mobilisation of resources: Public sector electrical undertakings are facing various difficulties in mobilising funds from different sources. The State Government is finding it difficult to provide finance to these undertakings due to the funds constraint and the use of resources mainly for welfare activities. Therefore, these undertakings should increase the internal sources and mobilise funds from outside sources, such as public deposit, conversion of loan into equity, and use of preference capital, such mobilisation through external sources requires the Government's decision. The State Government should appoint an expert committee to study the capital structure and profitability of all the enterprises and decide the issues on the merit of each case.

Management of cash: There exists no uniform and precise policy regarding cash management in the electrical companies taken up for this study. Hence, there is an urgent necessity to provide a good deal of attention in streamlining the organisation for cash management. Instead of the cashier being in charge of the cash section, one manager with high qualification and experience may be appointed for the management of cash. These companies should fix an appropriate size of cash balances to be held by them so that they can reduce the opportunity and carrying costs. Decisions relating to the preparation of cash budgets, controlling of cash and investment of idle funds must be entrusted to the cash section. In order to carry the optimum level of cash, the manager in charge of cash must be in a position to predict the cash inflows and outflows accurately. Inflow of cash can be increased by expediting the process of collecting debts and through quick transfer of funds. It was noted that the investment in receivables was high in all the four companies. Similarly, the collection period was also long. As such, if these companies are strict enough to disallow the excess credit periods, there would be significant improvement in the funds position of these undertakings. On the other hand, outflow of cash can be regulated through proper arrangement of the schedule of payments, reducing excessive investment in inventories, and controlling expenditure.

Management of receivables: The public sector electrical equipment undertakings should concentrate more on the formulation of attractive and coherent credit and collection policies. These policies determine the eventual magnitude of the firms' investment in receivables and thereby the return on them. It was observed that the public sector electrical undertakings selected for this study were too liberal and considerate in setting the credit terms. They were not offering any discount facilities, though their credit periods were extended to considerable lengths. Hence, there is an urgent and pressing need for formulating more viable credit policies. It was revealed from the study that accounts receivables often remained uncollected beyond the credit period allowed by the enterprises. Hence efforts should be made by these undertakings to step up the efficiency in the collection of debts. It is the responsibility of each of the enterprises to develop its own policy of collecting the debts. An assortment of tools and techniques can be pressed into service, based on their usefulness to particular situations. The enterprises have also to be cautious about the effects of each tool they wish to use against their customers. Each Company should have a separate cell for looking after the credit and its collections. This cell may be placed under the Finance Department or Marketing Department, wherever it is most suited. The cell should be made responsible for the formulation of credit policy and settling up of credit terms, credit analysis and expeditions, and follow-up of collection of receivables.

Bank borrowings for working capital: The use of bank credit for meeting working capital requirements was very high in these electrical companies, except in UEI. Efforts should be made by these companies to increase the internal sources and long-term funds for meeting permanent working capital needs. The State Government should take steps to enable the enterprises to generate more and more internal sources by improving the performance of their undertakings. It will minimise their dependence on the exchequer. These companies can also follow the policy of financing permanent working capital requirements through long-term borrowings and equity. Only variable working capital requirements may be met through short-term borrowings.

Operating costs: It was observed that the operating costs were high in these electrical undertakings. Therefore, it is imperative that the managements of these companies should control the operating expenses. It is only then that these companies would have a more favourable operating profit ratio. Similarly, the management should increase the operating income by increasing production and sales to the fullest possible extent. Particularly, the management of KEL and TELK should give special attention to the reduction of operating expenses because these companies have been incurring losses continuously. It is suggested that the management of these companies should try to exercise control over operating expenses through a proper financial policy.

Audit: The annual accounts of two electrical companies selected for this study, viz., TRACO and TELK, are pending finalisation for two years continuously. The arrears in the submission of accounts is an indication of lack of control and responsibility. The Government should stipulate a period by which the accounts of all the companies are finalised and brought up-to-date, for, only then can the real position of the industry be assessed. The audit conducted by the CAG is more effective than the audit by Chartered Accountants. The statutory audit carried out by the Chartered Accountants mainly deals with the maintenance of annual accounts, whereas the audits by the CAG go more deep into the various operational aspects and concentrate on the propriety of the various expenditures. So, it is advisable that the CAG audit should be strengthened so as to cover the audit of every enterprise, every year. The Government should take appropriate follow-up measures on the audit reports of the CAG.

The functioning of the internal audit system in these electrical undertakings is not perfect and it cannot benefit these enterprises. Hence, the internal audit system should be strengthened by these companies, in order to expose the imperfect accounting, imprudent management of inventory, mismanagement of cash, and so on. A new attempt must be made by the Government to evaluate the public sector electrical undertakings in the State. For this purpose, the best way will be to introduce the performance audit and revise the performance indicators. The need to improve the efficiency of these undertakings, especially of the loss making units, is imperative. It is, therefore, better that trade unions are given a clear picture of the health of these companies concerned and their co-operation to contribute wholeheartedly or to face the consequence of closure of companies is sought. The State Government can warn the management to take the responsibility for improvement. Otherwise, they will have to face curtailment of their perks, etc. The 'value for money' should be made applicable to all these electrical undertakings at the first instance.

Costing Department: A sound Costing Department is a prerequisite for making rational decisions, particularly relating to pricing. Unfortunately, the electrical undertakings selected for this study did not give any attention to maintaining a Costing Department. Even though these companies were following the cost plus pricing method, they did not have adequate facilities for proper ascertainment of the costs involved. Therefore, there is every necessity for maintaining a Costing Department in these companies. Further, this Department should be given a useful role in the fixation and revision of prices from time to time. The mechanism of cost ascertainment and cost control has to be strengthened in these undertakings. Standards should be fixed for each element of cost, and deviations should be analysed to find reasons and to take immediate steps to avoid unfavourable deviations in future. All these highlight the need for a Sound Costing Department in these enterprises.

Government Agency: In 1994, the State Government constituted the Public Sector Restructuring and Internal Audit Board (RIAB), and is functioning as a professional interface between the public sector undertakings and the administrative department within Government since then. RIAB is engaged in the appraisal of proposals from public sector undertakings at the administrative department level and provides recommendations to the Government. It is also engaged in the monitoring of performance and internal audit. However, RIAB is a very small organisation which could not look after the matters relating to all the public sector undertakings in the State on time. Therefore, the need for a professional institution in the form of RIAB for the electrical sector alone is very urgent for performing the public sector electrical undertakings in a planned manner.

Privatisation: Privatisation has been a topic of discussion in the country in recent years. State Governments are not in a position to bear huge losses and to provide finance to these public sector undertakings due to constraint of funds. The idea of privatisation has emerged from the feeling that the public enterprises in general have been making huge losses, while private enterprises operating in the same environment are earning substantial profits. However privatisation is not a remedy to prevent the Indian economy from the bad effects of the public sector. There is no country in which the government is not engaged actively and directly in setting up and managing industrial enterprises. An entire privatisation means the abandonment of the declared policy of the socialistic pattern of society. Thus, the only real remedy lies in improving the efficiency of public sector undertakings. Both the Government and the enterprises should make an all-round effort to ensure that a full-fledged system of control is installed in every aspect.

References

Backman, Jules, *Economics of Electrical Machinery Industry*, New York: New York University Press, 1960.

Bhasi, T.K., *Electrical Equipment Industry: Festo Elgi Private Limited – A Case Study*, Calicut: University of Calicut, 1985.

Bhushan, Bharat, *Technology and Work Organisation in the Indian Electrical Engineering Industry*, London: Department of Social and Economic Studies, Imperial College, 1982.

Chandra Bose, D., *Inventory Management in Public Sector Electrical Industry in Kerala*, Kochi: Cochin University of Science and Technology, 1995.

Dugar, S.M., *Law of Restrictive Trade Practices*, New Delhi: Taxman

Publications, 1976.
Gangadharan Pillai, V., *The Public Sector Enterprises in Kerala: Administrative Problems*, Trivandrum: Kerala Academy of Political Science, 1980.
Government of India, *India 2001*, New Delhi: Publication Division, Ministry of Information and Broadcasting, 2001.
Government of Kerala, *A Review of Public Enterprises in Kerala 2001*, Trivandrum: BPE, March, 2001.
Guru, D.D. and Ahsan, Q., *Public Enterprises*, Delhi: Amar Prakashan, 1987.
Hemalatha Rao, *Financial Performance of Public Sector Enterprises*, Jaipur: Print Well Publishers, 1988.
Khana, O.P., *Industrial Engineering and Management*, New Delhi: Dhanpat Rai Publications (P) Ltd., 1999.
Khera, S.S., *Government in Business*, Bombay: Asia Publishing House, 1963.
Nataraj Iyer, S., *Financial Performance of Public Sector Enterprises in Kerala*, Thiruvananthapuram: University of Kerala, 1995.
Newfarmer, Richard, *Transactional Conglomerates and the Economics of Dependent Development: A Case Study of the International Electrical Oligopoly and Brazil's Electrical Industry*, Greenwich: Ai Jai Press Inc., 1980.
Nishanth, M.E., *A Study on Transformer Industry with Special Reference to TELK*, Kochi: Cochin University of Science and Technology, 1999.
Perry, Josephine, *The Electrical Industry*, New York: Longmans, Green and Company, 1945.
Ramesh, P., *Market Survey on CATV Co-AXIAL Cables*, Kochi: Cochin University of Science and Technology, 1999.
Roy, R.C., *State Public Enterprises in India*, New Delhi: Uppal Publishing House, 1985.
Sapru, R. K. (Ed.), *Management of Public Sector Enterprises in India*, New Delhi: Ashish Publishing House, 1987.
Sreevalsam, T.K., *Administration of State Electricity Boards with Special Reference to Kerala*, Thiruvananthapuram: University of Kerala, 1976.
Syamala, S., *A Study of Inventory Management in Kerala Electrical and Allied Engineering Company Limited.*, Thiruvananthapuram: University of Kerala, 1996.
Thampi, Y., *Performance Evaluation of the United Electrical Industries*

Limited, Thiruvananthapuram: University of Kerala, 1994.

The Monopoly and Restrictive Practices Commission, *Report on the Supply and Exports of Electrical and Allied Machinery and Plant*, London: Her Majesty's Stationery Office, 1975.

UN Publication, *Organisation, Management and Supervision of Public Enterprises in Developing Countries*, Sales No. E 74 II.H.4.

Ushakumary, K., *A Study of the Linkages of Electrical Machinery Industry in Kerala*, Kochi: Cochin University of Science and Technology, 1992.

Wilson, P.R., Financial Planning and Control of Public Enterprises in Kerala, Thiruvananthapuram: Cochin University, 1981.

3

Textile Industry in the Public Sector

M. K. Manilal

The cotton textile industry is the first major industry to develop among the modern Indian industries. It is the base on which the pyramid of the industrial sector of the country has been built. What started largely as a spinning enterprise a century ago has now gradually developed into a mature composite industry. It provides employment to around 11.5 lakh workers, accounting for 18 per cent of all factory labour. Textile industry is one of the basic and important industries due to its wide user segment and large forward and backward linkages. Even today, it employs people directly and contributes 10 per cent of the total industrial production. It is one of the biggest sources for export, claiming 30 per cent of the total exports from India. The area under cotton cultivation in India is the largest in the world. The spinning capacity of Indian textile mills is the second largest after China's. India has the largest weaving sector and a long tradition of producing some of the finest and costliest fabrics in the world.

The industry has a very wide base with multiple products of multiple types. The industry produces spun yarn, fabric, hosiery, readymade garments and other textile goods. There are small units of hand spinning and hand weaving, handlooms, powerlooms, processing houses, spinning mills, composite mills, etc. There are different types of fibres starting from cotton to 100 per cent synthetic ones. The important feature of the pattern of production is the composition of output. Cloths produced in the mill sector can, be classified into five groups: (1) Coarse, (2) Medium B, (3) Medium A, (4) Fine, and (5) Super-fine. The first two categories of cloth generally meet the clothing requirements of the weaker sections of the society. The Government's textile policy has made it obligatory for the mills to produce these two categories of cloth in a certain proportion to their total output. The proportion of superior quality cloth to total output, however, has been increasing over the years. Various permutations and combinations of these factors make the spectrum of the industry very big.

The textile industry in India came with its first mill established in 1820 at Calcutta. But the first successful experiment was made by the mill established in 1860 in Ahmedabad. By the end of the 19th century, many textile mills started operating. By 1951, the mill sector started supplying 75 per cent of its production. In terms of fibre, cotton textile was the main segment, the share of non-cotton textile being less than 7 per cent till 1930. Though khadi and handloom production grew, the production was too small to affect the mill sector, which continued to increase. The history of the last 50 years witnessed various ups and downs in the industry. Till 1960 the mill sector continued to expand with good profitability. The tax structure and government policy were in favour of decentralised production. All new investment was diverted to the powerloom sector, and before it could be properly realised, the decentralised sector arose; as a competitor against the mill sector. So, after 1961, the mill sector started stagnating and declining. The last 90 years also witnessed rapid growth in the production of synthetic and blended fibres, and many changes in the processing technology, besides changes in the design of machines and processing of materials. This affected the cotton textile industry badly.

India enjoys comparative advantage in textile sale in the international market. Its exports, which helped the industry to survive even in, worst slumps. India claims around 2.5 per cent of the total world exports of all textile products including made-ups. The separate data on exports of each textile product indicate that readymade garments were the major export item during 1981 to 1990. India is the biggest yarn-exporter with a share of 28 per cent of the world market and is known for the quality of its fine count cotton yarns. The destinations of exports include various American and European countries. Cotton textile claims 70 per cent of the total exports. Raw cotton is being imported but the official import of fabrics has not been high till today. However, recent reports indicate that imported fabrics and garments have entered the Indian market in a big way and have badly affected textile production in powerloom and other sectors. In the past, cotton mill industry suffered on account of incompetent and selfish managing agents and directors who were more interested in their own profits. They did not take sufficient interest in the accumulation of financial reserves, or in the proper maintenance of machinery, or in modernisation.

The two most important factors which spelt disaster to the industry in the last three decades are the Government's textile policy and the growth of the powerloom sector. The result was that many cotton mills became inefficient and uneconomical. One-third of the cotton mills became sick and were closed down. The total number of mills closed as on December 2000 amounted to 382. The other reasons for sickness in the textile industry could be excess capacity, lower productivity of labour and machine, increase in the cost of inputs, particularly the key raw materials, as also lack of adequate working capital and lack of modernisation and technological upgradation.

On account of the various reasons, many cotton mills became sick and closed down. At one time, nearly one-third of the mills were closed down, throwing thousands of workers out of employment. Trade unions and political parties brought pressure on the Government to take over the sick mills. The Government set up the National Textile Corporation (NTC) to run these sick mills. The Government has been regularly pumping in money to rehabilitate and modernise these mills. However, these mills continue to incur losses which are borne by the tax payer, in the ultimate analysis. The textile industry, which is one among the oldest in the State of Kerala, has been contributing significantly towards industrial promotion, employment and export earnings. While considerable technological advancements have been achieved in this industry, there are also signs of incipient sickness due to low level of technology, increase in cotton price, demand -

supply mismatch, and low market price. During the 1970s, out of the total installed capacity of 6.91 lakh spindles, mills having around 2 lakh spindles became sick, leading to the take-over of three of them by the Kerala State Textile Corporation (KSTC) and four by the NTC.

At present, the textile industry in Kerala consists of 36 mills in the organised sector, nearly 6000 decentralised powerlooms and 57000 handlooms. There are also a few garment manufacturers. Out of the 36 mills in the State, 4 KSTC mills, 5 co-operative mills, and 2 State-owned mills are under the Industries Department. The 36 mills in Kerala directly employ nearly 20,000 workers. Indirectly a number of people in the handlooms and powerlooms are absorbed by this industry. The textile industry in Kerala is the second largest employer, next only to plantations.

Significance of the Study

The performance of the organised sector in Kerala presents a varied picture. While the years 1988 to 1990 had been very good for the textile mills of India in general, enabling them to come out of the progressive deterioration witnessed in the first five years of the last decade, mills in Kerala had not, by and large, fared well. Of the 36 mills, only 19 are in the private sector. Out of the total spindleage of 8.7 lakh in the State, more than 50 per cent is in the private sector. Many of these private mills have shown good profitability. On the other hand, mills in the public and co-operative sectors have been showing losses except in the year ending March 1990. Better performance of the private sector mills was achieved in spite of the fact that all the mills suffered from common disadvantages such as lack of availability of cotton and other raw materials in the State, frequent power cuts, and industrial unrest.

As on 31-03-2000, there were three spinning mills closed in the State, due to sickness, with an installed capacity of 76 thousand spindles and 2873 workers. There were 6 mills registered with the Board for Industrial and Financial

Reconstruction, as on 30-04-2000. The various factors which led the cotton mills to the present predicament require attention. The important problems, which affected the mills in the State adversely during the period under study include: low capacity utilisation of installed spindles and looms in the mills led to lower machine productivity and lesser profit; back-log of modernisation due to non-availability of adequate funds; and to inadequate cash generation from the operations in the earlier years; many of the mills have low profitability on account of increased cost of production due to low labour productivity and higher interest cost for borrowings and debts, and lower selling prices; the increase in power cost coupled with poor quality of power, usually affects the economical working of the mills; and the mills in the state depend on market outside the State for their raw material requirements and also for sale of finished products.

Review of Literature

Very few studies have been made about the various aspects of the cotton mills in the State. Regarding the public sector mills in the State mainly, some Government reports are in existence. A brief review of the available literature is attempted below.

The study by Padmanabhan analysed the problem of sickness in the organised mill sector of the cotton textile industry on an all-India basis. He analysed the composition of assets, liabilities and net working capital. He has found that the current ratio is useful in predicting the short-term solvency of a firm. Similarly, equity/debt ratio also proved effective in testing long-term solvency. Sreenivasan studied Indian textile industry and analysed the various branches of the industry, such as mills, power looms, handlooms, the knitting industry and Khadi, and their relationship. He has also studied the position of certain other industries closely related to the textile industry, such as the silk industry, the wool industry, man-made fibre industry and the textile machinery industry. He has also outlined the problems and prospects of the textile industry. Dhulasi Birundha undertook a study into the high variation in profits among mills of the same size in each year and for each mill over different years. She attempted to find the causes for the low profitability of the mills. In the study, four factors were identified for testing their impact on profitability. These four factors were: size of the firm measured in terms of total financial assets; technology adopted in terms of capital intensity; modernisation in terms of additional investment in machines; and capacity utilisation of spindles and looms in terms of the number of actual days worked by the mill. Among these four factors studied, technology and modernisation were found to have a greater impact on profitability in the mills. The study has also revealed a positive correlation between profitability and growth of the mills.

Kevin made a comparative study of the textile industry in Kerala and Tamil Nadu. He anaysed the profitability of the textile industry as well as of the individual mills. The study also analysed the cost structure, machine productivity, machine utilisation and labour productivity of the mills, in order to locate the factors responsible for inter-mill variation in profit. He intended to analyse the financial structure of the industry so as to assess its long-term solvency. He also studied the working capital management of the industry through fund flow statement. The study revealed that the profitability of the industry had declined during the period under study. The study has found that there is considerable inter-mill variation in profitability each year. The factors which account for the inter-mill variation in profitability have been identified as labour cost, interest payments, and gross value added. Machine productivity, machine utilisation and labour productivity are the three factors which determine the value of output of a mill, which in turn influence the gross value added. The study revealed the features of the industry like low profitability, low ownership contribution, high debt financing, excessive reliance on short-term fund, scarce initial resource generation, poor debt servicing capacity, negative working capital, insufficient liquidity, and overstocking of raw material and stores and spares.

The Government of Kerala constituted in 1990 an advisory

committee to study the problems and prospects of the textile industry in Kerala. The committee found that the mills in the public sector had not been well managed. The study revealed that efficiency and professionalised management are a sine qua non for the success of any industry in the State, which is a high wage island as compared to the neighbouring States. The study suggested modernisation of the existing textile units in the State, and also reduction of the work-force to the norms jointly recommended by the Textile Research Associations for modern and efficient units.

The study by South Indian Textile Research Association (SITRA) highlighted cost control and costing in spinning mills. The study analysed the causes for sickness and formulated the symptoms to forewarn sickness in a spinning mill. In most cases sickness in the textile industry is the result of the failure to control costs in time. Conditions to be fulfilled for a sick mill to become viable have also been arrived at. By emphasising the important and salient relationships between various managements, technical and cost factors; the study addresses itself to the needs of top management, managers and technical staff as well as cost accountants and accountants in a spinning mill. An inter-firm comparison of absenteeism is the fourth in the series of studies published by SITRA on absenteeism in the cotton mills. The survey was undertaken to enable each participating mill to compare its performance against absenteeism with others and to judge the extent of improvement or deterioration as a result of absenteeism over a period of time.

The study has revealed that there was a wide disparity in the rate of absenteeism among the member mills of SITRA. This phenomenon of abnormal variation itself suggests considerable scope for narrowing down the absenteeism rate in the mills with excessive absenteeism. The study further revealed that among the different components of absenteeism, unauthorised absenteeism was ruling very high. The member mills of SITRA were incurring a loss of 2.5 per cent in their capacity utilisation during 1993 due to absenteeism. The higher absenteeism rate in the public sector mills indicates the need for gearing up the absenteeism control mechanism in these mills. Productivity in spinning is a compilation of nearly four decades of SITRA's work in productivity measurement and improvement in spinning mills. The work comprises development of various concepts, defining suitable terminology, conducting surveys, applying the procedure developed, setting up of norms to reflect the top ten per cent productivity levels at various times in the industry and their periodic review and revision, as well as making projections to guide the industry to choose the possible alternatives open to them for future improvements.

Mohan Kumar analysed the relative performance of spinning mills of Kerala in different sectors. He has identified and analysed the factors affecting the productive and financial performance of various categories of spinning mills. The study revealed that the productivity of labour, capital, spindle and raw material showed the amount of gross value added per unit of each factor. A high index is an indication of the increase in gross value added, economies of scale, increase in efficiency, etc. The important factors which influence technical efficiency are identified as capacity utilisation, wage rate, and presence of a well-equipped research and development department. The report of the committee constituted for a study of the problems faced by the textile units under the Industries Department exposed the sickness in both public and private sectors of the industry.

The report revealed that the cotton yarn industry has been facing problems of high cost, demand - supply mismatch, low market price and consequent losses. This situation was aggravated by low demand from the South East Asian countries that are reeling under the currency turmoil. This committee has identified the performance parameters of profitable mills in the industry. The committee suggested modernisation of machinery, manpower and financial restructuring and a suitable capital gearing. The report of the committee to study the problems of private sector textile mills in Kerala identified the major problems of the industry,: such as backlog of modernisation, low profit, high cost of borrowings and debts, labour, power, and lack of consumption in Kerala. The committee suggested some rehabilitation measures, such as creation of seed capital fund, productivity norms, sales tax deferral and exit policy.

The KSTC was formed mainly to revive the sick mills nationalised by the Government in the State. It is against this background that the present study was undertaken to evaluate the working of the Kerala State Textile Corporation.

Objectives of the Study

The objectives of the present study are:

- to assess the organisational set-up and operation of the KSTC mills,
- to evaluate the performance of the KSTC mills in terms of quality and quantity of production, and
- to ascertain the problems confronted by the mills in the effective utilisation of available resources.

Out of the 36 mills in the State, four KSTC mills, five Co-operative mills and two State-owned mills are under the Industries Department. The NTC has six mills in the State, including one in Mahe. In the private sector, there are 19 mills in the State. The relevant data regarding the performance of the Corporation and the KSTC mills were collected from the head office and the office records of the mills. All the four mills owned by the KSTC were covered for data collection. The data collected from Co-operative mills and private mills were also made use of, for the study. One hundred (100) workers 20 supervisors and 10 managers each from all the four mills covered under study were selected as the sample to ascertain the performance of the mills, their efficiency, wages and incentives, and industrial relations. The size of the four mills of KSTC is more or less the same and hence, equal number of workers, supervisors and managers were selected from each mill. Data were collected from an equal number of respondents belonging to different departments of the mill, like mixing and godown, carding, preparatory, spinning, and cone winding.

Using a questionnaire developed for the purpose collected the primary data from the workers, supervisors and managers in the KSTC mills. The top executives of the Corporation and the managers of the KSTC mills were very co-operative in giving information about their organisations. Since the management arranged necessary facilities to interview the workers in the mill they responded freely. In addition to the questionnaire, an interview schedule was also used among the executives to ascertain the performance of the mills. Various discussions were also held with the officials, of the Corporation and the KSTC mills. Secondary data for the study were collected from the Corporation, KSTC mills, South India Textile Research Association, and Southern India Mills Association, Government publications, journals, periodicals and reports. To ascertain the growth of cotton mill industry, trend rate of growth and index numbers have been used. To analyse the financial statements of the Corporation, percentage of change, ratios, averages and average compound growth rate are used in the study. To analyse the variations in the overall organisational view and the KSTC mill-wise views, the 'Z' test has been applied. Weighted score method was adopted for ranking the various reasons for the problems in the KSTC mills.

Since data related to the KSTC mills before its take-over are not available, it would not be possible to compare the positions before and after its take-over. However, the management of the Corporation provided the data related to the KSTC mills, from the date of take-over i.e. from 1983 onwards. The views of the respondents from the KSTC mills influenced the special features of the individual mills and their conditions. However, care has been taken to assess the general view of the KSTC mills.

Findings

Cotton mill industry, the oldest manufacturing industry, occupies an important place in the Indian economy. The strategy of development plans had its due impact on the pattern of growth of the industry. In accordance with the overall objectives of the five-year plans, the mill sector of the industry has been accorded a comparatively low priority in the industrial development programmes. As a result of such a policy, the spinning capacity has been allowed to expand only at an average annual rate of about 1.4 per cent in the cotton mill sector and the weaving capacity declined during the period 1989-90 to 1999-00. Though the decline of weaving capacity in the mill sector might be due to socially desirable objectives and in conformity with the government's policy to protect the interests of the decentralised sector (handlooms and powerlooms), it has resulted in the stagnation of the mill sector of the industry. The problem has, however, been aggravated by the uncertainties of demand in the international market and the low purchasing capacity of the domestic market.

The government's policies resulted in a progressive decline in the share of the mill sector in the total output of the industry, especially in cloth production. The cotton mill industry has lost its prime position in cloth production. During the year 1999-00, it produced only 4.37 per cent of the total cloth production in the country. Yarn output per spindle, known as capital productivity, increased at the rate of 1.24 per cent per annum from 1989-90 to 1999-00. But cloth output per loom declined during the period. The per capita availability of cloth increased more significantly in the case of 100 per cent non-cotton fabrics from 1989-90 to 1999-00. It increased at the rate of 3.38 per cent per annum during the period. However, the per capita availability of cotton cloth declined during the period. The price trends of cotton mill cloth and yarn revealed that yarn prices ran ahead of cloth prices. It would appear from this that the mills might have found it more attractive to produce yarn than cloth. India's export performance in the textile sector in the recent years has been remarkable. Yarn exports increased at the rate of 9.75 per cent and mill-made cotton cloth at the rate of 1.75 per cent per annum during the period from 1989-90 to 1999-00. The textile sector contributes 35 per cent of India's total export earnings.

The cotton mill industry is in the grip of a chronic problem of under utilisation of installed spindles and looms. On an average, the spindles worked three-fourth of the capacity during 1989-90 to 1999-00. In the case of looms, they worked only about 44 per cent during the period. Even by a modest estimate, the output lost due to under-utilisation of capacity came to an average of about 587 million kg of yarn and 2184 million mts. of cloth per annum during 1989-90 to 1999-00. One of the most crucial problems confronted by the industry relates to economically inefficient and technically obsolete stock of plant and machinery in the industry. The impact of inefficient and outdated plant and machinery on the cost of production is very high. This has not only impaired the capacity of the industry to compete in the world market, but also prevented it from supplying adequate woven goods at cheaper rates in the domestic market. Even more importantly, it has reduced severely the profitability of the industry, thereby reducing its capacity to generate reinvestible surpluses.

The cotton mill industry is an energy-intensive industry. The recent power shortage has, therefore, adversely affected the performance of the industry. A situation where supply of power to the mills fluctuated severely, together with power cuts, sometimes as high as 70 per cent, forced the industry either to scale down their activities or to energise old diesel generator sets, the economy of which is highly unfavourable to the industry. Further, the major ills of the cotton mill industry are labour problems. Apart from the fact that a majority of workers employed by the industry are unskilled or semi-skilled, the incidence of absenteeism has been very high. The emergence of sick mills is one of the worst crises in the recent history of the industry. More than 23 per cent of spindles, 59 per cent of looms and 32 per cent of workers were idle in the cotton mill industry due to closure of mills during 1999-00. Nearly one-fifth of the cotton mill industry is considered sick.

KSTC - Structural Analysis

The average compound growth rate of the current liabilities during the period 1990-91 to 1999-00 of the Corporation was higher than the current assets. Interest accrued and due on government loan increased the current liabilities of the Corporation. The Corporation's current assets to current liabilities ratio, on an average of 1.24 during the period 1990-91 to 1999-00, revealed an inadequate margin of safety to meet its current obligations. The liquid assets of the Corporation had a negative compound growth rate and the declining trend of quick ratio indicated its liquidity position, which was also not favourable. The growth rate of net working capital of the Corporation was negative on account of the increase in current liabilities like interest accrued and due on government borrowings. The growth of the net assets was also not significant during the period, 1990-91 to 1999-00.

The average compound growth rate of the total debt of the Corporation was 3.90 per cent per annum, which was higher than the growth of capital employed. The Corporation's debt to capital employed ratio, on an average, was 0.51 and it indicated its dependence more on outsiders' funds for its activities. The net worth of the Corporation had a negative average compound growth rate of 15.9 per cent per annum during the period, 1990-91 to 1999-00. About 90 per cent of the net worth of the Corporation eroded during 1999-00, when compared to the year 1994-95, due to the accumulated losses. The growth of the total liabilities of the Corporation was more than two times of the total assets during the period, 1990-91 to 1999-00. The increase in the ratio of total liabilities to total assets of the corporation indicated that the amount of total funds provided by outsiders to finance total assets had an increasing trend. The financial risk of the Corporation increased considerably mainly on account of the increase in the total liabilities over total assets.

The income of the Corporation before finance charges, provision for depreciation and tax, had a negative average compound growth rate of 3.50 per cent per annum, whereas interest charges had a growth rate of 7.75 per cent during the period, 1990-91 to 1999-00. The average 1.64 finance charges cover of the Corporation indicated the excessive use of debt for its activities. It revealed that the Corporation was not in a position to offer assured payment of interest to the creditors. The income of the Corporation was not sufficient to meet finance charges obligations in certain years during the period, 1990-91 to 1999-00.

The average compound growth rate of cost of sales was 11.02 per cent per annum, which was higher than the average inventory holdings of the Corporation. The average inventory turnover of 23.58 times per annum indicated the corporation's ability to effect higher volume of sales with lower quantum of stock. This finding revealed the increase in the efficiency of marketing function of the Corporation. The average compound growth rate of raw material component in the inventory was 12.64 per cent per annum, which was higher than the average inventory of raw materials. The raw material inventory turnover of the Corporation showed an increasing trend and was on an average 5.96 times per annum, which revealed improvement in the efficiency of inventory management in the organisation. The work-in-process inventory turnover of the Corporation was on an average 36.2 times per annum, and it indicated that the organisation held ten days inventory of work-in-process to convert it into finished goods.

Receivables turnover showed an increasing trend and on an average 15.03 times per year, which indicated the Corporation's increased efficiency of credit collection. The average collection period per year did not exceed 32 days and it indicated the Corporation's better liquidity of receivables and credit policy. The total assets turnover showed an increasing trend and was on an average 1.32 times, and it indicated that the Corporation's utilisation of total assets had been increasing during the period 1990-91 to 1999-00. The average compound growth rate of sales of the Corporation was 10.21 per cent per annum during the period, 1990-91 to 1999-00. The Corporation generated on an average a sale of Rs. 1.32 for Re.1 investment in total assets, which also revealed the economical utilisation of assets for improving sales. The working capital turnover of the Corporation had also shown an increasing trend in spite of the decrease in the working capital in certain years. It indicated that the adverse working capital position of the organisation did not affect the sales. The capital employed turnover of the Corporation had also shown an increasing trend. It indicated its improving operating performance during the period, 1990-91 to 1999-00. On an average, the Corporation generated a sale of Rs. 2.08 from one rupee of capital employed in the organization.

The Corporation's negative average compound growth rate of 5.39 per cent per annum of gross profit indicated the poor efficiency of management to produce each unit of output. The growth of gross profit of the Corporation showed a negative rate of 5.39 per cent per annum. The gross profit margin of the organisation also declined during the period 1990-91 to 1999-00. These two factors indicated the poor efficiency of management to produce each unit of output. The operating expenses of the corporation grew at an average compound growth rate of 11.17 per cent per annum and in certain years it exceeded sales. The operating expenses ratio of the Corporation went high, and it indicated that the amount of operating profit was too low to meet the interest, dividend and other fixed demands. The average annual compound growth of net profit of the Corporation showed a negative rate of 11.33 per cent, and this also revealed the lack of efficiency in manufacturing, administering and selling the products. The earnings before interest and tax had a negative compound growth rate of 7.37 per cent per annum, and this too indicated the Corporation's lower operational and managerial efficiency.

Mill-wise Analysis of Production

The operations of Cotton Corporation of India and Maharashtra State Co-operative Cotton Growers Marketing Federation influenced the prices of cotton to a certain extent. The factors that influenced the prices of cotton in the medium term and long term were extra-factory consumption, size of the cotton crop, export and import policy, power supply, operations of he Cotton Corporation of India (CCI) and Maharshtra State Co-operative Cotton Growers Marketing Federation (MCSMF), financial health of cotton mill industry, and the Textile Commissioner's Stock Control policies.

The Corporation through a centralised purchase system was procuring raw cotton required for the KSTC mills from the private cotton suppliers. The Corporation did not procure cotton for the KSTC mills from the CCI or MCSMF mainly on account of the lack of credit facilities and other stipulations. The main problem encountered in the procurement of cotton for the KSTC mills was the poor quality of raw cotton made available by the Corporation to the mills. The second important problem associated with the procurement of cotton faced by the KSTC mills was financial constraints of the mills. The cost of raw material procured per one kg in Kottayam Textiles (KT) was high when compared to that in the other KSTC mills. Among the KSTC mills, Malabar Spinning and Weaving Mill (MSWM) procured the largest quantity of raw cotton and the yarn production of this mill was also the highest. The findings revealed that the prominent problem encountered in the management of cotton in the KSTC mills was decrease in weight of raw cotton during its storing and production process.

Among the KSTC mills, the trend rate of growth of spinning production was the greatest in KT at 0.8 per cent per annum, while in the case of MSWM it was negative at 0.3 per cent. The value of production per spindle per day worked in KSTC mills indicated that in the case of MSWM the value was the lowest when related to its spinning production, and was the highest in KT. The problem of poor quality raw material used in the KSTC mills was the main factor encountered in the processing of raw materials. The second prominent problem faced in connection with the processing of raw materials was the inefficiency of workers in the KSTC mills.

Since MSWM was producing low count of yarn the process waste of this mill was the lowest among the KSTC mills, and the yarn realisation of this mill was the highest. The SITRA norm of 5.3 per cent for re-usable waste for good working of an average spinning mill was not achieved in the case of Prabharam Mills (PM). But in the case of KT, the norm was satisfied fully and in the other two mills, except for a few years, it exceeded the limit. The average invisible loss of Prabharam Mills, Edaricode Textiles (ET) and MSWM exceeded the SITRA norm of one per cent. But in the case of ET, except for one year, the loss was within the limit. Due to the high incidence of process or saleable waste, the yarn realisation of the KSTC mills was not up to the SITRA standards. The process waste of PM was the highest among the KSTC mills and yarn realisation was the lowest. The yarn realisation of KT was below 80 per cent and this mill was producing the highest quality yarn among the KSTC mills. The overall view in the KSTC mills indicated that the wastage in the production process was high. The views of respondents from KT and MSWM did not differ significantly from the organisation's view. The prominent reason behind the high wastage in the production process of the KSTC mills was the poor quality of raw materials used for spinning. The second reason regarding high incidence of wastage in the production process in the KSTC mills was workers' inefficiency.

The cost of raw material per spindle per day worked in KSTC mills was, on an average, the lowest in KT. But in the case of MSWM the costs of raw material and production of yarn were the highest among the KSTC mills. The SITRA norm for raw material cost fixed at 58 per cent of the value of production was not exceeded in the case of KT and PM. But in the case of ET and MSWM, they did not attain the specified norm in many years. The important problem confronted in the availability of viscose staple fibre, the second important raw material used for spinning in the KSTC mills, was the limited supply of it to the mills. The findings revealed that there was no problem connected with the supply of polyester to the KSTC mills for their spinning activity.

Power cost per spindle per day worked in the KSTC mills was the highest in ET when compared to other KSTC mills. The committee constituted to study the problems faced by the textile units under the Industries Department fixed as power and fuel charges 8 per cent of the value of production, to earn a 5 per cent profit margin. The analysis revealed that in the case of KT, PM and ET the power charges were above 8 per cent for many years, but the power charges of MSWM were within the limits. The main problem identified in connection with the availability of power was irregular supply of electricity to the KSTC mills for their operations. The second important problem confronted in the availability of power was low quality of power or lack of proper voltage for the smooth working of the machines.

On an average, the capacity utilisation of KSTC mills was below 84 per cent of the installed spindles. KT achieved the highest capacity utlisation, and ET had the lowest among the KSTC mills. The main reason for the under-utilisation of installed spindles in the KSTC mills was labour absenteeism. The second important reason identified for the under-utilisation of installed spindles in the KSTC mills was lack of maintenance and service of the machines. The third reason for the stoppage of installed spindles was the power constraints like irregular supply and lack of proper voltage in the supply of current to the KSTC mills. Labour absenteeism in ET, PM and KT showed an increasing trend. The SITRA norm of 10 per cent rate of absenteeism was not maintained in ET and PM. Both the workers and managements were found responsible for the high rate of labour absenteeism prevailing in the KSTC mills, and the consequent under-utilisation of installed spindles.

Management of Human Resources

A good number of employees of the KSTC mills covered under the study belonged to the age group of 45 to 50 years. The majority of the managers belonged to the above age group. About 27 per cent of the supervisors were above 50 years of age. The age group of workers revealed that majority of them belonged to 40 to 50 years of age. The entire managers and 27 per cent of the supervisors had professional qualifications. A good number of KSTC mill workers were qualified below SSLC. The length of service of different levels of employees revealed that a good number of them had 21 to 25 years of service. Half of the managers had also the same length of service in the KSTC mills.

A good number of the supervisors had 26 to 30 years of service. In the case of 25 per cent of workers also, the length of service was the same. The labour productivity in the mills of Kerala was found lower when compared to the mills in the State of Tamil Nadu, and to all the mills in India. On an average, out of the KSTC mills, MSWM had the lowest labour productivity in spinning. The average production per spindle per 8 hours in grams (machine productivity) in the mills of Kerala was low when compared to mills outside the State. All the productivity indices in the spinning mills of Kerala pointed out that productivity with regard to labour and machine was low when compared to other parts of the country. The analysis of the operative hours required to produce 100 kg of yarn (HOK) in the KSTC mills that they did not achieve the SITRA standard.

The SITRA norm for the number of operatives engaged per 1000 spindles adjusted to 40's count (OHS) was also not achieved by the KSTC mills. Irrespective of the above findings, the labour productivity of the KSTC mills showed an increasing trend. The KSTC mills did not achieve the SITRA norm for machine productivity, i.e., production per spindle per 8 hours in grams adjusted to 40's count. The trend rate of growth of machine productivity declined for all KSTC mills, except for MSWM. The rate of growth declined at 0.3 per cent per annum in KT, PM and ET but in MSWM it showed an increase of 0.8 per cent. The general finding about the level of labour efficiency prevailing in the KSTC mills, the main factor associated with labour productivity, was that it was moderate. The findings on labour efficiency of ET and MSWM did not vary from the general findings of the organisation. Labour efficiency in the case of PM was low, but high in KT. Except for a few training programmes provided by the management to the workers there was no continuing or sufficient training to them to increase their efficiency.

In all the KSTC mills the labour cost showed an increasing trend. The labour cost per spindle per day worked in the case of MSWM was the highest among the KSTC mills. The labour cost of KSTC mills exceeded the SITRA norm of 11 per cent of the value of production. Due to high labour absenteeism in ET, its labour cost was the lowest among the KSTC mills. About 44 per cent of the workers of the KSTC mills got less than Rs. 4,000 as monthly income. Fifty per cent of the workers belonged to the Rs. 4,000 to 5,000 income group. The majority of the supervisors were in the Rs. 5,000 to Rs. 10,000 income group in the KSTC mills. The general finding about the structure of wages and salaries of the workers in the KSTC mills was that it was low. The wages to the workers in the KSTC mills did not vary in the case of KT, PM and ET. But in the case of MSWM the wages were very low. The overall finding regarding the structure of wages and salaries of the supervisors indicated that it was moderate. This general finding was found true in the case of KT, ET and MSWM. The finding about the wages and salaries to the supervisors in PM revealed that even though they were moderate, to some extent they were high. The general finding about the structure of wages and salaries of the managers in the KSTC mills was that it was moderate. The above finding did not vary in the case of KT, ET and MSWM. In PM it was found moderate, but to a certain extent it was high.

As regards labour welfare measures provided as a whole in the KSTC mills, they were moderate according to the workers. Slight variation in this respect was observed across the KSTC mills individually. The findings about welfare measures provided to the supervisors in the KSTC mills also indicated that they were moderate. There were no significant variations in the views about the welfare measures in KT and MSWM. In the case of ET, though they were found moderate, to some extent they were low. The welfare measures provided to the managers in the KSTC mills were also moderate as revealed by the findings. The same finding did not vary in the case of KT and MSWM. The finding about the incentives provided to the workers indicated that they were low in the KSTC mills. There were no significant variation about this in the case of ET and MSWM. The incentives provided to the supervisors were also low. This finding did not significantly vary in the case of PM. Slight variation was observed in the other KSTC mills. The incentives provided to the managers, as in the case of supervisors, were also found low. The above finding did not vary in the case of PM.

The general finding regarding safety measures provided in the KSTC mills to the workers was that they were moderate. There were no significant variations about this, in the case of KT and ET. The safety measures provided to the supervisors were also moderate and it was revealed that there were no significant variations about this in the case of ET and MSWM. The general finding regarding safety measures provided to the managers was that they were also moderate. It was found that there were no variations about these measures in the case of ET and MSWM. The employees-employer relation existing in the organisation as a whole was found to be good. This general finding did not vary in the case of ET and MSWM. But in the case of PM, this relation was found moderate or poor. The findings about the decision-making process in the organisation revealed that it was decentralised. This overall finding did not vary in the case of MSWM. In the case of PM and ET, it was centralised. The analysis revealed that demand for high wages and bonus was the main problem in relation to industrial unrest faced in the KSTC mills. Labour absenteeism was the second problem faced in the KSTC mills in relation to industrial unrest. General unrest prevailing in the cotton mill industry in the country was also found to be one of the problems faced in the KSTC mills in relation to industrial unrest.

Evaluation of the Performance of the Mills

The finance charges per spindle per day worked were the lowest in the case of KT and the highest in ET, among the KSTC mills. The finance charges of the KSTC mills showed an increasing trend. The SITRA norm of 5 per cent finance charges of the value of production was satisfied in all the KSTC mills except ET. The KSTC mills other than ET had an average of less than 3 per cent of the value of production as financial charges. But in the case of ET, it was on an average more than 5.53 per cent of the value of production. Difficulties in securing bank overdraft were the prominent problem for the KSTC mills in the management of working capital. The second important problem faced in the management of working capital was inadequacy in the credit period allowed by suppliers. A centralised sale of yarn was followed by the Corporation to market its yarn. The entire yarn output of the KSTC mills was sold outside the State through depot agents on a commission basis.

The stores cost and overhead expenses per spindle per day worked in KSTC mills revealed that the cost was the highest in the case of MSWM, and the lowest in KT. The SITRA norm of 3.5 per cent of stores expenses and 6.5 per cent of overhead expenses of value of production was not exceeded in the KSTC mills except for a few years. Out of the KSTC mills, ET had highest depreciation charges per spindle per day worked. Mainly on account of the old age of the machines the depreciation charges of MSWM were only one-fourth of the charges in ET. The SITRA norm of depreciation charges at three per cent of the value of production was satisfied only in MSWM, out of the KSTC mills.

The quantity of yarn sales of the KSTC mills during the 10 years under study indicated a declining trend. In the case of KT, the mill incurred net loss only during the period when the quantity of sales declined in the mill. But in the case of MSWM, even at the time of high quantity of sales the mill incurred losses. Yarn sales value of the mills indicated that KT got the highest prices when compared to other KSTC mills. In the case of MSWM, the yarn sales price per lakh kg was the lowest among the KSTC mills. The prices realised for yarn in the case of PM and ET were also found lower than in KT. Wide variation was observed in the case of PM, ET and MSWM with regard to contribution towards fixed cost and net profit. The contribution of KT, except for one year, was more than a certain limit. The Prices realised for yarn in the KSTC mills were moderate. This finding did not vary in the case of ET and MSWM. In PM, the prices realised for their yarn was low. The average net profit or net loss per spindle per day worked in the KSTC mills indicated that, except for KT, they incurred net loss. The SITRA norm of 2 per cent of net profit on the value of production was attained in the case of KT for four years during the period under study. In the case of PM, it was attained in two years, and in MSWM and ET, only for one year.

During the period under study the highest investments were made by KSTC in the MSWM, and the lowest in PM. ET, the newly set up KSTC mill, became a sick mill because its accumulated net loss exceeded the net worth during the period under study. In the case of MSWM, after its take-over, it did not improve the financial position and remained sick. Its negative net worth during the period indicated its ever-increasing accumulated net loss. The financial position of PM revealed that the mill had accumulated net loss throughout the period after its take-over, but it did not exceed the net worth. The performance of KT showed that the accumulated net loss of the mill at the time of take-over had changed and that it made net profit during the period under study. The trend rate of growth of average count of yarn produced by the KSTC mills except for the PM, showed an increasing trend. Low demand for yarn produced by the KSTC mills in the market was the main problem faced in the movement of finished goods. The second important problem in connection with the movement of yarn was seasonal demand for it in the market.

The study of the average age of critical machinery used in the KSTC mills revealed that except the machines used for drawing process, all other machines were more than 10 years of age, i.e., above the useful economic life. It was revealed that modernisation of existing plant and machinery in the KSTC mills was the main area requiring up to date renewal. The second important area of modernisation was the renewal of the very old factory buildings of the mills. The financial support from the government was found to be the main source of fund for modernisation in the mills. Institutional loan was identified as the second source of funds for modernisation in the mills. The efficiency of top management in formulating policies and programmes on time was moderate in the KSTC. The overall opinion about the efficiency of top management did not vary in the case of ET and MSWM. Though it was moderate in all the mills, in KT, it was low to a certain extent. The finding was that the research and development activity prevailing in the KSTC mills was poor or very poor. The overall finding about research and development did not vary in the case of PM and MSWM. But in KT, the research and development activity prevailing in the mill was found to be very poor. Protection of national interest and public purpose was the main reason identified against privatisation of the KSTC mills. The inefficiency of KSTC management was the main argument in favour of privatisation of KSTC mills. 'Not operating well' was the overall view revealed about the operation of the cotton textile industry in Kerala.

Suggestions

On the basis of the findings of the study, the following suggestions are made to improve the working of the Corporation and the KSTC mills.

Capacity utilisation: Due to labour absenteeism, the KSTC mills could not attain capacity utilisation of installed spindles beyond a certain limit. Both the management and the workers are equally responsible for this situation. The high rate of absenteeism in the mills naturally implies a very liberal policy of the managements towards absentee employees. Unauthorised absenteeism in the KSTC mills is found to be mainly on account of the work culture and laxity in the administrative control of the managements. It is noted that the unauthorised absenteeism prevailing in the KSTC mills is an exceptional one and not a common practice by the workers. The managements of the KSTC mills must implement prompt disciplinary measures as per standing orders, to bring down the rate of absenteeism among the workers. To improve the overall performance of the KSTC mills, the above step is to be adopted as an urgently needed one. To control sickness absenteeism, a close vigilance on the employees who are abusing sickness leave facility will be effective. Similarly, monitoring with Employees State Insurance (ESI) authorities, in the matter of liberal granting of sickness leave, will also be necessary.

In addition to the above measures, the managements may also create a group incentive scheme so as to bring down the loss in capacity utilisation, wherein the work of the absentee employees may be shared by other workers. The unauthorised absence on the part of the workers poses serious problems to the management in adjusting with the human resource requirements of the organisation. It is the responsibility of the KSTC mill managements to revamp the work culture by appropriate educational, disciplinary and counseling efforts.

Modernisation and productivity: In the KSTC mills, backlog of modernisation and low productivity are the two important factors affecting the operating profits of the mills. Productivity in respect of labour and machine in the KSTC mills is comparatively low, and it may be due to the lack of modernisation of machines in the mills. This low productivity leads to poor working, low profit and sickness of the mills. To increase the labour and machine productivity, the following measures are to be adopted in the KSTC mills. It is necessary to improve the operational efficiency through good supervision and control, as also by ensuring proper machinery up-keep and maintenance, increasing the work assignments of different categories of workers through improved working and work methods, by implementing operative training and work methods, by combining the jobs, by changing the mill layout, and so on. It is essential to replace the existing machines by high-speed, semi-automatic and automatic machines. The first two measures are intended to utilise the existing resources at an optimal level, whereas the third measure requires modernisation of machinery involving huge capital investments.

Quality of raw cotton: Cotton required for the KSTC mills is now procured from the private cotton suppliers registered with the Corporation. A centralised purchase system is evolved for this purpose and a committee constituted is authorised to do it. Because of the liberal credit facilities offered by the private cotton suppliers, the Corporation covers most of the requirement of cotton from them. Credit purchase of cotton from private suppliers always affects the quality as well as its availability at the required time for production. However, the Corporation does not generally resort to purchase from institutions such as CCI, MCSMF, Gujarat State Co-operative Marketing Federation, etc., due to lack of credit facilities and other stipulations. The CCI and MCSMF handled nearly 40 per cent of the entire cotton in the country. The findings revealed that the main problem encountered in connection with the procurement, management and processing was the poor quality of raw material used in the KSTC mills. In addition to that, the main reason for high process waste in the mills was also found to be poor raw material quality. The Corporation has to purchase cotton from CCI and MCSMF, mainly for procuring quality cotton to the mills in order to avoid all types of wastage and loss. It is necessary to provide quality cotton to the KSTC mils in order to increase yarn realisation as well as to produce high count yarn. The Corporation should take necessary steps to lift bans on credit facilities and other stipulations imposed by the CCI and MCSMF.

Financial restructuring: The net worth of the Corporation during the period under study declined considerably, indicating that within a short period of time, it might become negative. The working capital position of the Corporation was also not favourable during the period. These two findings indicated the necessity for financial restructuring of the Corporation. The Government has provided Rs. 394.49 lakh as long-term loan to the Corporation and this combined with the Government equity of Rs. 863.19 lakh makes the total Government investment Rs. 2,257.68 lakh. During this period the accumulated losses of the Corporation stood at Rs. 1,770.18 lakh, out of which Rs. 1,573.97 lakh was accounted for towards depreciation. In this situation the Corporation needed to convert Government loan to equity so as to avoid a financial crisis in the Corporation. In case the accumulated loss is set off against the share capital post-loan equity conversion, the tangible share capital in the Corporation will be Rs. 487.5 lakh, and together with a reserve of Rs. 110.02 lakh, the net worth of the Corporation would be positive at Rs. 597.52 lakh.

Since the Corporation cannot service the huge existing Government loans, it is an urgently needed measure to convert Government loan into equity. This measure is needed to avoid referring the functions of the Corporation to the BIFR, under the Sick Industrial Companies Act of 1985 in future. It is needless to say that the operations of the KSTC mills depend on the effective management of working capital through cut down of costs, especially in the procurement of raw material. The cost of raw-material forms the major part of the cost of production, and it was as high as about 60 per cent of the value of production in the KSTC mills. The poor machinery conditions and the resultant low quality of products that cannot attract remunerative prices are the major reasons for this. This problem can be solved by modernisation of the existing machinery and by effective marketing of the products.

Sale of Yarn: The yarn produced by the cotton mills is consumed by the weaving sector, and the majority of which are in the un-organised sector. In the case of KSTC mills, the yarn produced by them is sold in the Mumbai market through Depot agents appointed on commission basis. The Depot agents are appointed for a term of one year on the basis of sales agreements. Yarn is despatched to the sales depot by stock transfer, on a regular basis. It has been the policy of the Corporation to have sales on a continuous and daily basis at the prevailing market rates, without resorting to any sort of speculation, so that the adverse effects of price fluctuations will be the minimum and the overall sales realisation the better. In short, the KSTC mills do not permit direct sales to consumers.

The Corporation's main argument in favour of this type of sales is to avoid bad debts and to overcome the lack of demand in the home market. However, the findings revealed that though the prices realised for yarn was moderate in the Mumbai market, low demand was the main problem encountered in the movement of finished goods. Such being the situation, the Corporation can explore home market to sell the yarn produced by their mills. The main advantage of the home market is to minimise the transportation cost of the finished goods. The present procedure is to transport the yarn from the KSTC mills which are situated at Chengannoor and Kottayam, to the Mumbai depot for sales. Secondly, there is wide scope for market in the Kozhikode and Kannur belt for yarn because of the presence of wide handloom weaving sector in the State.

Rationalisation of manpower: In all the KSTC mills, it is needed to limit the wage cost to 11 per cent (as per SITRA standard) of the value of production. The findings revealed that in all the KSTC mills, it exceeded the specified norm. In this situation, manpower rationalisation is inevitable in the KSTC mills. It is noted that VRS has been implemented in all the mills to tackle this situation. But the main difficulty in this connection is lack of funds to implement this scheme. Government support is required so as to operate the scheme in the mills without delay. Rationalisation of manpower leads to improvement in labour productivity, which in turn can increase the overall profitability of the KSTC mills.

Management Information System: In the context of controlling cost, reporting to management plays a key role. The management information system and variance analysis are treated as part of standard costing in cotton mills. The overall efficiency of the management depends to a large extent on the quality of decisions. The general findings about the decision-making process in the organisation revealed that it was decentralised. It is noted that both effective and purposeful decision-making should be based on proper information system. A scientific MIS improves the quality of the decisions. In all the KSTC mills, it is required to provide information to all levels of management to enable them to make faster and sound decisions. This process will help to utilise the available skills and resources more effectively to increase productivity and profitability in the mills. Good and sound decisions are possible only with the aid of correct facts and figures. The development of sophisticated equipment and techniques for collecting such facts and figures and presenting them to management is required in the KSTC mills to improve the quality and effectiveness of managerial performance. In all the KSTC mills, the managers and supervisors have to solve the ever-increasing number and size of complex problems. This necessitated the development and use of an effective information system.

References

Balakrishnan, M.S., *An Interfirm Comparison of Absenteeism*, SITRA, Coimbatore, 1994.

Dhulasi Birundha, *An Economic Study of Profits in Spinning and Weaving Mills in Madurai City*, Ph.D. Thesis (unpublished), Madurai Kamaraj University, Madurai, 1985.

Dutt Ruddar, Sundaram, K.P.M., *Indian Economy*, S. Chand and Company Ltd.

Government of Kerala, *Findings and Recommendations of the Advisory Committee for the Textile Industry in Kerala*, June 1991.

Government of Kerala, *Report of the Committee Constituted for Study of the Problems Faced by the Textile Units under the Industries Department*, November 1999.

Government of Kerala, *Report of the Committee to Study the Problems of Private Sector Textile Mills in Kerala*, 1999.

Industrial Researcher, *Textile Industry: Performance in Last Decade and Future Prospects*, Pranava Industrial Services Pvt. Ltd., January - March 2001.

Kevin, S., *A Study of the Textile Industry in Kerala with Comparitive Reference to Tamil Nadu*, Ph.D. Thesis (unpublished), Cochin University of Science and Technology, Cochin, 1988.

Mohan Kumar, P.S., *Cotton Textile Industry - A Comparative Analysis of Different Sectors*, Reliance Publishing House, New Delhi, 1997.

Office of the Textile Commissioner, *Compendium of Textile Statistics 2000.*

Padmanabhan, M., *The Sick Mill Problems - The Indian Cotton Textile Industry*, Ph.D. Thesis: (unpublished), University of Bombay, Bombay, 1974.

Ramaswami Manikam, *Awaiting a New Lease of Life*, Survey of Indian Industry 2001, The Hindu.

Ratnam, T.V., Indra Doraiswamy, Seshadri, S., and Rajamanickam, R., *Productivity in Spinning*, SITRA, Coimbatore, 1996.

Ratnam, T.V., Indra Doraiswamy, Seshadri, S., and Rajamanickam, R., *Cost Control and Costing in Spinning Mills*, SITRA, Coimbatore, 1992.

Sreenivasan, K., *Indian Textile Industry*, SITRA, Coimbatore, 1984.

4

Financial Management of Public Sector Undertakings

V. Anil Prasad

Public Enterprises occupy a vital position in the national economy of almost all countries in the world irrespective of their political orientation. However, the ultimate cause of the emergence of public enterprises varies from one country to another. In western countries, it was the unworkability of the laissez faire policy and widespread social tension created by capitalism that resulted in the emergence of public enterprises. The classical economic view of laissez faire aimed at full employment, full investment and maximum wealth. However, in actual practice, under employment, exploitation, inequality in the distribution of wealth, poverty and plenty, and distress and luxury were the results. At this stage, State intervention was the only remedy possible. Public enterprises were the result of ideological commitment under communism. The ideology of communism necessitated all factors of production to be brought under the direct control of the State. Public enterprises were created in most of the third world countries in the post World War II period as a matter of economic necessity rather than any ideological commitment.

Developing countries, many of which attained independence after World War II, were under strong pressure to bring about rapid economic progress. These countries lacked the necessary conditions under which private enterprises could be expected to attain rapid economic progress. The economies of such countries were characterised by low level of savings and investment, lack of technical, managerial and entrepreneurial talents, under developed economic infrastructure and basic industries, non-existence of capital market, etc. Such being the circumstances, the Governments of these countries were left with no alternative but to participate directly in the economic process, which was mainly promotional and entrepreneurial in nature. Faced with the problem of raising the standard of living of people in the shortest possible time, the developing countries had before them two models of economic planning and public enterprises, and the Western Model of development through private enterprises. Since the Soviet Union (as it existed earlier) had attained within five decades a measure of economic and technological development, which the western democracies had taken two centuries to achieve, the Russian Model was an obvious choice.

During the pre-Independence period, the role of the public sector in Indian economy was almost nil. After the attainment of Independence, the most important problem faced by the Government was to accelerate the pace of economic development, keeping in view a political and economic philosophy suited to its needs and aspirations. Economic planning was accepted as the philosophy for economic progress, and the Planning Commission was set up with the responsibility for planning for the entire country. Private enterprises could not be expected to implement the plans, policies and programmes fully in line with the national economic goals. Policies laid down by the Planning Commission were on the lines of setting up basic industrial; undertakings by the Government. This was justified on the ground that it was extremely difficult for the enterprises under private ownership to raise adequate finance for projects, which involved huge outlays. Moreover, undertakings in the sector were naturally guided by profit motive rather than public interest.

Thus, without resorting solely to any of the two extremes of democracy, with private enterprises on the one hand and totalitarianism with public sector on the other, the national leadership followed a pragmatic policy of opting for the democratic political set up of the West, together with the system of economic planning and dominant role of public sector of the socialist countries. Various Industrial Policy Resolutions clearly demarcated industries into different categories in this regards. The development of public sector undertakings was accelerated through the Five Year Plans, and now these enterprises are regarded as the milestones of the progress of the economy. In spite of the rapid increase in investment and dominant role of the public sector in the economy, there has been considerable criticism about the public enterprises in India. While the Government has been pushing ahead with more and more public sector undertakings, there has been considerable criticism about the poor performance, and in some cases the utter failure of Government undertakings in the country.

The history of the public sector in Kerala is much longer than that of the State sector of India in general. Even before independence, Kerala had made considerable progress in the area of industrial development under the Princely State of Travancore and Cochin. At present the State-level public enterprises provide the industrial infrastructure and act as accelerators of rapid economic development. During 1999-2000, there were 97 Government companies and nine statutory Bodies under the State Government, as against 88 Government companies and eight Statutory Bodies in 1989-90 and 77 Government companies and seven statutory Bodies in 1981-82. The total capital investment at the end of 1999-2000 stood at Rs 1,37,770.40 crore, providing employment to 1,25,814 persons.

Statement of the Problem

Together with the central public sector undertakings, the position of most of the public enterprises in the States has also attracted vehement criticism from various corners. The dismal performance of undertakings promoted and managed by various State Governments is going almost unnoticed by the social scientists. While there has been growing literature on the central public enterprises, research literature as well as statistical information about State-level undertakings is scanty.

One of the major reasons for the poor performance of public enterprises is the lack of financial discipline in them. In the initial stages, the prime objective of public sector undertakings was the welfare of people and hence the financial management area remained almost neglected. The modern techniques in excellent utilisation of funds remained out of reach for the public sector undertakings. At the same time, the industrial and commercial undertakings in the private sector were able to attain efficiency and effectiveness through the application of modern tools and techniques in the management of their financial resources. In the majority of the public sector undertakings in Kerala, sadly enough, a large chunk of their capital has show erosion. The Review of Public Enterprises in Kerala 1998-99 stated that 56 among the 106 enterprises had carried forward losses amounting to Rs. 2,263.43 crore as on 31-03-1999. In 41 enterprises, the net worth had fully eroded, becoming negative by the end of 1998-99.

Review of Literature

A brief review of the available literature on the working of State-level public sector undertakings is attempted here. Most of the studies conducted in the area are in the form of case studies, where the working of a single firm has been evaluated. In some other cases, only a limited area of financial management has been covered.

Hemlata Rao conducted a study on the financial performance of Karnataka Electricity Board and pointed out that defective planning, high cost of manpower, excessive dependence on loan, wasteful energy consumption, etc., were some of the practical problems faced by the Board. Choyal, B.R., in his study on the financial management of the State Warehousing Corporations in Haryana, Madhya Pradesh, Andhra Pradesh and Orissa, analysed aspects of the financial structure, working capital, fixed assets investments, profitability and funds flow. Sahay S.N. conducted a study on the financial management of State-level enterprises in Bihar. Financial management variables such as capitalization, capital structure and resources of long-term funds were analysed, in respect of six sample units from the State.

Sharma, G.D. reviewed the working of the State enterprises in

Rajasthan covering the internal organisation, personnel policy, forms of management, capital structure, inventory control, price and profit policy, etc. Chouhan, A.B. made an attempt to study the organisation and working of public enterprises in Gujarat. The edited volume 'Public Enterprises in India - A study of State Government Undertakings' by Khan and Arora contains 11 papers dealing with public enterprises in eight States. The paper highlight certain important aspects of administration of State-level public enterprises. Studies on the financial management aspects of public enterprises in the other states include: Financial Management of Jammu and Kashmir Enterprises by Khurshid Ali, Management of Working Capital with Reference to selected State Enterprises in Andhra Pradesh Public Enterprises by Shankaraiah A., Vishwanathan V., and Finances of Andhra Pradesh State Electricity Board by Nagaraja Naidu V.

The management set up and administrative problems in the Kerala State Road Transport Corporation, Kerala State Electricity Board, Trivandrum Rubber Works Limited, and Kerala State Industrial Development Corporation were evaluated by Gangadharan Pillai, V. and he arrived at the conclusion that political interference, inefficiency of management, defective recruitment system, lack of finance and indiscipline among workers were the major problems in these enterprises. In the study conducted by Beena, P.L., regarding the performance of manufacturing enterprises in the public and private sectors in Kerala, she analysed the trends in capacity utilization indices, trends in their total and partial factor productivity, and the growth and financial performance of both the sectors in Kerala. Nair P.P. made a detailed analysis of the working of nine State Government undertakings in Kerala. He concluded that there was under-utilisation of all factors of production.

Wilson P.R. evaluated the existing system of financial planning and control and its role in reducing losses and increasing profits through his study, 'Social Planning and Control in Public Sector Undertakings in Kerala'. Nataraja Iyer S., in his study on the financial performance of public sector enterprises in Kerala, analysed the productivity performance, profitability performance, financial solvency and contribution made by public enterprises in Kerala. Prasad G. and Rao K.V. conducted a study on the financial management of public enterprises in the southern states taking two enterprises each from Kerala, Tamil Nadu, Karnataka and Andhra Pradesh. In his article, 'Performance and Development of Public Enterprises in Kerala', Narayanan, R. concluded that the low profitability of State-level public enterprises was due to labour unrest and management failure, lack of corporate culture, poor marketing approaches, financial difficulties in the from of heavy interest, and lack of professionalism in management.

A close observation of the literature in the area reveals the fact that a scientific study on the management of financial resources by public sector undertakings in Kerala is yet to be made, and hence the present study.

Objectives of the Study

The present study was undertaken with the following objectives.

- To examine the methods of financing and capital structure adopted by the public enterprises in the State.
- To assess the strategies evolved by the public enterprises in ascertaining the feasibility of investment decisions.
- To ascertain the basis for the management of short-term funds by the public enterprises.
- To analyse the performance of public enterprises in terms of the working results.
- To suggest measures for improvement of the management of funds based on findings of the study.

The present study is confined to the financial management of enterprises owned and managed by the Kerala Government. The study excludes non-financial problems. However, some non-financial problems which have an impact on finance have also come incidentally under the purview of the study,. Further, the present study is intended to cover only those undertakings which are engaged in manufacturing activities, and so does not include the other undertakings that fall under categories like promotional, developmental, welfare, service, and marketing enterprises since the working capital cycle is complete only in respect of the manufacturing enterprises, and also due to the significance of capital expenditure projects in those enterprises.

The Review of Public Enterprises in Kerala 1989-90 covered 100 units including eight Statutory Bodies. These 100 units were categorised under 14 sectors as given in Table 4.1. Of these 100 units, two were under liquidation and one had been taken over by another unit. Another three units were formed during the year. Out of the 14 sectors, five sectors (Developmental and Infrastructure, Trading, Welfare agencies, Public utilities and 'others') were not engaged in manufacturing activities. The present study covers the other nine sectors, and all the units included in them are Government Companies.

Table 4.1: Sectoral Classification of Public Sector Undertakings in Kerala during 1989-90

Sl. No.	Sector	No. of units
1.	Development and Infrastructure	10
2.	Ceramic and Refractories	6
3.	Chemicals	11
4.	Electrical	5
5.	Electronics	10
6.	Engineering	11
7.	Plantation and Agro-based	12
8.	Textiles	4
9.	Wood-based	3
10.	Traditional	7
11.	Trading	3
12.	Welfare Agencies	7
13.	Public Utilities	5
14.	Others	6
	Total	100

Out of the 69 enterprises in the nine sectors, only 59 were alive throughout the period of analysis. Three enterprises had not begun their business operations until April 1, 1990, and seven others had become inactive before March 31, 1999. From these 59 enterprises, nine were chosen for the purpose of the present study, at the rate of one from each sector.

Table 4.2: Percentage of Capital Invested in Each Sample Units in the Sector

Sector (1)	Name of Unit selected (2)	Capital Invested		Percentage of (4) to(3)
		Sector (Rs. lakh) (3)	Units (Rs. lakh) (4)	
Ceramics	Kerala Ceramics Ltd.	1397.73	1303.92	93.29
Chemical	Kerala Minerals and Metals Ltd	27108.40	14321.98	52.83
Electrical	Transformers and Electrical Kerala Ltd	10569.68	4656.99	44.06
Electronics	The Kerala State Electronic Development Corporation	12500.45	9531.23	76.25
Engineering	Autokast Ltd.	8304.32	2588.00	31.16
Plantation	Meat Products of India Ltd	6394.17	195.57	3.06
Textiles	Kerala State Textile corporation Ltd.	3828.37	1889.78	49.36
Wood-based	Travancore Plywood Industries Ltd.	393.15	349.91	89.00
Traditional	Kerala State Cashew Development corporation Ltd	7882.31	3833.95	48.64
Total		78378.58	38671.33	49.34

For this purpose, the unit with the highest capital investment in each sector as on April 1, 1990 was taken into consideration, except in the case of the Plantation sector, since in that sector, the major activity of many units was confined to plantation, The meat Products of India Limited was chosen, wherein the major activity was production of meat products.

The sample units and their capital investment as on 1st April 1990 are presented in Table 4.2. The Table 4.2 also contains the total investment of all active units in the sector and the percentage of capital invested in each unit.

For the purpose of collection of primary data, the employees were grouped under three categories, viz., executive level, supervisory level, and non-supervisory level. Since the number in each category varied widely, the proportionate sampling was not found suitable. So the number of respondents from the executive and supervisory levels was decided by ensuring fair representation, and in the case of respondents from the non-supervisory level, the following scale was adopted.

Number of employees	Sample Size
Up to 250	25
250 to 400	40
Above 1000	100

The sample design is shown in Table 4.3.

Both primary and secondary data were used for the purpose of the study. A structured questionnaire was prepared for the collection of primary data, which was pre-tested. Discussions were also held with high-level executives of financial institutions, both in the private sector and the public sector, and the top-level officers of the Industries Department, Government of Kerala. The analysis and interpretation of the data were effected by suitably incorporating the views expressed by these groups. Secondary data were extracted from various publications related to the public sector undertakings such as Review of Public Enterprises published by the Bureau of Public Enterprises, Economic Review published by the State Planning Board, Reports of the Comptroller and Auditor General, Reports of the Committee on

Public Undertakings, RBI Bulletins, Public Enterprises Survey published by the Central Bureau of Public Enterprises, Economic Survey of the Governments of India, Reports of the Centre for Monitoring Indian Economy, etc. A nine-year period beginning with the financial year 1990-91, and ending in 1998-99, was chosen for the analysis of secondary data. However, data for the year 1999-2000 were also included, wherever found appropriate.

Table 4.3: Population and Sample

Category	Executive Level		Supervisory Level		Non-supervisory Level	
	Population	Sample	Population	Sample	Population	Sample
Ceramics (KCL)	19	10	34	20	380	40
Chemical (KMML)	43	20	173	30	1841	100
Electrical (TELK)	115	15	327	40	1140	100
Electronics (KELTRON)	649	50	45	25	1610	100
Engineering (AUTOKAST)	46	25	59	25	397	40
Plantation (MPIL)	10	8	7	5	105	25
Textiles (KSTC)	53	20	13	10	1334	100
Wood-based (TPI)	18	10	87	25	231	25
Traditional (KSCDC)	45	20	525	40	20669	100
Total	998	178	1270	220	27707	630

Most of the secondary data were extracted from the final accounts of the companies. But, in many cases, accounts were not up-to-date; so, provisional figures were depended upon in some cases. One of the tools used for analysis is that of financial ratios, and these ratios are applied on figures drawn from financial statements. Neither financial statements nor accounting ratios are fee from limitations, and, to that extent, the present study is also not free from that limitation.

Findings

Growth of public enterprises: Public sector undertakings in India achieved tremendous progress over the last five decades. Both Central and State Governments have invested huge amounts of capital in this sector. The Central Public sector enterprises grew appreciably from a mere five, with an investment of Rs. 29 crore in 1951 to 240, with an investment of Rs. 2,52,554 crore by the end of March 2000. Like the Central Government, various State Governments have also brought the Public sector to enormous growth. By the end of March 2000, the total investment in State level public enterprises in Kerala reached Rs. 13,770.40 crore. The role of the public sector in the 'State cannot be underestimated, for the presence of it is felt in every walk of life. Like the public sector in the other States, most to the public utilities such as road transport, electricity, water supply, public distribution etc., are predominantly handled by the public sector in the State. In addition to Public Utilities, State enterprises are also engaged in the production and distribution of various types of consumer and capital goods. Several industrial and commercial undertakings have been promoted by the Government in the public sector.

Unfortunately, in spite of the growth in investment and the dominant role in the economy, the public enterprises owned by both Central and State Governments have attracted severe criticism due to their dismal performance. One of the major reasons for the poor performance is the lack of financial discipline in these undertakings. Various agencies such as Committee on Public Undertakings, Bureau of Public Enterprises, Administrative Reforms Commission, Estimates Committee, and the Comptroller and Auditor General, have, after regular reviewing, highlighted the poor performance of these undertakings. While there have been a lot of studies on the functioning of Central sector undertakings, only limited attempts have been made to evaluate the reasons for the poor performance of State level enterprises, especially in the finance area. It is well admitted that the efficiency of these enterprises cannot be measured in terms of profits alone. Other criteria like contribution to the exchequer, generation of employment, development of small-scale industries, elimination of monopoly, development of backward areas, provision of infrastructure facilities, etc., are also relevant.

However, in a developing country like India, where funds are very scarce, the huge investment in the public sector lacks justification, even as they fail to generate reasonable return. While public enterprises were a craze for policy makers in the early 1950s, now the policy of the Governments, both Central and State, is to sell the public sector units to private entrepreneurs. As part of the new economic policy, the Central Government has already started disinvestments in the public sector units. In Kerala, even though an attempt was made by the UDF Government in 1992 in this direction, no progress could be made thereafter. However, during the last five years, it was a closed chapter as the LDF Government was ideologically against disinvestments. However, the 'White Paper' prepared by the new UDF Government clearly stated its intention to disinvest in the weak public sector units as a means to raise additional resources, and at the same time to avoid further drainage of resources.

Financial Management: Since the inception of public enterprises, one of the major problems faced by them has been the lack of financial discipline. An attempt has been made in the present study to identify some of the problems faced by the state level public enterprises in Kerala, in the financial management area. With this intention, four areas in management of funds were analysed in the present study. The major findings from each area are summarised here.

Financing and Capital Structure: The investment in the public sector has shown an increasing trend over the last nine years. The majority of these enterprises failed to generate internal resources, and heavily depended on the Government and financial institutions for funds to carry on the business operations. The major sources for financing were share capital, long-term loans and bank borrowings. Negative net worth was a common feature of the public sector undertakings in Kerala. Of the nine sectors evaluated, the net worth as on March 31, 999 was positive only in two sectors. In the Electronics and Traditional sectors accumulated losses reached around two times, and in the Electrical sector, it constituted three times, of the paid-up capital. Except in the Chemical sector, the share of reserves and surplus in various sectors was negligible. The State level public enterprises in Kerala failed to generate adequate amount of retained earnings. The debt-equity ratio was found negative in the majority of the sectors due to negative net worth. This indicates that even borrowings were not adequately represented by tangible assets. A comparison of debt with share capital helps to understand the policy of financial management with respect to leverage. In all the sectors expect Ceramics, the average ratio exceeds the generally accepted standard of 1:1. The total debt multiplied 24 times of the paid-up capital in the Wood-based sector, three times in the Electrical, three times in the Engineering, and two times each in the Electronics and Traditional sectors.

The interest coverage ratio was used to evaluate the ability of the firm to serve the huge amount of debt that they mobilized. The analysis reveled that EBIT was negative in most of the sectors, and where EBIT was positive, it was not sufficient even to cover interest. It was only in the Chemical sector that the borrowings were within the limit, and payment of interest was not at all a problem. Asked about the dependence on excess debt, the employees from all the three levels covered under the study agreed that lack of adequate internal resources was the major reason. The opinions of the respondents were found significantly alike in many sectors. The Chemical sector was the only exception where debt was very low. Regarding the reasons for low interest coverage, the employees at the lower levels covered under the study opined that lower turnover was the major reason, while the executives viewed that high operating cost was the major problem. However, the difference in ranking was not significant. All of them viewed that insufficient sales and irregular cash flows were the reasons for non-repayment of loan amounts.

Maintaining a large volume of debt, which prevents creation of return that is adequate even for paying interests, caused severe problem in many State-owned enterprises in Kerala. Non-payment of interest in time has led to accumulation of interest which again added to the principal loan amount. Continuous losses made by these enterprises forced them to depend on long-term capital to meet operating expenses. There had been several instances where long-term funds were diverted for operational requirements. The employees also agreed that a large part of long-term fund was used for meeting operating expenses, due to insufficient sales proceeds. Like any other industrial concerns, the public sector units also depended on the commercial banks for their working capital borrowings. However, the banks, generally, were reluctant to lend money to the public sector undertakings due to the latter's poor state of affairs. So, many public sector units were facing the problem of arranging short-term finance. A comparison between long-term and short-term borrowings revealed that in most of the enterprises short-term borrowings constituted only less than 20 per cent of total borrowings. The important sources of long-term borrowings were non-Government sources. Direst borrowing from the Government was the major source only in the Traditional and Textile sectors.

Asked about the degree of autonomy with regard to resource mobilisation, the majority of the employees covered under the study believed that the financial executives had a decisive role in it, though they did not have complete freedom. Shortage of fixed capital and delay in getting finance are the major problems in relation to fixed capital. Usually, the Government takes a very long time to sanction the schemes of rehabilitation submitted by the enterprises, and, in the meantime, the position of the enterprises may have become worse. The majority of the employees at all the three levels favored financial restructuring as a remedy to bring the firm back on the track, and they preferred mainly conversion of debt equity as the mode of restructuring. Methods such as waiving of interest and moratorium on interest also got remarkable ratings A few employees were not favourable to restructuring and they believed that the proposal would not be approved by the Government, or it would take a long time to fulfill the cumbersome formalities, or it would not help the firm to recover from the bleak state of affairs. Most of the respondents preferred Government equity as the best source of fixed capital, because of the notion that it was cost free. This proved that they were not confident of earning adequate return form capital. Some respondents were of the view that the raising of long-term loans would automatically bring in some financial discipline in the management of business

There were mixed responses from the employees covered under the study regarding private participation in the equity. While employees from the lower level were generally against private participation, the majority of employees at the executive and supervisory levels favoured it. Those who welcomed private participation believed that it would relieve the financial problems to some extent and make the enterprises accountable to the public. But those at the lower level feared that the majority of share holding by private entrepreneurs would adversely affect their interest. While executives and supervisors favoured private participation mainly because of undue political influence in the functioning of public enterprises and due to lack of commitment on the part of workers, non-supervisors favoured it mainly because of political interference, heavy loss and lack of professional managers. Employees who were against private participation believed that only enterprises in the public sector could act as a model employer and contribute to the society in a different manner.

Around 45 per cent of the employees from the executive level, 40 per cent from the supervisory level and 13 per cent from the non-supervisory level were indifferent regarding the idea of compulsory participation in the equity by personnel in the organization. A majority of the remaining employees belonging to the executive and supervisory levels were against this idea. However, the majority of the respondents at the non-supervisory level favoured compulsory participation in equity by executives and supervisors. Interestingly, they were not so much interested in participating themselves in the equity.

Capital Budgeting: Investment decisions in the sector, on many occasions, are guided by various social considerations. The social considerations may relate to development of backward areas, generation of employment, export promotion, taking over of sick units, and so on. The poor financial performance of public enterprises is often traced to defects in their project planning and implementation process. Delay in completion of projects and the consequent cost escalations were common features in public enterprises. There were many instances of project cost escalation in different sectors. The majority of the respondents also agreed that the delay involved was very high. According to the respondents, the major role causing delay in implementation. Anyhow, labour problems and political interference were rated only low by the respondents. There were also instances of unfruitful investments in many undertakings. Certain investments did not yield anything to the revenue at all.

The amount of gross fixed assets increased only marginally in the different sectors over the period of analysis. The highest trend percentage was 232, obtained in the Plantation sector. In the Traditional sector, gross fixed assets diminished by 50 per cent. In most of the sectors fixed assets formed only less than 50 per cent of the capital invested. Fixed assets exceeded capital invested only in the Chemical sector, where a part of retained earnings too was used for investment in fixed assets. In all other sectors a part of capital invested was either used for financing working capital or had been lost in business operation. The proportion of fixed assets and current assets was consistent throughout the period of analysis. In six of the nine sectors, investment in fixed assets exceeded investment in current assets. The turnover of fixed assets was very low in almost all sectors. In seven out of the nine sectors, fixed assets turnover did not even reach two. This indicates the poor fixed asset utilisation in public sector undertakings. One of the reasons for low fixed assets turnover was unfruitful investment in fixed assets. There were many cases of imprudent investment in fixed assets which did not help the firm to improve its turnover. The percentage capacity utilisation showed that in no sector capacity was utilised in full during the period of analysis. In three sectors, capacity utilisation was less than 30 per cent. In four other sectors, it ranged between 50 to 70 per cent by the end of 1999-2000.

In many sectors, the paid up capital was in excess of the fixed assets, which indicated that only a part of the paid up capital was invested in fixed assets, while in some other sectors, in addition to share capital, borrowings were also used for financing fixed assets. In several public enterprises, long-term capital was not raised mainly for investment in fixed assets. A comparison between trend of fixed assets and trend of capital invested showed that in the majority of the sectors capital invested increased much faster than fixed assets. It led to the conclusion that in many undertakings, long-term capital was raised not primarily for investment in fixed assets. The respondents also opined that long-term funds were raised mainly for the purpose of meeting operating expenses.

There were also instances where the viable project proposals supported by techno-economic feasibility studies were turned down by the Government, consequent to which companies could not earn the possible return. In some cases, projects were generated at the Government level even without any consultation with the company. However, only a few executives regarded that projects were designed without any consultation with them. Since the proposals for replacements and modernization projects originated from the enterprise itself, the majority of the respondents viewed that they had a decisive role in this regard. The public enterprises seldom used scientific methods for evaluation of economic feasibility, such as Pay back period, Net Present Value, Return on Investment, etc. Instead, they blindly followed the project reports prepared by some outside agencies. In most cases, there were no alternative projects to compare with. Even the opportunity cost was not considered for comparing the expected return from the project under consideration. The public sector units made only very little effort in research and development. In all sectors, investment for research and development was found inadequate and this was attributed to poor profitability.

Working capital management: The efficiency with which total current assets and each component of it is managed, greatly influences the working results of an enterprise. The analysis of working capital management in the State-owned enterprises in Kerala revealed that the amount invested in total current assets increased considerably in almost all the sectors and it constituted, on an average, more than 50 per cent of the net assets in them during the past nine years. In the majority of the sectors, it was even above 70 per cent. However, the current ratio reached the standard of two only in the Chemical sector. In the majority of the sectors, it was even less than one, evidencing inadequacy of current assets to meet current liabilities. This indicated that the public sector undertakings in the State were facing the problem of negative working capital. The quick ratios calculated to check the adequacy of quick assets revealed that in no sector other than the Chemical, quick asset was sufficient by the end of 1998-99. The majority of the respondents also agreed that working capital was insufficient. Shortage of working capital was also selected by the respondents as the major problem in relation to working capital management. The other important problems were difficulty in getting working capital loans, non-availability of raw materials, etc. Non-availability of working capital loans, poor sales and excess inventory were reported by the respondents as the major reasons for the shortage of working capital. Accumulation of trade liabilities and excess borrowing for working capital loans caused the net working capital to become negative in many public sector undertakings. The low level of current assets and the presence of non-trading liabilities also contributed to this phenomenon.

Inventories were the major components of current assets in many sectors. Inventories exceeded more than 50 per cent of current assets in four sectors. In the Ceramics and Chemical sectors, it was even greater than 70 per cent. There was the presence of slow-moving, non-moving and obsolete inventories in several sectors. At the low organisation level, the respondents were more and more dissatisfied with the manner in which inventories were managed. Compared with the standard, the size of inventories was found to be in excess in five sectors, and much below the standard in another two sectors. The majority of the respondents viewed that the inventory was sufficient for their operations. The executives who believed that inventories were in excess of actual requirement asserted that long manufacturing cycle was the major reason for that. However, the respondents at the other two levels opined that defective purchase policy was the major reason. The majority of the respondents who were of the opinion that there was shortage of inventories believed that lack of adequate working capital had led their firms to the situation. The turnover of inventory was very low in the various sectors, which indicated that the level of inventory was much excessive in relation to the level of activity. Low production and sales also caused turnover to fall down. The analysis of structure of inventories revealed that raw material was the major component in four sectors, while in two sectors finished goods constituted the major part of the inventory. In the wood-based and Engineering sectors, work-in-progress was the important component, and in the Chemical sector, stores and spares ranked first. In the public sector, there existed the problem of over-stocking of raw materials. Except in the Traditional sector, stock of raw materials exceeded the standard of one month's requirement. Respondents at the supervisory and non-supervisory levels regarded management of raw material as poor. Several cases of defective purchase procedure were noticed in various public sector units. In most of the public sector units, scientific inventory control techniques were not used for the efficient use of inventories.

There were differences in the opinions of respondents

regarding the problems in relation to raw material procurement. According to the executives, lack of finance and delay in getting raw materials were the major problems, whereas most of the supervisors viewed low quality of materials as the important problem. The non-supervisors held the view those unnecessary purchases were the major problem in raw material procurement. While respondents at the higher levels were satisfied with the present purchase system, those at the lower level were not satisfied with it. Overstocking of finished goods was a problem only in some public undertakings. The majority of the respondents considered the movement of finished goods to be fast or normal. Those who viewed the movement of finished goods as slow opined that high price and severe competition were the major reasons for it. Analysis of receivables turnover revealed that in the Electrical and Electronic sectors the turnover was very low and as a consequence the collection period worked out to 345 and 480 days respectively by the end of 1998-99. The CAG Reports also noticed faulty management of receivables.

There existed no precise policy regarding cash management among the public enterprises. The percentage of cash holding to total current liabilities showed wide variation during the period of analysis in almost all the sectors. While the majority of the respondents at the executive level rated management of cash as satisfactory, the majority of those at the other two levels were not satisfied with it. In most of the cases, no attempt was seen made to estimate the periodical cash requirements. In certain cases, failure to invest the surplus cash in short-term deposits resulted in loss of interest.

Profitability: There exists much controversy as to what should be the criteria to be adopted for the performance evaluation of public enterprises. While some argue that profitability is to be considered as an important criterion to judge the public enterprises, some others are of the opinion that it would not be appropriate to evaluate the performance of public enterprises in terms of the profit they earn. In spite of the profit objective, these enterprises are supposed to act as agencies for reducing regional imbalances, checking concentration of economic power, generating employment opportunity, augmenting more public revenue, providing public utility services, etc. However, there is another argument in this regard that only those enterprises which were financially profitable had the strength and capacity to undertake the wider dimensions of social obligations. Judged from this angle, it is important for every public enterprise to give due consideration for economic objectives for making contributions to the exchequer and for their own development.

Keeping this controversy in view, the respondents were asked to rank the important criteria for evaluating the performance of public undertakings. While respondents from the executive level highly rated 'model employer' as the important criterion of efficiency, those from the other two levels rated 'profitability' the highest. The analysis of profitability revealed that many public sector enterprises were running at heavy losses. Even the gross margin (the aggregate of gross profit and depreciation) was negative in the majority of the enterprises during many years. The net revenue was not sufficient even to cover depreciation in these enterprises. In seven out of the nine sectors, gross profit was negative and net margin was negative in eight sectors n 1998-99. In two sectors, the percentages of net margin fell down below 100 in many years. It indicated that the total expenditure in those years was more than double the sales revenue.

The return on assets was positive throughout the period of analysis only in the Chemical sector. By the end of 1998-99, return taken in terms of operating profit was negative in seven out of the nine sectors. In the wood-based sector, the operating loss averaged at 76.19 per cent of the total assets over the nine-year period. In the year 1996-97 itself the operating loss was 128 per cent of the total assets. This means that during that year alone the full amount of assets had eroded even before providing for interest. The return on capital employed as well as return on owners' equity could not be analysed because of the problem of negative working capital and negative net worth. The return taken in terms of earnings after tax was not positive throughout the period of analysis in any sector. The Chemical sector has earned remarkably high rates of return on equity capital in recent years. In all the other sectors, the earnings after interest and tax were negative at the end of the period of analysis. The turnover of investment in the various sectors brings to light the inability of the management to utilise the investment effectively. In seven out of the nine sectors the average turnover of investment was less than one. The highest average turnover of 1.62 was noted in the Chemical sector. By the end of 1998-99 the highest turnover of investment was noted in the wood-based sector, followed by Ceramics with 1.51 times and Chemical with 1.49 times. In all other sectors, investment turnover was less than one. Low investment turnover was one of the problems in the public sector units.

In several sectors personnel expenses stood very high in relation to sales. By the end of 1998-99, personnel expenses exceeded 30 per cent of the sales in five sectors and in another two sectors; it was between 20 per cent and 30 per cent. In the wood-based sector, personnel expenses constituted 103.44 per cent of the sales during 1998-99. In relation to the level of activity prevailing in the firm, there was overstaffing in the majority of the public sector undertakings in Kerala. The selling expenses were not so high in the public sector units in Kerala. The average ratio of selling expenses to sales ranged from 1.41 per cent to 5.13 per cent during the period under study. The units selected to represent different sectors in the present study employed about 50 per cent of the total capital investment in those sectors. However, none of these enterprises could distribute any amount of dividend to the Government. Out of the 108 public sector undertakings owned by the Kerala State, only eight had been paying divided continuously during the period of analysis.

According to the employees at all the three levels, the major problem in relation to finance was the repayment of debt. The other important problems, according to them, were related to working capital, interest payment, and high cost of production.

Several reasons were noticed by the CAG for the adverse working results in various public sector units in the state. Several instances of imprudent management, negligence on the part of top executives, misappropriations and production flaws were pointed out in his reports from time to time. However, neither the Government nor the companies seemed to have taken any effective step to avoid such unhealthy events and all these irregularities were being repeated in one form or another.

The respondents from all the three levels rated high production cost as the foremost reason for low profitability. The other important reasons, according to them, were heavy interest and low capacity utilization. Though rated very low, inferior quality of products, defective pricing policy, political interferences, lack of professional managers, outdated technology, high competition, non-viable projects, poor sales promotion, etc. were also noted by the respondents as some of the other reasons for low profitability. According to the respondents, profitability could be improved mainly by reducing interest burden, by increased capacity utilisation, and by effective cost control. High cost of power, high cost of materials and overstaffing were reported as the major reasons for high cost of production. While respondents at the higher level complained about excess staffing, those at the lower level complained about excess managerial positions. Low productivity, outdated technology and excess material consumption were also noted by some respondents as the reasons for high product cost. The CAG, in his report, noticed many instances such as failure to execute orders in time, excess consumption of materials, under-utilisation of manpower, inferior quality of products, high intensity of product rejections, avoidable cost of electricity, faulty pricing policy, etc. which led to cash losses in the public sector units.

In most of the public sector undertakings, the costing system was completely absent. Even where there was a system of cost accounting, the efforts for cost control were less effective. Application of costing techniques was also completely absent in almost all the sectors. In most of the public enterprises in the state, they did not have an internal audit system. Accounts for many years were pending finalisation in many undertakings and, hence, a timely external audit was also not possible. In spite of the repeated pleas from the Committee on Public Undertakings and CAG, no effort seemed to have been made in the public enterprises to implement the system of performance budgeting. It is alarming that even the traditional budgeting was not properly followed in most of the public sector units. While respondents from the higher levels were generally reluctant to admit the fact, the majority of respondents from the lower levels admitted that the system of budgetary control was not working properly.

Suggestions

Effective steps are to be implemented to ascertain the magnitude of over-capitalisation in every public sector undertaking in the state. The managements of over-capitalised firms may be asked to prepare their own rehabilitation packages to wipe off excess book value and to make proposals regarding their future activities, to make their firms financially viable. The process should ensure the involvement of personnel from all the levels and from the trade unions. A team of experts may be constituted to evaluate each such proposal. The State Government should set up a fund for rehabilitation of potentially viable public sector units. The fund shall be created by sale of minority equity of profitable public sector units, sale of totally unviable units, and also by sale of unproductive and unwanted assets possessed by public sector undertakings. Public deposits can also be attracted by offering guaranteed return.

The need for a balanced capital structure in the public enterprises cannot be overlooked. Instead of the standard debt-equity ratio of 1:1 for every firm, a more realistic approach is needed in determining the debt-equity ratio, taking into account the nature of the industry as well as its gestation period. In a capital-intensive industry, the proportion of equity shall be fixed higher than that of debt. Again, while financing new projects, it is prudent to finance the major part of investment by way of equity during the period of gestation. The proposal for conversion of debt into equity should be subjected to critical analysis, and decision on the issue must be based on the merit of the case. The settlement should be on a 'once for all' basis.

The rehabilitation packages should be accompanied by a Memorandum of Understanding (MoU). MoU is an agreement or a contact reached out as to the carrying out of certain obligations by the Government as well as the public enterprises in their working. The contract will form the basis for an action plan or a corporate plan of the enterprise, and performance of the enterprise will be evaluated with reference to the contact. Before signing the MoU, the concerned enterprise should involve all the parties responsible for carrying out the tasks. Specifically, the workers' representatives should be involved in the process of designing the enterprise plan, so that the workers may play a real part in drafting the contract. The MoU helps in defining clearly the relationship between the enterprise and the Government, and clarifies their respective roles in order to achieve better performance. It will help both the parties in several ways. The MoU is also an attempt to bring a proper balance between accountability and autonomy.

Clarity of objectives is most essential for the public sector undertakings. There should not be any controversy between financial profitability and social welfare. No public enterprise should be allowed to hide their inefficiencies under the guise of social objectives. While certain types of industries falling under public utility may give more importance to social objectives, those engaged in the manufacturing of consumer durables should be guided strictly on financial terms. Only profitable undertakings can be regarded as good contributors to social objectives. Loss-making public enterprises tend to be poor employers, and fail to ensure the quality of products. They do not have the resources to respond to environmental needs, and they are a drain on the public exchequer.

Most public enterprises in the State lack a well-organised financial division. In many of them, the post of financial manager has often remained vacant. It is most essential that the finance division be organised from the project stage itself. Many earlier studies have pointed out the need to improve the status of the financial managers, but still they are treated as middle-level managers who have no say in the top level decisions affecting finance function. So it is recommended to improve the status of finance managers to the Board level.

In relation to project planning and implementation, it was seen that, while new project proposals arose mostly from Government level or Ministerial level, only proposals for replacement and modernisation did arise from the enterprise level. When the Government takes the initiative in project proposals, it is doubtful whether they are subjected to detailed evaluation of financial viability. Quite often projects will be announced by politicians of the party in [illegible] to win the support of the people without assessing the financial feasibility. The Government should strengthen the Bureau of Public Enterprises by setting up a project appraisal division as part of it, and entrust them to assess the feasibility of a project at a particular place before announcing it in public. Regarding capital expenditure projects in the existing units, the firms concerned should be encouraged to come forward with their own proposals accompanied by feasibility reports.

The Government should show its determination not to accept projects without a Detailed Project Report. Every project proposal should be subjected to critical appraisal using modern techniques in the light of the financial objective of the firm. The managers of public sector units must be convinced of the need for ascertaining the cost of capital and the need to follow modern techniques of capital budgeting, incorporating risk and uncertainty in project implementation. Project implementation in public enterprises is characterised by time and cost escalations. In order to overcome this, an expert body should be constituted in the State to monitor project implementation in public sector undertakings. Project implementation techniques such as PERT, CPM, etc. can be made use of to ensure completion of projects within the scheduled time and to avoid cost escalation. Timely release of funds by the Government and elimination of procedural delay are most essential to keep up the schedule.

In order to check the problem of excess inventory in public enterprises, inventory norms should be specified for each and every public sector unit, keeping in view their operational requirements. The Government should ensure adequate supply of raw materials to the public sector units through policy formulations, wherever possible. The management should take effective steps to identify non-moving inventory and to curtail unnecessary investments in inventories. Inventory control techniques such as ABC analysis, FNSD analysis, value engineering, PERT/CPM, etc. will be of great utility in carrying out inventory management functions.

The existing purchasing procedure should be revitalised by delegating more powers to the officers of the company, still ensuring accountability. Concrete efforts should be made to fix the maximum, minimum and reorder levels, and purchases should be based on economic order quantity calculated based on ordering and carrying costs. The storage of materials should be made systematic. Those enterprises which have not so far applied the perpetual inventory system should take immediate steps to implement the system, and bin cards should be kept to identify exact stock position of materials.

Even though the management of receivables in general was found satisfactory, there were instances where imprudent credit granting resulted in loss of several lakh of rupees. In order to avoid this, credit granting should be made on the basis of efficient credit investigation. In some sectors, collection period stretched to one year or even more. Preparation of ageing schedule of debtors will help to identify customers with overdue debt. Effective measures should be taken to recover these debts as soon as possible. Defaulting customers should not be allowed further credit. Sophisticated statistical techniques such as point scoring, numerical scoring credit scoring, and discriminate analysis can be used for conducting credit analysis of customers.

Preparation of periodic cash budgets should be made compulsory in the public sector units so as to identify the cash requirement at different periods. The Miller-Orr Model can be used to evaluate the cash position in the firm and to take appropriate decisions regarding purchase or sale of short-term securities. This will help them to avoid keeping of idle cash. The Baumol Model can be used to ascertain the optimum cash balance to be kept by the firm, keeping in view the transaction cost, total cash requirement, and opportunity cost of holding cash.

In view of the excess dependence by certain public sector units on bank borrowings to finance the working capital needs, it is advisable to assess the fixed and variable working capital requirements. Firms should follow the policy of financing permanent working capital requirement through, long-term sources such as equity, long-term borrowings, retained earnings, etc. only variable working capital requirement may be met through short-term borrowings.

The major supplier of finance for public sector units is the Government, which provides capital in the form of equity and loans. Nowadays, the Government is facing severe financial strain, and is even finding it difficult to arrange funds for meeting revenue expenditure. So, the public sector enterprises are left with alternatives such as borrowings from non-Government sources, public deposits, and retained earnings. Financial institutions are also reluctant to provide loan to public sector units, due to the latter's inability to find resources for payment of interest as well as for repayment of principal loan amount. The need for earning adequate operating profit is imperative for theses undertakings, both for creating adequate internal resources and for attracting public deposits and financial institutions. Under-utilization of capacity, increased cost of production and defective price policy are the major reasons for the poor financial performance of many public sector undertakings. So the Government should take effective steps for improving the profitability by reducing cost and increasing operational efficiency.

The mechanism for cost ascertainment and cost control has to be strengthened in these undertakings. Standards should be fixed for each element of cost and deviations should be analysed to find reasons and to take immediate steps to avoid unfavourable deviations in future. All these highlight the need for a sound cost accounting department in the public sector undertakings. Once the cost has been brought under control, the price of the product should be fixed definitely in such a way as to cover full cost and reasonable profit. The pricing policy in the public sector is subject to the distinction between society-oriented pricing and profit-oriented pricing. The socio-economic classification of public enterprises suggested by Prof. Ramanadhan, as early as 1967, may be taken as the basis for resolving this controversy such as enterprises with mainly non-economic and social functions; enterprises with both commercial and non-commercial functions; and enterprises with mainly commercial functions. The Government may fix the appropriate pricing policy for each of these categories; in the case of enterprises in the third category, the management may be given adequate freedom to fix the price of their products. It is highly necessary that products of public enterprises must be priced in such a way as to generate resources for further investment.

Low capacity utilisation is one of the basic problems in public sector undertakings. Owing to under-utilisation of capacity, many of these undertakings cannot even reach the break-even level of activity. The Bureau of Public Enterprises should be entrusted with the task of ascertaining the reasons for low capacity utilization in each individual unit and to suggest steps to improve the capacity utilization. A better coordination among public enterprises and also between public enterprises and Government Departments can be helpful in improving capacity utilization in several public sector undertakings. The management of public sector units can also go a long way in improving capacity utilisation by tackling the problems at the enterprise level.

The excess manpower at work force level and managerial level have led to heavy burden of administrative costs in public enterprises. This situation necessitates a scientific approach to human resource management in these undertakings. The size of manpower should be commensurate with the level of activity of the undertaking. In many cases, the manpower requirement is fixed in anticipation of full capacity utilization and the failure to attain the target has led to the problem of excess manpower. Political interference in the recruitment process also leads to this phenomenon. The excess manpower should be wiped off through the implementation of suitable schemes, such as VRS, redeployment, or deputing to other suitable positions. In order to eliminate political interference, the recruitment in public enterprises may be entrusted to an independent agency. The Kerala Public Service Commission may be entrusted with the process of recruitment to all positions in the entire public undertakings in the state. The other aspects related with human resource management such as manpower planning, training and development, motivation, evaluation, compensation, etc. shall be dealt with at the enterprise level, whereby problems of indiscipline, lack of commitment, apathy to work, etc. can be tackled to a great extent. The tendency of workers to do overtime work, for which the firm has to incur wages at a higher rate, should be curtailed. There were instances of overtime even in the case of those firms which faced the problem of excess staffing.

The annual accounts of several public sector undertakings are pending finalisation for years. Effective steps must be taken by the Government to make sure that the final accounts are kept up-to-date. The audit conducted by the CAG is more effective than the audit by Chartered Accountants. The statutory audit carried out by Chartered Accountants mainly deals with the regularity of the maintenance of accounts, whereas the CAG's audits go more deep into the various operational aspects and they alone help in pointing out the various deficiencies without fear and favour. So it is advisable that CAG audit should be strengthened so as to cover every enterprise in each year. The Government should take appropriate follow up measures on the audit reports of the CAG of India. The internal audit system in several organisations is inoperative, and wherever it exists, it has not been working properly. So the internal audit system should be introduced in every public sector undertaking and it should be made effective. A good internal audit system helps an undertaking to bring out the loopholes in its various activities. A minimum tenure should be fixed for the managing directors to facilitate some sort of permanency in their posts. While constituting the Board of Directors of a public sector undertaking, the Government should take steps to include professionals from the relevant fields. Politicians should not be provided with any position in these undertakings. The managerial positions in these organisations should be filled with persons having professional qualifications and experience.

In order to make the budgetary control system effective, the BPE should formulate general guidelines to be followed by different public sector units in relation to preparation and follow up of budgets. When the budget is used as a tool for control, the subordinates should also be participated in the process of setting targets. Performance budgeting helps to a great extent in linking inputs with outputs. It spells out, in concrete terms, the functions, activities, operations and tasks to be performed by the various segments of the organisation in order to accomplish its objectives. The use of various physical inputs for achieving the desired output are spelt out on the basis of scientific norms, standards, measurement units, and correlation of the financial and physical aspects of each performance unit so that the same relationship is used as a guiding frame for evaluating the actual achievement later. Again, Zero Based Budgeting (ZBB) can be used in place of the traditional ways of preparing budgets with the past figures as the basis by adding a certain percentage. In ZBB each items of expenditure must be justified in view of its necessity and nothing is provided just because it was provided in the previous years. Timely implementation of modernisation schemes is very essential for the public enterprises to compete with their counterparts in the private sector. Procedural delays should be avoided in sanctioning the feasible schemes for modernisation. Many public sector units have found it difficult to set up their own research and development wing. So, the possibility of setting up a Research and Development wing as part of the BPE to assist the public enterprises in the State as a whole, or at lest for some sectors, should be evaluated by the Government.

Disinvestment in the equity of public enterprises has been a topic of discussion in recent years. Governments are no longer in a position to bear the huge losses from public sector units and there is no justification in running these enterprises just to maintain the employees. However, the Government should be selective in its approach towards disinvestments. In the case of loss-making enterprises, those in promotional and development sectors as well as in public utilities such as road transport, power supply, water supply, etc. should be under Government control for the simple reason that they were formed with different distinct welfare objectives, and not for profit alone. Thus, disinvestments should be thought of only in the case of commercial undertakings. Even in that case, disinvestments in profitable enterprises should be restricted to a minor portion of the share holdings. In the other enterprises, privatization should be resorted to only as the last step. Every effort should be made to make these enterprises run profitably. The enterprises selected for privatization at the preliminary stage should be given some more time to prove their efficiency. Enterprises which continue to incur losses in spite of all efforts shall be selected for privatization in the final stage. A Disinvestment Board shall be constituted by the Government with experts to value the assets and to fix the consideration. The fund so raised can be utilized for rehabilitating potentially viable public sector units. While privatizing public enterprises, the Government should see that the interest of employees is protected.

The present study, undertaken with a view to evaluating the financial management of public enterprises, attempts to point out that the public enterprises have a vital role to play in the country in evolving and maintaining a price mechanism, in adding revenue to the exchequer, in creating employment opportunities, in neutralising the competitive market and in providing basic needs to the society.

References

Beena, P.L., Performance of Manufacturing Enterprises in the State

Sector and Private Sector in Kerala – A Comparative Study, Dissertation, Jawaharlal Nehru University, 1991.

Chauhan. A.B., Organization and Working of Public Enterprises in Gujarat, Vijayanagar, Sardar Patel University Press, 1978.

Choyal, B.R., Financial Management of State Enterprises, Jaipur, Printwell. Publishers, 1986.

Dutt, Rudder and Sundaram, K.P.M., Indian Economy, New Delhi, Sulthan Chand and Co. Pvt. Ltd, 1989.

Gangadharan Pillai, V., The Public Sector in Kerala Administrative Problems, Trivandrum, Kerala Academy of Political Science, 1980.

Government of Kerala, Review of Public Enterprises in Kerala, 1999-2000.

Hemlata Rao, Financial Performance of Public Enterprises, Jaipur, Printwell Publishers. 1987.

Khurshid Alli, Financial Management - A Study into the Public Sector Undertakings of Jammu and Kashmir, Srinagar, Gulshan Publishers, 1985.

Krishnama Chary, P., Investment Management in Public Enterprises, Printwell Publishers, 1990.

Nagaraja Naidu, V., Finances of Andhra Pradesh Electricity Board. Thesis submitted to Osmania University.

Nair, P.P., Efficiency of State Enterprises Investment in Kerala, Lok Udyog, August 1990.

Narayanan, R., Performance and Development of State Level Public Enterprises in India (Ed.), Sankar, T.L., Nanda Gopal and Misra. R.K., Hyderabad, Institute of Public Enterprises, 1989.

Nataraja Iyer, S., Financial Performance of Public Sector Enterprises in Kerala. Ph.D Thesis, University of Kerala, 1995.

Prasad, G and Rao, K.V., Financial Management of Public Sector Enterprises, New Delhi, Ashish Publishing House, 1989.

Sahay, S.N., Financial Management of Public Enterprises in Bihar, Thesis Submitted to Patna University, 1982.

Shanakaraiah, A., Financial Management of Public Enterprises - A Study of Budgeting in State Undertakings of Andhra Pradesh, Delhi, Seema Publications, 1983.

Sharma, G.D., Working of State Enterprises in Rajasthan, New Delhi, Sterling Publishers Pvt. Ltd., 1975.

Sing, V.S., Public Enterprises in India, New Delhi, Deep and Deep Publications, 1986.

Vishwanathan, V., The Finances of AP State Road Transport

Corporation, Thesis submitted to Osmania University. 1979.

Viyyanna Rao, K., Management of Working Capital With Reference to the Selected A.P. Public Enterprises, Thesis Submitted to Nagarjuna University, 1981.

Wilson, P.R., Financial Planning and Control of Public Enterprises in Kerala, Ph.D. Thesis, Cochin University, 1981.

Ziauddin, Khan and Ramesh, K. Arora (Ed), Public Enterprises in India - A Study of State Government Undertakings, New Delhi, Associated Publishing House, 1975.

5

Promotion of Tourism: Role of State Enterprises

G. Joseph Antony

Tourism is a fast growing economic and industrial activity of immense global importance. It has become a very effective instrument for generating employment, earning foreign exchange, improving infrastructure, helping regional development and thereby facilitating overall development of an economy. World tourism is now a 350 billion dollar business, with every tenth human being a traveller. Tourism industry contributes 10.9 per cent to the world's Gross National Product and employs over 200 million people, which is about 11.2 per cent of global work force. Tourism industry is the largest economic force with an annual turnover of 3.5 trillion dollars. It is the world's biggest export industry, which, according to the World Tourism Organisation, generated about US$ 372.6 billion during 1995 by some 567 million tourists world wide. Tourism thus became a major foreign exchange earner of several developing and even developed countries.

In India also tourism continues to be a major channel of development as a massive foreign exchange earner, big generator of employment and a genuine promoter of cultural ties. The foreign exchange earnings for the year 1995-96 through tourism were over Rs. 9000 crore. The sector is also estimated to have given employment to over 75 lakh people in 1994-95. Its importance can further be gauged from the fact that it is the third largest foreign exchange earner after the two export-oriented industries, namely; ready-made-garments and gems and jewellery. In terms of net revenue, it is the single largest earner of foreign exchange in India. It assumes increasing importance in the national development and can rightly be an effective means of national integration. The great potential to break barriers of caste, creed and motivating linguistic groups to communicate with one another, to promote inter-regional understanding and championing an outlook of world community underlying in tourism is well recognised by social scientists.

India has been immensely blessed with worthy tourist attractions which lured travellers from time immemorial. She enjoys a unique position among the "world's renowned tourist destinations. Indeed many unmatched and unparalleled peculiarities place her in a superior and advantageous position. The ancient architecture exhibited by magnificent structures dotted all over the country, the *onion* – topped Islamic edifices-chiselled stone-work on the walls of temples, sand-stone-built houses in Jodhpur, Asia's first Christian church, the first Islamic mosque, the 5000 year old civilisation, five seasons every year, religious and harvest festivals, 7516.5 kilometers of coastline, national parks with wild animals, deserts with walled cities, the high plateau of Ladakh - the fantasy of Central Asia - and 1652 spoken languages form colourful feathers in the cap of our country. The beautiful beaches of Goa and Kovalam, architectural elegance of holy temples, ageless charm of heritage -monuments like the legendary Taj, the lure of snow-clad mountains, grandeur of the mighty rivers like the Ganges and the Brahmaputra, awe-inspiring sand dunes of the Thar, and the exotic beauty of various mediaeval forts and royal palaces have, in their own inimitable ways, been beckoning the travellers since long.

The word tour is originated from the Latin word tornus, which was later, changed into tourn, standing for lathe or turner's wheel. As the full turn of the wheel or lathe forms a circle or circuit, the word tornus or tourn also means a round journey in which one returns to starting point. The word tour was first used for a journey in which one travels and visits a number of places in circuit or sequence, thus meaning a circuitous or circular journey. Tourism encompasses travel for pleasure and holiday, wanderlust, health, business and trade, pilgrimage and social purpose, historical and geographical research, educational studies and training, foreign affairs and other official functions. The perspective of travel spreads over many fields of human activity-cultural, religious and sociological and thereby influences the social and economic aspects of international trade, transport and finance. Tourism has become an export-oriented business for travel agents, transporters, hoteliers, retail dealers selling curios and other items and for many others connected with tourism.

Tracing back to the history of the development of tourism, trading people went from one place to another. It is well supported by the civilisation of Mohanjodaro and Harappa where wheel and money were already in existence. Centuries back, the King of Babylon, Shulglect, protected roads, rest houses and gardens for travellers. Romans used to travel for pleasure. They rode hundred miles in a day on horseback to see monuments of Egypt. Olympic games were also a reason for their travelling from their houses to Olympia. In fifth century the downfall of Roman Empire accounted for the set back of tourism there.

India had also travel facilities. When Alexander the Great reached India, he found well-maintained roads, rest houses, police stations and wells. Chinese travellers also gave an account of travel facilities in India. European travellers also visited India between 12th and 14th centuries. People travelled for religious cause too. The travels of emissaries of Ashoka, the Great and Faheiyan are examples. A large number of pilgrims visited the shrines in Europe. The adoption of Christianity also initiated travel to, the Holy Land. Hinduism, Buddhism, Islam and other religions contributed towards travel. Travels were also made to explore the world. Travels of Vasco De Gama and Christopher Columbus belong to this kind.

The people of economically strong countries visited other countries to show their feeling of dominance and to impress others by their way of life. Romans visited Greece and other Eastern Countries to show them their styles of life. The famous traveller Marcopolo visited Kerala in 13th century A.D. The Chinese traveller Vang Twa Yan came down to Kerala in 1940.

The famous African traveller Ibn Batutah visited Kerala seven times and wrote an account of the place. The Arabian Traveller Sulaiman visited here in 851 A.D. Jewish traveller Rabbi Benjamin had also written about this place. St. Thomas, a disciple of Jesus Christ visited Kodungalloor in 52 A.D.

The Portuguese, Dutch, British and French came down for trade and commerce. Thus, tourism had its origin centuries ago, developed through ages and now reached with international acceptance as an industry earning foreign exchange and generating employment opportunities. In India, tourism was accorded the status of an industry by the Government in the Seventh Five Year Plan. Deliberate and intense efforts were made both in the Centre and the State sector for the development of Tourism Industry by way of increasing allocations for tourism through planning from Rs. 1.58 crore in Second Plan to Rs. 364.61 crore in the Eighth Plan. The tourist arrivals have increased from 17,000 in 1951 to 2.12 million in 1995-96. It is estimated that during the year 1995-96 foreign exchange earnings crossed Rs. 9100 crore. In spite of these, the growth rate of tourism sector is much lower than that of countries like Spain, Thailand, U.K, and Singapore. Tourist arrivals in India recorded only two per cent increase during 1995- 96, which was merely a drop when compared to other Asian Countries. One of the main reasons for the low tourist arrivals is the poor state of infrastructure. Paucity of fund accounts for the lack of infrastructure and poor quality of existing infrastructure.

The World Tourism Organisation (WTO) projects an increase of 10 per cent over the estimated arrivals in the current year (1997-98) for India. India's possible target of receiving five million foreign tourists will have to be backed up by infrastructure sufficient in number and standard of service. It seems very urgent that our infrastructure will have to be doubled the existing capacity in terms of hotel rooms, airline seats, airports, inland transport and telecommunications. The time has come for the Government of India to plan and act adequately enough to keep pace with the growing demands of tourism sector.

Statement of the Problem

Tourism, in its broadest, generic sense, can do more to develop understanding among people, provide jobs, create foreign exchange and raise living standards than any other economic force known. Tourism is the second largest industry in the world, the first being oil industry. By the end of 20th century, this industry will become the biggest industry in the world. To keep pace with the alarming growth of the Tourism Industry on the global rounds, the Government of Kerala plans suitably to bring economies from the development of Tourism. Inaugurating the children's swimming pool at Akkulam on 5th May, 1994, the then Chief Minister of Kerala who was also in charge of Tourism, announced the proposed development of tourism between Akkulam and Veli spending five hundred crore of rupees. He also stated to the press, of the various development schemes with a view to attracting five lakh tourists at the end of this century to Kerala.

The various proposals on the anvil include the formation of Tourist Investment Agency in the joint sector with Central Tourism Department, Central Tourism Finance Corporation, State Government and Private Agencies. The other proposals are the declaration of Tourism Policy, formation of a company to invest 1500 crore of rupees to develop Akkulam and Bakel and the implementation of different tourist projects sanctioned by the Central Government. The exotic spices, enchanting natural beauty, tranquility of backwaters, fury of the lashing monsoon, the colourful fairs and festivals and the cosmopolitan outlook of the people are the proverbial features of Kerala which lured tourists from time immemorial. In Kerala, tourism industry offers much potentiality to enrich the economic, stature and to create employments to multitudes.

Considering the commercial viability of exploiting the treasures of tourist attractions to achieve social and economic benefits, the Government of Kerala declared tourism as an industry in 1986. The much-awaited 'Tourism Policy - Kerala' has been announced in 1995 by the state government. The Government of Kerala wanted to give an industrial base to the tourism activities to earn profit and foreign exchange. With this end in view a public limited company was incorporated on 29th December, 1965 by name Kerala Tourism and Handicrafts Development Limited. Later on 15th July 1970, the corporation was renamed as Kerala Tourism Development Corporation Limited. It is the only Government Company floated with an authorised capital of Rs. 13,00,00,000 to conduct tourism industry for the State. The Corporation owns, operates and manages 15 hotels, 3 yatrinivases, 11 motels, 41 restaurants and beer parlours, 3 bars and 4 boat clubs at different places throughout the State.

Considering the socio-economic significance of tourism, Kerala Tourism Development Corporation Limited is expected to promote tourism industry at large through many developmental schemes and projects involving huge investments. Objective evaluation of the role of the Kerala Tourism Development Corporation Limited in promoting tourism in the light of its past performance and expected future prospects becomes imperative, particularly in the context of large scale investments, added social responsibility and in the context of tourism industry being processed to become the biggest industry of the world by the turn of this century. It is against this background an attempt has been made to evaluate the role of Kerala Tourism Development Corporation Limited in the promotion of tourism.

Review of Literature

Indeed, literature on tourism has been almost enriched with worthy contributions of books, articles, reports, theses and lectures by academic stalwarts and others. Literary pieces of academic excellence and interest reviewed in the context of launching the present research work are to be briefly referred here.

Arora K.K. in his doctoral thesis entitled Tourist Industry in Kumaon explains the problems of tourism industry in Kumaon and pointedly reports that almost every country aims at earning a good deal of economic benefits from the tourism industry. Negi J.M.S. in his book Tourism and Hoteliering, critically evaluated the infinite multiplier effect ensures from the economic benefit of tourism industry. The quarterly economic report of Indian Institute of Public Opinion outlined the multiple contributions of tourism industry to the economy of India. Emmanuel De Kardt undertook a study relating to tourism in the context of socio-economic development. In his book Tourism - Passport to Development he highlighted the role of peripheral tourism area requirements and planned development of tourism industry. The Political Economy of Tourism in the Third World scribbled by Stephen G. Britten dealt with the economic advantages the third world can derive by developing tourism as an industry. Selvam's Tourism Industry in India - A Study of its Growth and Development Needs evaluated the present status and needs of tourism industry in India. It also highlighted the contribution of foreign exchange to the country's economic growth. Ummat, R.C., in his article Forecasting Tourism - Why Dither projected that by the end of this century, tourism industry becomes the biggest industry of world.

Smart William.W., Gearing Charles,E. and Var Truget in their joint article Determining the Capital Investment Policy for Tourism Sector of a Developing Country have given a detailed description of creating new destinations for tourists. They have also developed a decision structure for the investment allocation for the tourism industry. The UNCTAD in its report Elements of Tourism Policy in Developing Countries discussed the different and wide resources and stated that the resources must be identified and developed by conducting appropriate surveys. Fred Lawson and Manual Band Bavy stated in their book Tourism and Recreational Development, A Hand book of Physical Planning that resources are the inherent attractions of an area. They further explained that resources include tradition, folklore, songs, customs, way of life and attitude. Raymond Noroncha described in his working paper the significance of natural resources and the influence of climate, culture and history to attract tourists to a destination. Jag Mohan Negi's Tourism Development and Resource Conservation, analysed the importance of tourism resources and identifies the easily accessible ones. The author holds that the spiritual value of tourism in Indian sub-continent should be preserved and given publicity.

Hotels and Catering Costing and Budget authored by Boardwan, R.D. dealt with the study relating to costing and budgeting of hotel and catering industry. The author explained the fixed, variable and miscellaneous expenditure of hotel and catering establishments and exhibits a marginal costing analysis of a tourist hotel. Jag Mohan Negi also made an in-depth study on tourist hotels, its administrative problems, the cost and benefit of hotel business and the role of hotels in tourism development. The findings of the study are of high professional value and it is highlighted in his book Hotel for Tourism Development. The cost benefit analysis and the multiplier effect of tourism industry are brought under study by Robert Christie Mill and Morrison Alasataire M. The opportunity cost, socio-economic cost, benefits of tourism industry and the marketing problems of the business are explained in their book entitled The Tourism System.

Indian Airlines and Tourism authored by Ajith S. Gopal read the concessions granted by Indian Airlines to various tourists and the average length of stay of tourists at different places. The author stated that the tourists stay for the largest period in India when compared to that in any other country. WTO conducted a comprehensive study on tourist project evaluation. Manual on Evaluating, Tourism Projects dealt with the aims of tourism projects and its prospects for tourism development. It also highlighted the expenditure and staff pattern of a tourism-oriented hotel. Ram Laxman in his article No longer a Bargain Destination presented the statistics regarding the number of tourists visited and the foreign exchange earned. It concluded that Indians charge more from tourists than other developing countries. Anil Chakraborthy highlighted in his article, Conducted Tours - A Lucrative Business, the advantages and problems of conducted tours organised by travel agents.

Wilson's write up ITDC's Performance thrown light on the working of ITDC which is the largest accommodation chain spread throughout the country. Sarojit Dutta presented in his article, Eastern Region - yet to make up to its Potentials, a few problems like accessibility to forests, non-availability of transport and accommodation, political condition etc., faced by the tourists there. Garg, R.B.I, in his article What Ails Indian Tourism, wrote about the problems faced by Indian Tourism Industry such as untapped resources, unavailability of suitable accommodation, customs procedures, poor image of the country, lack of transport, security and safety measures etc. The prospects of tourism industry in Orissa were analysed in Prospects of Tourism in Orissa by Mishra R.C. Tourism development is a real challenge and offers unlimited opportunities. The author has estimated the tourism accommodation needs by the turn of this century.

Kaul R.N. conducted an analytical study on tourism related industries with special emphasis on accommodation, transportation and marketing aspects. The valuable findings of study are outlined in three volumes- Dynamics of Tourism Vol. I, The Phenomenon Vol. II, Accommodation Vol. III. The first volume dealt with the economic policies and programmes required for the contribution of tourism industry to the optimum growth of the economy of a country. The second volume discussed the requirements of accommodation establishments and the problems connected with the preservation of national heritage and recommend the need for granting incentives and concessions to hotel promoters. The growth of transportation and the estimated need for the tourism-linked transportation are highlighted in the third volume. Misra, S.K. in his article The Chief Executive Speaks: Public Sector in Tourism-A Survey, wrote that by the end of 1990 India will receive 3.5 million tourists and that India's tourism machinery should be geared enough to accommodate them. Agarwal Govinda's article Tourism Management in Nepal, dealt with the tourist arrivals and the foreign exchange earned by Nepal. It also described the application of marketing concept of tourism.

In the editorial of the tourism special volume of Capital the writer laid emphasis on the need of customers satisfaction and gave many references to the speech delivered by the then President of International Air Transport Association. Successful Tourism Management authored by Pran Nath Seth read the evolution and historic development of tourism industry in multiple dimensions. It also studied through tourism and infrastructure the needs of tourism industry in India. Peter Murphy in his book Tourism - A Community Approach, explained that tourism is a business both for the individual entrepreneur and for the community. Kumar H.L. opined in his book Personnel Management in Hotel and Catering Industry, that yearly renovation, remodelling, provision for modern amenities and comforts and proper selection of hotel employees would constitute the essential ingredients of modern hotel and catering industry.

Employment generation in tourism and leisure industry was analysed by Hilary Metcalf in his report Employment Structure in Tourism Leisure. He identified the various categories of employees in tourism industry and their work responsibilities. He also laid out the necessity and importance of proper human resource development for the tourism business. Tourism Planning, written by Glare A. Gunn, threw light on the detailed planning of tourism and stated that tourism industry development is one of the greatest challenges of the regional tourism planner. It is also remarked that handicrafts, entertainments and small business would offer added attraction for both the local and foreign tourists. Cooper, C.P. conducted a study relating to recreation and hospitality management, the findings of which he narrated in his book Progress in Tourism Recreation and Hospitality Management. The author explains the significance of proper organisation, leadership and Co-ordination and the importance of human resources in providing integrated recreation.

In Tourism in India - A Perspective to 1990 Ahuja S. P. and Sharma S. R. evaluated the tourism development in India and described that developing countries should give immediate attention to identify the important geographical zones and assign special importance to tourism product development. They also recommend both luxury and economic class amenities for the future growth of tourism. Sudheer S. V. undertook an in-depth study, the findings of which are exhibited in his doctoral thesis entitled Tourism in Kerala - Problems and Prospects. He prefaced his treatise with problems and status of tourism as an industry in Kerala and analysed the potential of natural resources and the various facilities available to the tourists in Kerala. The researcher pointedly remarked that the lack of professionalism among the personnel retarded the efficient functioning of State Department of Tourism.

Commercial Viability of the Tourist Infrastructure of the Tamil Nadu Tourism Development Corporation forms the report of the research study conducted by Soundara Rajan A. The doctoral thesis deeply analysed the assessment of the potential and the impact of tourism development in Tamil Nadu. It also highlighted the role and viability of the infrastructure development under TTDC in terms of money and profitability. He forwarded several creative recommendations for the substantial and all round development of TTDC. Development of Tourism in India authored by Lajipathi Raj H. gave a broad spectrum analysis of tourism industry in India, governmental and institutional role in tourism promotion, problems for development of tourism, tourism awareness and domestic tourism. It also outlined the profile of foreign tourist arrivals in India from 1980 to 1989.

The sociological and historical development of tourism, the types of tourism, tourism infrastructure, incentives and attractions desirable at a tourist site are the main subjects of discussion in the Dynamics of Modern Tourism described by Ratandeep Singh. In his book the chapter on Hill stations of India would rightly amuse the reader and inform him of the historical back ground of many hill stations. Infrastructure of Tourism in India is another book written by Ratandeep Singh wherein he widely analysed the state of tourism industry in India, planned approach to tourism development, tourism infrastructure, tourism marketing, fairs and festivals, wild life etc. Ratandeep Singh in his book Tourist India – Hospitality Services, gives a detailed account of all hill stations, wild life sanctuaries, historical and archaeological monuments and natural beauty sites. This book makes up as a valuable guide to the tourists going to the Himalayas or seaside, resorts or even desert or jungle. This is a very informative book on the tourist sites of India.

A meticulous survey of available literature on tourism irresistibly revealed that no scientific, empirical and exploratory studies have been so far made to evaluate the role of Kerala Tourism Development Corporation Limited in the promotion of tourism. It is in this context that a research study of the present nature is highly warranted. The researcher has, hence, fully devoted to carry out an indepth research study for an intellectual analysis, logical interpretations and critical evaluation of the working of Kerala Tourism Development Corporation (KTDC) in the promotion of tourism and to submit the creative suggestions emerging there from for a better and more efficient performance of KTDC in the days to come.

Objectives

The present study aims at the following objectives:

- To assess the potential for the development of tourism as an industry in Kerala.
- To evaluate the management of funds by the KTDC.
- To analyse the views of the tourists on the facilities provided by the KTDC.
- To suggest measures for improvements based on the findings of the study.

The data for the study were acquired from varied sources. Both primary and secondary sources were relied upon. The sample for the study consisted of 685 tourists who availed the services and facilities provided by the KTDC. Of these, 541 respondents were foreign tourists and 144 domestic tourists. The respondents covered under the sample were selected on a random from the hotels and other units of KTDC.

Both foreign and domestic tourists were interviewed personally during the period October 1996 to March 1997. A questionnaire was specifically developed for the collection of data from the tourists covered under the sample for the study. A pilot study was conducted among 50 tourists and the questionnaire was finalised on the basis of that study. The questionnaires advocated to the tourists were obtained back from them by remaining with them on an average of 45 minutes each. This has benefited in making informal discussions on matters directly related to their feelings during their stay at Kerala. In addition to the primary sources mentioned here, informal discussions were held with the officials at different levels working at head office and the sample units of KTDC. Informants were also contacted and this category consisted of officials in state department of tourism, tourist guide, secretaries of district tourism promotion councils, tour operators in the private sector and traders. The observation made at the time of holding the interviews and discussions were also useful in analysing and interpreting the data. Secondary data were mainly collected from the office records of KTDC and the published annual accounts and reports of the KTDC for a ten-year period from 1986 to 1995. Besides these sources, data collected from State Department of Tourism, State Department of Economics and Statistics, State Planning Board, State Bureau of Public Enterprises, World Tourism Organisation and other reports and periodicals were also made use of the study. The data collected from primary and secondary sources mentioned above were analysed by using mathematical tools like percentages, ratios and chi- square tests.

In the present study whatever data furnished by the tourists in the questionnaires advocated to them were to be relied upon. In certain cases it was observed that the tourists were showing a passive attitude in providing answers. However utmost care was taken to overcome this limitation by holding personal discussion with a view to making a cross-check of the correctness of the answers. Another limitation of the study is that the data related to the management of funds in respect of the financial years 1993-94 and 1994-95 were subject to the final statutory audit.

Findings

Potential for the development of tourism as an industry in Kerala: Kerala also comes under the group of 23 states which declared tourism as an industry. Government of Kerala declared tourism as an industry in 1986. Those engaged in tourism promotion activities in the state would become automatically eligible for the concessions/incentives as applicable to the industrial sector from time to time. The State Government offers assistance to the potential entrepreneurs for the self-employment programme in the tourism sector. The areas selected for this purpose are transport, catering, sightseeing, entertainment and shopping. The entrepreneurs are being given one-month training and 15 per cent investment subsidy limited to Rs. 25,000. The State Government grants financial assistance and subsidy for the development of watercrafts and waterfronts. Running of floating restaurants and floating cottages is encouraged and made eligible for financial assistance and subsidy. A scheme was introduced by the State Government to encourage tourism in rural areas. Private entrepreneurs are invited to invest in tourism projects in the newly developed areas. The project is sanctioned and supervised by the District Tourism Promotion Councils. Self-employment scheme for tour operation has been introduced by the State Government. The local tour operators are selected for training and financial assistance under this scheme.

The successful candidates of the training programme are being granted an interest free loan of Rs. 25,000 each for a period of two years to set up their own tour operating business. The State Department of Tourism (SDT) has initiated schemes to promote the construction of motels along the side of the highways. SDT supplies designs; estimates and project reports free of cost and arrange a loan up to Rs. 5 lakh through Kerala Financial Corporation. SDT has also a scheme for constructing way-side toilets by hotels, motels and petrol bunks adjacent to the state and national highways. The designs will be supplied by SDT which grants a subsidy of 50 per cent of the total cost subject to a maximum of Rs. 10,000.

According to the world survey on tourism held in 1988, seventy per cent of the international tourist traffic is drawn towards any country solely by the natural attractions in the shape of beaches, hill resorts, wildlife sanctuaries, backwaters and cultural heritage. Golden beaches, tranquility of backwaters, fury of the lashing monsoon, wildlife sanctuaries, evergreen forests, diverse flora and fauna, ancient temples and churches, hill resorts, the colourful fairs and festivals and the rich cultural heritage are the major tourist attractions of Kerala, which can be fully exploited to generate a number of socio-economic benefits like more employment opportunities and foreign exchange earnings. The ancient time-tested, scientific systems of medicine like Ayurveda, Yoga and Naturopathy contributed much to the health tourism in Kerala.

Kerala offered a wide range of accommodation facilities ranging from costly star hotels to budget hotels. The latest additions are heritage hotels, paying guest accommodation and 'Kettuvalloms'. A wide network of communication facilities backed by the latest technology is all along available. The major tourist centres are well linked by roads and rails. There are international airports developing at Trivandrum, Cochin and Calicut. A special wing of the state police designated as 'Tourist Police' was given proper training and the charge of being vigilant in the destination areas of tourists. Lifeguard facility, the first of its kind in the country, is being made available at beaches in Kovalam and Varkala to ensure the safety of tourists taking sea bath. Trained guides appointed by private travel agencies and the KTDC are sought by the tourists to accompany them.

Tourist traffic to Kerala showed an increasing trend over the past ten years. The total tourist inflow to Kerala was 4058628 during the year 1995 registering a sharp increase of 192.2 per cent over the previous year. Foreign tourist arrivals recorded an increasing trend during the last period of six years from 1990 to 1995. There was an increase of 36.7 per cent in 1995 over the previous year. Domestic tourist arrivals also indicated an upward trend during the same period. The increase in 1994 over the previous year was 204.8 per cent. The immediate past years witnessed a galloping rise in the tourist traffic. Among the foreign tourists the highest number hails from United Kingdom (20 per cent) and the lowest number from Pakistan as per the statistics of 1995.

The highest number of tourists visited was in Kochi (39.58 per cent) and the maximum bed nights spent was recorded at Trivandrum which accounts for 42.3 per cent of the total bed nights spent in Kerala. The lowest figure both in the case of number of tourists and bed nights spent was shown against Guruvayoor. It shows that there is no scope for the pilgrim-tourism among the foreigners. It was interesting to note that the highest number of domestic tourists visited was recorded against Guruvayoor (33.3 per cent) in 1995. Most of the domestic tourists belong to pilgrim category. Importantly adequate marketing techniques are required to attract more pilgrim-tourists to other centres.

Road and rail continued to be the main mode of travel for the tourists frequenting Kerala. It constituted 62.5 per cent of the total traffic, whereas 34.8 per cent of tourists came by air and 2.7 per cent by ship in 1995. It was noted that much developments are to be carried out on road and rail transport to keep pace with the growth rate of tourist traffic.

Earnings from tourism industry showed a promising growth since 1986. From the base year 1986, the earnings recorded a sharp growth rate of 519.3 per cent, 580.2 per cent and 830.1 per cent in 1993, 1994 and 1995 respectively. This proves that earnings from tourism industry have been ever on the sharp growth surpassing other industries. Government of Kerala realised that tourism offers high potential to the economic growth of the State and decided to broad base the developmental plans for the tourism industry by declaring 'Tourism Policy' of the State in 1995. The main purpose of the policy was to give a clear derivation and guidance for the various activities and programmes to be launched for the effective and successful development of tourism in the State.

Government of Kerala resolved to define and demarcate the functional areas of the SDT, KTDC, KITTS and the District Tourism Promotion Councils. The State Government proposed to organise tourism clubs in colleges to create awareness of tourism among the youth. The State Government also decided to introduce an insurance scheme for the tourists visiting Kerala. They may be given financial aid when they meet with casualties of running short of funds for the return journey.

Kerala Tourism Development Corporation Limited - Management of Funds

Long term funds: The total capitalisation of the KTDC increased from Rs. 190.73 lakh in 1986 to Rs. 2,551.80 lakh in 1995 representing an increase of 280.20 per cent. There was an increasing trend in all the constituents in the capital structure. Reserves and surplus including grants and subsidies from governments showed the highest growth of 19,173.5 per cent in 1995 from 1986. The average debt to equity ratio for the period under study - 1986 to 1995 - was 1.03:1. It was stated that KTDC had a satisfactory position. Since it has started earning huge profits from 1994 onwards, the inclusion of more debt can be considered for availing the benefit of trading on equity. Funded debt of the Corporation increased from Rs. 352.96 lakh in 1986 to Rs. 802.99 lakh in 1995. During the period, the total capitalisation increased from Rs. 828.92 lakh to Rs. 2,129.23 lakh. The average ratio of funded debt to total capitalisation for the period under review was 0.43. KTDC maintains a safe and better position with regard to this ratio throughout the period of study - 1986 to 1995. KTDC could procure more funds from outsiders, if necessary, since the ratio is allowed up to 0.55.

During the period of ten years of study from 1986 to 1995, the net worth of the Corporation had increased from Rs. 475.96 lakh to Rs. 1,336.94 lakh and the total assets from Rs. 910.73 lakh to Rs. 2,551.80 lakh. The average ratio of net-worth to total assets for the period was 49.50. KTDC had been less dependent on the outside sources to acquire its assets. The fixed assets of the

Corporation increased from Rs. 425.67 lakh in 1986 to Rs. 1203.45 lakh in 1995. The average ratio of fixed assets to net worth was 0.87, which indicated that the shareholders fund was more than the fixed assets during the period under review.

Working capital management: The working capital changed from Rs. 29.80 lakh in 1986 to Rs. 95.63 lakh in 1995. The percentage of change in working capital revealed that it varies from year to year to a great extent. It moved up and down throughout the period of study. The position of working capital was negative in 1987 and 1988. It connotes that KTDC had no proper management of working capital. Nevertheless the latest position of working capital is so positive and safe that it can adequately ensure both liquidity and solvency of the Corporation.

The current ratio of the Corporation varied from 0.83:1 to 2.50:1 during the period under study. The current ratio was above standard level only in 1994 - 2.50:1. In all other years it fell below the standard level 2:1. The average current ratio during the period under review came to 1.45:1. The current ratio recorded below the satisfactory level pointedly denoted that KTDC should initiate deliberate attempt for a better working capital management. The average quick ratio of the Corporation during the period under study came to 1.35:1, which was above the satisfactory level 1:1. The highest ratio was recorded at 2.35:1 in 1994 and the lowest ratio at 0.76:1 in 1987. The liquidity position based on the quick assets had been satisfactory since 1989. The cash ratio during the period ranged from 0.12 to 0.94 with an average of 0.40. This ratio rose beyond the satisfactory level of 0.50:1 only in 1992 (0.54), in 1993 (0.80) and in 1994 (0.94). In all other years the liquid cash position was not adequate enough to meet out the current obligations. This also leads to the conclusion that a proper management of working capital is to be designed in the KTDC.

Profit

The average percentage of operating cost to net income during the period of ten years from 1986 to 1995 came to 107.46. The operating cost exceeded net income in all these years except from 1992 to 1995. KTDC has started earning operating profit since 1992. The position of operating profit was improved to 111.56 per cent in 1995 from that of the base year 1986. Provision and expenses formed the major item of expenditure in KTDC. Provision and expenses to net income ranged from 24.73 per cent in 1990 to 42.04 per cent in 1992 with an average of 31.84 per cent for the period 1986 to 1995. There was no marked variation on percentage of this expenditure to net income during the period under study. The second major item of expenditure was salaries, wages and other benefits. The percentage of this expense to net income ranged from 21.07 to 65.04 with an average of 34.75. In 1990 an exorbitant rise on the percentage of this expense to the net income was recorded (65.04). In all other years there was no wide difference. The percentage of administrative expense to net income ranged from 7.73 in 1993 to 12.91 in 1996 with an average of 10.09 during period under study. This expense and net income had increased to 638.13 per cent and 873.75 per cent respectively from those of the base year 1986. There had been no marked variation on the ratio of administrative expense to net income from the average for the ten year period under study.

The percentage of electricity, water and fuel expense to net income ranged from 4.30 in 1992 to 8.22 in 1989 with an average of 6.01. It was seen that no wide change occurred on percentage of this expenditure to net income during the period from the average except in the year 1989. The average percentage of running and maintenance cost of vehicle to net income for the period under study came to 6.89. It ranged from 2.89 per cent in 1995 to 11.20 in 1986. Advertisement and publicity expense to net income ranged from 1.27 per cent in 1993 to 2.64 per cent in 1995, with an average of 1.87 per cent during the ten year period from 1986 to 1995. There was no marked change in the percentage of this expenditure to net income during the period under review. Interest and bank charges to net income ranged between 2.25 per cent in 1995 and 24.59 per cent in 1990 with an average of 12.68 per cent during the period 1986 to 1995. Pointedly, this expense had sharply fallen down below the average in the last 5 years of study. KTDC had reduced the employment of borrowed capital which accounted for lowering down of this expenditure.

Views of the Resident-tourists of KTDC Units

The profile of the resident-travellers, who were interviewed and discussed with, for the present study, featured the following:

On an enquiry about the country of origin of the 685 resident-travellers of the KTDC units, it was seen that 23.3 per cent of them belonged to the United Kingdom, 20.7 per cent to Germany and 21 per cent to India. In the case of number of foreign tourists, U.K stood first followed by Germany. Of the total tourists covered under the study 69.9 per cent were males and 30.1 per cent females. Most of the tourists belonged to Europe (66.2 per cent). Majority of the tourists were hailing from the age group of above 30 years (79.6 per cent). Most of the domestic tourists were under the monthly income group of Rs. 10,000 to Rs. 40,000 (92.4 per cent). Majority of foreign tourists belonged to the monthly income group of Rs. 40,000 to Rs. 1,60,000 (74.86 per cent). The occupation of the most of the domestic tourists was 'business' (54.2 per cent) and majority of the foreign tourists belonged to the occupation 'others' (other than business and profession). Most of the both foreign and domestic tourists were married (69.5 per cent). More tourists stayed in India for less than four weeks (52 per cent). 'Entertainment' had been the main purpose of visit in India (71.8 per cent). More tourists stayed in Kerala for the period less than 2 weeks (52.3 per cent). Majority of the foreign tourists visited India for one to two times (60.4 per cent). Tourists frequented Kerala for one to two times came to 78.3 per cent of the total tourists covered under the study. More foreign tourists visited Kerala for the first time.

Source of information about KTDC: Books and travel guides were the main source of information about KTDC - to both foreign and domestic tourists - irrespective of their occupation. It was found that 54.5 per cent of respondents covered under study came to know about Kerala from books and travel guides. On a sex-wise classification of the tourists covered under the study, it was found that more female tourists had the information about KTDC from friends and travel agents. On the basis of age, tourists falling below 40 years of age got information about KTDC from books and travel guides, but those with above 40 years of age had the information from 'friends and travel agents'. On the basis of income, more tourists with monthly income up to Rs. 1,60,000 came to know about KTDC from books and travel guides and those who had the monthly income of above Rs. 1,60,000 got the information from the source of 'friends and travel agents'.

Advertisement of KTDC: On an analysis of the opinions collected from the tourists covered under study, it was found that majority of both foreign and domestic tourists, irrespective of their nationality, sex, age, occupation and income, were not attracted by the advertisement of KTDC.

Stay at KTDC hotels: The different options for the opinions of the respondents on the stay at KTDC hotels given in the questionnaire were 'excellent', 'good', 'satisfactory', and 'poor'. More tourists, irrespective of nationality, sex, age, occupation and income, entertained 'good' opinion on their stay at KTDC hotels. Room rent is a major source of revenue to the tourism industry. Majority of the foreign tourists, irrespective of age, sex and occupation, were of opinion that the room rent charged at KTDC hotels was reasonable. Of the domestic tourists only 43.1 per cent had the same opinion. Foreign and domestic tourists entertained different views on the room rent charged at KTDC hotels. Almost all foreign and domestic tourists interviewed for the present study were of the view that there was proper up keeping of rooms at KTDC hotels (92.6 per cent). Data collected on the basis of age, sex, occupation and income conform to the same conclusion.

Conducted tours of KTDC: In Kerala, only KTDC operates the wide network of conducted and package tours. Nevertheless, only 20.9 per cent of the respondents took part in the conducted tours and majority of them (69.9 per cent) entertained 'excellent' opinion on the conducted tours. A cross tabulation of the views of the tourists on the basis of age, sex, occupation, income and nationality asserted the same conclusion. The tourists who did not participate in the conducted tours revealed that paucity of time and preference for other vehicles were the reasons for their not availing this facility. They were not aware of the better facilities offered in the conducted tours of KTDC. The views of the tourists on the conducted tours and on the advertisement of KTDC correlated that more effective publicity would be required for the activities of the KTDC in and outside the State.

Tourist reception centres of KTDC: KTDC runs four tourist reception centres at Trivandrum, Ernakulam, Kumily and Kozhikode and information counters at the hotel units and head office. It provides tourist information, undertakes reservation services and monitors conducted tours. Majority of the resident-tourists covered under the present study availed this service (64.1 per cent). It was also found that 63.8 per cent of the tourists, who availed this service, entertained 'good' opinion on the various services rendered by the tourist reception centres and information counters. The analysis made on the basis of age, sex, occupation and income also led to the same conclusion.

Hospitality of the staff of KTDC hotels: Among the tourists sought for the data 69.8 per cent respondents stated 'good' opinion on the hospitality of the staff at KTDC hotels. It could be rightly concluded that KTDC could all along win the appreciation of the tourists, irrespective of nationality, age, sex, occupation and income, on the hospitality of the staff of KTDC hotels. From the discussions held with a few staff at different units of KTDC, it was rightly observed that they had job satisfaction and could serve the customers with courteous behaviour and pleasing personality. Moreover, the relationship between employees and management was very cordial and the management implemented many welfare measures for the employees.

Quality of the food served at KTDC hotels: It was importantly found that 90.2 per cent of the respondents viewed the food items served at the KTDC hotels to be 'good'/'satisfactory'. Almost all the tourists covered under the study belonging to different sex, age, occupation and income had the same opinion in this regard. The opinion of the tourists pointedly showed that the price charged for the food items at KTDC hotels was quite reasonable. It was evidenced from the views of the 74.2 per cent of the tourists irrespective of age, sex, occupation and income. But the domestic tourists had a different view.

Role of KTDC in the promotion of tourism: The information gathered from the interview and discussions with both the foreign and domestic tourists led to the irresistible conclusion that KTDC has been discharging its functions with a view to promoting tourism as an industry and that it has a very significant and lead role in the development of tourism industry in the State. Almost all the respondents (97.2 per cent) sought for the interview held the same view.

The ancillary services of KTDC: The ancillary services include information, tourist guide, health club, reservation of rooms and air tickets, retail shops and transport. It was seen that majority of the tourists covered under the study (52.8 per cent) did not avail any of these services. Lack of time, information and necessity were the reasons for not availing these services by the tourists. Among the various services, more travelers availed information.

General observation: Almost all the tourists interviewed for the present study made a few observations from the experience they had in the State. The principal observations were the road traffic was over crowded and congested particularly in the urban areas, the sanitary facilities at the public places were inadequate, the law and order situation was not satisfactory to ensure the safety of the passengers and many of the urban roadways and areas and some places of tourist importance had not been kept clean and hygienic.

Recommendations

Based on the foregoing findings, the following recommendations are made to improve the present situation.

KTDC, being a government agency and a promising marketer of tourist-products, is expected to flourish and grow, provide wealth and welfare of the people and enhance standard of living. Tourists frequenting the KTDC hotels and availing the facilities and services offered, return with appreciation on the overall performance of the Corporation. Nevertheless more resident tourists did not avail the facilities like conducted tours and health club on account of the lack of information and other reasons. Proliferation of hitech advertisement and publicity carrying information about the wide network of the facilities and services provided by KTDC can no more be delayed to attract more new foreign and domestic tourists and to encourage the existing tourists to patronize the various services now made available.

Majority of the domestic tourists were not of the opinion that the room rent charged at KTDC hotels was reasonable. This is on account of the low level of income earned by them as compared to their counterparts in foreign countries. It is highly necessary that KTDC should plan and construct economy class structures too, to provide budget accommodation to suit the preference of the domestic tourists. Likewise more domestic tourists were of opinion that the food items at KTDC hotels were not charged reasonable. Considering the general economic backwardness of the Indian citizens, KTDC should think of granting concessions and discounts to the domestic tourists on the charges of food and room rent so as to attract more domestic travellers. Electricity has now become a key factor even for the existence of industry in Kerala. Lifts and air conditioners at the hotel units cannot always work due to the dearth of electricity supply. It is very imperative to install more powerful generators in the hotel units to suit the requirements of electricity for each unit.

Development programmes in terms of both quality and quantity are to be broad-based on the changing and growing needs and views of the consumers. It stands to reason for the KTDC to onset a research and development wing to streamline the development programmes on the basis of surveys revealing the changes in the tourism markets and reflecting the growing needs, tastes and fashions of both the foreign and domestic tourists. Since KTDC has a lead role in the promotion of tourism industry in Kerala, it should spearhead such research work and disseminate information to other undertakings in the tourism sector of the State.

Tourism is a highly sophisticated business involving consumers of different nationalities and of heterogeneous nature. Now, tourism industry lacks professionalism at different levels of staffing and needs a guaranteed supply of high-quality and well-trained manpower to keep abreast of the growing demands. The lack of an effective human resource development strategy may be the Achilles' heel of the tourism sector worldwide. KTDC is expected to prioritize tourism education and training to its employees throughout their career. The management of KTDC can either conduct their own programmes of human resource development or seek the services of professional institutes like KITTS for equipping the employees to rise to the level of growing professionalism.

KTDC has started earning huge profits since 1994. The ratios of debt to equity, funded debt to total capitalisation and net worth to total assets of the past years invariably permit the inclusion of more debt for availing the benefit of trading on equity. The financial management of KTDC can very well think of employing the borrowed capital so as to reap the gain of trading on equity. An analysis of current ratio, quick ratio and cash ratio revealed that KTDC had no proper management of working capital. The position of working capital has been improved since 1994. Nevertheless the management of working capital requires revamping so as to make a proper trade between liquidity and profitability. It is suggested that each component of current assets is to be thoroughly analysed in such a way as to study its impact on the day to day working of the Corporation. The present study reveals that the management of cash and other current assets badly requires more attention.

It is quite inevitable on the part of KTDC as a Government owned agency to arrange sightseeing programmes through conducted tours with a view to providing opportunity to the tourists to enjoy and appreciate the beauty and unique attractions of the God's Own Country. It was noted that the present arrangements made by the Corporation have not been fully utilised by the tourists, especially foreign tourists. While holding personal interview with the tourists covered under the present study, it was observed that majority of them were not aware of this facility. This state of affairs calls for urgent and necessary steps from the Corporation. It is suggested that the KTDC could give wide publicity in this respect outside India so that foreign tourists could think in advance for availing this facility at large. Similar publicity is also required in the case of other ancillary services like health club, tourist guide, and transportation and reservation facilities.

The general observations made from the discussions held with the tourists covered under study called for the urgent attention of the State Government. The police-machinery should be geared up to ensure the safe and free movement of tourists throughout the State. It is also suggested that more infrastructure developments may be well planned to smoothen the road traffic in the urban and semi-urban areas. Government would also initiate regular and routine measures to ensure a more clean and hygienic city and tourist centres with proper sanitation to win the appreciation of the tourists. It stands to reason that the Government would be always alert in identifying the negative effects of tourism. It is also suggested that adequate legislations would be made to give more teeth to the law for checking the evils of tourism.

Tourism industry has been a blossoming flower enriched with profound fragrance of socio-economic benefits, which would substantially elevate the stature of the State. The dawn of the twenty-first century would witness the tremendous growth of tourism industry surpassing all other industries in the world. WTO's forecast was announced at a news conference during the International Tourism Bourse in Berlin on March 9 1997, which stated that the growth of tourism industry would be unstoppable in the twenty-first century roaring to 1.6 billion international arrivals annually by the year 2020. Imagination staggers! It is expected, in this context that the Government of India and Kerala would rightly pave the way to gain a reasonable market share of the world total in respect of international arrivals and receipts.

References

Agarwal, Govind,R., *Tourism Management in Nepal*, Prashasan, Vol.33, March 1982.

Ahuja S.P. and Sharma S.R., *Tourism in India - A perspective to 1990*, The Institute of Economic and Market Research, New Delhi, 1990.

Anil, Chakraborthy, *Conducted Tour - A Lucrative Business*, Capital - Vol. 185 September 1980.

Arrora K.K., Tourist *Industry in Kumaon* (Ph.D. Thesis) Agra University, Agra, 1971.

Bhardwaj, Brij, Tourism *and Infrastructure*.

Boarduran R.D., Hotels *and Catering Costing and Budget*, William Heineman Ltd, London, 1978.

Britton, Stephen,G., *The political Economy of Tourism in the Third World*, Annals of Tourism Research, Vol. 9.1, Pergamon, U.S.A 1982.

Cooper C.P, Progress *in Tourism Recreation and Hospitality Management*, Belhaven Press, New York, 1989.

De Kadt, Emanuel, *Tourism -Passport to Development*, Oxford University Press, New York, 1979.

Editorial - Capital, Tourism Special Volume - 8th September 1982.

Garg R.B.I, What *Ails Indian Tourism,* Eastern Economist, Vol.77, July - September 1981.

Gopal, Ajith.S., *Indian Airlines and Tourism, Eastern Economist*, Vol 73, December 1979.

Gunn Glare A., *Tourism Planning*, Taylor and Francis, U.S.A., 1989.

Kaiser, Charles and Helber, Larry E; *Tourism Planning and Development*; CBI Publishing Company, Boston, 1978.

Kaul, R.N., Dynamics *of Tourism, Vol. - I, The Phenomenon, Vol. II - Accommodation, Vol.111 - Transportation and Marketing*; Sterling Publishers, Delhi 1985.

Kumar,H.L., *Personnel Management in Hotel and Catering Industry*, Metropolitan Book Company, New Delhi, 1986.

Lawson, Fred and Band Bovy, Manual: Tourism *and Recreational Development - A Handbook of Physical Planning*, CBI Publishing Company, Boston, 1977.

Laxman Ram; No *Longer a Bargain Destination*, Capital, Vol. 85; 29th September, 1980.

Metcalf, Hilary., *Employment Structure in Tourism and Leisure*, University of Sussex, Brighton, 1987.

Mill, Robert Charisty and Alasataire M., Morrison, *The Tourism System*, Prentice Hall International, USA, 1984.

Mishra, R.C., Prospects *of Tourism in Orissa*, Yojana - Vol. 36, No.5. New Delhi, March 1992.

Misra.S.K., *The Chief Executive Speaker; Public Sector in Tourism - A Survey*, State Enterprises, October- December, 1982.

Murphy, Peter, E., *Tourism - A Community Approach*, Methuen, New York, 1985.

Negi Jagmohan, *Tourism Development and Resource Conservation*, Metroplitan Book Company Pvt. Ltd., Delhi, 1990.

Negi, Jagmohan, Hotels *for Tourism Development*, Metropolitan Book Company, Delhi. 1984.

Negi.J.M.S., *Tourism and Hoteliering*, Githanjali Publishers, New Delhi, 1982.

Noroncha, Raymond, World Bank Staff Working Paper, 1979.

Paul, Babu.D. and Sharma, Alkesh; *Kerala: An Ideal Tourist Destination*.

Quarterly Economic Report of Indian Institute of Public Opinion - October 1982.

Rai Laji Pathi H., *Development of Tourism in India* - Printwell, Jaipur, 1993.

Rajan, Soundara.A., *Commercial Viability of the Tourist Infrastructure of the Tamil Nadu Tourism Development Corporation* - Doctoral thesis. University of Kerala, 1993.

Rehman S.S.H.; *Strategy for Boosting Tourism*, Yojana, New Delhi, Vol.40. No. 8, August 1996.

Sarojit Dutta, *Eastern Region, yet to make up to its Potentials*, Capital, Vol.185, September, 1980.

Selvam M., Tourism *Industry in India. A Study of its Growth and Development Needs*, Himalaya Publishing House, Bombay, 1989.

Seth Rabindra; *Tourism in India: An Overview*.

Seth, Pran Nath, Successful *Tourism Management*, Sterling Publishers, New Delhi, 1985.

Singh Ratandeep, Dynamics *of Modern Tourism*, Kanishka Publishers, Distributors, New Delhi 1996.

Singh Ratandeep, Infrastructure *of Tourism in India*, Kanishka Publishers, Distributors, New Delhi, 1996.

Singh, Ratandeep, *Tourist India, Hospitality Services*, Kanishka Publishers, Distributors, New Delhi, 1996.

Sudheer.S.V - *Tourism in Kerala - Problems and Prospects,* Ph.D. thesis, University of Kerala, 1992.

Tourism Policy - Kerala, State Department of Tourism, Trivandrum, 1995.

Ummat R.C., Forecasting *Tourism - Way Dither*, Capital, Vol. 73; October - December 1979.

UNCTAD, *Elements of Tourism Policy in Developing Centuries*, Report of the Secretariat, UN, 1973.

William,W. Smart; Charles, E. Gearing and Turget; Var, Determining *the Capital Investment Policy for Tourism Sector of a Developing Country*, Management Science - Vol 20(4), December 1973.

Wilson P., *ITDC's Performance*, Capital, .Vol.185, September, 1980.

WTO, Manual on Evaluating Tourism Projects, General Programme of Work for 1978-79, Madrid, 1980.

6

Cashew Industry in the Public Sector

M. N. Dayanandan

Cashew processing has been an export-oriented traditional industry in India. It is of great significance to the national economy on account of the fact that it earns more than Rs. 300 crore annually by way of foreign exchange. The year 1990-91 witnessed an all-time record in terms of export value of cashew products (Rs. 446.52 crore) with a net foreign exchange earning of Rs. 411.51 crore. The state of Kerala enjoyed monopoly of cashew industry and trade till the mid 1960s. Of the total 273 processing factories in India in 1966, 211 were located in Kerala. Despite the loss of monopoly in the subsequent years, the State still had 252 factories, which accounted for about 50 per cent of the total processing factories in the country as on March 31 1991. The credit for about 80 per cent of the export of cashew production in India goes to Kerala. The processing industry is significant also to the economy of the State in as much as it provides employment to more than one lakh workers, mostly women.

The cashew industry in the private sector was unregulated till the year 1952. There was no uniformity in the system of work or wage payment. Consequent on prolonged strikes and other trade union activities by workers, minimum wages were introduced in the industry in 1953, and were subsequently revised in 1960. To evade payment of minimum wages and other statutory benefits to workers, the factory owners resorted to all possible methods, including closing down of factories and shifting the processing to cottages. Following the continued strike by workers, the Government of Kerala abolished the cottage processing system and revised the minimum wages in 1967.

Statement of the Problem

Most of the cashew processors in Kerala closed down their factories and shifted processing to the Kanyakumari District of Tamil Nadu, the neighbouring State, where wage rates were comparatively lower. The large scale shifting of processing to Tamil Nadu culminated in acute shortage of raw nuts in Kerala, and rendered about one lakh workers in the State jobless. At this juncture, the Government of Kerala intervened to protect the interests of workers by starting its own public sector company, viz. The Kerala State Cashew Development Corporation Ltd. (KSCDC) in 1969. The birth of the Corporation was meant to put the industry on a sound kneel and to create stability, to provide a model employer, and above all as a socio-economic measure. The Corporation started functioning in 1970 with one factory and 1,000 workers. It tookover more and more closed factories, and, by 1975, the number of factories under its control rose to 34 with 36000 workers on the rolls. Another initiative aimed at rescuing the industry was the formation of the Kerala State Cashew Workers Apex Industrial Co-operative Society Ltd. (CAPEX) in 1984. The objectives of the Society are to organise the cashew industry on a commercial basis and to provide assistance to the affiliated societies for procuring and processing raw nuts and marketing cashew products.

The Industry continued to face shortage of rawnuts. To prevent the diversion of nuts to outside the state, the Government of Kerala introduced monopoly procurement of indigenously produced rawnuts in 1977. The scheme was abandoned in 1983, but re-introduced in 1988. The re-introduction of the scheme in 1988 landed the Industry in another crisis. Most of the private processors refused to open their factories and lift the nuts procured by the government agency, as a measure of protest against the monopoly procurement scheme. In this predicament, the Corporation was obliged to play a more responsible role. The Government of Kerala tookover 36 closed factories and entrusted them for operation to the Corporation. With this the number of units under the control of the Corporation increased to 70. While the take-over was hailed by workers and trade unions, the wisdom of entrusting the units to the Corporation was questioned by many, on the ground that it has not succeeded in fulfilling its mission. However, the take-over of the 36 closed factories by the government changed the structure of the industry in the state.

The cashew industry in Kerala consists of - the public sector institution namely the K.S.C.D.C. with 70 cashew processing factories, three tin factories and one tannin factory; the co-operative sector institution namely the CAPEX with nine affiliated co-operative societies; and the private sector with 173 processing units.

Review of Literature

Inspite of its importance, the different aspects of the cashew processing industry have seldom been subjected to scientific enquiry in a substantial manner. Very few studies have been made, and published literature is almost non-existent except for some government reports. A brief review of the available literature is attempted below.

The study by John Thomas Chirayat highlighted the salient features of the cashew industry, its relevance to foreign trade, and the growth of trade unionism in the industry. It also threw light on the method of processing, employment, productivity and welfare activity in the industry in the early 1960s. A study conducted by the State Planning Board discussed the problems faced by the industry in the 1960s. The Reserve Bank of India Study Group on Financing of Cashew Industry reviewed the practices and procedures followed by commercial banks in regard to monetary advances to the industry, made some recommendations regarding the procedures and method to be followed and the credit limits and financial discipline to be enforced by commercial banks. They found that the capital base of the industry was low to augment the capital base. Emam Beevi reviewed the evolution of minimum wages and examined the effect of state legislation on wages and working condition in the cashew industry in Kerala. She found that the average daily earnings of workers increased as a result of the fixation of minimum wages, but the annual average earnings decreased owing to the diversion of processing activity to Tamil Nadu as well as to the resultant reduction in the employment days in Kerala.

The proceedings of the National Seminar on Cashew industry, which covered 19 papers, gave a detailed discussion of the problems and developments in the industry. There was general agreement among the participants that the basic problem of the cashew industry was chronic shortage of raw nuts. The seminar discussed the need to increase production of raw nuts, to use improved processing machinery, to keep down the cost of production, and to establish ancillary industries to ensure the commercial use of the by-products of cashew. The seminar noted the low equity base of the industry and suggested that the industry be reorganized in the form of limited companies so that the profits could be ploughed back to strengthen the equity base. Regarding exports, the seminar noted the wide fluctuations in the price of kernels, and suggested that India, Brazil and Mozambique, the three major producing countries, should make a joint effort to bring about some measure of stability in the prices. Kannan analysed the major issues involved in the cultivation, distribution, processing and marketing of cashew, and examined the prospects of development of cashew industry in India. A major finding of the study was that the government policy of promoting exports was without adequate appreciation of its linkages with the processing sector and the cultivation of crop in the agricultural sector. The study also found that despite the high level of profitability in the Industry, the level of wages had been very low. The workers also had experienced an erosion of quantum of employment owing to the diversion of processing activity to Tamil Nadu.

A committee formed to suggest strategies for the development of industries found that organised labour and minimum wage legislations had not succeeded in ensuring to the workers a reasonable wage or continuity of employment. The committee observed that the social purpose of setting up the K.S.C.D.C. had not been achieved in a substantial manner, as it provided employment only to 32,000 workers for 100 days a year and that at a high cost. The committee came to the conclusion that the maladies of the industry stemmed from the reluctance of the government and the unions to face the fact that there were practically no advantages in organising the industry on a factory scale since the cashew processing industry did not involve high technology. The committee suggested that organising the industry in the household sector was more logical and advantageous to both manufacturers and workers. Dharmarajan made a study of the cost structure of the industry in Kerala. Karnataka and Tamil Nadu. Balan Pillai examined the extent to which collective bargaining in cashew industry in Kerala could be held responsible for its decline. It was found in this study that both market forces and industrial relations forces were relevant in explaining the decline of the Industry, but the role of the latter as evidenced by collective bargaining was only a minor one. Studies by Krishnaswamy, Thomas Mathew, Rema, and Balasubramanian dealt with the marketing and pricing trends of both rawnuts and kernels.

Eventhough, the organising of the industry in the public sector was a landmark in the history of the industry; no scientific study has so far been made on the working of the Corporation or its impact on the socio-economic development of cashew workers. It is against this background, that the present study is undertaken to evaluate the working of the Cashew Development Corporation.

Objectives

The objectives of the present study are:

- To determine the extent to which the Corporation has succeeded in procuring adequate quantity of rawnuts at reasonable costs to ensure the round the year working of its factories.

- To assess the relative efficiency of the Corporation in the processing of rawnuts and marketing of final products.
- To evaluate the relative efficiency of the Corporation in the management of funds.
- To compare and contrast the socio-economic condition of cashew workers in the Corporation with that of their counterparts in the private sector.
- To suggest measures for improvement, wherever possible, based on the findings of the study.

There were 220 processing units in the state as on 31st March 1988. Of these, 34 were owned by the Corporation, nine by the co-operative sector institution CAPEX, and 177 by private processors. Data relating to the performance of the Corporation were collected from the head office and the 34 units of the Corporation. To facilitate comparison, data were also collected from 34 working units in the private sector, selected at random from among the 177 units. Care has been taken to include both small and large-sized units, so as to render the sample representative. The sample private sector units constituted 19 per cent of the total units in that sector, and the total units under study accounted for about 31 per cent of the units in the industry. The co-operative sector units were excluded from the study, as their impact on the industry was found to be negligible. Ten workers each from all the 68 processing units covered under the study were selected as sample to ascertain the socio-economic condition of the workers. Since size difference among the units is not important, equal numbers of workers were selected from all the units. The sample selection was made in such a way that the proportion of each category of workers was approximate to its respective weight in the industry. Accordingly, data were collected from five peelers, four shellers, one roaster/borma worker, one grader and one 'other category worker', subject to a maximum of ten workers from each unit.

Both primary and secondary data were collected for the study. Primary data relating to the working of the processing units in the public and private sectors were collected by using a questionnaire developed for the purpose. The officials of the Corporation and the owners of the private sector units were generally co-operative. However, owners of three private sector units selected in the sample refused to give the required data and consequently substitutes for these three units had to be taken. Primary data relating to the socio-economic condition of workers were collected by using a pre-tested interview schedule. Data were collected by visiting the residential house of the workers. The visits were extremely useful in making personal observation and assessment of their living condition. The responses of the workers were, by and large, encouraging. However, a few workers in the private sector were reluctant to say anything about their daily earnings and the working condition in the factories. They responded freely only after being convinced that they would not be personally identified. In addition to collecting the responses of workers, discussions were also held with the officials of the Corporation and government departments and the leaders of various trade unions. Secondary data collected from the Corporation, government departments, government publications, journals, periodicals and reports were used for the study.

The study covers a nine-year period from 1979-80 to 1987-88. It was originally planned to collect data for a ten year period starting from 1978-79. However, when the pilot study was made, it was known that 1978-79 was an abnormal year, when many units did not operate. Therefore, that year was dropped and the study was limited to the nine years succeeding. Data on the socio-economic condition of workers pertain to the financial year 1989-90. To compare the financial data of the Corporation and the private sector units, averages, ratios and percentages have been used throughout the thesis. Scoring technique is employed to rank the responses of the Corporation officials, the private processors and the cashew workers. Index numbers are used to examine the trend of assets and liabilities. Karl Pearson's simple and partial correlation techniques are employed to measure the relationship between variables. To test the significance of the co-efficient of correlation, 't' test has been applied. Chi-square test has been used to test the significance of the difference in the responses of workers in the two sectors.

The term 'public sector units' and 'public sector workers' are used in the sense of 'units of the Corporation' and 'workers in the Corporation' respectively, for purposes of analysis and discussion throughout the study. It is hoped that the findings of the present study would be useful to planners and policy makers in formulating future programmes for smoothening the working of the cashew industry. In a situation where the country has been facing serious problems related to adverse balance of payment position, it is felt that there is utmost need for strengthening this industry as an earner of foreign exchange.

The accounting year of some of the private sector units covered under the study did not correspond exactly to that of the Corporation. However, care has been taken to ensure that the data collected relate to the same processing season so as to render the comparison logical and relevant. Data related to the socio-economic condition, supplied by the workers, were in many cases furnished from the respondents' memories. Since no other systematic records were available to countercheck the accuracy, the data supplied by the respondents had to be solely depended upon for the purpose of analysis. However, in almost all cases, on-the-spot observation was helpful to make the data more accurate.

Findings

The major findings of the study are summarised below:

Procurement. processing and marketing: The K.S.C.D.C. was not able to procure adequate quantity of rawnuts for the continuous working of its factories. The quantity of nuts procured varied between 18 and 44 per cent of the total requirements. The share of the Corporation in the nuts procured during the period of monopoly procurement varied from 24 to 38 per cent. The major problems of monopoly procurement, according to the private processors, were uncertainty in the supply of nuts, loss of business secrecy and bargaining power, and unsatisfactory quality of nuts. For the officials of the Corporation, the major problems related to unsatisfactory quality of nuts, higher handling charges and loss of business secrecy and bargaining power. The officials of the Corporation and the small processors in the private sector favoured the monopoly procurement scheme, while the large private processors wanted the scheme to be discontinued. The study revealed that monopoly procurement had a favourable effect on the working of the Corporation even though the Corporation was less efficient in the procurement of rawnuts than the private sector units. The share of the Corporation in the rawnuts procured during the period of free trade varied between five per cent and 25.03 per cent of the total requirements. The major problems of free trade, according to the private processors, were profit making by middlemen, competition by processors and diversion of nuts to other states. According to the officials of the Corporation, the major problems were competition among the processors, diversion of nuts to other states, and higher prices of rawnuts. The share of the Corporation in the nuts procured during the period of free trade was only about 50 per cent of its share during the period of monopoly procurement.

The share of the Corporation in the imported nuts during the period of partial decanalisation varied from 9.13 to 56.94 per cent. Poor import due to inefficiency of the Cashew Corporation of India and uncertainty in the supply of nuts, were the major problems of canalization policy. While the officials of the Corporation and small private processors favoured canalisation of imports, large private processors stood against it. The share of the Corporation in the nuts imported during the period of the O.G.L. system varied between 25 and 51 per cent. Competition by importers, higher prices, and cumbersome import procedures were the major problems of the O.G.L. system according to the private processors. At the same time the major problems, as reported by the officials of the Corporation were competition by importers, absence of quality guarantee and higher prices. The major problems involved in the import of rawnuts. Were competition from other countries, development of processing centres in rawnut exporting countries, and restrictions by government of rawnut exporting countries. The analysis of data also revealed that significant correlation did not exist between kernel price and the quantity of nuts procured by the Corporation.

Rawnut cost showed an increasing trend in both the private and public sectors. The cost per bag of rawnut cost per bag was lower during the period of monopoly procurement and higher during the period of free trade in the Corporation, when compared to that of the private sector units. Positive correlation existed between rawnut cost and production cost in both the sectors. The rawnut cost as percentage of sales revenue was higher for the Corporation in most of the years when compared to that of the private sector units. The co-efficient of correlation between rawnut cost and sales revenue of the Corporation was significantly lower than that of the private sector units. This shows that the sales revenue was not commensurate with the rawnut cost in the Corporation.

The processing cost per bag of the Corporation was 50 to 100 per cent higher than that of the private sector units. Processing cost as percentage of production cost and as percentage of sales was higher for the Corporation. Labour cost per bag was 50 to 100 per cent higher for the Corporation than that of the private sector units. Labour cost as percentage of production cost varied from 11 to 21 in the Corporation as against 7 to 13 in the private sector units. Labour cost and production cost were positively correlated in both the sectors. Factory overheads constituted less than 1.5 per cent of production cost in the private sector units, while they varied from three to nine per cent in the Corporation. No correlation was noticed between factory overheads and production cost in both the sectors. Packing cost was on an average 3.53 per cent of the production cost in the Corporation and 3.21 per cent in the private sector units. Packing cost and production cost were positively correlated in the private sector units. However, no such correlation was found to exist in the Corporation. The average number of days of employment in the Corporation was 75.78 as against 125 in the private sector units. The correlation between the number of days of employment and processing cost was not statistically significant in both the sectors. Higher processing cost of the Corporation is attributed to the disproportionate engagement of shellers and peelers, idle capacity and delays in processing, decline in the yield per bag and the percentage of holes in the total yield, improper packing and consequent rejection and reprocessing. Fluctuations in the price of Kernel, and competition from other countries, were the major problems of export, according to the officials of the Corporation and the private processors.

More than 90 per cent of the revenue of the Corporation was from the sale of cashew kernels. The sales revenue also showed an increasing trend in both the public and private sector units. But the sales revenue per bag for the Corporation was lower than that of the private sector units in most of the years under study. Both the marketing cost per bag and marketing cost as percentage of sales revenue were marginally lower in the Corporation than in the private sector units. The co-efficient of correlation between marketing cost and sales revenue was insignificant in both the sectors, which meant that the variations in marketing cost were not commensurate with the variations in sales revenue.

Management of Funds

The average amount of funds per factory was lower in the Corporation compared to the private sector units. The short-term fund was far in excess of the long-term fund in both the sectors. While the short-term fund was 111.97 per cent of the total funds in the Corporation, it was 70 per cent in the private sector units. The short-term fund of more than 100 per cent in the Corporation indicates that its accumulated loss had exceeded the capital invested. The average fund per bag was lower in the units of the Corporation in most of the years under review. However, short-term fund per bag was higher in the Corporation.

The owned fund of the Corporation was negative throughout the period under study as the accumulated loss exceeded the share capital. The imbalance in the capital structure of the Corporation was the result of heavy loss incurred in 1978-79 and the consequent borrowings and interest burdens. Government loan, trade credit and other current liabilities, and bank borrowings were the major sources of funds of the Corporation. In the private sector units the major sources were bank borrowings and trade credits and other current liabilities. The debt component in the financial structure of the Corporation was higher than that of the private sector units, as evident from the analysis of the debt-equity ratios. The interest charge in the Corporation was, on an average. Rs. 85.01 per bag in the private sector units, the interest charges constituted, on an average, Rs. 27.49 per bag only about one-third of that in the Corporation. While the interest coverage ratio of the Corporation was negative in most of the years under study, the private sector units had a comfortable coverage ratio varying from 1.21 to 3.1 times.

The values of fixed assets per factory and fixed assets per bag were lower in the Corporation compared to the private sector units. Building, land, plant and machinery were the important items of fixed assets in both the sectors. The growth of fixed assets was positive in the Corporation but negative in the private sector units. The average value of current assets was also lower in the Corporation in most of the years under study. The most important components of current assets were inventory, and loans and advances in both the sectors. The average annual growth rate of current assets was higher in the Corporation than in the private sector units. The lower current assets per bag and the lower current asset to fixed asset ratio of the Corporation (especially after 1983-84) indicate that the Corporation was following an aggressive current assets policy compared to the private sector units.

The current asset to fixed asset ratio of more than 15 in the cashew processing industry reveals the low capital intensity and the dominance of the trading aspect of the industry. The operating assets-turnover ratio was on an average 3.48 times in the Corporation as against 2.23 times in the private sector units. The turnover ratios of fixed and current assets were higher in the Corporation compared to those in the private sector units. The analysis of fixed assets to long-term fund ratio showed that the Corporation followed an aggressive financing plan while the private sector units followed a conservative financing plan. Neither the Corporation nor the private sector units was following a uniform policy in the financing of fixed assets, as evident from the insignificant correlation between fixed assets and long-term fund.

The net working capital per factory and net working capital per bag in the Corporation were positive in four years and negative in five years. The private sector units had positive net working capital varying from Rs. 59.02 to Rs. 197.28 per bag. The growth of net working capital was negative in the Corporation and positive in the private sector units. The analysis of the current ratios and quick ratios reveals that the liquidity position of the private sector units was satisfactory, while that of the Corporation was poor. The inventory per bag in the units of the Corporation was, on an average, Rs. 296 as against an average inventory of Rs. 238 in the private sector units. The inventory-turnover ratio was higher in the Corporation in most of the years under review. The dependence of the Corporation on bank borrowings, to finance, its inventory holdings, was less in all the years, except during 1986-87 and 1987-88 compared to the private sector units. The Corporation had on an average, receivables of less than one per cent of sales, whereas the private sector units had receivables of about ten per cent. The Corporation's average collection period was three days as against 36 days in the private sector units. This indicates that the Corporation was very restrictive in extending credit. Loans and advances formed, on an average 11.07 per cent of the total current assets in the Corporation, as against 23.15 per cent in the private sector units. The loans and advances-turnover ratio of the Corporation was higher than that of the private sector units throughout the period under study.

The cash balance held by the Corporation was lower than that of the private sector units in most of the years under study. However, it had a higher average cash balance because of an abnormally high proportion of cash holdings during the years 1979-80 and 1980-81. Wide fluctuations in the cash-turnover ratios of the Corporation indicates that the Corporation faced liquidity problems and that it was less efficient in the management of cash, compared to the private sector units. The analysis of the working capital policy and the components of current assets lead to the conclusion that the Corporation did not succeed in managing the working capital in an efficient manner.

Profitability

The gross profit per bag of the Corporation varied widely over the years and showed a negative trend in four years. At the same time the gross profit margin of the Corporation was either negative or low in most of the years, while the private sector units could keep a steady margin of 11 to 13.5 per cent during the period under study. The negative/low gross profit margin of the Corporation was the result of lower sales revenue and higher production cost. The principal determinants of gross profit in the Corporation were sales, rawnut cost, labour cost and manufacturing expenses. In the private sector, sales, rawnut cost and labour cost alone were the principal determinants.

The operating profit per bag and the operating profit margin of the Corporation were negative in most of the years covered under the study. The private sector units showed consistently positive gross profit margin varying from 2.62 to 7.08 per cent. From the result of the study it was noticed that an insignificant positive correlation was noticed between operating profit and administrative cost and between operating profit and selling cost. This indicates that these costs were not the principal determinants of operating profit in both the sectors. The net profit per bag and the net profit margin of the Corporation were negative in all the years except 1983-84. The net profit margin varied between 1.24 per cent and 4.79 per cent in the private sector units. Significant negative correlation was found to exist between profit before taxes and interest charges in the Corporation. This leads to the conclusion that interest charges were a major cause of negative net profit of the Corporation.

While the private sector units earned positive return on assets throughout the period under study, the Corporation showed it only in two years. Return on assets and investment in assets were not significantly correlated in the Corporation. However, significant negative correlation was found to exist between return on assets and fixed assets in the private sector units. The variation between the two sectors in the return on assets was mainly because of the variation in the profit margin. The variation would have been wider, but for the efficient utilisation of assets in the Corporation. The Corporation could earn a positive return on capital employed only in four years, while the private sector units earned positive return throughout the period under study. The relationship between profit before interest and taxes and capital employed, was not significant in both the sectors.

Socio-economic Condition of Cashew Workers

About 93 per cent of the cashew workers covered under the study were women. The leading age group of workers was 31-40 years. Among the married workers 27 per cent in the private sector married workers and 35.1 per cent in the Corporation had more than three children. The average family of workers in both the sectors consisted of five members. About 37.9 per cent of the allies of workers in the private sector and 42.6 per cent in the Corporation had their size higher than the average. The average number of earning members per family was two in both the sectors. The analysis of annual family income revealed that about 76 per cent of the workers in the private sector and 69 per cent in the Corporation had an annual family income of less than Rs. 9,000. The leading income group was Rs. 6,000-9,000. More than 80 per cent of the workers in both the sectors were socially and economically backward castes. About 64.7 per cent of the private sector workers and 75.3 per cent of the workers in the Corporation were illiterate or only primary-educated. A majority of the illiterate workers were found engaged in unclean operations.

About 75 per cent of the workers in the Corporation and 50 per cent of the workers in the private sector received less than 100 days of employment. Significant difference was noticed between the public and private sector workers with regard to the number of days of employment received by them. The number of average days of employment was 93.82 in the Corporation and 110.25 in the private sector. The difference in the number of days of employment between the two sectors was found significant at 5 per cent level. The average daily earning of workers was higher in the Corporation. The difference between the two sectors in this respect was significant at 5 per cent level. The average annual earning from cashew industry was higher for the private sector workers on account of their larger number of employment days.

Cashew processing was the main source of income of roasters and other category workers. For shellers, peelers and graders in both the sectors, other wages and salaries formed the main source of income. The share of cashew processing in total income of workers was the highest in the lower income groups. Average family expenditure was higher for the workers in the Corporation. The difference in the average expenditure between the workers in the two sectors was significant at 5 per cent level. The pattern of expenditure was similar for the workers in both the sectors, food constituting the largest single item of expenditure. The private sector workers had, on an average, excess of income over expenditure while the workers in the Corporation had an income deficit. However, significant difference was not seen in the deficit/surplus of the workers between the two sectors. About 40 per cent of the workers in the two sectors had a surplus income. The remaining workers had either deficit income or expenditure equal to income. Significant difference was not seen in the distribution of workers with surplus/deficit income between the two sectors.

About 50 per cent of the workers in both the sectors had land holdings of 1-10 cents. Very few workers had land holdings of more than 50 cents. About seven per cent of the workers in the two sectors were landless. No significant variation existed in the size of land owned by the workers of the two sectors. A vast majority of the workers in the two sectors lived in their own houses. Difference in the nature of houses between the public and private sector workers was found insignificant. Workers who lived in *pucca* and *katcha* houses were more in the Corporation. Those who lived in thatched houses were more in the private sector. The variation in the type of houses of workers in the public and private sectors was statistically significant.

The position of the workers in the Corporation was better than that of the private sector workers with regard to facilities available in the house, such as kitchen, bathroom, latrine, electricity and drinking water. Only very few workers in both the sectors could accumulate assets such as land, buildings and livestock. The average investment in land and buildings was higher in the case of the workers in the Corporation. The difference in the average value of assets accumulated by the public and private sector workers was found statistically insignificant except in the case of buildings. A majority of the workers in both the sectors had debts. No significant difference was noted in the average value of debt between the workers of the two sectors. Friends and relatives, nationalised banks and money lenders were the major sources of debt for workers in both the sectors.

A vast majority of workers in both the sectors were members of trade unions. Among the trade unions, C.I.T.U. had the largest membership followed by I.N.T.U.C., A.I.T.U.C. and U.T.U.C. in both the sectors. But only a small percentage of trade union members regularly participated in the trade union meetings and study classes. The level of participation in the union activities was higher in the case of the workers in the Corporation. About 70 per cent of the workers in the private sector and 87 per cent in the Corporation claimed that they received benefits from trade unions. General help settlement of disputes, higher wage rates and job security were the benefits received by the workers in both the sectors. More than 90 per cent of the workers in both the sectors were either members or sympathisers of any political party. Of the political parties C.P.I. (M) had the highest influence on the workers in both the sectors. The influence of C.P.I. (M) was the highest in the lower income group of the public sector workers. The Indian National Congress had the highest influence on the private sector workers. Workers with different political ideologies were found in all the trade unions. A higher percentage of Congress sympathisers was found in C.I.T.U. and A.I.T.U.C. than the percentage of C.P.I.(M) or C.P.I. sympathisers in A.I.T.U.C. The inconsistency in the political and trade union affiliations of workers was found to be less in the Corporation.

Cultural participation was also very low among cashew workers in both the sectors. Only five workers in the private sector and four workers in the Corporation' were members of cultural organisations like library, arts and sports club or women's association. Workers with no specific educational aspiration for their children were relatively less in the Corporation. With regard to higher education also, the workers in the Corporation had shown more interest. The difference in responses between the public and private sector workers was significant at 5 per cent level. Workers with no aspirations regarding the occupation of their children were found to be more in the private sector. The majority of workers in both the sectors preferred government jobs for their children. The percentage of workers with such aspirations was slightly higher in the Corporation. Only a few workers in both the sectors were interested in putting their children in the cashew processing work. The difference in responses between the public and private sector workers was statistically significant.

The majority of workers in both the sectors had either no comment to offer or liked to give a subordinate status to women. The number of workers who favoured equal status to women was higher in the Corporation. The responses of the workers in the Corporation regarding the status of women in the society were significantly different from those of the private sector workers. The attitude of the workers in the Corporation towards the dowry system was more progressive and the difference in responses between the workers of the two sectors was statistically significant. The majority of workers in both the sectors were in good health. However, a higher percentage of workers with good health were found in the private sector. The responses on the health condition of the public sector workers were significantly different from those of the private sector workers.

Suggestions

Based on the findings of the study enlisted above the following suggestions are made to improve the working of the Corporation.

Supply of rawnuts: Owing to the shortage of rawnuts, the Corporation could not work for more than 100 days a year. Therefore, every effort should be made to ensure adequate supply of nuts. The continuation of the monopoly procurement scheme could ensure reasonable quantities of indigenously produced rawnuts. To increase the supply in the long run, the Corporation should consider the possibility of starting its own cashew plantations inside and outside the state. To maximise the import of rawnuts it can make permanent arrangement with the major rawnut exporting countries

Rawnut cost: The rawnut cost of the Corporation showed an increasing trend. Since rawnut cost constitutes about 75 per cent of the total cost any small change in this cost component will have a great effect on the profitability of the Corporation. Therefore, measures will have to be taken to reduce the rawnut cost. The Comptroller and Auditor General (C.A.G.) had sported that the Corporation had no prescribed policy for the fixation of rawnut price and that there were instances of avoidable expenditure in connection with the procurement of rawnuts. Great care should be taken to fix the drying involved, and the kernel price in the international market.

Processing cost: Another area of concern is the increasing processing cost. Labour cost and factory expenses are the major components of processing cost. Workers should be made cost-conscious and processed. Measures like the supply of adequate quantity of nuts leading to increased number of days of work, engagement of shellers and peelers in the right proportion, effective supervision of different operations, and optimum utilisation of existing facilities, can go a long way in educing the processing cost per unit. One factor that leads to increasing labour cost is the decline in output per worker. Fixation of minimum stipulated output and linking of D.A. to output will to a remarkable extent, help to improve labour productivity and reduce labour cost per bag.

Sales revenue: The sales revenue of the Corporation is not commensurate with the rawnut cost. The Corporation has no definite policy; it seems, as to the fixation of export sales, price of kernels of various grades. The report of the C.A.G. is replete with instances of short realisation of revenue and extra expenditure incurred in connection with the sale of kernels. Kernel price movements in the international market should be closely followed and, care should be taken to fix the selling price on the most favourable terms.

Capital structure: A major cause of the poor financial performance of the Corporation is heavy borrowings and consequent interest burden. Since the accumulated loss has exceeded the share capital, the Corporation is depending totally on borrowings for its financing requirements. To do away with the ill effects of past losses, the capital structure of the Corporation should be reorganised and the accumulated loss will have to be written off. The entire government loan should be converted into equity capital. The government policy of granting loan to tide over a crisis, when the crisis itself is generated owing to the lack of sufficient equity base, is questionable. Conversion of government loan into equity capital will not only enlarge the capital base and reduce interest burden, but also pave the way for efficient management of the working capital of the Corporation. In the long run, the Corporation will be able to formulate its own financing policies without looking for the financial support of the government.

Professionalism in management: The Corporation had to work under eight different Managing Directors during the period 1980 to 1990. Frequent change of the chief executives often hampers the interest of the Corporation, which is engaged in the sensitive export business where speculation and forward trading are rampant. The Managing Directors were in most cases, deputed from the civil service. To ensure stability of management, professionally qualified persons, willing to work for a minimum period of five years, alone should be appointed as Managing Director. The findings of the study reveal the fact that there is lack of professionalism in all the functional areas of management. The functional managers should also be persons experienced in the professional line. The government should give autonomy to the Corporation to devise its own policies. Autonomy in the functioning, and development of professionalism in the management, will be conducive to improved overall performance on the part of the Corporation.

Welfare measures for workers: The survey of cashew workers showed no significant difference in the living conditions of workers in the Corporation and the private sector units. The existing welfare schemes, which provide for assistance to workers for the education and marriage of their children, are inadequate. Absence of a fruitful pension scheme is also worth mentioning. Proper welfare and social security schemes will have to be devised and implemented to improve the living conditions of workers. The workers are not at all satisfied with the way in which the E.S.I. Scheme is functioning at present. The government should take suitable measures to improve the functioning of the E.S.I. hospitals so as to satisfy the medical needs of workers.

References

Balasubramanlan. P.P., "Prospects of Utilisation of Cashew Apple in India", The *Cashew*, Cochin, Vol. I, No. 2, (April-June 1987).

Beevi, Emam A.J., *Impact of Minimum Wage Legislation on Cashew Industry*, M.Phil. Dissertation (unpublished). Trivandrum: Centre for Development Studies, 1978.

Chirayat. John Thomas, *A Study on the Cashew Industry in Kerala*, Industry Study Series. Report No. 1, Trivandrum: Labour and Industrial Bureau, 1965.

Dharmarajan. P.G., *A Study of the Cost Structure of the Cashew Industry in Kerala, Kamataka and Tamil Nadu*, Ph.D. Thesis (unpublished). School of Management Studies, University of Cochin, June 1984.

Government of Kerala, *Cashew Industry in Kerala* (mimeo), Trivandrum: State Planning Board, 1969.

Government of Kerala. *Report of the High Level Committee on Industry Trade and Power, Vol. II, Report on Large, Medium and Traditional Industries*, Trivandrum: State Planning Board, May 1984.

Indian Bank (ed.), National *Seminar on Cashew Industry*, Quilon, December 1981.

Kannan K.P., *Cashew Development in India: Potentialities and Constraints*, New Delhi: Agricole Publishing Academy, 1983.

Krishnaswamy, L., "Marketing and Pricing Policy of Cashew-nut", Cashew *Bulletin*, Cochin, Vol. XIII, No. 8 (August 1976).

Mathew, Thomas M., and Rema. M., "Cashew in India: Yesterday, Today and Tomorrow", *Indian Cashew Journal*, Cochin, Vol. XVI. No. 1, 1986.

Pillai, Balan K., *Economic Impact of Collective Bargaining on Cashew Industry in Kerala*, Ph.D. Thesis (unpublished), Trivandrum: Department of Economics, University of Kerala, 1986.

Reserve Bank of India, "*Report of the Study Group on Financing of Cashew Industry*" R.B.I. Bulletin. Bombay, May 1973.

Theme Title 2
Small and Traditional Industries

7

Export of Traditional Items: Promotional Measures

S. Jayakumari

The classical and neo-classical economists attached much importance to international trade in economic development. They considered it as a vital factor and Robertson, for example, calls foreign trade an "engine of growth" Marshall declared, "the causes which determines the economic progress of nations belong to the study of international trade". There is no doubt that foreign trade of a country in general is a reliable indicator of its level of economic activity. Knowledge of the volume of goods exchanged, the nature of goods entering the foreign trade transactions, and the countries with which exchange of goods take place, helps to get valuable information about the working of an economy.

Indian Scenario

Developing countries, in general, are predominantly overpopulated agricultural countries. They invariably import manufactured goods and export primary commodities, mainly agricultural based. The entire trade is concentrated in a few commodities and in a few countries. India is no exception to this. There are certain limitations in the export promotion of agricultural or agricultural based commodities. Most of the developing countries export these goods and therefore there is keen competition. More over, in order to reduce dependence on foreign supply of raw material the developed countries try to find out substitutes or alternative sources. Sometimes, nature itself may cause fluctuations in production. Sometimes international factors create problems. The result is uncertainty of export earnings. Export instability introduces an element of uncertainty and makes the planning difficult. The developmental efforts of India necessitated heavy import of capital goods and technology. With limited export earnings and greater pressure to import developmental goods, an adverse balance of trade becomes imperative. India however imported more than her exports and her balance of trade always remained unfavourable throughout the planning period. Consequently there has been a serious and constant strain on India's limited foreign exchange reserves. India has been taking loans from World Bank and its associates and also borrows sizable amount from abroad on a commercial basis. The country, had short-term as well as long term commitments. Foreign borrowings can sustain only short term temporary deficits, but continuous and ever increasing deficit cannot be met by external assistance.

Ultimately trade deficits began to build up steadily from 1979-80 onwards from Rs. 2,724 crore to Rs. 10,640 crore in 1990-91. There was also a sharp increase in government's budget deficit during this period. A lot of unfavourable domestic and international developments changed the situation worst in 1991-92 which resulted in a serious balance of payment problem for the country. In order to come out of the situation, the government, along with other short-run stabilisation measures, initiated a structural reform process. Liberalisation of external trade is an integral part of the reform process. This results in globalisation of industries and trade which calls for diversification of exports as well as the screening and regulation of them, and this implies a careful consideration of commodity composition and direction of trade. India has started diversification of her export structure during the 80's and has succeeded in it to a considerable extent. But even then the exports are not sufficient to meet the import requirements. Imports invariably exceed exports. So to increase exports, India has to make necessary changes or adjustments in her export industries. Under the globalised environment there will be severe competition in export front and this competitive pressure will lead to improvement in the quality of the export products and results in rapid growth in exports and it will serve as an inducement to foreign investment in the country. This will lead to more production and development. Thus, only export promotion through structural changes in export industries, changes in commodity composition and diversification of products and markets can accelerate the growth of economic development in India.

The impact of trade reforms is evident from the changing structure of India's foreign trade in terms of diversity of markets and products and also in the form of higher degree of trade openness, resulting from higher exports growth and associated increase in the capacity to import. Following the various policy initiatives taken by the Government, there was a perceptible improvement in India's export performance in the initial phase of the reform period. The benefits of trade liberalisation undertaken during 1990s are evident from the higher average growth rate of exports during 1990s at 9.3 per cent per annum which was higher than the 7.9 per cent growth recorded during 1980s. Exports grew from $18 billion in 1990-91 to $43.7 billion in 2001-02. India's export growth performance of 9.3 per cent during the 1990s was substantially higher than global export growth of 5.5 per cent. But the faster growth however made little difference to India's relative position in world trade during the decade. India's share in world trade grew from a negligible 0.5 per cent in 1994 to 0.7 per cent in 2001.

India's trade GDP ratio showed substantial improvements during 1990s as compared with the 1980s. On an average basis the export GDP ratio increased from 4.6 per cent in 1980s to 8 per cent in the 1990's and further increased to 9.4 per cent in 2001-02. The import GDP ratio increased from 7.2 per cent in 1980s to 9.5 per cent in 1990s and further increased to 10.8 per cent in 2001-02. Similarly the export import ratio increased substantially from 64 per cent during 1980 to 84 per cent in 1990 and to 85.2 per cent during 2001-02, reflecting the increased alignment between India's export and import performance. All these developments put together contributed to a distinct change in the structure of India's trade, after the reform process.

Diversification of exports constitutes an important element of India's export promotion strategy. Reflecting the policy trust as also evolving pattern of industrial development, India has gradually transformed from a predominantly primary products exporting country into an exporter of manufactured goods. Aided by various export promotion measures, the share of manufactured goods in India's total exports increased from 70.7 per cent during 1987-90 to 75.3 per cent during 1992-97 and further to 77.4 per cent during 1997-2002. The commodity composition with in the major groups has also undergone a considerable transformation. Exports of engineering goods and processed agricultural products showed marked improvement in the post reform years, where as the shares of traditional export items such as tea, coffee, cereals etc declined. China was among the fastest growing market for India's exports during the period of study. The growth is from $ 48.7 million of Indian exports in 1991-92 to $925.7 million during 2001-02 implying a growth of 34.2 per cent per annum. Other countries that recorded growth of more than 30 per cent per annum were very small; they are Ethiopia, Vietnam and Myanmar. USA, U.K and Japan were the largest markets during the period of study.

Export Trade of Traditional Items from Kerala

Kerala which lies at the southern most part of peninsular India has only 1.18 per cent of the total land area of India, with a population of 318.39 lakh as per 2001 census. Kerala's share in the population of India is 3.1 per cent which shows the highest density of population among the Indian states. The state has a long coastal belt, a mountainous range and a mid region. Kerala has abundant rainfall, sunshine and a range of temperature and a wide range of soil types which suit the different crops. Kerala has a wide spectrum of plantation crops unlike in any other part of the country. Kerala stands first among the Indian states in literacy rate of both men and women in rural and urban areas. During the Portuguese invasion, the craftsmanship and skill of the people were developed to a great extent. This gradually led to the formation of a skilled labour force in the state. The access to the sea induced her maritime trade from very ancient times. Ancient Kerala was famous for her trade in the products of her own and collected from other parts. Her fame as the "land of spices" attracted the Europeans to the shore and changed the history of the country itself. But when the Europeans left the country, they had formed organised plantations of coffee, tea, cardamom, pepper, cashew, rubber and cinnamon and they even preached the cultivation of Cocoa, Nutmeg, Clove etc. which could be exported. The Europeans also paved the way for the development of coir industry in the country; the first coir factory was founded by James Darah, an English businessman, at Alleppey in 1859.

Kerala exports a large variety of products even now. They are coir and coir products, coffee, cashew, tea, marine products, rubber and rubber products, coconut oil, pepper, cardamom, ginger, turmeric, cotton piece goods, timber, minerals, rice and other food grains, electronic items, electrical items, computer software etc. A substantial portion of the export earnings of Kerala is from traditional items. The important traditional export items identified and approved as traditional items by the Government of Kerala are cashew, coffee, tea, pepper, cardamom, ginger, turmeric, marine products and coir and coir products. The contribution of Kerala towards the export of traditional items from India is substantial.

Cashew industry had its humble origin in Kerala in 1920 when Swaminathan established the first cashew-processing unit in Kollam (Quilon). There after Kerala had been a monopoly over the global cashew market till 1980. Till recently Kerala had been the largest producer of raw-cashew and she had the largest areas under raw-nut cultivation. But during 2001-02 Maharashtra became the largest cultivator and producer. However it is Quilon which engineered the mass production of cashew and became the cashew capital of the world a distinction it holds even today. The government of Kerala entered into this business with the formation of the Kerala State Cashew Development Corporation in 1969. The infrastructure developed within the state in the

Cashew industry is commendable. There are about 400 factories which can process 5,00,000 M.T of Cashew, a skilled and trained labour force of 2,10,000, a large number of enthusiastic entrepreneurs, efficient transport and communication and a well equipped laboratory (at Quilon) which can provide technical consultancy and analytical services to processors, exporters etc. Thus Kerala is endowed with all the requisites for the development of cashew export. Yet the performance is disappointing.

During 1990-91 Kerala had exported 88.3 per cent of the total cashew exported from the country in quantity terms. But at the end of the period of study the contribution of Kerala had declined to 55.7 per cent. The earnings also declined accordingly, it was from 88.3 per cent to 54.4 per cent. The share of Kerala in the total import of raw nut had also increased correspondingly from 5.93 per cent to 54 per cent in quantity and 5.75 per cent to 53 per cent in value, resulting in a decline in the earnings from 94 per cent to 47 per cent of the export price of cashew. But in the all India level the earnings had decreased from 70 per cent to 40 per cent.

Marine products export sector achieved spectacular growth in the State only after 1970. There after its growth is tremendous. Kerala is a maritime state with a long coastline of 599 K.M and 3600 sq. K.M of Exclusive Economic Zone (EEZ). Fishing and related activities provide livelihood to a vast majority of the population in the State. The estimated fisher folk population in Kerala during 2001-02 was 1085 lakh. In view of the strategic location in the area with an extensive coastal belt, with a wide network of inland water bodies, Kerala State has the requisite natural endowments for emerging as a leading fish producing State in the country. Kerala coast is known for its plentiful resource of marine fish, over 475 different species of fish have been identified in Kerala coast. In Kerala Marine product export sector is considered as the most promising export sector. The export earning from this sector increased from Rs. 33.70 crore during 1971-72 to Rs. 950.55 crore in 2001-02. Shrimp is the most important item exported from the State. It constitutes 38.52 per cent of the export earnings, which amounted to Rs. 549.49 crore during 2001-02. Kerala had maintained her first position among the marine products exporting states of the country till recently. But now Andhra Pradesh ranks first.

It is due to poor fish landings in the State of Kerala and the increased production of culture fisheries in Andhra Pradesh. Kerala is facing a resource depletion crisis. Kerala's share in the export of marine products in India was 67 per cent in quantity and 79 per cent in value during 1970-71. Gradually the share declined to 38.56 per cent in quantity and 41 per cent in value during 1980-81, and during 1990-91 it reached to 37 per cent in quantity and 35 per cent in value and during 2001-02, the share further declined to 17.14 per cent in quantity and 15.9 per cent in value, thus showing that Kerala's performance is deteriorating gradually.

For many centuries past, a wide range of spices crops have been grown in the State winning it the fame as the 'Land of Spices'. Pepper, cardamom, ginger, turmeric, cloves, cinnamon and nutmeg thrive very well under the eco-geographical condition prevalent in Kerala. Kerala continues to enjoy a near monopoly in area and production of pepper. Pepper produced in Kerala fetches a premium price in the international market due to its intrinsic quality. The cardamom produced in the State has certain distinct characteristics like colour, flavour and fragrance which have created a specific market demand for it. The third important spice exported from Kerala is ginger. Almost the entire quantity of dry ginger (Cochin ginger) exported from the country is of Kerala origin. The distinct features of ginger produced in Kerala are its high volatile content and strong pungent taste.

These characteristics make the product distinct from those produced in other states. Further the low moisture content and lower fibre content of Kerala ginger has created a specific export market. Another important spice exported from Kerala is turmeric. The varieties of turmeric grown in Kerala have good export market demand. The entire quantity of 'Alleppey turmeric' grown in the state is exported, because of its high circumin content. In addition to these spices, a number of minor spices are also cultivated and exported from Kerala. They are cinnamon, Cassia, nutmeg, mace, clove etc. The demand for spices has changed from whole or ground spices to oils and oleoresins. These value added spices are produced and exported from Kerala on a large scale.

Kerala is known as the 'Home of coir industry'. Coir is the natural hard fibre obtained from the fibrous husk of coconut. It is an important traditional industry in Kerala, which employs 3.6 lakh workers and nearly 76 per cent of them are women. It is only second to agriculture in the State. A large number of people, directly and indirectly, depend on this industry for their livelihood. Though coir industry is developed in almost all coconut growing states in India are manufacturing of value added coir products is concentrated in Kerala only, all other states produce mainly coir fibre. Coir industry in the state had an export orientation from the very beginning. More than 90 per cent of the value added coir products exported from the country is from Kerala. A large variety of coir products namely, Handloom mats, Handloom matting, powerloom mats and mattings, curled coir, rubberised coir, tufted mats, coir geotextiles, coir pith, coir rugs, coir rope etc. are exported from Kerala.

Statement of the Problem

Following the policy initiatives taken by the government there was a perceptible improvement in India's export performance, both at the overall level and across commodities. The commodity composition of India's export basket changed in favour of technology intensive industrial products such as engineering goods, high value agricultural products etc. Most of India's export promotion measures aim at fostering non-traditional exports. As a result of all these measures and the industrial development taking place in the country, the prominence of traditional items began to decrease in the export basket. India has potential for significantly increasing the exports of many of these traditional items. But India failed to exploit the potential satisfactorily.

Though the other developing countries advanced so much in the field of export of such commodities, there exists a lot of scope for substantially increasing the exports of many of these products. A primary analysis showed that the structure of India's export trade has changed a lot. The non- traditional export item gained prominence, after the reform process and the traditional items lose its prime position in the export basket. This change in the composition of items brought certain far-reaching implications in the economy of Kerala, as Kerala is a major contributor of traditional items. This study is concentrated on the export trade of four such traditional items of Kerala namely *cashew, marine products, spices and coir* for a period from 1991-92 to 2001-02.

All the four export items selected for the study suffer from poor export performance. Even though the quantity and value of export increased during the period of study, the percentage share of Kerala in the total export from the country had declined considerably. In the case of cashew the decline in the percentage share of Kerala is from 88 per cent to 55.7 per cent in quantity, and it is 88.3 per cent to 54.3 per cent in value, during the beginning and at the end of the study period. In marine products' export sector the decline was from 36.58 per cent to 17.14 per cent in quantity and from 35 per cent to 15.9 per cent in value. But in the spices sector the decline is not so sharp. In pepper the share of Kerala in the total quantity of pepper exported from the country was 98.78 per cent at the beginning of the study period, but at the end, it fell to 89.37 per cent and in value the decline was from 97.55 per cent to 88.34 per cent. In cardamom the share of Kerala in quantity terms had decreased from 80 per cent to 70 per cent and in value terms it had decreased from 80 per cent to 72 per cent.

In ginger the decline in quantity is from 39.28 per cent to 32 per cent and in value it is from 58 per cent to 56.4 per cent. In turmeric export there is no decline, but the increase is too negligible. In the coir export sector even though more than 95 per cent of the value added coir products belongs to Kerala, the coir fibre and coir yarn are also exported which are manufactured in other States and the export of which is increasing. So when considering the total export of coir and coir products, the percentage share of Kerala shows a decline. The contribution of Kerala towards the all India export of coir and coir products in quantity was 99.5 per cent during 1991-92 and it declined to 75 per cent during 2001-02 and in value the decline was from 99.8 per cent to 93.93 per cent.

A primary analysis has shown that the export trade of traditional items of Kerala is affected by a multitude of problems. The government affirms its commitment to the development of this sector. Yet the performance of the state lags behind most other states. The greatest problem that the export sector of the state faces is an absolute lack of any co-ordinated effort on the part of the state government to study these problems in a consolidated manner and arrive at a feasible solution to the major problems confronted by the exporters of traditional items of Kerala. This study has been an effort in this direction and tries to analyse the problems faced by the exporters of traditional items of Kerala after the liberalisation movement in the country.

Review of Literature

The Government of India set up several committees during the 1970's and 80's for evaluating the export performance strategy and promotional measure. Notable among them are the Alexander Committee (1978) the Dagil Committee (1979), the Tandon committee (1980), the Abid Hussain Committee (1984) and the Narasimham Committee (1985). Reports of these committees mainly stressed the adverse effects of the inward oriented export strategy of India and pointed out the weakness of the Indian export sector. Based on the recommendations of these committees, certain policy measures in the direction of trade liberalisation were initiated by the government.

The Alexander Committee recommended simplification of import licensing procedure and provided a framework involving a shift in the emphasis from controls to development. The Committee called for the removal of anomalies in the administration of subsidies and a thorough overhauling of India's export and import policies. The Dagli Committee also called for removal of anomalies in the administration of subsides. The Tandom Committee on Export Strategy for the eighties made an evaluation of the export performance of the country and made a number of recommendations. The committee stressed the efficiency aspects of export growth in the economy that would result from the pursuit of dynamic comparative advantage. The Abid Hussain Committee on Trade Policies pointed out that the export promotion measures taken by India are quite inappropriate. Even though there are certain incentives to the exports, these are very negligible. The Committee stressed the need for harmonisation of foreign trade policies with other economic policies and argued for growth-led exports and a phased reduction of effective (rather than nominal) protection.

The Alexander Committee and the Abid Hussain Committee have gone into the various aspects of trade policies and have emphasised the importance of promotion policies. Recommendations of these committees pertain broadly to the rationalization and strengthening of the export promotion measures, simplification of procedures and improvement of export capability through expansion of production-base, technological upgradation etc. The Abid Hussain Committee also favoured announcement of trade policies for longer periods in order to impart a degree of continuity and provide facility for long-term planning of export business. The Narasimham Committee recommended that import substitution activities, which do not save foreign exchange, should not be encouraged.

Some scholars have conducted individual studies about the export trade of India. They have analysed various aspects such as export strategy, export performance and procedures, export promotion measures etc. Some of the evaluative studies relating to the topic are discussed here. One such notable study was conducted by the present Prime Minister Manmohan Singh in 1964. He has commented on the adverse effects of import substitution and the indiscriminate protection to the domestic industries. According to him the sheltered domestic market acted as a deterrent to efficiency improvement and thus the prospects of newly established industries, were further diminished. He pointed out that in the mid 1950's in India while export industries like jute and cotton textiles were denied foreign exchange for their much needed modernisation, a much too liberal approach was followed in allocating foreign exchange to many non-essential industries in the name of import substitution. He established that the "export fatalism" in trade policy of this period and lack of policy efforts to intensify exports were the major reasons for the dismal export performance in the 1950s.

Benjamin Cohen (1964) traced the reason for the fall in the share of India's traditional exports in the foreign markets. He opined that the increased domestic production cost and increased domestic demand resulted in an increase in the price of Indian exports. The relatively higher prices of the Indian exports reduced their competitiveness in the foreign markets and resulted in a fall in the share of Indian traditional exports in the world markets during the fifties. The absence of a well thought out economic policy also acted as a hindrance to the expansion of Indian exports. He observed that only through the formation of an integrated strategy, export promotion is possible.

Jagdesh N. Bagwathi and Padma Desai (1970) were of the opinion that it was the export pessimism resulting in the neglect of export promotion, and certain government measures with bias against exports which were responsible for the stagnation of India's export earning in the 1950s. They farther evaluated the export policy of India after the first and second five year plans; as the Indian Export policy has been evolved over the period from indifference, pessimistic neglect to growing encouragement. Ragnekar (1975) analysed the factors behind the change in the composition of Indian exports during the post devaluation period. He pointed out that since the beginning of the planning era there has been a sharp increase in capital investment in industrial sector and it resulted in an increase of per capita and national income of the country. These excess capacities increased domestic demand for primary goods within the country and hence resulted in excess production of manufactured goods.

The import substitution strategy of the government also induced the production of manufactured items like engineering goods and all these resulted in a fall of primary exports and increase in manufactured exports. Jagdesh N. Bhagwati and Sreenivasan, T.N (1975) conducted a detailed study to investigate the relationship of the exchange control regime to growth via static efficiency and other factors. The authors have calculated the loss in aggregate exports due to India's declining share in the world trade in traditional items. India's share fell in every case and the total loss in earnings over the decade was calculated to be 16.5 per cent of all earnings generated by these commodities. They argued that though export promotion policies fostered non-traditional exports, these measures were obvious of the efficiency considerations in export production. They were of opinion that domestic (domestic production, availability etc.) rather than external factors were largely responsible for the slowdown of India's exports during the study period.

Animesh Halder's (1976) study on 'India's Export Pattern Analysis on Potential Diversification', examined the importance of the role of exports within the context of India's balance of payments position. It also looked into the pattern of foreign demand in order to analyse the question of export diversification. The study also examined India's export performance with reference to commodity composition, geographical distribution, and competitive position in her export trade. In order to indicate the direction of diversification, the stability pattern of the country was analysed in terms of both commodities and markets.

Further he has analysed the supply possibilities of Indian export. Halder has made an attempt to estimate the change in India's export earning on a quantitative basis. The aim of this estimate was to see whether India incurred a loss or gain on her export earnings between 1957 and 1966 within the context of the change in world exports. His opinion was that India's failure in its export performance was largely due to its inability to compete successfully in a highly competitive world market. Deepak Nayyar (1976) in a study on India's Export and Import Policies in the 1960s examined the export policies of India during the period. He opined that the export promotion measures adopted during the first half of the 1960s succeeded in boosting the total exports. They helped to increase some of the non-traditional exports. According to him, apart from the selective export promotion policies, excess capacity in Indian industries is a major reason for the expansion of the non-traditional exports, particularly those originating from the engineering industries.

He opines that the devaluation of rupee in 1966 was a futile exercise, because devaluation was companied by removal of various subsidies and introduction of export levies on various products. This reduced the extent of de facto or net devaluation. He observed that exclusion of traditional exports from the scope of subsidy measures is regarded as an effective way of taxing these exports. But the promotion of non-traditional exports is concentrated on very few commodities even though there is scope to boost exports of many other items with high potential in the international market. In the sphere of trade policies Panchamukhi's study is of paramount importance. In his book 'Trade Policies of India-A Quantitative Analysis' (1977) he emphasised the importance of trade policies as a determinant of trade patterns and has highlighted a number of significant issues regarding the problem of quantitative measurement of policies and their effectiveness. He made a reasonable attempt to discuss some selected aspects of the trade policy system and has furnished a unified trade theory for developing countries.

Martin Wolf (1982) conducted a study on India's exports based on World Bank Reports and some other notable studies. He has commented on the adverse effects of import substitution and the indiscriminate protection on the productive efficiency and exports. He opined that the import restriction starved the export sector of quality raw materials and components at competitive prices, and the high input cost due to protection had increased the cost of exportable and discouraged export development.

Rameswar Tandon's study 'Some Perspectives on India's Trade Policy' (1983) was a critical evaluation of India's export strategy. He stated that the domestic policies of the Government via export controls and quotas, export duties and policies aimed at promoting domestic consumption and inflationary pressures inhibited the expansion of export earnings. He criticised many of the export promotion measures and their implementation. Deo Raj Singh (1985) in an empirical study on 'Pattern of Foreign Trade and Planning in India' provided an integrated picture of trade and growth aspects of Indian economy during the plan period. He examined the importance of foreign trade in India's economic development. The study encompassed the pattern of trade and economic growth during the planning period. He examined the trend of foreign trade from pre-plan period till 1980-81 and analysed the relationship between growth and volume of trade, commodity composition, direction of trade and terms of trade and said that there is a significant scope left for a leap forward through improved financial, technical and management planning.

Bhashyam (1988) conducted a study on the export promotion measures adopted in India during the period from 1965-66 to 1976-77. He tried to measure the export performance of India during the period in the light of the global perspective. According to him the increase in the export earnings in India could not cope up with the tremendous increase in world trade, and he observes that a promotion policy which suits the needs of the individual firms engaged in export, would definitely yield better results. Bhattacharya (1989) conducted a study on the input- out-put framework to show the import intensity of exports. The study concluded that the policy of export linked import liberalisation followed in India raised the import content in a large number of sectors. It has enabled the export sectors to increase their capacity to pay for their imports. Sidharthan (1989) carried out a study on the basis of data collected from large public limited companies published by the Reserve Bank of India. The study has brought out a sharp uptrend in import intensity immediately after liberalisation and its continuation at that high level. In sharp contrast, the export intensity of many industries declined following the intensification of liberalisation process since 1985, thereby contributing to a large trade gap during the sample period.

A study done at the Indian Institute of Foreign Trade (1990) showed that import liberalisation had a very positive impact on the Indian economy in terms of accelerated production and export. The impact of import liberalisation measures viz. widening the coverage of the OGL list and reduction in tariff rates had been very significant in the food sector. Production was also found to have had a strong impact on both export and imports. The rapid rise in incremental exports of food, garments, engineering and textile groups during the period from 1980-81 to 1986-87 may be attributed to the growing imports of capital goods consequent on increasing import liberalisation. Francis Chenmilam in his empirical study (1991) analysed the export climate of India with particular reference to marine products export. He emphasised the need for increasing exports by adopting new technology, quality up gradation, market expansion, product diversification and consumer packing. He critically evaluated the role of MPEDA in boosting up the exports of marine products.

Leela conducted a study (1993) about the export growth achieved by India. According to her, the processes of liberalisation and economic reforms have opened the economy for an accelerated growth. A series of economic reforms have been announced and they include relaxation of the industrial regulatory involvement, liberalisation of international trade, easing of exchange control, encouraging foreign investment, reforms in the financial sector and in taxation as well as in government subsidy and disinvestment in public sector enterprises. These measures have far reaching impact on Indian Economy in general and on the corporate sector in particular. Ramakrishna (1993) conducted an empirical study and examined the relationship between import-substitution and export and economic growth in India. Growth trends in India's foreign trade both at aggregate and at disaggregate level are studied. The study revealed that there is a unidirectional and positive causation between exports and economic growth in India, which supports the export promotion hypothesis.

In an attempt to learn important lessons from the past, Muneesh Kapoor (1997) presented an analytical overview of the balance of payments and the concomitant evolution of external policies since independence. The robust export growth witnessed since 1993-94 becomes a critical minimum or a viable external sector with the ratio of current receipts to GDP providing a measure of the degree of sustainability of the current account deficits. As the country proceeds towards capital account convertibility, the major concern would be the management of capital inflows. In such a scenario, the level of reserves needs to be built up higher than the current level. Since huge capital inflows put upward pressure on the exchange rate, to avoid bad effects, it is imperative to ensure that the domestic inflation rate is roughly the same as that prevailing in the case of country's trading partners.

Dulal Bhattachanya (1999) analysed India's contemporary foreign trade scenario. According to him, in view of the globalisation taking place currently all over the world, India has taken a major initiative to diversify its export base and its destinations, and the management philosophy to be applied in case of India's foreign trade front should follow the accepted principle of globalisation. Sujanm Hajr had conducted a study on India's trade policy regime-non tariff issues and W.T.O norms and opines that being a founder member in the W.T.O, the possibility of misalignment between India's non- tariff measures and the relevant W.T.O norms cannot be ruled out. He suggested India need to initiate time bond programmes to bridge such gaps.

These changes however can substantially reduce the scope of the existing export promotion schemes. The study also discussed certain policy options, which may encourage Indian exports without violating the W.T.O norms.

Objectives of the Study

The present study was undertaken with the following objectives:

- To examine the trend of export trade of traditional items o Kerala in relation to cashew, marine products, spices and coir
- To ascertain the existing mechanism for the export of selecte traditional items of Kerala.
- To assess the influence of export promotion measures of th Government and other institutions on the export trade of th selected traditional items.
- To investigate into the hindrances in boosting the volume c export trade in respect of the selected traditional items.
- To suggest measures wherever possible based on the finding of the study.

The present study is confined to the export trade of selecte traditional items of Kerala namely cashew, marine product spices and coir. The reference period ranges from 1991-92 2001-02. However, larger duration has been considered appropriate context, where such an extension would help tl analysis of trends in a more historical perspective and the da were more easily accessible. But while dealing with the item wi export from Kerala in marine products and spices, the analysis possible only for shorter duration due to the difficulty in getti data on a state wise basis.

Data relating to the study were collected from both prima and secondary sources. Both descriptive and analytical metho are used for the study. The fieldwork for the study has be conducted during the period from April 2001 and June 20(Primary data have been collected by interviewing the exporte The interview schedule used for the purpose was designed af conducting a pilot survey in the Alapuzha district of Kerala, a the findings were utilised to give final shape to the questions to incorporated. The findings have also been augmented by inter discussions with men of knowledge such as the office bearers Cashew Export Promotion Council, Marine Product Exp Development Authority, Spices Board, Coir Board, Sea Fc Exporters Association, Coir Exporters Association, Cocl Chamber of Commerce and the exporters. Secondary data w collected from Cashew Export Promotion Council, Mar

Products Export Development Authority, Spices Board, Coir Board, Kerala State Planning Board, Bureau of Economics and Statistics, Cochin Port Trust, Office of the Director General of Foreign Trade, etc. In addition to these sources, appropriate secondary data were collected from Economic Review, Reserve Bank of India's Bulletin on Currency and Finance, Centre for Monitoring Indian Economy, Books and Journals etc.

A random sample technique is adopted to select the sample units. As there are four types of export items covered under the study, sample is selected from each item using random numbers, so as to make the total sample size 25 per cent of the population. All the exporting units in Kerala, registered with the Cashew Export Promotion Council, MPEDA, Spices Board and Coir Board up to March 31, 2001, were considered for selecting the sample. Twenty five per cent of the sample is selected from 90 cashew exporters, 148 marine products exporters, 53 spice exporters and 102 coir exporters and the sample for the study covered 98 exporters consists of 23 cashew exporters 37 marine product exporters, 14 spice exporters and 24 coir exporters. Mathematical and statistical tools have been used to make the study meaningful and purposeful. Percentage and averages are used to measure the relative changes in the export of traditional items from Kerala and India. An annual average growth rate is used to measure the export growth in different markets and products during the study period and for making comparison of the export growth of traditional items of Kerala with that of India. Correlation and regression techniques are used to measure the trend of exports in traditional items during the post-liberalisation period and the pre-liberalised period. Chi-square test of association is used to test the significance of the result of analysis of data.

The study suffers from some limitations, due to the non-availability of state wise data, on longer period it was felt appropriate to adopt market wise analysis and product wise analysis of Kerala for short duration. The majority of the exporting units are concentrated in areas like cashew in Kollam, marine products in Kochi and Kollam and Coir in Allappuzha, etc. limits the selection of large geographical area. However utmost care is taken to make the finding of the study scientific, rational and logical.

Findings

The most important findings of the study are summarised below.

Cashew: India exports 49,874 M.T. of cashew in the 1990-91, out of this 44,060 MT was from Kerala, it consisted of 88.3 per cent of the total export from India. But in 2001-02 the total quantity of cashew exported from India increased to 97,550 M.T out of which 54,330 M.T. was from Kerala, it formed only 55.5 per cent of the total export from India. In value terms the exports of cashew kernels from India was Rs. 442.2 crore in 1990-91, out of this Rs. 390.67 crore worth of cashew was exported from Kerala that is 88.3 per cent of the total export was from Kerala. But in 2001-02 the exports from India increased to Rs. 1776 cores and that of Kerala was Rs. 964.49 crore which formed only 55.7 per cent of the total earnings from cashew export. Within a period of 12 years there is a decline in the contribution of Kerala, in quantity by 32.6 per cent and in value 34 per cent. This shows that even though there is increase in quantity of exports and earnings from exports, the percentage contribution of Kerala in all India export is declining. When comparing the rate of growth of exports in India and Kerala, in quantity terms the average annual growth rate of India was 0.07 per cent and that of Kerala were 0.03 per cent, and in value terms it was 0.16 per cent and 0.10 per cent respectively. So the rate of growth of cashew export of Kerala was less than the rate of growth of all India both in quantity terms and value terms.

With regard to market share, there was difference in the share of export by different countries during the period of study, India exported cashew kernels to 26 countries during the period of study. On an average basis these countries can be arranged in a descending order as USA, Netherlands, Japan, U.K, UAE,

Australia, Singapore, Germany, Hong Kong, and so on. In the absence of separate market wise data of Kerala it is assumed that Kerala followed the same pattern of market. The rate of growth in these different markets varied very much both in quantity terms and value terms. In quantity terms the maximum growth rate was possessed by Russia with 386.56 per cent followed by Norway with 295.62 per cent. Next was Lebanon and Greece. In value term Russia ranked first with 452.57 per cent followed by U.K. with a growth rate of 287.81 per cent and Lebanon with 281.84 per cent and Norway with 263.10 per cent. So Russia was the fastest growing market both in terms of quantity and value. In value terms U.K came second, but in quantity it became third, die second was Norway. Lebanon had a higher growth rate both in quantity and value, in value terms it was third and in quantity terms the fourth. Greece stood as fifth both in quantity and value terms.

The cashew nut shell liquid (CNSL) is a by-product of cashew industry which is extracted from the cashew nutshell at the time of processing of cashew-nut. It has innumerable industrial applications. In the year 1990-91, India exported 5658 M.T. of CNSL worth Rs. 5.56 crore, in Kerala it was 2490 M.T. worth Rs. 1.65 crore. The quantity as well as earnings of CNSL began to decrease from this and reached at 4148 M.T with an earning of Rs. 5.93 crore on all India basis and for Kerala it reached at 3335 M.T with an earning of Rs. 2.68 cores in 2001-02. In 1990-91 the share of Kerala in the all India export of CNSL was 44.01 per cent in quantity and 30 per cent in value. But the share of Kerala increased to 80.40 per cent in quantity and 77 per cent in value in 2001-02. This shows that in the export of CNSL, Kerala's share has grown both in quantity and value terms during the period of study. When the rate of growth of CNSL export from India and Kerala is considered, the average annual growth rate of India in quantity was 0.21 per cent and in value it was 0.014 per cent, while that of Kerala was 1.14 per cent and 0.78 per cent respectively.

This means that the growth in export of CNSL in Kerala was more than that of India. CNSL was exported to 12 countries from India during the period of study, out of this Korean Republic had the biggest share followed by Japan, U.S.A. and U.K. But when the growth rate is taken into account U.K had the highest growth rate both in quantity terms and value terms followed by U.S.A. Even though Korean Republic imported large quantities of CNSL from India every year, the growth rate was negative for Korea and Japan; it showed that Korea and Japan had declining trend for import of CNSL from India. For USA, the growth rate in quantity was 72.83 per cent and in value it was 62.70 per cent. It means that the value increased only at a lesser pace than quantity for CNSL exported to U.S.A from India.

India from the very beginning of the industry, imported raw-nuts from foreign countries and processed these nuts in local factories and exported to various markets. After concerted efforts in agricultural sector, the local production of raw nut began to increase and thereby reduced the import content to 54 per cent of the total consumption for processing. The increase in the area of cultivation and the production of raw nut for the period of study is analysed to understand the trend in this direction. From that it is found that Maharashtra, Andhra Pradesh, Kerala, Orissa, Tamil Nadu, Karnataka, Goa and West Bengal are the important states where raw- nut cultivation were undertaken, in the year 2001-02, Maharashtra had the largest area under cashew nut cultivation, but till 1994-95 Kerala was the number one cultivator. From 1995-96 there was drastic reduction in the area of cultivation of raw cashew nut in Kerala and as a result the percentage share of Kerala in the total area of cultivation began to decline and reached at 15.58 per cent in 2001-02, from a share of 29.14 per cent in 1991-92, but in Maharashtra the share increased from 4.28 per cent to 18.57 per cent during this period and the increase in Andhra Pradesh in area of cultivation was from 13.35 per cent to 17.53 per cent and in Orissa from 11.26 per cent to 14.29 per cent. On an all India basis the increase in the area of cultivation was from 5,33,550 ha to 7,70,000 ha, that is an increase of 44 per cent within 11 years.

When the average annual growth rate is considered, the maximum growth was achieved by Maharashtra, followed by Orissa and Andhra Pradesh. But in Kerala and Tamil Nadu, there were negative growth rates in area of cultivation; it shows that in these two states the area of cashew nut cultivation decreased at a faster rate. When the all India situation is considered, the average annual growth rate was only 3.45 per cent which was less than the growth rates of Maharashtra, Orissa and Andhra Pradesh. In the production of raw cashew nut, Kerala was the number one producer till 1998-99, there after Maharashtra became the number one producer. In 1991-92 the share of Kerala to the total production of raw nut in India was 47 per cent but in 2001-02 the share had declined to 18.51 per cent. In the year 2001-02 Maharashtra became the number one producer with 22.73 per cent followed by Kerala, Andhra Pradesh, Orissa, Tamil Nadu, Karnataka, Goa and West Bengal. When the rate of growth of production is considered, the highest rate was achieved by Maharashtra followed by Tamil Nadu, Andhra Pradesh and West-Bengal. But in Kerala the average annual growth rate in production of raw-nut was -2.13 per cent, which shows a decline in the production at a higher rate.

Most important feature of India's cashew export is the import of raw cashew nuts for processing. India is trying to reduce the import content by increasing the domestic production yet it constitutes a major part. India imported raw nuts from 20 major markets and from certain other small markets during the period of study. The import of raw nuts increased from year to year. In 1990-91, it was 82639 M.T. and in 2001-02 it reached at 355,443 M.T in quantity and in value it increased from Rs. 134 crore to Rs. 949.3 crore during the period. In Kerala the quantity imported increased from 4,898 M.T. to 1,91,579 M.T. and in value the increase is from Rs. 7.71 crore to Rs. 502.46 crore during the same Period. In 1990-91 the percentage share of Kerala's raw-nut import was only 5.93 per cent in quantity and 5.75 per cent in value. But in 2001-02 the share of Kerala increased to 54 per cent in quantity and 53 per cent in value. In Kerala the increase in quantity was about 40 times and the increase in value was 65 times in comparison with the 4 times increase in quantity and 7 times increase in value in India. When comparing the growth rates of import in India and Kerala, compared, it is found that the average annual growth rate of India in quantity was 0.15 per cent and in value it was 0.23 per cent, while the growth rate of Kerala in quantity was 1.21 per cent and in value it was 1.52 per cent. It indicates that the growth of important of raw cashew nuts to Kerala is increasing faster than the import of raw-nuts to India both in quantity and value terms during the period of study.

The actual earnings from the export of cashew can be determined only by finding out the difference between the earnings from the export of cashew kernels plus the earnings from the export of CSNL and the value of imported raw cashew nut. In Kerala in 1990-91 out of the total export value of cashew kernel and CNSL, 1.97 per cent was spent for the import of raw cashew nut, but in the year 2001-02 the import value of raw cashew nut was 51.85 per cent of the export earnings. Even though the quantum of earnings increased from year to year, the net earning from the export of cashew decreased from 98 per cent to 48 per cent in Kerala during this period. In India in the year 1990-91 the import value was 29.93 per cent of export value, but in 2001-02 the import value was 53.25 per cent of the export value. That is, the actual earnings have decreased from 70 per cent to 47 per cent during the period. It means that the percentage earnings from cashew export had decreased in India and Kerala, and the decrease was more sharp in Kerala than in India during the period.

The overall import growth rate of India was 0.23 per cent and the export growth rate was 0.16 per cent. In Kerala the average annual growth rate of import was 1.52 per cent and the average annual growth rate of export was 0.10 per cent. This means in India and Kerala, the import of raw cashew nut had grown faster than the export of cashew and the growth was at a higher pace in Kerala than in India during the study period.

Marine Products: Marine products export from India has been growing from 15,732 M.T. in 1961-62 to 1,71,820 M.T. in 1991-92 and reached at 4,12,538 M.T. in 2001-02. The value also increased from Rs. 4 crore in 1961-62 to Rs. 1376 crore in 1991-92 and reached at Rs. 5957 crore in 2001-02. The share of Kerala in the all India export of marine products was significant from the very beginning. But there was a gradual decline in Kerala's share, though there was an increase in quantity and value. The share of Kerala in 1970-71 was 67 per cent in quantity and 79 per cent in value. In 1980-81 the respective percentages were 38.56 and 41 in 1990-91 it became 36.58 and 35 respectively. In 2001-02 it declined further and reached at 17.14 per cent and 15.9 per cent of quantity and value respectively. As a result Kerala's average annual growth rate of exports lags behind India. The average annual growth rate of India in quantity was 11.83 per cent while that of Kerala was only 4.82 per cent. In value terms the average annual growth rate of India was 20.36 per cent and that of Kerala was only 12.77 per cent. It indicates that Kerala's marine product export had grown at a lesser pace than India's both in terms of quantity and value during the period of study.

An analysis of the comparative export performance of India and Kerala in different markets during the period showed that the European Union was the number one market followed by USA and Japan for Kerala's marine products, both in quantity and value terms, if European Union is treated as a single market. But if it is ranked on country basis USA was the number one country for Kerala exports in quantity and value. On all India basis, Japan was the number one market both in quantity and value terms USA came only second.

When the rate of growth of export in these different markets in quantity terms achieved by Kerala and India are considered, the growth of Kerala's marine products exports in Japan and European Union were less than the growth for Indian marine products' export in that markets. In USA and Chinese markets, there were negative growths for Kerala's marine products. In South East Asia, Middle East and a group of other countries the growth for Kerala's marine products exports was higher than that of India's. In terms of value also there was the same trend. The growth of Kerala's marine products export in Japanese market was only 4.74 per cent while that of India was 13.34 per cent. In USA, European Union and in China, the growth rate for Kerala was very low, when compared to all India level. But in South East Asia, Middle East and a group of other countries, the growth rate of Kerala exports was higher than that of all India level.

A product wise analysis during the period of study show that out of the different types of products exported from Kerala, shrimp was the most prominent item both in quantity terms and value terms. In quantity term the descending order of magnitude was frozen shrimp, frozen cuttle fish frozen squid and frozen finish. In value terms also, the decending order of magnitude was frozen shrimps, frozen cuttle fish, frozen squid and frozen fin fish. But when the all India situation was taken, in quantity term frozen fin fish was the biggest item followed by frozen shrimp, frozen cuttle fish and frozen squid. In value terms shrimp came first followed frozen fin fish, frozen cuttle fish, and frozen squid. So for Kerala shrimp was the most prominent item both in terms of quantity and value but in India fin fish was the most prominent item in terms of quantity but in terms of value shrimp was number one.

But the surprising feature about shrimp in Kerala, irrespective of it position was both in quantity terms and value terms; it had a negative growth rate. In quantity terms the growth rate for Kerala's shrimp export was 0.73 per cent and that of India was 5.64 per cent and in value the respective rates were 3.92 per cent and 19.42 per cent. This indicates that the quantity of shrimp export declined very sharply in Kerala and the fin fish export was growing in Kerala both in quantity terms and in value term than in India. Frozen cuttle fish export had a negative growth in Kerala in quantity, but in value there was a negligible growth but on all India basis cuttle fish export was growing both on quantity basis and value basis and value had grown faster than quantity. In squid export also, Kerala's exports had a negative growth both in quantity terms and value terms, but in India the squid export increased at a higher rate both on quantity basis and value basis. There is yet another group consist of live, chilled and dried forms of fish, ornamental fish, aquarium fish, clam meat, mussel meat etc which have a higher growth rate both in quantity terms and value terms both in Kerala and in India.

Spices: India has been exporting spices from very ancient times. On analysis of data relating to spices export from India from 1960-61 to 2001-02, it is found that the quantity of spices had increased from 45,653 M.T. to 2,45,000 M.T. during the period; in other words an increase of more than 2,00,000 M.T. within a period of 40 years, that is a five times increase. The value also rose from Rs. 16.39 crore to Rs. 1625.35 crore, a 100 times increase in value. But difference in the rate of growth achieved by the exports during the pre-liberalisation period and the post liberalisation period is more. The growth rate in quantity during the pre-liberalisation period was 3.85 per cent and in value it was 13.6 per cent. But during the post liberalisation period, the rate of growth was 10.34 per cent in quantity and 21 per cent in value. A detailed analysis of the export of spices during the post liberalisation period, that is 1991-92 to 2001-02 is made in the study. There were 17 major product groups of spices which were exported from India during the period from 1991-92 to 2001-02, the relative importance of each one differs considerably during the period of study. On an average basis chilly ranked first in terms of quantity of export and pepper was the second. In terms of value Pepper ranked first followed by oil and oleoresins and chilli. Out of these export items, Kerala exported pepper, cardamom (small), ginger, turmeric, curry powder, spice oils and oleoresins.

Pepper occupied a prime position among the spices exported from India. Pepper had an average of 17 per cent share in quantity and 30 per cent share in value in the total export of spices from India during the period of study. Pepper was exported in different product forms such as black pepper, white pepper, pepper powder, dehydrated green pepper, frozen pepper, pepper in brine, etc. Another important form of pepper export was as oil and oleoresins. Pepper is cultivated in India from Kerala, Karnataka, Tamil Nadu, Pondicherry and Andaman. Kerala was the number one producer of Pepper in India. The state produced on an average 95 per cent of the total pepper produced in India, and the state had more than 95 per cent of the area of cultivation of pepper also. The share of Kerala in the all India export of pepper was substantial. In quantity terms it ranged from 99 per cent to 90 per cent, and value ranged is from 98 per cent to 89 per cent during the period of study. But the percentage share of Kerala in the all India export of pepper decreased annually in quantity and value and the share of other areas increased correspondingly. During the period of study the average annual growth rate of pepper export on quantity basis from India was 11.38 per cent and for value it was 25.42 per cent, the corresponding rates for Kerala was 10.15 per cent and 25.52 per cent. The growth in export of pepper from Kerala on quantity basis was less than India and on value basis it was more than on all India level.

Cardamom is the next important spice exported from Kerala. It constituted a minor share in the total quantity of spice exported from India. In quantity basis its share ranged in between 0.38 and 0.36 per cent, but in value its share ranged in between 4.09 per cent and 3.43 per cent during the period of study. Small cardamom was cultivated from Kerala, Karnataka and Tamil Nadu during the study period. Out of this, Kerala occupied the prime position with an average of 55 per cent in the area under cultivation and 67 per cent in production. Cardamom was exported mainly in three forms - cardamom full, cardamom seed and cardamom powder. Kerala's share in the total export of cardamom on quantity basis was 90 per cent at the beginning of the period of study and 90 per cent at the end of the period of study. From the point of view of value, it was 90 per cent and 72 per cent during the same period. Kerala's share declined both in quantity terms and value terms by 10 per cent and 8 per cent within a period of 11 years. This decline in the share of Kerala was due to the increased domestic use of cardamom. During the period of study, the all India average annual growth rate of cardamom export in quantity was 41.10 per cent and on value basis it was 27.03 per cent. The respective percentages of Kerala were 34.61 per cent and 16.67 per cent. So it indicates that the rate of growth of cardamom export in Kerala is at a lesser pace than that of India both in quantity and value terms.

Ginger is cultivated in 22 states in India and Kerala had the largest area under ginger cultivation in the country, on an average it was 20 per cent of the total area under ginger cultivation in India. And the state's production of ginger was on an average 19 per cent of the total production during the period of study. Ginger is the important spice exports from Kerala. It constituted 10.3 per cent of the total exports of spices from India in quantity in 1991-92 but it was only 3.26 per cent of the total export of spices at the end of the period of study. The value also varied from 5.74 per cent to 1.54 per cent at the same period. Ginger is exporting mainly in three forms, fresh ginger, dry ginger and ginger powder. Out of the total quantity of ginger exported from India, Kerala's average contribution was around 30 per cent in quantity and 51 per cent in value during the period of study and Kerala's share in the total export of ginger from India decreased both on quantity basis and value basis by 7 per cent in quantity and 1.5 per cent in value during the period. By comparing the rate of growth of export of ginger in India and Kerala, it was found that the all India growth rate on quantity basis was 5.70 per cent and in value it was 11.21 per cent while that of Kerala was 4.18 per cent and 21.67 per cent respectively. This means the growth in the quantity of ginger export was at a lesser pace in Kerala than India, but in value the growth was at a higher pace in Kerala than on all India basis. The high rate of growth in value of Kerala's ginger export shows the high demand for the export items like Cochin ginger and Calicut ginger which fetches more value in the international market and which are exported only from Kerala.

Turmeric is another important spice exporting from Kerala. During the study period every year India had exported substantial quantity of turmeric, it was 13.84 per cent of the total spices exported from India in 1991-92, it became 14.28 per cent in 2001-

02 and in value terms the respective percentages were 10 and 5.21. Turmeric was cultivated in 18 states in India, Kerala had only 8th position in the area of cultivation, her share was only 2.5 per cent in area of cultivation and 1.5 per cent in production during the study of period. India exported turmeric mainly in three forms-turmeric fresh, turmeric dry and turmeric powder. Out of the total export of turmeric from India, Kerala contributed on an average 12.3 per cent in quantity and 15.3 per cent in value during the period of study. Kerala's share in the total export of turmeric was more or less constant in both quantity terms and value terms, throughout the period of study. Even though Kerala was a meagre producer of turmeric in India, the state earns a substantial amount by way of export of turmeric, because the whole of Alleppey turmeric which is exported from India belongs to Kerala. It is a costlier item and the demand for which was higher in the international market. The rate of growth of turmeric export from India in quantity terms was 7.28 per cent and in value it was 11.29 per cent, while that of Kerala were 8.49 per cent and 10.21 per cent respectively. The rate of growth of turmeric export on quantity basis was high in Kerala than in all India basis, but in value the rate of growth of Kerala was less than on all India basis.

In addition to these items, spices were also exported in forms of spice mix, curry powder, paste and masalas and above all in spice oils and oleoresins. The demand and price of spice oils and oleoresins increased from year to year and in the year 2001-02 it formed 1.8 per cent in the total quantity of spices exported from India and in value it constitutes 24 per cent of the total value of spices exported from India, in 1991-92 the respective percentages were 1 per cent and 16 per cent respectively. But the share of Kerala in the oil and oleoresins cannot be calculated in the absence of separate state wise data, as no agency collects the state wise details.

India exported spices to various markets and so for further analysis it is condensed into different zones. Out of these zones, East Asia came first in quantity of exports and American zone came second followed by West Asia and EEC. On value basis

American Zone came first followed by East Asia, EEC and West Asia. The growth rates of these markets on quantity basis show that West Asia had the highest growth rate followed by Rest of Africa and North African Zone. On value basis, Rest of Africa had the highest growth rate followed by East Asia and American zone. From this it is found that even though the largest quantity was imported by East Asia, followed by American Zone and West Asia, the export to West Asia was increasing year by year at a higher rate. In value basis Rest of Africa and East Asia had grown faster than American Zone. Even though on the basis of quantum of earnings American Zone came first, the rate of growth in quantity and value were less when comparing West Asia and Rest of Africa.

Coir: Coir is a versatile natural product extracted from coconut husk. It is of great significance in the global context but it is of considerable socio-economic importance to India and especially to Kerala. It is the most important traditional industry of the State. India earns valuable foreign exchange by way of exporting coir and coir products. In the year 2001-02 India exported coir and coir products worth Rs. 320 crore out of which Rs. 297 crore belong to Kerala i.e. 95 per cent of the country's coir export was from Kerala alone. Though coir industry is developed in almost all coconut producing states of India, manufacturing of value added coir products was concentrated in Kerala only. All other states produce mainly coir fibre. The coir fibre is of two types-white fibre and brown fibre. White fibre is extracted from retted husk by using traditional methods and brown fibre is extracted from dry or green husk by using mechanical devices. White fibre is produced mainly in Kerala which is superior in quality than brown fibre.

The production of coir in India in terms of fibre had increased from 2,19,600 M.T. in 1991-92 to 3,69,600 M.T. in 2001-02. But the increase was only in brown fibre, and the production of white fibre remained constant for seven years and there after there was a decline in production. The percentage share of white fibre in the total fibre production had decreased from year to year; it was 29 per cent at the beginning of the study and decreased to 15 per cent at the end of the period of study. But in brown fibre, the percentage share increased from 21 per cent in 1991-92 to nearly 31 per cent in 2001-02. The other items where production increased were in coir products and rubberised coir, in all other items the production had either decreased or at a stagnant state. This reflected in the growth rates also, that is, white fibre had a negative growth rate of -0.41 per cent and brown fibre had a higher growth rate of 10.48 per cent. It indicates that the production of white fibre in the country decreased at a higher rate and the production of brown fibre increased at a higher rate. The highest growth rate was possessed by curled coir, followed by rubberised coir and coir yarn. The wide spread use of curled coir and rubberised coir in automobile industry for making automobile seat and insulation pad and in furniture is the reason for the growth in production.

Coir industry in India has had a strong export orientation from the very beginning. During the 19th century there was a trade boom in hard fibre and it witnessed rapid expansion in the export of coir and coir goods except for a period of two world wars, the shipment of coir from India has been steadily increased till early 1960s there after there was a constant decline. The coir export which was 73,200 M.T during 1950s declined to 62,300 M.T in 1960's and 45,700 M.T in 1970's and 26,700 in M.T in 1980's. But in contrast to this, there was a continuous upswing in the earnings; the increase was from Rs. 8 crore in 1950's to 30 crore in 1980s. The decline in the off take of coir yarn in the agricultural field and the fall in production of coir products in the Western European coir industry and the introduction of highly competitive synthetic products were the major reasons for the decline in exports. It was from 1990 that there was an upward trend in coir export, which was the result of the liberalisation movement in India along with the growing environmental awareness and green movement sweeping across the world over, which resulted in a growing affinity towards natural products. This basic change in consumer attitude provides an export market quite favourable to coir. As a result, coir export achieved spectacular growth after 1991. This is clear from the growth rates of coir export before and after liberalisation. The growth rate of quantity in pro-liberalisation period was -2.97 per cent and in value it was 6.35 per cent whereas during the post liberalisation period the corresponding growth rates were 10.59 per cent and 19.79 per cent respectively.

Kerala exported different types of coir products, the relative contribution of which varies considerably. By analysing the data on exports, it is clear that handloom mat was the biggest item of export in terms of quantity followed by coir yarn and handloom matting, the percentage contribution of each of them wase 40, 31, and 12.5 respectively. Another noticeable change is that, during the end of the study period, the relative contribution of coir pith, geotextiles and tufted mats showed an increasing tendency which indicate increasing demand for these products in foreign countries. The order of magnitude was the same in value terms also. The only difference was in the relative percentages of contribution. They were 50 per cent for handloom mats, 17 per cent for coir yarn and 15 per cent for handloom matting.

To measure the relative growth in exports of various coir products, the average annual growth rate is taken into account. The average annual growth rate in quantity of exports was the highest in tufted mats followed by coir fibre, geotextiles and coir yarn. The average annual growth rate in value of exports was the highest in coir, other sorts followed by tufted mats, handloom mat and coir rope. It indicates that the demand for tufted mat in foreign countries is increasing very fast and it is a more durable and costly product than other types of mats and which can be produced only in mechanised factories. The application of geotextiles increased domestically and internationally in soil engineering and it had resulted in the increased demand for that product in foreign countries. Handloom mats constitute the biggest item of export among all coir products exported from Kerala and it had a higher growth rate of value also, which indicates a growth in the price per unit.

Kerala exports coir and coir products to a number of countries. The growth of these different markets differs very much, which is clear from the growth rates in quantity achieved by these markets. Out of the different markets the highest growth was achieved by USA with a growth rate of 6.48 per cent followed by Australia with a growth rate of 5.53 per cent and Netherlands with 4.59 per cent growth and U.K with 2.79 per cent growth. In value terms also the highest growth rate was USA's and the second was that of U.K and third, Netherlands. From this it is clear that the market for coir and coir products in USA is growing very fast in both quantity terms and value terms and so it is the most promising market for Kerala's coir exports.

Category of exporters: The exporters selected for the study belong to four forms of business organisations such as sole trader, partnerships, private limited companies and public limited companies. Sixteen per cent of the exporters are sole traders, 32 per cent are partnerships, 46 per cent are private limited companies and 5 per cent are public limited companies. Majority of them are private limited companies and others are partnerships. The exporters surveyed are either merchant exporters or manufacturer exporters. 95 per cent exporters belong to manufacturer exporters. Only 5 per cent are merchant exporters. They consist of 8.1 per cent marine products exporters and 14.3 per cent spices exporters. The exporters may be registered exporters or unregistered exporters. Registration is granted by the respective boards or councils or authorities concerned. All the exporters surveyed are registered exporters.

The exporters covered under the study had experience in their fields ranging from a minimum of 5 years to a maximum 30 years and more. Forty per cent exporters had an experience of less than 15 years, another 40 per cent had an experience of more than 25 years and 20 per cent exporters had an experience of 15 to 25 years. Those who had more than 25 years of experience consist of 88 per cent coir exporters, 70 per cent cashew exporters and 14 per cent spice exporters. All marine products exporters have less than 25 years of experience. This shows that coir and cashew export business has long standing in Kerala than marine products and spices.

Products exported: The exporters covered under the study export marine products, spices and coir in different product forms. But cashew exporters export only cashew Kernels and CNSL. The marine products exporters export mainly shrimp, cuttle fish, squid, fin fish etc. Each of these items is exported in different product forms like frozen, chilled, live, etc. in addition to a variety of value added items like IQF, breaded, battered, ready to cook and ready to eat fish products in pouches such as surumi squid rungs etc. Different types of spices like pepper, cardamom, ginger, turmeric, chilli, coriander, cumin, fennel, garlic cassia, nutmeg etc in different product forms such as whole, fresh, powder, curry powder, spice massala, oil and oleoresins, mint oil, frozen, brined etc. Coir is also exported in different forms like fibre, yarn, mats, mattings, curled coir, coir rope, rubberised coir, coir rugs, coir pith, tufted mats, geotextiles, etc. All these exporters export different types of products according to the orders received by them.

The exporters exported their products in consumer packs with a brand name and also in bulk without a brand name, in both cases there is the necessity of packing. Brand and package are the two attributes of a product. All the sample exporters exported in bulk without a brand name and along with this 22.4 per cent of them exported in consumer packs with a brand name also. They consist of 22 per cent cashew exporters, 38 per cent marine products exporters and 21 per cent spices exporters. The coir and coir products are exported in bulk only. It indicates that consumer packing began to popularise among the exporters of marine products, cashew and spices of Kerala.

Availability of raw material: All the four types of export industries are located in Kerala as there were plenty of raw materials in the state at the initial stages of the industries. But the position has changed very much and nowadays there is acute shortage of raw materials like raw cashew nut, seafoods and coir yarn. The survey results showed that on all overall 96 per cent exporters are facing the problem of non availability of raw materials and particularly 91 per cent exporters in cashew and 94 per cent exporters of marine products are facing this problem very much and the influence is comparatively moderate in spices and coir. So the exporters have to depend on various sources to get sufficient raw materials. Ninety per cent exporters collected raw materials from within the state and 91 per cent exporters collected it from other states. They consisted of 91 per cent cashew exporters, 89 per cent marine products exporters, 79 per cent spices exporters and 100 per cent coir exporters. Minority has their own raw materials also. All cashew exporters (24 per cent of the total) import raw cashew nut from foreign countries. So it is the common practice among the exporters of Kerala to collect raw materials from other states or import it from other countries

Sources of product for export: Ninety five per cent of the exporters covered under the study belong to manufacturer exporters. Hence the products exported by them are their own products. Five per cent are merchant exporters and they collect the export items from the manufacturers within the state. So it is inferred that in Kerala majority of exporters are manufacturer exporters and hence they export their own products.

Processing centre: Processing centre means the place where goods are processed for export. The entire manufacturer exporters have their own processing centres, only the merchant exporters (only 5 per cent of the total samples) use the processing centres of others.

Method of canvassing orders for export: The sample exporters use different methods for canvassing orders for export. They either canvass orders directly, or through commission agents or through traders outside or through friends and relatives. Majority of the exporters use these different methods simultaneously, that is, 95 per cent collect orders directly, 83 per cent collect it through commission agents and 13 per cent collect orders through traders outside. So the common practice among the exporters of Kerala for canvassing orders is direct collection and through commission agents.

Market studies: The study revealed that seventy eight per cent of the exporters who are surveyed are influenced by market studies. Out of these, marine products exporters and spices exporters are influenced more by market studies. But majority of the sample exporters do not conduct market research themselves. They depend on the results of such study conducted by institutions like Cashew Export Promotion Council, MPEDA. Spices Board and Coir Board. So it is found that the exporters of Kerala utilise the results of market research in formulating their marketing plans and strategies, even though they are not usually conducting such studies independently.

Modem Electronic devices: Modem electronic devices are widely used now in the field of exports, especially for speedy settlement of transactions. Ninety seven per cent of the sample exporters use different types of electronic devices. It shows that electronic devices are widely used by the exporters of Kerala.

High cost of production: High cost of production is an inhibiting factor for Indian exports. Increased cost of production is the net result of a large number of factors namely increased material cost, increased interest rate, higher bank charges and port charges, supply bottlenecks, high inventory requirements, technological factors, low productivity, power shortage, break downs etc. Eighty per cent of the sample exporters state that high cost of production affected their export activity very much. More than 90 per cent of exporters of cashew and marine products and more than 70 per cent coir exporters support this view and this is comparatively less (43 per cent only) in spices. From this it is understood that high cost of production adversely affected the export of traditional items of Kerala.

Competition: Competition in the international trade has many dimensions. There is competition from national exporters and from exporters of other countries. The competition may be from the same product or from competing products. The Indian exporters are generally small sized and they concentrate on limited items by taking advantage of proximity to raw materials, cheap and skilled labour etc. So naturally there may be competition between these firms. The survey results show that more than 70 per cent exporters face this problem severely and for 27 per cent exporters it affects moderately. This problem is more severe in cashew and marine products than in spices and coir. So it is found that competition from firms within the country affected the exporters of Kerala very much. The Indian exporters also face competition from developed as well as developing countries and in particular for traditional items of export, the competition from developing counties is very severe also. More than 75 per cent of cashew and marine products exporters and 64 per cent spice exporters hold the view that this type of competition is a serious problem from them but 88 per cent of the coir exporters are not affected by this problem. It is found that the export of traditional items of Kerala except coir face severe competition from exporters of other countries. But in the case of coir they have to face the competition from synthetic products and other natural hard fibres like sisal, hemp, etc. and from grass products.

Availability of finished product: The quantum of finished product is sometimes affected by a number of factors like supply of raw material and power, transportation problem, labour problem etc. In such cases the exporters are not able to adjust the supply according to the export orders accepted by them. Seventy per cent of the sample exporters hold the view that it is a serious problem. This problem very seriously affects the cashew exporters than the exporters of marine products and spices, where this occasionally create some problems and in coir exports this is not a serious problem as they can stock raw material or finished product for a fairly long period without any contamination or loss.

Availability of skilled labour: Skilled and cheap labour is required in plenty for industries like cashew, marine products and coir. In Kerala there is adequate labour force with skill and expertise, but the wage rates are high and the labour laws are stringent in the state. To avoid this, certain exporters of cashew and marine products started processing centres in the neighbouring states also for doing certain laborious, intensive work. Plenty of skilled workers are required for coir industry. But those types of skilled workers are available in plenty only in Kerala. This is the reason for the concentration of coir manufacturing industry in Kerala. The availability of skilled labour is not a problem for the exporters of traditional items from Kerala.

Technological factors: In export business technology determines the competitiveness of the product. So the exporters are compelled to adopt latest technology, the adoption of which requires additional investment. In international markets, more demand is for value added products like IQF, surumi, buttered, breaded, ready to cook or ready to eat marine products and different value added spices products like oleoresins and spices oils in spice sector, and different forms of, tufted mats, rubberised coir, curled coir etc in coir sector. But only 47 per cent of the sample exporters are influenced by technological factors out of the 95 per cent of the marine products exporters and are affected by them. This means technology plays an important role in marine products export than other types of exports.

Up-gradation of quality: The quality of the final product varies according to the quality of the raw material, processing facility, hygiene, quality consciousness of the workers etc. International marketers are more conscious about quality requirements than home market. They have imposed stringent health parameters for all types of food products and so the exporting firms could cope up with such changes which are insisted by them from time to time. They insist on frequent up-gradation of processing facility according to their healed parameters. The coir exporters also must upgrade the quality of coir products and standardise them. Fifty seven per cent of the sample exporters are affected by the non-upgradation problems. Ninety-seven per cent of the marine products exporters are adversely influenced by non up-gradation of quality. In spices it is 43 per cent, in coir it is 42 per cent and in cashew it is 17 per cent. So quality up-gradation is a very serious problem for marine products exporters than those of spices cashew and coir. In general the exporters of traditional items of Kerala must upgrade the quality of export goods to boost their exports.

Marketing Management of Export Items

Price of product: A product can compete in the international market only if it is price competitive. Price and quality are two deciding factors which help to market the commodity successfully in a foreign market; often Indian products are high priced due to several reasons. Ninety five per cent of the sample exporters are influenced by high prices of their product in the international market. High prices affected 96 per cent cashew exporters, 97 per cent marine products exporters, 93 per cent spices exporters and 92 per cent coir exporters. That is, high prices of the product adversely affected all the four types of exports.

Quality of the product: International marketers are more conscious about quality than home marketers. So quality improvement is a pre-requisite for successfully competing in the highly competitive international market. Poor quality will act as a deterrent in India's export trade. Eighty per cent of the sample exporters hold the view that low quality of the product affects their export business. The influence of poor quality of the export goods is less in coir products than marine products, spices and cashew because in food items the quality is a serious problem than non-food items but they can use only quality inputs like dye, chemicals etc. which are permissible by importing countries.

Execution of orders: To execute the order means fulfilling the order as it is. Any fault in fulfilling the export order will result in a loss to the importer, and sometimes it may lead to litigation and the exporter may have to pay compensation to the importer. Out of the exporters surveyed, 46 per cent are influenced by delay in execution of orders. This is found more in cashew, that is, 87 per cent. But in marine products and spices it is less than 50 per cent and coir is the least affected item. It is found that 54 per cent of the exporters of traditional items of Kerala are prompt in the execution of the export orders received by them. So it is not a serious problem for the exporters of traditional items of Kerala.

Distribution system: The nature of the physical distribution system prevailed in any market is an important aspect in export marketing. Because of the crucial importance of distribution in developing business, an exporter has to take very important decision about the channels of distribution; other wise it will detrimentally affect his exports. Eighty eight per cent of the sample exporters are not influenced by ineffective distribution; they adjust the distribution system according to the situation prevailing in that market. So distribution is not a major problem for the exporters of traditional items of Kerala.

Sales promotion measures: All countries use sales promotion measures as an effective means of getting entry into export market. Eighty nine per cent of the sample exporters are not influenced by poor sales promotion. They either resort to the sales promotion activities of the respective boards or councils concerned or they arrange it by themselves with the help of ITPO. In all cases it is not a serious problem which affects the export of traditional items of Kerala.

Packaging: Packing refers to the protective covering used for shipment of goods and packaging refers to the package in which the product reaches the consumer. In export marketing packing as well as packaging is very important aspects, which demands very careful attention than in domestic marketing, as it can influence the volume of export trade. Ninety seven per cent of the exporters covered under the study are not affected by poor packing or packaging, this shows that the exporters of Kerala are well versed with the packing requirements of foreign countries. It is the usual practice of the exporters of Kerala to export commodities in bulk. Often these are re-packed by the importers. So in such cases packaging does not pose a problem for them. Nowadays export of products in consumer packs is gaining popularity among the exporters of spices and marine products.

Planning of the activities: Planning for export is an extremely difficult and often neglected function. An export plan may be short term export plan or long term export plan and in addition to this there should always be a contingency plan. In the absence of proper planning one could not succeed in export. Out of the sample exporters 93 per cent is not affected by improper planning. It is found that majority of the exporters of traditional items of Kerala plan their export activities well in advance, so it is not at all a problem for them.

Management control: Management control refers to the process of evaluating the completed work and work in progress to ensure that it is earned out according to the plan and programme envisaged at the commencement of operation. The efficiency of the export organisation largely depends on management control. All the sample exporters hold the view that their management control is adequate and effective.

Communication measures: Exports always demand efficient and economic communication facilities; in the absence of proper transport and communication facilities export will suffer. Ninety eight per cent of the exporters surveyed support that in Kerala, there are appropriate communication facilities and so it will not affect their export business adversely.

Export import policies of the government: EXIM policy is an important instrument of a government to regulate the exports and imports of the country to spur economic growth. It gives guidance regarding the policy of the government on exports and imports. All the exporters surveyed hold the view that it influences their export business. 70 per cent of the exporters opine that the influence of EXIM policy on their export was very great and 30 per cent is of opinion that it only affected their business moderately. From this it is found that EXIM policies of the government influenced the export of traditional items of Kerala.

Clearance of the product for export: Getting the formal approval of the customs authorities at the port for loading the goods on board the ship is termed as clearance. Only after completing the customs formalities an exporter can load the cargo on board the ship. Any delay in this process may cause problems to the exporter. This type of delay affects 57 per cent of the exporters surveyed. The cashew and marine products exporters were severely affected by this problem, they were 13 per cent in cashew and 32 per cent in marine products, in total 84 per cent marine products exporters, 57 per cent cashew exporters and 71 per cent spices exporters are influenced by this. But majority of coir exporters are not influenced by this. From this it is found that delay in clearance of the product for export affects the cashew and marine products exporters more adversely than spices and coir.

Shipment facilities: Shipment is the more popular method of despatching goods to an importer than despatch by air. All the procedural aspects from the time the product meant for export leaves the export warehouse till it is loaded on board the ship and the relevant documents for such loading are collected from the shipping company is termed as shipment. Poor shipment facilities create obstacles for the expansion of export trade. It affects 94 per cent of the exporters covered under the study moderately that is they felt this problem occasionally and on such occasions they resort to ports in other states for exporting.

Export incentives: Government of India provides a number of incentives like drawback of customs and excise duties, reimbursement of difference between domestic and international prices etc, for encouraging exporters. But due to administrative and other reasons, there may be delays in the disbursement of these incentives and in such cases the exporters are put in difficulties. This may happen frequently in export business and 82 per cent of the exporters surveyed were influenced by this. Out of this 22 per cent cashew exporters 38 per cent marine products exporters and 29 per cent spices exporters are seriously influenced by it. So delay in getting export incentives is a serious problem affecting the export of traditional item of Kerala adversely.

Realisation of exports proceeds: In export trade the exporter may sometimes offer liberal credit terms to his importer, these may be short term or long term. Even if no credit is given the exporter has to wait till the shipping documents reach the importer. All these cause delay in getting the export proceeds. This is a serious problem affecting the export trade. Sixty three per cent of the sample exporters are affected by die delay in realisation of the export proceeds, out of this 22 per cent cashew exporters, 38 per cent marine products exporters and 29 per cent spice exporters are more affected by this delay. Others are only moderately affected. This shows that delay in realisation of proceeds seriously affected the exporters of Kerala.

Inadequate negotiation of documents: The submission of relevant set of documents to the bank and the process of obtaining payment consequently are known as negotiation of documents through bank. The bank carefully scrutinises the documents and if all the conditions in the letter of credit have been complied with, it purchases the bill and payment is made to the exporter. If the documents presented are inadequate, the banker refuses to make payment and the exporter will be in a dilemma. But the exporters surveyed hold the view that they are well versed with the documentation and so it does not pose a problem for them.

Financial structure for counter trade: Counter trade can be described as a transaction in which the proceeds of exports will be realised in kind fully, or partly in cash and kind and may involve two, or more than two countries in one transaction. It is simply a trade arrangement that contains a requirement to purchase products as a condition for sale, the balancing of exports and imports could wholly or partly be in cash, goods or services. India also resorted to counter trade to solve her problem of increased imports due to the developmental activities and stagnant export earnings, but it is only in non- traditional export items and so it is not felt by the exporters of Kerala, who export traditional items. All the exporters covered under the study hold the view that counter trade is not a problem for them.

Devaluation of Indian Rupee: Devaluation is the official reduction in the value of domestic currency in terms of gold or foreign exchange. Devaluation is resorted to help correction in the balance of payments disequilibrium by increasing exports and diminishing of imports. Devaluation of currency generally gives stimulus to the country's exports, but frequent devaluation has adverse effects on the exports of a country. The exporters surveyed hold the view that devaluation of Indian Rupee has moderately influenced their export activities.

Globalisation: Globalisation has exercised an influence on the exporters of Kerala, as they are compelled to increase the quality of the export goods and reduce the prices. Fifty three per cent of the exporters surveyed agreed that globalisation influenced their export business. There is some influence of globalisation on cashew exporters, and spices exporters but the influence of it on the marine products exporters is more severe than its influence on others.

Export promotion measures of the government: The government implemented various policy decisions with the objective of promoting exports. They include various concessions, incentives, subsidies and facilities to the exporters. These measures are aimed at making the export business more profitable enough to lure entrepreneurs to this sector and achieve the ultimate objective of boosting exports. Sixty nine per cent of the exporters are of opinion that they are moderately influenced by the export promotion policies of the government.

Services of institutional agencies: There are a number of institutions which help in promoting exports. Some of them are governmental organisations and some others are not. An attempt is made here to highlight how these organisations are helping the exporters of traditional items. W.T.O is the only international body dealing with the rules of trade between nations. The purpose is to help trade flows as freely as possible by removing obstacles and it also ensures transparency and predictability in trade policies and rules. The survey results show that 97 per cent of the sample exporters are not adversely influenced by W.T.O in the export of traditional items from Kerala. Chamber of Commerce is a non-profit making association among business people and it plays a prominent role in the export promotion activities by providing valuable information about foreign markets and importers and also they help members by interpreting government policies and in making meaningful representation to government. The study revealed that exporters of traditional items of Kerala have not experienced any influence by chambers of commerce over their exports business. Trade associations are similar to chambers of commerce. But the difference is that it is an association of similar type of business people like cashew exporters, marine products exporters, etc. The members may have common grievances and problems and they can collectively bargain for it through trade associations. Trade associations are playing prominent role in the export front of Kerala and they are more influential among coir exporters than others and the trade associations are more popular than chambers of commerce among the exporters of traditional items from Kerala.

Foreign Banks by virtue of their long association with groups of countries in a region may possess specialised information about those groups of countries and they can sometimes serve as good links between the buyers and the exporters. But the study shows exporters lack any help from foreign banks. At the same time the survey shows that 70 per cent of the exporters of traditional items of Kerala are influenced by the nationalised banks. They consisted of 71 per cent cashew exporters, 70 per cent marine products exporters, 93 per cent spices exporters and 58 per cent coir exporters. That is the nationalised banks have been exercising significant influence on the export of traditional items from Kerala. In addition to nationalised banks private banks also provide the same service to the exporters and they influenced 65 per cent of the sample exporters of traditional items from Kerala and only 35 per cent exporters are out of its purview. It indicates that in Kerala nationalised banks as well as private banks are popular among the exporters and nationalised banks exercise a little more influence than private banks.

EXIM bank is the major financial institution for co-ordinating the working of various institutions engaged in financing exports and imports in India. ECGC is a company owned by the government of India, the objective of which is development of India's export trade by offering security to the exporters and banks in the provision of credit to their clients. Out of the exporters covered under the study only 36 per cent are influenced by EXIM bank or ECGC and the influence is more among spices exporters and the next is marine products; for the other two types, there is not much influence by these institutions.

Trading corporations are started by government to give proper guidance and advice to the exporters. The study revealed that the trading corporation has not exercised any influence on the exporters of Kerala. Besides, the Government of India set up various institutions for promoting exports, among them are the various commodity boards and export promotion councils. The Board which relates to the items under study are the Coir Board, Spices Board, and the Marine Products Export Development Authority and the Cashew Export Promotion Council. Sixty per cent of the exporters surveyed are influenced by these agencies. They include 74 per cent cashew exporters, 60 per cent marine product exporters, 86 per cent spices exporters and 29 per cent coir exporters. The degree of influence exercised by these agencies over the exporters of traditional items from Kerala is not so significant it is only moderate.

The director General of Foreign Trade (DGFT) advises the central government in the formulation of the export import policy and shall be responsible for the execution of the export import policies of the government. The exporters surveyed unanimously opined that DGFT influence their export activities moderately. So the office of the DGFT exercises some influence on the exporters of traditional items of Kerala. India Trade Promotion Organisation (ITPO) is a government undertaking for organising export development programme including fairs and exhibitions in India and abroad, buyer seller meet, and such other activities for the promotion of exports. The exporters who are surveyed are not so influenced by the working of ITPO. Government of India set up certain other organisations also for the promotion of exports from the country. They are FIEO, IIFT, Indian Council of Arbitration and Indian Institute of Packaging. All the exporters hold the view that these institutions moderately influence their export business. Even though these institutions help Indian exporters in general the help the individual exporter receives in particular is only limited.

International trading environment: Quantitative restriction (QR) is an important method of trade barrier imposed by countries with the object of regulating export and imports of the country. It is included in non-tariff barriers (NTBs). The exporters covered under the study are of opinion that they are not affected adversely by the quantitative restrictions. The government of India fixed minimum price for certain agricultural commodities like coir to ensure the minimum price to be received by the small-scale manufacturers who supply the products to the exporters. These price restriction influences 67 per cent of coir exporters of Kerala and the other types of exporters are not affected by this. Quotas and licensing procedures are imposed by countries as a protective measure against their foreign trade, both the cases the government of the respective countries fixes either a quota or imposes licensing to control the imported goods to that country. The exporters of Kerala covered under the study are of opinion that they are not adversely affected by these systems. Foreign exchange restrictions can be exercised by countries by state monopolising the foreign exchange resources and not releasing foreign exchange for import of items which the government does not approve of, for various reasons. The exporters are of opinion that they are not yet affected by this system and in the cashew export sector there are governmental institutions to handle the import of raw nuts.

State trading means government involvement in foreign trade either directly or through government owned organisations, in place of or in addition to private traders. The study revealed that State Trading has not adversely influenced the business of the sample exporters of Kerala. Within the multilateral trading system, a few member countries form themselves into small advantageous groups to negotiate and arrive at settlement of a preferential tariff rate to carry on trade among them. This type of arrangement had not influenced the business of the exporters covered under the study adversely.

Different methods are followed by countries for computation of customs duty. Specific duty is one method of arriving at customs duty. It is a flat sum per physical unit of the commodity imported or exported. Forty seven per cent of the exporters are moderately influenced by this type of duty, that is, majority of the exporters of traditional items of Kerala are not influenced by this type of duty; out of this cashew and coir exporters are affected more than that of marine products and spices exporters. The study also shows that the influence of advalorum duties on exporters of traditional items from Kerala is negligible, and more influence is exercised by specific duties than advalorum duties. But majority of the exporters (90 per cent) hold the view that anti dumpling duties have no influence on their export business. Export processing zones are industrial estates which form enclaves within the national customs territory and are usually situated near international port or air port. EPZs are created by developing countries for promoting export oriented manufacturing industries and the entire production of such zones is normally exported. Such export processing zones have no influence on the export of traditional items of Kerala.

Adequate and timely financing is essential for the success of export business. For this government of India has devised a number of schemes like pre-shipment finance, post-shipment finance etc. through banks and various other institutions. Majority of the sample exporters are not affected by poor credit facility. Only 34 per cent exporters felt some type of difficulty. Fifty seven per cent cashew exporters, 60 per cent marine products exporters, 79 per cent spice exporters and 75 per cent coir exporters never felt any difficulty in getting timely and appropriate credit. So credit is not a serious problem for these exporters.

Countries which possessed something in common began to get together as an economic union for mutual benefit like free movement of factors of production, removal of barriers to trade etc. The formation of such trading blocks became popular among countries after World War II. But the formation of such blocks has not exercised any adverse influence on 91 per cent of the exporters. So the formation of trading blocks is a not a serious problem for the export of traditional items of Kerala. Trade agreements are agreements entered into between two countries with the object of increasing trade between them. All the exporters surveyed are of opinion that such systems have not influenced their export business.

Prior to undertaking real exports, it is advisable for such a firm to analyse different foreign markets to identify those which show the maximum promise for successful marketing. This is known as identification of promising markets, which helps the exporter to increase his exports by concentrating on such markets. Such identification influenced only 44 per cent of the exporters. The exporters revealed that the usual practice among them is not to conduct market surveys but collect information from the respective boards or councils concerned or collect the necessary information from their agents abroad and it influences the spice exporters more and the influence is a little bit low in marine products, spices and coir. So identification of promising market is not an important issue to the exporters of traditional items of Kerala.

Suggestions

In the light of the findings of the study, the following suggestions are made for the development of the export sector of the State in Cashew, Marine products, Spices and Coir. Though there are certain suggestions which are applicable to all items, there are certain issues particular to each item, which requires special measures.

Cashew: In spite of Kerala's long tradition both in cashew cultivation and cashew nut processing, the raw nut production is far from the requirement. The processing capacity of the factories and skill of the workers remain unutilised. The labour force hardly gets employment even for one-third of the year due to the shortage of raw material. This threat to raw material availability could lead to erosion of global market. The heavy dependence on imported raw nuts is to be reduced. At present the import dependence of Kerala has increased to about 40 per cent of the raw nut for processing, and many of the raw material sources are the country's current or potential competitors, which increases that threat in future. This must be tackled through increased domestic production through larger area coverage and productivity improvements. In Kerala the productivity of the crop has started declining along with the decline in the area of cultivation. At the same time area and production are increasing steadily in other producing states in the country. The recent decision of the government to include cashew in the list of plantation crops will help in area expansion under this crop if proper steps are taken in this direction. Immediate attention of the authorities is required in this matter.

In order to increase export earnings from cashew, it is necessary to expand the export of CNSL. For that, efforts should be made to find out new markets and new applications of CNSL. Another important thing pertaining to earnings from export is that, 'brokens' occur in processing of cashew kernels. The average price of 'brokens' has been less by about four per cent in comparison to average price of wholes. Nutrition value and taste being the same, brokens must find favour with world confectionery industry. In most of the importing countries, law stipulates that imported food must be pure, wholesome, and safe to eat and produced under sanitary conditions. So the reduction of pesticide residues must be properly ensured, in addition to filth, spoilage, and contamination or mislabelling. So proper care should be exercised to comply with the sanitary and psytosanitary (SPS) measures of the importing countries, in order to maintain the export market.

Marine Products: The marine fish production in the state has been stagnant for many years. The main reason for this situation is the over fishing due to the enormous increase in the number of fishing crafts. The proliferation of the mechanised boats and trawlers along the coastal line of the state and the indiscriminate use of gears and nets in violation of the Marine Fisheries Regulation Act, have led to large scale destruction of egg bearing and juvenile fishes. It needs effective regulatory measures. A preliminary survey conducted by Central Marine Fisheris Research Institute (CMFRI) reveals that the total annual economic loss estimated is Rs. 600 crore due to the use of this various destructive gears. Along the Kerala coast, there has been already a ban on monsoon trawling from 1989 onwards as part of the implementation strategy and to oversee the conservation measures. The government is following a participatory approach combined with regulatory measures for resource conservation but the regulatory measures should be enforced effectively to combat with the situation.

In Kerala 20 per cent of the landings are wasted being interior in quality due to the improper handling on board fishing vessels and at the landing centres. So the infrastructure facilities at the landing centres as storage, lighting and handling facilities must be improved to increase exports. Fish production in the state should be improved by promotion of fish culture in the natural water bodies and paddy fields. This will facilitate eco-friendly fish culture in the state which can provide employment opportunities in addition to increased exports. There is growing demand all over the world for value added marine products. Due to convenience, consumer preference is towards ready to cook or ready to eat marine products in pouches. So the export of such items should be encouraged in the place of block frozen or IQF items. Along with this brand image should also be created.

Maintenance of hygiene in processing plants, landing centres, fishing crafts and personnel working in these areas are important aspects for improvement of quality in marine products. So proper training must be given to them to ensure quality of the goods exported. The state has to move towards international standards of product hygiene in order to retain market share. The sanitary and psytosanitary agreement under the W.T.O stipulates maximum permissible chemical residue and other standards. There were reports of a number of environmental contaminants like mercury, cadmium, nickel, pesticide residue etc in Kerala catch. So the MPEDA has set up a full-fledged laboratory at Cochin for the fast analysis of these environmental contaminants, the service of this laboratory is to be extended to other places also.

Spices: The most important advantage for the spice industry in Kerala is the availability of high quality spices. The most important and valuable export item among spices is pepper. The pepper produced in Kerala is considered superior due to its intrinsic quality. Consequent to the liberalisation of imports low quality pepper began to be imported from Vietnam, Indonesia etc. In the case of cardamom there is the threat of import from Guatemala, which is also inferior in quality. These are imported in the light of Indo-Sri-Lankan Free Trade Agreement, and it should be modified immediately. In addition to this presently import for re-export enjoys duty free status, a minimum value addition needs to be prescribed to avoid such import.

The quality issues reported in consignments exported from Kerala include presence of pesticide residues, mycotoxins and microbial contaminants. As Quality control is very important in the post W.T.O context to retain the market share, because the SPS norms are gradually becoming a weapon to discriminate trade. The Spices Board should enforce quality standards in the absence of pre-shipment inspection and certification by exporters with the status of trading house, star trading house, or within process quality control system, in which case a self certification is necessary. There is a lot of potential for value added products like oil and oleoresins. But due to the scarcity of products with required quality to produce oil and oleoresins, Kerala lags behind the demand. Steps must be taken to resolve the situation. There is an emerging international market for organic spices throughout the world. The consumers in developed countries are willing to pay an additional 10 to 40 per cent for organic produce. Kerala should exploit the situation and detailed action plan should be taken to promote organic agriculture.

Since there is only limited scope for increasing area under pepper, ginger and turmeric, as a monocrop, the existing potentialities of cultivating these as an intercrop in coconut, arecanut, plantain and young rubber plantations may also be exploited to increase production. Along with this the state has to bestow specialised attention for upgrading the productivity of pepper through an organised replanting programme of high yield clones. For sustaining raw material advantage in the future, it is essential to finance research activity for disease tolerant varieties of spice crops. The government should motivate and finance cultivators to replant with better clones. Technological upgradation of processing is very much essential, as traditional methods of processing results in loss of flavour and quality. The Board shall provide and assist the growers in acquiring the essential equipments for that.

Coir: Even though Kerala is the largest producer of coir in the country, the husk, which is the raw material for coir utilisation is not sufficient, that is Kerala uses only 30 per cent of the available husk for coir making. This results in acute shortage of coir fibre, which is the main problem of the coir industry in Kerala. At present the co-operatives are entrusted with the task of collection of husk. This proves to be ineffective and alternate methods must be evolved for collection and utilisation. Too much dependence on manual labour for extraction of fibre and spinning of coir yarn increases the cost. Presently the coir industry in Kerala depends heavily on Tamil Nadu for fibre, where the fibre is extracted through mechanical devices. The fear of labour displacement and unemployment led persistence to the traditional methods of production. So to increase productivity and reduce cost, mechanization is required for fibre extraction and spinning of coir yarn. Hence proper mechanisation is to be encouraged by the government without losing the present employment level in the industry, and then only the product will be priced competitive.

In the international market, heavy dependence on mats and mattings is the major problem of coir industry in Kerala. The competition is severe for both because of the availability of cheaper substitutes like grass mats from China and from other natural products and from synthetic products. So steps must be taken for product diversification through research and development. But practically there is no research and development in coir industry. Srilanka advanced very much in the export of coir pith as a soil conditioner. In that way Kerala can effectively use coir geotextiles in soil engineering. But the product is not familiar in many countries due to the absence of publicity on such lines. So proper publicity is to be given to the uses of coir geotextiles systematic studies do not exist in coir sector for market information, analysis and dissemination of information. This erodes competitiveness of the industry. There is no systematic bench marking of quality of coir products and mandatory testing of products. So steps must be taken to correct the situation by introducing proper standardization.

General: The exporters at the time of survey raised the issue of high price of their products. They argued that the products are not price competitive in the international market. These high prices are the result of high raw material cost, high labour charges, high interest rates, high handling charges, high port charges, power shortage, and labour problems. Government should take necessary steps to solve such problems, and then only the exporters can export their products at competitive prices. The practice of exporting products in bulk without a brand name is not advisable. The exporters should be encouraged to export in consumer packs with their own brand names. Otherwise these products are re-packed and re-processed by the importing countries and marketed with their own brand names and the importers make large profits. This should be avoided by encouraging consumer packing and branding by the respective Boards and the government.

Diversification of products and markets are the two areas which require immediate attention. The traditional export items face competition in the international market from developing countries like Srilanka, Indonesia, Vietnam, Myanmar, Philippines, Malaysia, China, Guatemala, Thailand, Brazil, etc. All these countries developed new products, adopted new technologies, increased productivity and expanded markets. So their products became cost effective and they popularised their products more effectively in the international markets. So immediate steps must be taken in these directions to compete effectively in the international market. The exporters must be educated in hygiene, quality, promptness, loyalty, dependability, reliability, etc. All these will increase the image of the exporting country as a whole.

The role played by the state government in the export promotion is quite inadequate. The Kerala State Export Development Council and Kerala Industrial Infrastructure Development Corporation are the two state government institutions in this field. KINFRA is the nodal agency for the proposed Assistance to States for Developing Export Infrastructure and Allied Activities programme of the Central Government in Kerala state. But the activities of these two institutions are quite insufficient when considering the export potential of the state. The State has immense potential in exporting value added forms in the selected items of the study. So proper attention must be given by the state government in starting an organisation which can provide the necessary infrastructure for export identity, export potential and encourage exports in such areas, provide advice in necessary matters to the government and the exporters, provide a forum for solving the problems of the exporters and provide necessary incentives to encourage exports. Even though exporters had provided necessary incentives to encourage exports. Even though export is a central subject, the state government should take active interest in boosting the exports from the state which can act as a catalyst for the economic development of the state and thereby the acute unemployment problem can be solved to a great extent.

References

Bagawathi, J. N. and Desai, Padma, *India Planning for Industrialisation*, New Delhi: Oxford University Press, 1970.

Bagwathi, J.N. and Sreenivasan, T.N., *Foreign Trade Regimes and Economic Development: India*, Vol. IV, New York: Colambia University Press, 1975.

Battacharya, Dulal, *Management of India's Contemporary Foreign Trade Scenario*, Batra G. S. and Dungwal R.C. (Ed.) New Trends in

International Business, Vol. VI, New Delhi: Deep and Deep Publications, 1999.

Bhasyam, S. *Export Promotion in India*, New Delhi: Commonwealth Publishers, 1988.

Bhattacharya, Manas, *Import-Intensity of Exports*, Indian Economic Journal, Vol. 36,

Cohen, I. Benjamin, The Stagnation of Indian Exports 1951-61, *Quarterly Journal of Economics*, Harvard University: Mass col: 78, No. 4, November 1961.

Francis, C.A., *Export Development Process and Potential* – A Stud with Special Reference to the Marine Products Industry in India, Ph. D. thesis, Cochin University of Science and Technology, Cochin, 1991.

Government of India, Ninenth Five Year Plan, New Delhi: Planning Commission, 1997.

Government of India, Report of the Committee on Controls and Subsidies, New Delhi: Ministry of Commerce, 1979.

Government of India, Report of the Committee on Export Strategy for the 1980s, New Delhi: Ministry of Commerce, 1980.

Government of India, Report of the Committee on Import Export Policies and Procedures, New Delhi: Ministry of Commerce, 1978.

Government of India, Report of the Committee on Trade Policies, New Delhi: Ministry of Commerce, 1984.

Government of India, Report of the Committee to Examine Principles of a Possible Shift from Physical to Financial Control, New Delhi: Ministry of Commerce, 1985.

Haberlar, Gottfried, International Trade and Economic Development 5th Anniversary Commemoration Lecturers at the National Bank of Egypt, Cairo, 1959.

Halder, Animesh, *India's Export Pattern: Analysis on Potential Diversification*, Calcutta: Minerva Associates, 1976.

Indian Institute of Foreign Trade, Impact of Import Liberalisation on Exports, New Delhi: IIFT, 1990.

Kapur, Muneesh, *India's External Sector Since Independence: From Inwardness to Openness*, Reserve Bank of India Occasional Papers, Vol. 18, 1997.

Leela, P. *Export Experience of India*, Allahabad: Chung Publications, 1993.

Marshall, A., *Principles of Economics*, London, Macmillan, 1947.

Nayyar, Deepak, *India's Exports and Export Policies in the 1960's*, London: Cambridge University Press, 1976.

Panchamukhi, V.R., *Trade Policies of India: A Quantitative Analysis*, New Delhi: Concept Publishing Company, 1978.

Ramkrisha, *Import Substitution, Export and Economic Growth in India*, Ph.D. thesis, Osmania University, 1993.

Rangnekar S. B., Is the Indian Export Structure Changing, in J. C. Sandeswara (Ed.), Problems of Indian Economic Development, 1975.

Robertson, D.H., *The Future of International Trade*, In Essays in Monetary Theory, London, Staples Press, 1948.

Sidhartahn, N. S., *Impact of Import Liberalisation on Export Intensities*, A Study of the Indian Private Corporate Sector, Indian Economic Journal, Vol. 37, No. 2, 1989.

Singh Deo Raj, *Pattern of Foreign Trade and Planning in India*, New Delhi: Criterion Publication, 1985.

Singh, Manmohan, *India's Export Trends*, Oxford: Clavendane Press, 1964.

Sujan, Hajra, *India's Foreign Trade Policy Regime: Non-Tariff Issues ad WTO Norms*, Reserve Bank of India Occasional Papers, Vol. 20, 1999.

Tandon, Rameshwar, *Some Perspectives on India's Trade Policy*, Allahabad: Chugh Publication, 1983.

Wolf, Martin, *India's Exports*, London: Oxford University Press, 1982.

8

Marketing Management of the SSI Sector

S. Rajitha Kumar

The development experience of Kerala has attracted the attention all over the world. An important feature of this has been the impressive achievements in contributing to the physical quality life of the people in the state. Despite its low per capita income Kerala has attained the physical quality of life index that are more in line with high income economy. It is often described as the 'Kerala Model' of development.

It is widely accepted that there exists a strong correlation between industrialisation and economic development. A number of factors contribute to the industrial growth of a region. A strong industrial base with backward and forward linkages provides a favourable foundation for the rapid development of a region. Although the State of Kerala is endowed with a lot of natural resources, it has inherited a weak industrial base. An examination of the performance of the state in the industrial sector since the formation of the state in 1956 has been quite disturbing. The industrial performances compared to the national level development measured by any conventional parameter have been on the low. The share of the manufacturing sector in the state domestic product is relatively small and the growth rate of it is marginal when compared to the national figures. An analysis of the industrial structure of the state reveals some important aspects. The industrial sector is dominated by traditional industries and there is an inadequate development of large scale industries. Besides, small scale industries are still dominant in the number of industries in the state. The trends in total productivity of the Small Scale Industrial (SSI) sector have been showing a declining tendency since 1970s. The SSI sector in Kerala has been facing a number of problems mainly in relation to marketing and distribution of the products and services.

Statement of the Problem

The marketing problems of SSI sector have assumed a greater importance in the present context because of a number of factors. First, the competition from large scale units is fast increasing and becoming more and more intensified. Many small units find it difficult to compete with the large manufacturers who are far better equipped with modem methods of marketing. Secondly, because of the growing number of small units spread over different parts of the country, there is at present inter-unit competition within the SSI sector itself. Thirdly, with the production of a varied variety of products both by the small and large scale units, market for many products is fast changing from 'sellers' to 'buyers' market. Fourthly, lack of government assistance in the form of large purchases from the small scale producers. Fifthly, unorganised sales due to lack of co-operative marketing organisations. Sixthly, absence of market researches either by the small entrepreneurs or by government. Effective marketing has, therefore, become a vital necessity for the small scale sector to meet the new challenges in the market.

It is against this background that the present study was undertaken with a view to analysing the marketing management of the SSI sector in Kerala. It is hoped that a study of this nature would provide an acute insight into the problems of marketing of the SSI sector. It may also be helpful in formulating a specific strategy for the improvement in the marketing management of this sector.

Review of Literature

Several studies have been undertaken on the marketing problems of SSI sector of various states in India. An attempt is made here to present a brief review of such studies.

The International Planning Team (1954) in its report on small industries in India stated that small manufacturers depended on dealers for marketing their products and, therefore, did not get a fair price. The Industrial Policy Resolution of 1956 laid stress on the organised marketing of their products as one of the important aids for the promotion of small scale industries in the country. Dhar, P.N., in a study (1958) on investment, output and employment by small scale industries in Delhi, observed that small manufacturers depended on dealers for marketing their products and therefore, did not get a fair price. The report of Japanese delegation (1959) of small scale industries stated that the most knotty point in the operation of small scale and cottage industry was that it was isolated from the market and unable to understand quickly and accurately the trend of the market. In a study (1960) in Bombay made by Lakdawala, D.T., and Sundesara, J.C., it was observed that majority of the SSI sector sold their products direct to consumers.

International Labour Organisation (1961) observed that the survival of small scale industrial units depended upon their products on a competitive market in which large industries were also selling. It was also suggested that co-operative societies or government aided agencies should undertake market survey and market research since these would be too expensive for individual small firm. Singh Baljit in a case study (1961) of small scale industrial establishments of Moradabad stated that small entrepreneurs depended on dealers for marketing their products and therefore, did not get a fair price.

UNESCO Research Centre of Social and Economic Development (1962) in South Asia opined that small entrepreneurs did not get fair price for their products because they depended on intermediaries for marketing their Products. Ramakrishna (1962) also held the same view. Shetty, M.C., in a study (1964) in Maharashtra stated that majority of small scale units sold their products to wholesalers. Since they depended more on intermediaries for marketing their products, the small entrepreneurs did not get fair price.

Oommen, M.A., made a study (1967) on the small industry development programme of Kerala. The study evaluated the small scale industry development programmes and examined how far the various objectives of the small scale industry laid down in the five year plans would be achieved. It went deep into the employment creation and entrepreneurial resources mobilisation aspects. The development programmes that were taken up for study were: the modernisation of the techniques of production of the major traditional industries of Kerala, namely coir and handlooms, the industrial estates, the rural industries project and the special programmes of assistance covering the modem small scale industries namely finance, marketing and service. With regard to marketing the study stated that there was not much marketing assistance programme. The need for orientation of favour in goods based on local resources and skills was felt. The agencies to provide knowledge of better techniques and management could not make a major impact. This was due to the lack of adequate technical personnel, research facilities and follow up action. It was suggested that service extension centres must be located in areas where industries were concentrated.

The Economic and Statistical Research Department of State Bank of India conducted a survey (1968) in Varanasi on potential for financing small scale industries. The study revealed that the role of government sponsored institutions in marketing arrangements was not significant. Wholesalers and retailers had an important place in the marketing arrangements of small scale industries at Varanasi. The study also found that, quality control and standardisation measures were adopted only by a limited number of units. Wanchoo also emphasised (1968) the need for quality control.

A symposium held (1969) in the name of the late Vaikunthabai Metha, the man after Mahatma Gandhi, with the idea of the Khadi and Village Industries, discussed in detail the various problems in the small scale sector. With regard to marketing it was opined that wider outlets must be planned which will enable the small scale sector to compete with the large scale sector. It stressed the need for quality control and organised marketing structure. More improved facilities are required in the field of communication, supply and storage. Singh, Nau Nihal stated (1970) that continued production of an obsolete product, and failure to realise that business begins with the customer and not with the product, were pointed out to be the major reasons for the failure of small industrial units. Jain,O.P., in a study (1971) on the problems faced by the small scale industries of some countries with regard to export found that the outstanding problem for most of the exporting firms was lack of information relating to such major areas as export procedures, market research and locality agents.

Richman, Barry, M. and Copen, Melvyn, R., stated (1972) that the marketing of the products of small scale industries has been a problem for quite sometime. The problem was getting more and more complex as markets were becoming highly competitive day by day. Some of the units became sick as a result of the failure of their marketing operations. In a study (1972) the National Council of Applied Economic Research revealed that inadequate knowledge of foreign markets and insufficient realisation of production problems at home were the basic hindrances to the maximum exploitation of export possibilities. A study (1972) undertaken by the National Council of Education Research and Training emphasised that the optimal functioning of an economic system depended upon the even matching of the capability and efficiency levels attained by its productive and distributive systems. The study also suggested that marketing was probably the least developed aspects of the Indian economy and that there had been very little systematic attempt to study its problems in India. The seminar organised by the National Alliance of Young Entrepreneurs in 1973, on marketing services for small scale entrepreneurs stressed the need for an institution of marketing research and feasible studies on product or industry basis so as to enable new entrepreneurs to take up selected lines of manufacture.

Ahmad, Nisar carried out a study (1974) on the operational problems of the small scale and cottage industries in India with special reference to the state of Jammu and Kashmir. On analysing the marketing problems the study inferred that in the field of distribution the industries were limited by the keen competition not only from the large scale firms but also from competing firms in other States of India. The findings of the Working Group for the Fifth Five Year Plan (1974) were that the major drawback in the small industries development programme was the lack of proper distribution system for disposal of their products.

Sharma, A.P., in his work on marketing problems of small scale industries presented at the National Seminar on Marketing Strategy for small industries at Vigyan Bhavan in March 1975, classified the marketing problems of small scale industries into those associated with the product and those with the market for the product. The former arose from lack of standardisation, differences in the quality of materials used and lack of precision. The latter stemmed from inadequate resources at the disposal of small scale industries for identifying market outlets and tapping them profitably. Sapru, K.N., in his paper (1975) on marketing problems of small industries at the same seminar stated that because of their small size and lack of resources, the small industries, by and large, were unable to adopt modem marketing methods. Market research, market forecast, branding, effective publicity and even proper type of after sales service were beyond the means of many a small industrialist. They were, therefore, often victims of circumstances. In times of crisis, they found it very difficult either to predict conditions or to overcome difficult situations. Tambi, J.M.L., in his paper (1975) on marketing strategy for small scale industries presented at the same seminar, emphasised that large scale units had an edge over small scale sector in the matter of marketing because of economies of size and scale, sufficient financial strength to face temporary set backs and competence to hire professional managers, specialising in different branches of management. Sharma Krishnalal, in his book Entrepreneurial Performance in Role Perspective (1975) argued that since small entrepreneurs depended more intermediaries for marketing, they did not get fair price for their product.

Neelamegham, S. (1977), in a paper on Marketing Strategy for Small Business stated that marketing was at present a neglected step-child in the small sector. There were many firms, which could be proud of their modem plant and up-to-date machinery. The units, which could boast of their marketing skills and organisation, were very few in number. By and large, small units continued to be production-oriented rather than market-oriented. Many companies in the small sector had never measured their market potential for their products. He also argued that products of many small units suffered from poor quality, lack of good finish and lack of consistency in standards. Their after sales services were also to be improved. As a result of their poor marketing skills, many small units found it difficult to sell their products effectively in the market in the face of stiff competition especially from large scale units.

The Working Group (1977) on Marketing Assistance to Small Scale Industries reported that market studies had not been updated and that there was no arrangement for systematic collection of marketing information by any organisation in respect of the domestic market. A survey relating to the Rural Small Scale Industry in the People's Republic of China revealed (1977) that most of the small scale enterprises were producing items for which there was a ready local market. Nagaraj, A.V., and Srinivasan, E.S., in their paper on Problems of Sick Units in India presented at a Seminar on Rehabilitations of Sick Industry in Small Scale Sector held at Hyderabad in Andhra Pradesh in 1977. They grouped in internal causes of sickness into four namely marketing, production, financing and organisation. They pointed out the inadequate and improper assessment of demand, poor quality of the product and absence of a clear marketing strategy of the SSI sector. In 1977, the Department of Industries Andhra Pradesh, collected data on sick with in the small scale sector in the state. The analysis revealed that the cause of the failure of small scale units in the various regions of the state was due to the marketing problems.

A study (1978) of marketing of industrial products of Punjab reported that quality appreciation of a Punjabi entrepreneur was poor because he had developed efficiency in the long years of experience without the support of a formal technical education and he did not understand the importance of quality particularly during the process of manufacturing. The Small Industries Extension Training Institute emphasised (1978) the need for greater co-ordination between the various agencies assisting small industries, to ensure production of quality goods at competitive rates without which the small industries would continue to face serious marketing problems. The working group on small scale industries for the Third Five Year Plan (1979) also recommended similarly.

The significance of marketing was brought out (1979) by Paul Hoffman, former Administrator of the United Nations Industrial Organisation as it was illusory to think that a country could be industrialised by building factories - industrialisation means building markets. Small Industries Extension Training Institute made a study (1979) on the identification of product opportunities in Kerala observed that a market study had considerable importance in a State like Kerala where tremendous possibilities for developing markets for a variety of small industry products were available especially because of certain favourable factors such as high density of population, highest rate of literacy, compact markets, well developed infrastructure and surplus electricity.

Bala, Shasi, had conducted a study (1980) on the management of small scale industries. Government policy and its implementation were studied in the perspective of the benefits and problems of the small industrialist. She made an attempt to make it a comprehensive study of all aspects related to the management of small scale industries. The field survey for the study was done in Ludhiana District of Punjab. The study stated that the procedure for choosing the method of scale was determined by trial and error and small industries did not make organised sales. Regarding the selection of area of sales, the selection was made not on the basis of any market research or information. Borooah,

H.K., in a study (1980) on the prospects and problems of small scale industries in Lakshimpur District in Assam revealed that lack of up-to-date marketing practices and deficiency in entrepreneurial zeal were the major causes of staggish growth of the small scale industrial sector in that district. Bannock Graham, made the comment (1981) that a small firm could not significantly influence its marketing mainly because of too many competitors.

Kapoor, T.N., Chand Bidhi and Kapoor, S.K., in their study (1983) were able to identify the marketing problems faced by the small scale industries and their awareness and extent of utilisation of government assistance for marketing, conducted on the basis of data collected from two centres Chandigarh and S.A.S. Nagar (Mohali) in Punjab stated that the marketing problems of small industry had assumed a greater importance in the present context because of a number of factors namely: growing competition from large scale sector as well as from within the small scale sector; and with the production of a varied variety of products both by the small and large scale units, market for many products is fast changing from 'sellers' to 'buyers' market. They argued that, at present, marketing was a neglected step-child in the small sector. They concluded that many small units found it difficult to sell their products effectively in the market in the face of stiff competition especially from large scale units, due to their poor marketing skills. The Committee on Pubic Undertakings on National Small Industries Corporation Lt., (1983-84) reported that marketing was identified as one of the critical areas in which institutional support was required by the small scale sector. There were major gaps in information such as customers' needs, quality control, standardisation and optimal production process, which need to be bridged.

Reddy Subby. T., and Apparao, P.B., in a paper presented at the National Seminar on Sickness in Small Industry held at Ananthpur (AP) in 1986 tried to distinguish between the apparent and real causes of sickness in the small scale industry stated that the poor quality of the product, the high cost of production, operations in a sellers' market, competition with large scale producers in all these resulted in marketing problems, which constrained the entrepreneur to operate below the break-even level, and which resulted in the under utilisation of installed capacity and increases the burden of fixed overheads. All these factors collectively landed the entrepreneur into a financial crisis. Tilak, M.B.G., in his paper industrial sickness in medium and small scale industries presented at the same seminar stated that marketing was one of the important factors responsible for the success and growth of an industrial enterprise. Poor quality control of the products seldom reduced the market segment of the industry. Inadequate facilities of market research and inadequate funds to launch a publicity campaigns quite often led to a situation in which the product did not receive its due market share. Sometimes big business houses tended to ditch the units and ultimately to squeeze them out of the market by intensive and extensive advertisement and publicity.

Lajipathi Rao, H., and Reddy Subbi, T., in a paper 'Small Industry Sector Marketing - Panacea for Sickness' presented at the same seminar stated that the strength of the small industry sector lied in its improved ability to compete with quality products in the world market which, in turn, depended on the health of this industry in India. They also pointed out that thousands of small and cottage units were dotted over the industrial map of India. These units manufactured a wide range of products, posing a challenge to the marketing manager. Many of these units were manned by people with little or no marketing experience. Hence the imperative need for assisting them in their marketing operations. If this assistance was not forthcoming, they would be playing blind man's buff in the marketing arena.

Gupta, M.C., conducted a study (1987) on entrepreneurship in small scale industries in few selected units of Uttar Pradesh. In this study an attempt was made to analyse the marketing practices adopted by entrepreneurs. He observed that due to limited sphere of activities and economic resources, the small units were neither in a position to conduct market research nor to employ well-qualified personnel to perform marketing functions. Most of the entrepreneurs were not well informed in regard to the competitive position, consumers' choices and prospective markets of their products and consequently were deprived of adequate profits. Lack of standardisation, absence of trade or brand names of the products were some other marketing problems of the small entrepreneurs. The study also stated that brand consciousness of customers was also a big problem to the entrepreneurs. It also observed that marketing facilities provided by the government had not been granted to the entrepreneurs in general.

Munshi, N.M., carried out a study (1988) to supplement the knowledge about the forces that influenced management with special reference to the units of small scale industries established in the Saurashtra region of Gujarat State. The study pointed out that small manufactures paid more attention to the production and distribution than to product research and development. It was feared that the marketing management was time consuming and cost involving management for which units with their limited financial resources could not afford to adopt. Modern marketing was the challenge for the well developed and developing small units of small scale industries. It should be accepted in these times when market strategies were developing very rapidly.

Baishya Prabin, conducted a study (1989) on the role of small and cottage industries in Assam and observed that some of the traditional industries faced stiff competition from the modern sector due to which even the existing capacities were not fully utilized. The study also remarked that absence of a proper marketing channel for the product was a prominent problem for the small scale industrial sector. Anmbili Kumar, V., conducted a study (1989) on the working of small scale industries in Kerala with reference to Trivandrim district. He tried to know the different methods of marketing and to ascertain the problems in marketing the products and services. The study brought about the results that the small scale industrial units faced various problems for marketing the products, competition between similar units and lack of demand were predominant. It also stated that no small scale industrial unit conducted marketing research in the required manner.

Tewari, Vinod, K. Philip, Joseph and Pandey, Amar Nath conducted a study (1991) on the working of small scale industry in Karnataka State. Their analysis of operational problems on small scale industries revealed that marketing problem was found to be one of the most difficult problems faced by sample entrepreneurs across all the performance groups. Among the nature of marketing problems, the problems like inadequate and irregular order form the parent units, lack of ISI mark, and stiff competition due to imports, grouped as others, were found to be the most difficult problems. The second most difficult marketing problem was found to be the demand on credit, followed by the competition from SSI units, long distance, scattered demand, slackness in demand, and competition from large scale industrial units. Competition from the SSI units was found to be the most difficult problem in the very successful groups followed by the slackness in demand. Reddy, Jaya Prakash, R. has made a study (1991) on small and tiny industrial units of Prakasan District in Andhra Pradesh. The study observed that, on analysing the marketing problems, many units suffered in marketing their output because of their poor or sub-standard quality. It was also found that units were demand based but there was no sufficient demand to meet their output.

Thomas, T. Thomas opined (1992) in the ultimate analysis on various issues related to marketing confronted by the small scale industries that there was no single for all marketing problems of the small scale industries. As the market was diverse so could be the problems. Again even as time shifts the solution to the same problem could change. It was, thus, dynamic nature of the whole marketing process that made it a challenging proposition. A systematic and scientific study of the market and that of necessary marketing inputs was suggested to chalk out a feasible and effective marketing strategy for the small enterprises.

Patra, S.C., made a study (1993) on the establishment and growth of small scale industries in India The study had an objective to through light on the marketing activities of small scale industries. The analysis of marketing activities of small scale industries led to the conclusion that because of their small in size and lack of resources, small scale industries by and large, were unable to adopt modem marketing methods. Market research, effective advertising and after sales services were beyond the means of many small industrialists. Small scale entrepreneurs face difficulties to enter the market independently. The study also stated that the involvement of government was limited to the strengthening of marketing efforts of small scale industries. Resia Beegam, S., carried out a stu (1993) on the problems of women entrepreneurs in Kerala. The study aimed at locating the problems of women entrepreneurs at different states in running the units. Regarding the analysis of marketing problems the study came to a conclusion that competition from large units was the main problem faced by the women entrepreneurs in marketing their products.

Taleyarkhan Homi J.H., in a paper (1993) on problems of small scale industries argued that marketing surveys and outlets must be much more developed. More research and development work needs to be done for this. Full installed capacity is not utilised because of lack of it. Very often the small man does not know where to market his product and there is no one to guide him. He should be made aware of the various facilities which are available. All information he needs or is required from him must be made available to him from one source so that he is not driven from pillar to post. Chander Suresh and Singh, Hardeep in a study (1993) on the awareness of Government Marketing Assistance Schemes amongst the Small Textile Units of Amritsar, concluded that the awareness regarding various marketing assistance schemes among small entrepreneurs was very low. A large number of the respondent units were not at all aware of those schemes.

A through review of the existing literature, leads to the conclusion that there is utmost need for the conduct of exhaustive study on the marketing problems of the SSI sector in Kerala and hence the present study.

Objectives of the Study

The study aims at the following specific objectives:

- to assess the working of the SSI sector in Kerala in general;
- to examine the methods of marketing adopted by the SSI units;
- to study the sales promotion measures of the SSI units in the state;
- to evaluate the consumer preferences for the products of the SSI sector; and
- to suggest measures for improvement of the present position.

The study was undertaken in two stages. In the first stage the magnitude of the marketing problems was tried to be ascertained from the entrepreneurs concerned. Survey was conducted in three revenue districts in the state, namely, Thiruvananthapuram, Ernakulam and Palakkad. The SSI units in the state are largely concentrated at these districts. Incidentally, these districts are respectively located in southern, middle and northern parts of the state. The lists of the SSI units in these districts were obtained from the District Industries Centres concerned. A sample of 600 units was designed under stratified random sampling giving proportional representation to consumer goods, industrial goods and services. An interview schedule was developed after a pre-testing among 50 entrepreneurs for the collection of data. The entrepreneurs covered under the sample were personally interviewed and obtained the responses. In the second stage the consumer preferences for the products of the SSI sector were tried to be ascertained. Judgment sampling was adopted for this and 1,500 consumers giving due representation to rural, semi urban and urban centres were personally met to obtain the views. A questionnaire was advocated for the collection of data from the consumers. Various quantitative tools like percentages, weighted scores and chi square test were employed for the analysis and interpretation.

There were difficulties to get the questionnaire filled in by the consumers. They were to be contacted personally to obtain the responses at their convenience. Besides, some entrepreneurs were reluctant to show the documents and records maintained by them for counter checking the data provided at the time of interview. Since the study has primarily depended upon the views of the entrepreneurs and consumers covered under the sample, an element of subjectivity cannot be ruled out, in spite of earnest efforts to overcome this limitation.

Findings

Major findings emerged out of the present study are summarised below:

Factors motivated to the establishment of units: Data were collected from 600 SSI units located in Rural (300), Semi urban (200) and Urban (100) centres by using an interview schedule specifically developed for the study. The sample consists of units which were engaged in the manufacture of varied categories of activities like food products, hosiery and garments, wood products, rubber based products, repairing and services and other forms of services. It is noted that the units producing food products were dominated in the sample (160 numbers) followed by units manufacturing miscellaneous products like nails, nuts and bolts. Taking into account the fact that the units covered under the study were engaged in varied activities, it was felt appropriate to classify them under three groups namely consumer goods, industrial goods and services for further analysis.

It is interesting to note that a definite aspect cannot be pinpointed to be the common motivating factor. An independent job was the prime motivator for 30 per cent of the entrepreneurs covered under the study. Acquisition of profit and accumulation of wealth (15.67 percent) were the motives for some other group of industrialists. Application of knowledge was cited to be the prime motivator for 15 per cent. The location wise analysis of the units like rural, semi urban and urban also revealed the same responses with slight variations. It was also noted that 58 per cent of the respondents belonging to the industrial products were motivated by an opportunity for an independent job, the other responses did not provide much variation.

Average value of production: The data brought about the fact that the average value of production for a five year period from 1990-91 to 1994-95, taking the first year (1990-91) as the base year was showing an increasing ..end throughout. However, cost of production for all the elements like material, labour and expenses was also increasing and as such it need not be compulsory that the average production in increasing volume could not be taken as an indicate for increase in production every year. The data provided also confirmed that the increase in production in monetary value throughout the five year period under study was true for the south, central and north regions and for the consumer goods, industrial goods and services.

Problems in production: To analyse this issue, the problems in production were classified into three such as raw materials, labour and other inputs. The responses obtained regarding raw materials were tabulated by assigning the weights 3, 2, and 1 for the first, second, and third preferences respectively. The non-availability of raw materials in time was marked to be the most prominent problem followed by high price. However, the location wise analysis brings about the nature of problems in a slightly different manner. High price was the most prominent problem for units located in urban centres while non-availability of materials in time was the main problem for units in rural centres. Units located in semi urban centres consider high price and non-availability in time in equal way. The data when cross tabulated on product wise brought about the fact that 153 units dealing with consumer goods, 107 units dealing with industrial products and 64 units dealing with services were not at all concerned with the problem in the availability of raw materials. With regard to the remaining units, as far as consumer goods units were concerned high price was the prominent bane while units dealing with industrial products were confronted mainly with the non-availability of raw materials in time. The services units were suffering from the problems of non-availability of raw materials in time and high price.

Regarding labour high cost was the most prominent problem

for units located in semi urban centres whereas lack of technical skill was the major bottleneck for units located in urban centres. It is worth mentioning in this regard that neither the region wise classification like south, central and north nor does product wise classification like consumer goods, industrial goods and services make wide variations to this phenomenon. On the problems related to the availability of other inputs needed for production it was responded by most all entrepreneurs that they were facing the lone problem of power cut declared in the state during the summer season.

Capacity utilization: The data collected for the present study revealed that the small scale industrial units were not utilising their installed capacity in full. The average capacity utilisation for the five year period from 1990-91 to 1994-95 was ranging from 60.92 per cent to 78.42 per cent. The location wise analysis confirms the fact that there are only slight variations among units located in rural, semi urban and urban centres with regard to the average capacity utilisation. The region wise data brought about the fact that the units located in southern, central and northern parts of the state had the problems of under utilisation of capacity more or less same extent. This finding was corroborated on cross tabulation of the data by classifying the units under the heads consumer goods, industrial goods and services. The analysis led to the conclusion that the 'difficulties in marketing' was the prominent reason for underutilisation of capacity followed by financial difficulties.

Average value of sales: The average value of annual sales effected by the units covered under the study for a five year period from 1990-91 to 1994-95 were subjected to an analysis. There was an increasing trend with regard to the sales for every year. This tendency had been consistent with regard to the units located in rural, semi urban and urban centres. The price increase might have resulted in the increase of sales and that was how the respondents were commenting upon the increase of sales in monetary terms. The details of average value of annual sales on area wise like south, central and north and product wise like consumer goods, industrial goods and service goods also confirmed the fact that the increase in volume of sales in monetary terms was a general phenomenon. It was felt that the tendency was revealing the inability of the SSI units in taping the potential market in urban centres as well as rural centres.

Area of sales: The details indicated that 43.83 per cent of the SSI units were effecting more than 80 per cent of the sales with in the districts. The location wise analysis also revealed that a good number of units in rural (40.67 per cent), semi urban (52.50 per cent) and urban (36 per cent) areas were effecting sales of more than 80 per cent within the districts. It was also interesting to note that there were units in rural (15 per cent) and semi urban (7 per cent) centres in which case the sales were completely effected outside the districts. In an attempt to establish a relationship between nature of products and sales within the districts, by cross tabulating the data it was noted that 30.67 per cent of the units producing consumer goods, 35.50 per cent of the units producing industrial products and 100 per cent of the services units were marketing more than 80 per cent of their output within the districts. With regard to the products marketed purely outside the districts there were only a very few units producing consumer goods (9 per cent) and industrial products (16 per cent) were observed.

It was observed that 38.50 per cent of the units were disposing of their products/services within the home districts. In regard to the sales outside the home districts but within the state it was noted that there were only 11.17 per cent of the units having the extent of sales over 80 per cent. The market network of all the services units was limited to the home district. The data when cross tabulated the data in respect of the sales outside the districts but within the state, revealed that only 11.67 per cent of the units manufacturing consumer goods and 16 per cent of industrial products could manage more than 80 per cent of their total sales outside the districts. The data clearly indicated the poor performance of the SSI units in exploring the market potential outside the state. Only 36.17 per cent of the units covered under the study were able to capture the market at the national level. The units, which could manage more than 80 per cent of the total sales outside the State, were estimated to be only for 4 per cent. This included 6.5 per cent of the units manufacturing industrial products and 3.67 per cent of the units producing consumer products. The data collected for the present study also brought out the fact that only five percent of the units were engaged in export trade. This included 3.33 per cent of the total units engaged in the manufacture of consumer goods and 10 per cent of the units manufacturing industrial products. From the foregoing analysis on the market network of the SSI units in the state, it was concluded that the SSI sector in the state did not succeed in extending their market network at the national and international level.

Data indicated that the increased demand was the most prominent base for the selection of area of sales followed by scope for increased sales. This phenomenon was common for the units located in rural, semi urban and urban centres. An analysis of the above mentioned responses by cross tabulating the data in accordance with the nature of products once again confirmed that the increased demand was the prominent basis for selection of area of sales for consumer goods, industrial goods and the services followed by the scope of increased sales.

Channel of distribution: It was noted that the units had set up the channel of distribution in a varied manner like by appointing sole agency, appointing wholesalers, distributing direct to the retailers, marketing of the product direct to the consumers, supplying goods direct to the government, supplying to the parent units and selling goods direct to other industrial units. It was noted that the SSI units were making use of the services of the intermediaries for marketing their products/services. Much variation was not observed among the units on the basis of the location like rural, semi urban and urban.

However, the analysis of the same data on the basis of nature of products revealed the details in a different dimension. The units manufacturing industrial products were marketing their products to other industrial units. Of this, 96.50 per cent of the units supplied direct to other industrial units whereas the remaining 3.50 per cent units supplied their products to the parent units. The services units were resorting to three channels namely direct to consumers (52 per cent), parent units (12 per cent) and direct to the other industrial units (36 per cent). The services of the intermediaries were needed only in the case of units manufacturing consumer products. There were units making use of one channel or more than one channel.

The data collected in this regard were cross tabulated with a view to ascertaining the average share of sales in percentages to various groups. The observations in this regard also corroborated with the above mentioned conclusion that the units manufacturing consumer goods were largely making use of the constituents in the channel of distribution. It was noted that 56.67 per cent of the consumer goods were marketed through the intermediaries like distributors, wholesalers and retailers. However, the point that 30.43 per cent of the total sales were effected direct to the consumers requires special mention.

Rate of commission/margin to the intermediaries: The data indicated that majority of small scale industrial units were under the clutches of intermediaries in the sense that the intermediaries were able to secure more than 20 per cent as margin for the goods. It was noted in this connection that in the case of 39 per cent of the units covered under the study the commission/margin charged by the intermediaries was more than 25 per cent. With regard to this aspect, much difference was not observed among the units located in rural, semi urban and urban centres. However, on an analysis on the basis of the nature of products revealed that the intermediaries were taking advantages to the maximum extent from the units manufacturing consumer goods. Services units were absolutely free from the clutches of intermediaries and the units producing industrial products were also being exploited by the middlemen only to a limited extent.

Methods of securing orders: It was noted that 142 units out of 600 units covered under the study were making use of more than one method in canvassing orders. This included 53 units from rural centres 44 units from semi urban centres and 45 units from urban centres. Of the total units making use of more than one method 128 units were relying on two methods six units three methods and eight units four methods. On an analysis of the responses regarding the methods of canvassing orders, it was observed that in majority of the cases the units were forced to approach the intermediates or the consumers for marketing their products/services. This was found to be same with the units located in rural, semi urban and urban centres with slight variations. The units located in rural centres were getting more orders direct from the consumers compared to the units located in other centres. The product wise analysis revealed that, of the 142 units having more than one method for securing orders 98 units were coming under the category of units producing consumer goods and remaining 44 units were engaged in the production of industrial goods. In the case of services units, in 64 per cent cases consumers were directly approached by the units and in the remaining cases consumers placed orders with the units. It was also noted that the units producing consumer goods were having more problems in securing orders.

Problems faced in effecting sales to government departments: The weighted score indicated that the most prominent problem was procedural problems and delayed payment of bills followed by 'exceptionally low price'. It was also noted that the first and second problems cited by the respondents did not vary on the basis of the location of units. The fact that the responses corroborated in respect of a cross tabulation of the data on the basis of nature of products/services also requires special attention. It may be concluded on the basis of these responses that while measures for assisting small units are inevitable, the modus operandi is not best suited to achieve the objectives.

Participation in exhibition/trade fair: One hundred and sixteen units (19.33 per cent) out of 600 units covered under the sample participated in exhibitions and trade fairs. This included 52 units in rural, 43 units in semi urban and 21 units in urban centres. All these units were engaged in the production of consumer goods.

Break up of sales into cash and credit: Considering the merits and demerits of the cash and credit sales it was thought of estimating the break up of cash and credit sales for the units covered under the study. The data presented depicted that a major portion of the sales (60.53 per cent) were effected on credit basis. This was true in regard to the units located in rural, semi urban and urban centres with slight variations. An analysis of the average break up of sales on the basis of nature of products/services brought about the results in a different manner. The consumer goods units were selling 66.20 per cent of the goods on credit and units manufacturing industrial goods were selling 76.75 per cent of the goods on credit basis. However, the service units were able to manage 76 per cent of the sales on cash basis.

Average credit period allowed: It was noted that 99 units out of 600 units covered under the study were not allowing any credit sales. Of the remaining 501 units, 292 units were able to collect the debt either within a fortnight (107) or within one month (185). The remaining units were forced to allow credit for a period ranging from one month to four months. There were no firms allowing credit period for more than four months. Only slight variations were noted on the location of the units and the average collection period. However, the product/service wise analysis revealed that units engaged in the production of consumer goods and industrial goods had to allow more credit period compared to the service units. Only 31 per cent of the service units were able to manage their transactions wholly on cash basis while the other units were able to collect the credit within one month.

Storage facilities: The data collected with a view to ascertaining the storage facilities available to the units covered under the study revealed that all the units were keeping the finished products in their own godowns. None of the SSI units covered under the study was keeping their finished products in the state owned Warehousing Corporations or other private agencies.

Pricing: It was noted that the entrepreneurs were making use of varied methods to fix the price of the products/services. Of the 600 entrepreneurs interviewed for the study 58 were using more than one method. Majority of the entrepreneurs were not aware of the intricacies as well as scientific principles involved in different methods. As such, the merits and demerits of these methods were not well known to many of the entrepreneurs. Nearly one-half of the respondents (46.35 per cent) were explaining their strategy for fixing the price as adding a margin to the unit cost of production. The remaining entrepreneurs were resorting to other methods.

Cost plus pricing was the method adopted by a good number of units producing consumer goods (47.29 per cent), industrial products (46.02 per cent) and services units (44 per cent). It may be concluded from the analysis based on the data furnished and the observations made at the time of interviews that the small scale industrial units in the state were not adopting the methods of pricing in a scientific manner. This was mainly due to the fact that the entrepreneurs did not get reliable data on numerous factors associated with pricing like, cost, demand, competition and so on. The entrepreneurs were also not making use of the methods of costing for ascertaining the cost of production by segregating the total cost into variable cost and fixed cost. A large number of entrepreneurs (84.17 per cent) were of the opinion that the prices quoted by them were reasonable. The units manufacturing industrial goods (90.50 per cent) were more satisfied with the reasonableness of the prices followed by units manufacturing consumer goods and units rendering services (81 per cent each).

Advertisement: It was noted that only 37.83 per cent units were advertising their products. This included 41.33 per cent of the units in rural areas, 28.50 per cent of the units in semi urban areas and 46 per cent units in urban areas. The product wise analysis indicated that 42.33 per cent of the units manufacturing consumer goods, 39 per cent of the units manufacturing industrial products and 22 per cent of the service units were trying to motivate the consumers through advertisements.

In an attempt to ascertain the media selected by the

entrepreneurs interviewed for the study, it was observed that 65.56 per cent of the respondents had resorted to advertising in newspaper and journals. None of the units had given advertisement in television and this might be due to the huge cost involved. Majority of the units manufacturing consumer goods (69.63 per cent), industrial products (49.38 per cent) and services units (50 per cent) were mainly depending upon newspapers, magazines, and journals for advertising their products. Offering complements in the form of key chains, diaries, calendars as media of advertisements popular for industrial products (31.87 per cent) and service units (50 per cent). It was noted that the units located in rural areas had to spend more in advertising their products. There were organisations incurring annual expenditure on advertisement up to Rs. 80,000, whereas there were 373 numbers of units with no expenditure on advertisement. The product wise analysis revealed that the consumer goods had to spend more on advertisement followed by units producing industrial goods.

Branding: Majority of the units (60.83 per cent) covered under the study were not using any brand name. Of the 235 units using brand name 134 units were located in rural areas, 63 units in urban centres and 38 units in semi urban centres. Sixty three per cent of the units located in urban centres were using brand names for their products. Product wise analysis brought about the fact that branding was done more for consumer goods (53.67 per cent) whereas it was only 37 per cent for industrial products. None of the service units was using brands for their services.

Nature of competition: A vast majority of the units (527) covered under the study were facing competition in the market. This included all the units located in urban centres 89 per cent of units located in semi urban centres and 83 per cent of the units located in rural areas. The extent of competition was more in the case of consumer goods (90.67 per cent) followed by the units producing industrial goods (88.50 per cent) and service units (78 per cent). It was tried to ascertain the nature of competition under three heads namely competition from big units, competition from small units and competition from both big and small units. Majority of the units (43.45 per cent) stated that their main competition was from big units followed by competition form within the small units (29.60). There were also units having competition form both big and small units (26.95 per cent). Majority of the units (49 per cent) located in semi urban centres were facing competition from within the small scale sector. The product wise analysis revealed that the units producing consumer goods facing competition from small units (37.13 per cent) whereas the units producing industrial goods were facing competition mainly (60.45 per cent) from large scale units. The findings of the present study corroborated with the findings of the study conducted by Nisar Ahamad in Jammu and Kashmir that small scale and cottage industries of Kashmir were facing keen competition not only from the large scale units but also similar units in other states of the country.

Marketing Research: An attempt was made in the present study to ascertain the views of the entrepreneurs regarding the conduct of marketing research for effective marketing of the product and services. Out of 600 units covered under the study only 61 units carried out marketing research. This included 28 units in rural areas 12 units in semi urban areas and 21 units in urban areas. With regard to the nature of the products it was noted that the units producing consumer goods had taken more advantages from marketing research. It was known from the study, that in most of the cases surveys were carried out among consumers and intermediaries.

Since 89.83 per cent of the total units were not carrying out marketing research, despite its vital importance and usefulness in the industrial and commercial activities, it was felt appropriate to identify the reasons why the marketing research was not thought of. A structured question using the answers 'not needed', 'not known' 'non availability of skilled personnel' and 'insufficiency of funds' was used for the purpose. Not even a single entrepreneur was ready to admit that he was unaware of the uses of marketing research. Majority of the entrepreneurs (74.21 per cent) were of the opinion that it was not needed for their enterprises. Marketing research was not conducted by 22.08 per cent of the units owing to insufficiency of funds.

Product wise analysis revealed that all the service units covered under the study did not think of making research since it was not needed for their units. This argument did not stand valid since the service sector was facing stiff competition subsequent on the emergence of 'new products'. The majority of the units producing consumer goods (55.87 per cent) neglected the need for marketing research simply by stating that it was not needed. However, the argument of the units producing industrial goods (84.38 per cent) could be valid on the ground that they were supplying goods in accordance with the requirements of the industrial units. Thus, the analysis on marketing research led to the conclusion that the small scale industrial units did not realise the importance of marketing research.

Nature of marketing problems: The entrepreneurs were asked to mark five prominent problems faced by them in the order of priority. The responses collected in this regard were subjected to ranking by assigning the weights 5, 4, 3, 2, and 1 respectively for the answers in the priority of 1, 2, 3, 4, and 5. Competition was the most important problem for the small scale industrial sector in the State followed by lack of market information, inadequacy of advertisements, price of the products, and inadequacy of demand. There was not much variation to the general trend between the units located in rural, semi urban and urban centres with regard to the nature of marketing problems. The data when cross tabulated on the basis of nature of products/services also brought out the results in the very same manner. Competition was accounted for as the main problem associated with marketing followed by lack of market information, inadequacy of advertisement, price of the product and inadequacy of demand for the units producing consumer goods and industrial goods as well as service units.

Views of the Consumers: The sample size consisted of 1,500 consumers of which 800 were drawn from rural areas, 450 from semi urban areas and 250 from urban centres. Male respondents constituted 60 per cent and female respondents 40 per cent. Majority (56.87 per cent) of the consumers covered under the study were in the age group of 30- 50 years. Occupation is very important in relation to the purchasing power of consumers. The consumers covered under the study had various occupations like government employment (33.13 per cent), private employment (25.60 per cent), agriculture (21.13 per cent), trade (13.87 per cent) and industry (6.27 per cent). The income of the consumers was also considered for the study because the real purchasing power of the consumers was influenced by the level of income. Majority (65.73 per cent) of the consumers covered under the study were having monthly income below Rs. 4,000. The consumers having a monthly income below Rs. 2,000 were to the extent of 31.20 per cent.

Occasion for bulk purchases: It is customary on the part of the consumers to make bulk purchases during festivals and similar occasions. As far as the state of Kerala is concerned the festivals include Onam, X'Mas, Bakrid, Ramzan, Vishu and Deepavali. It was shown that 94.93 per cent of the consumers covered under the study were effecting bulk purchases of goods during festival season. Onam, which is celebrated by the people of Kerala irrespective of caste, creed and other considerations, is the most prominent occasion in which bulk purchases are being made. There were only 5.07 per cent of the consumers having no preferences on special occasions for effecting bulk purchases. This consisted of 4.75 per cent of the rural respondents, 5.34 per cent of the semi urban respondents and 5.60 per cent of the urban respondents. The data related to the nature of occasions for bulk purchases were cross tabulated on the basis of monthly income. Chi square test also confirmed that monthly income had nothing to do with the bulk purchases during special occasions.

An attempt was also made to identify the reasons for bulk purchases during occasions majority (52.24 per cent) of the consumers covered under the study were of the opinion that wide choice was the main reason for their bulk purchase during festival seasons. It was admitted by 29.99 per cent of the consumers that they were attracted by special discounts and concessions. The very same data when cross tabulated on the basis of monthly income brought out the fact that the respondents from various strata of income were largely attracted by the wide choices during festival seasons. It was also observed that the increase income during festival seasons by way of bonus, exgratia benefits, clearing of debts and receipts of advances also provided inclination to buy more goods during festival seasons.

Influence of advertisement: It was stated by majority of the consumers covered under the study (77.73 per cent) that they were being influenced by advertisement. The only difference was with regard to the level of influence. A few of the consumers (10.13 per cent) admitted that they were highly influenced whereas a good number (43.73 per cent) of consumers were influenced only to a limited extent. The phenomenon in this regard was apparently same for all the categories of residents like rural respondents, semi urban respondents and urban respondents. This similarity was, it was observed, mainly on account of the peculiar position of the state of Kerala well known for its 100 per cent literacy. The data on this account when cross tabulated with the income level of the respondents confirmed the results in the very same manner. In the study an attempt was also made to know the medium of advertisement having greatest influence on consumers. Since the consumers were found to be exposed to more than one media at the time of pilot study it was requested to specify three media in the order of preference by assigning rank numbers 1, 2, and 3. The responses were subjected to weighted scoring assigning the weights 3, 2 and 1 respectively for the answers specified as 1, 2 and 3. Television (44.16 per cent) was emerged as the most powerful medium followed by the newspapers (26.21 per cent) magazines (14.22 per cent) and radio (11.56 per cent). Posters and Banners were found to be influenced by only a small section of the respondents (3.85 per cent). The most interesting observations in this regard were that the level of variations on the influence of various media among the rural, semi urban and urban respondents was insignificant. The data when made related to monthly income also confirmed the findings with slight variations. However, the ranking remained the same.

The data related to the medium of advertisement having greatest influence were cross tabulated on the basis of age structure and occupational status and the results thereon were also the same, indicating television as the most prominent medium followed by newspapers. This led to the conclusion that the products of the SSI sector were being pushed back by the products from big units which could afford to giving advertisements in Television and other costly media.

Preference for buying the products/services: A large number of consumers under the study (45.67 per cent) were purchasing the products and services with the first preference for high quality and branding. This phenomenon was found to be true for the respondents of all the locations like rural, semi urban and urban centres. The data when cross tabulated by considering income and age as independent variable separately it was once again observed that a good number of the respondents irrespective of their level of income and age structure were interested in buying goods and services of high quality and branding. The phenomenon was found to be the same for large number of the consumers covered under the study with occupation like government employment and private employment. The agriculturists (30.60 per cent), traders (37.98 per cent) and industrialists (40.43 per cent) were also found to be interested in goods and services of high quality and brands.

Views on quality of SSI products/services: The responses in this regard were found to be really interesting. A large number of consumers covered under the study from rural areas (41.88 per cent) have viewed the quality of SSI products to be good whereas majority of the consumers from semi urban (46.45 per cent) and urban (41.60 per cent) centres viewed the quality of the SSI products to be bad. It was further observed that majority of the consumers (39.96 per cent) having low income were of the view that the quality of SSI products was good. Majority of the consumers (26.44 per cent) in the higher income strata viewed the quality to be bad. This difference on the observation of the quality of SSI products was noted on a cross tabulation of the same data occupation wise. A good number of the agriculturists (34.07 per cent), Traders (47.12 per cent) and government employees (47.69 per cent) viewed the quality of SSI products/services to be bad while industrialists (46.81 per cent) and private employees (39.84 per cent) were of the opinion that the SSI products were acceptable to them from the point of view of quality. From the foregoing analysis it was quite evident that the measures for the standardisation of the SSI products was inevitable for attracting the consumers with varied interest and tastes.

Views on price: A large number of consumers viewed that the prices of the products and services of SSI sector were either high (47.60 per cent) or very high (20.33 per cent). The observation of the consumers was of the same nature for the rural and semi urban people. But 34.80 per cent of the urban people viewed price as very high while 30.40 per cent viewed it as high. The data when cross tabulated on the basis of the monthly income of the respondents also brought out the results in the very same manner with the observation of majority of respondents from all income levels that the prices were either high (47.60 per cent) or very high (20.33 per cent). Occupation wise analysis also led to the conclusion that products and services were marked with high prices.

Views on finish/appearance: Finish of the products is highly favoured as a success strategy for the manufacturing and services units. On an enquiry with the consumers covered under the sample it was made known by the majority (30.67 per cent) that they viewed the finish/appearance of products/services from small scale sector as moderate. This phenomenon was found applicable for all categories of consumers like rural (27 per cent), semi urban (39.11 per cent) and urban (63.20 per cent). Income wise analysis also brought out the results in a similar manner.

Views on availability: Majority of the respondents were of the opinion that the SSI products were either easily available

(20.80 per cent) or moderately available (37.53 per cent). The location wise analysis revealed the fact that the SSI products were easily or moderately available in all the centres. However, a good number of the respondents (25.87 per cent) were observing scarcity with the availability of SSI products/services. Income wise, age wise and occupation wise analysis did not show any difference on the view with regard to the availability of products/services.

Views on packaging: The consumers were asked to indicate their views on the packages of SSI products. It was stated by majority of them that the packages of SSI products was poor appealing. This was the view of majority of consumers from rural, semi urban, and urban centres. The views when cross tabulated depicted the above mentioned information in the same way irrespective of the level of income, age structure, and occupation. The analysis on the packaging led to the conclusion that the effective selling of the SSI products was largely hindered by unattractive packaging.

Views on variety: The data related to the views of the consumers covered under the study on the availability of variety of products and services from the SSI units. Majority of them opined that the SSI sector was successful in providing variety of products and services. This view was endorsed by majority of the consumers irrespective of their place of residence level of income, age structure, and occupation.

Frequency in buying SSI products/services: It was against this observation that the consumers were asked to state the frequency of buying the goods/services made available by the SSI sector. It was stated by majority of them that they were exercising the option of buying goods and services of the SSI products (19 per cent) who insisted to have the products/services of SSI products always. This view was endorsed by majority of the consumers irrespective of location, level of income, age structure and occupation.

Sources of availability of SSI products/services: The data related to the sources of the consumers covered under the study for buying the products were collected with a view to ascertaining the prominence of the intermediaries. It was noted that the products of the SSI sector were marketed to the ultimate users largely by the retailers. Trade fairs and exhibitions were also contributing a lot in marketing the SSI products. Only slight variations were noted among the consumers with regard to their view on the basis of their place of residence, level of income, age structure and occupation.

Area requiring attention in boosting sales: The consumers were given the choice of indicating five in the order of preference from among the nine factors included in the questionnaire based on the data collected through pilot study. Nine factors provided in the questionnaire were quality, price, advertisement, colour, design, availability, salesmanship, discount and variety. The responses were subjected to weighted scoring by assigning the weights 5, 4, 3, 2 and 1 respectively for factors indicated in the order of preferences as 1,2,3,4 and 5. Data indicated that quality considerations (27.20 per cent) should be the first factor that required utmost consideration by the SSI sector followed by price (16.36 per cent), advertisement (15.60 per cent) availability (15.38 per cent) and variety (8.30 per cent) in that order. Only slight variations were noted on the views when cross tabulated by taking place of residence, monthly income, age structure and occupation as independent variables.

Recommendations

Based on the findings of the present study, it is proposed that the following measures be considered for the revamping of small scale sector.

From the manufactures' point of view the success of their marketing strategy depends on the closeness with which it is related to the needs and linking of their target group of customers. For, it has to be a manufacturer's endeavour not only to attract the public by offering what they like the most but also to have their patronage by meeting their satisfaction on a continuous basis. The clue to such a strategy lies in their extent of understanding various forces that influence consumers' decision making and behaviour. The present study has attempted to examine some of the important dimensions of consumer behaviour relating to the purchase and consumption.

The government and the industrial promotion agencies under the government control should take greater interest in marketing the products of small scale industrial units. The main problem faced by them in the area of marketing is the competition from big units. The requirements of government departments, wherever possible, should be met from the products and services of SSI units.

Through show room display and publicity during festival seasons, the marketing of products developed by SSI units can be strengthened. In addition, the state government can set up a Marketing Corporation with autonomous status to procure the products of SSI units at reasonable intervals and market them in an organised manner through its sales depots to be located within and outside the state. The strategy and weaknesses of the important attributes affecting the product/brand choice as revealed by the study may be used as an index for an improvement in the marketing strategy of SSI products by the marketers. The Corporation would be able to market the products under a common brand name. So far as the distribution set up is concerned, it may be worth examining that the Corporation could dispense with the extra middlemen. This needs to be examined in the light of the findings of the present study that majority of the consumers preferred to buy standardised products. This would also enable them to meet the other expectations relating to reliability of the sellers.

With the reduction in the number of unwanted intermediaries, their contacts will become more direct, thereby improving manufacturer dealer relationship and ultimately, the consumers' satisfaction. The maintenance of good manufacturer dealer relationship would also warrant that the manufacturers should understand the needs and expectations of the dealers, and develop and motivate them to carry out the tasks required effectively.

Dealer training programmes, dealers' conferences and special promotional programmes offered to carry out the tasks required effectively. Training programmes, conferences and special promotional programmes can also be arranged effecting. To strengthen the marketability of products of SSI industrial units, the Marketing Corporation can draw the services of professionally qualified persons who have the aptitude for industrial development, and dedication to the cause. The Corporation can also carry out marketing research. New product requirements of the market should be traced and such information should be imparted to the small industrialists through orientation and training programmes.

At present, only a negligible portion of the products of the SSI units is exported. Export potential is to be ascertained through the active involvement and encouragement of the government. If viable demand in foreign markets is traced out, the SSI units can make use of their full production capacity. The formation of marketing consortium at the regional level for different types of industries may also contribute a lot in promoting marketing of the products of SSI units. Such consortium should be entrusted with the task of pooling the products of the SSI sector, ensuring the quality of the products and popularising the products among the consumers. Inadequacy of funds and lack of expertise are the major problems that hinder the SSI units from undertaking marketing research of their own. The SIDCO and other agencies responsible for the promotion of SSI units should take the initiative to conduct marketing research and to provide the SSI units with the relevant information which would be required for changing the production pattern and marketing strategies. The prospective entrepreneurs can also be properly guided under such an arrangement. In addition to this comprehensive industrial potential studies and market surveys be undertaken by the Directorate of Industries and Commerce, Government of Kerala to identify the possible products, feasibilities and market possibilities. Such a survey may also keep in mind the level of technology required, whether the products are fast moving or slow moving. In order to improve the marketing channels, a constant counseling service may be organised to meet the special needs of small units in different districts.

Advertising in one form or other has emerged as the major source of information used by the consumers. The only other source that got a good rating was the displays at the retail stores. Advertising has to rise above from being just a source of information and this means that the advertisement contents and appeals used need more thinking. Likewise, the existing advertising media mix used, need to be reexamined in terms of it's reach as well as the credibility associated to it by the decision maker for such products. While radio and television commercials would continue to play their important role, with the increase in literacy of the state the vernacular press along with others ought to be experienced with. Needless to mention, the marketers and their marketing agencies should undertake detailed studies on attitudes and motivations of the consumers, and develop consumer profiles in order to carry out changes in their marketing and advertising programmes.

The present packaging need also to be reviewed in view if the desires expressed by the consumers giving emphasis to the factors like, economical and convenient to handle packages, development of new package sizes, and more information on the packages. The desire of the consumers for the package to contain information on aspects such as the expiry date, ingredients used in the product, maximum retail price including taxes, directions regarding storage and handling of the product should be given top priority.

Fast changing attitudes of people towards different products and purchase factors, as brought out by the present study, necessitate that marketers should remain in touch with the preferences, motivations, expectations, attitudes, perceptions and opinions of the consumers. It may not be sufficient for the marketers to cater to the changing wants and preferences of the consumers or to content with the changed policies of the competitors. Instead, they should act judiciously, which requires that they must plan. The marketing plans must be based on identifying and anticipating the consumer needs and their changing desires and aspirations. Research in consumer behaviour should, thus, be carried out on a continuous basis by the marketers to keep them in the forefront, thereby improving the productivity of their marketing efforts. Consumer behaviour has always a scope for research studies, because the attitudes and perceptions of consumers are changing with the passage of time. Such type of consumer research will enable the manufactures, distributors and dealers to formulate effective sales and advertising strategies.

References

Ambili Kumar, V., Working of Small Scale Industries in Kerala with Reference to Trivandrum District, Ph.D. Thesis (Unpublished), University of Kerala, Trivandrum, 1989.

Baishya Prabin, Small and Cottage Industries - A Study in Assam, Manas Publications, Delhi, 1989.

Bala Shashi, Management of Small Scale Industries, Deep and Deep Publications, New Delhi, 1984.

Bannock Graham, The Economics of Small Firms, Oxford, Basil Black Well, 1981.

Barry, M.Richman, and Melvyn, R.Copen, International Management and Economic Development, Tata Mc Graw Hill Publishing Company, Bombay, 1972.

Borooah, H.N., Prospects and Problems of Small Scale Industries in Lakshimpur District, Gauhati University, Gauhati, 1980.

Chander Subhash and Hardeep Singh, 'Awareness of Government Marketing Assistance Schemes Amongst the Small Textile Units of Amritsar: A Study', SEDME, Vol. XX(1), National Institute of Small Industry Extension Training, Hyderabad, March 1993.

Committee on Public undertakings, 88th Report National Small Industries Corporation Ltd., Government of India, 1983-84.

Dagli, Vadilal (ed.), Decentralised Development - A Symposium, Vaikunthabai Metha Smaraka Trust, Bombay, 1969.

Development Commissioner, Small Scale Industries, Interim Report of Working Group on Marketing the Assistance to Small Scale Industries (Mimeographed), Ministry of Industry, Government of India, New Delhi, 1977.

Dhar, P.N., Small Scale Industries in Delhi: A Study in Investment Output and Employment Aspect, Asia Publishing House, Bombay,

1958.

Government of India, Report of Japanese Delegation on Small Scale Industries, Ministry of Commerce and Industry, New Delhi, 1959.

Government of India, Report of Working Group on Fifth Five Year Plan for Small Scale Industries, Development Commissioner, Small Scale Industries, Ministry of Industry, Government of India, New Delhi, 1974.

Government of India, Small Scale Industries, Development Commissioner, Small Scale Industries, National Printing Press, New Delhi, 1971.

Gupta, M.C., Entrepreneurship in Small Scale Industries, Anmol Publications, New Delhi, 1987.

International Labour Organisation, Small Scale Engineering Industries in the Punjab: Economic and Labour Conditions, International Labour Office India Branch, New Delhi, 1961.

Jain, O.P., Small Industry Exports, S. Chand and Company Private Ltd., New Delhi, 1971.

Lakdawala, D.T., and Sandesara, J.C., Small Industry in Big City: A Survey in Bombay, Bombay University Press, Bombay, 1960.

Munshi, N.M., 'Marketing Strategies and Practices in the Units of Small Scale Industries of Saurashtra Region (Gujarat State)', The Indian Journal of Commerce, Vol. XLI, Part I, No. 154, January - March 1988.

Nagaraj, A.V., and Srinivasan, E.S., 'Problems of Sick Units in India', Seminar on Rehabilitation of Sick Industry in Small Scale Sector - Background Papers, Directorate of Industries, Andhra Pradesh, Hyderabad, 1977 (memo).

National Council of Applied Economic Research (NCAER), Study of Selected Small Scale Industrial Units, NCAER, New Delhi, 1972.

National Council of Educational Research and Training, New Perspective in Marketing, Cambridge Printing Works, New Delhi, 1972.

Neelamegham, S.,(ed.), Marketing in India Cases and Readings, Sharma, A.p., 'Marketing Problems of Small Scale Industries', Vikas Publishing House Private Ltd., New Delhi, 1988.

Nizar Ahamad, Problems and Management of Small Scale and Cottage Industries, Deep and Deep Publications, New Delhi, 1974.

Oommmen, M.A., Small Scale Industry in India Economic Growth - A Case Study of Kerala, Research Publications in Social Sciences, New Delhi, 1967.

Padolecchia, Siro, P., Marketing in the Developing World, Vikas Publishing House Private Ltd., New Delhi, 1979.

Patra, S.C., Promotion and Management of Small Scale Industries, Discovery Publishing House, New Delhi, 1993.

Punjab Industrial Consultancy Organisation and the Administrative Staff College of India, Hyderabad, Market Survey of Industrial Products of Punjab, Vol. II, Directorate of Industries Punjab, 1978 (memo graphed).

Ramakrishna, K.T., Finance for Small Scale Industry in India, Asia Publishing House, Bombay, 1962.

Reddy, R. Jaya Prakash, Problems and Development of Small Scale Industries in India, Ashish Publishing House, New Delhi, 1991.

Reddy, T.S. and Venugopal Reddy, L.V. (eds.), Sickness in Small Industry, Himalaya Publishing House, Bombay, 1988.

Report of the Working Group, Small Scale industries: Programmes of Work for the Third Five Year Plan, Ministry of Commerce and Industry, Government of India, New Delhi, 1970.

Resia Beegam, S., A Study on the Problems of Women Entrepreneurs in Kerala, Ph.D. Thesis (Unpublished), University of Kerala, Thiruvananthapuram, 1993.

Seminar Report, 'Fostering Small industries', Eastern Economists, Vol. 61, No.8, August 1973.

Sharma, Krishanlal, Entrepreneurial Performance in Role Perspective, Abhinas Publications, Delhi, 1975.

Shetty, M.C., Small Scale and Household Industries in a Developing Economy, Asia Publishing House, Bombay, 1964.

Singh Baljit, The Economics of Small Scale Industries: A Case Study of Small Scale Industrial Establishments of Moradabad, Asia Publishing House, Bombay, 1961.

Singh, Nau Nihal, Scientific Management of Small Scale Industries, Lalvani Publishing House, Bombay, 1970.

Small Industries Extension Training Institute, Identification of Product Opportunities in Kerala: A Market Study, Small Industries Extension Training Institute, Hyderabad, 1979.

Small Industries Extension Training Institute, New Industrial Possibilities in Malappuram (Kerala), Small Industries Extension Training Institute, Hyderabad, 1978.

State Bank of India, Economic and Statistical Research Department, Survey Potential for Financing Small Scale Industries - Varanasi Centre (Part I), State Bank of India, Bombay, 1968.

Taleyarkhan Homi, J.H., 'Problems of Small Scale Industries', Southern Economist, Vol. 32, No. 11, Southern Economist Pvt. Ltd., Bangalore, October 1993.

Tewari Vinod, K., Joseph Philip and Amar Nath Pandey, Small Scale Industry Success and Failure, Concept Publishing Company, New Delhi, 1991.

The International Planning Team, The Ford Foundation, Report on Small Industries in India, Government of India, New Delhi, 1954.

Thomas T. Thomas, 'Marketing for Small Industries - A Rethinking', Vyavasayakeralam, Vol. 5, No. 16, Directorate of Industries and Commerce, Thiruvananthapuram, May 1992.

UNESCO Research Centre of Social and Economic Development in South Asia, Social Aspects of Small Industries in India, United India Press, New Delhi, 1962.

Wa nchoo, N.N., 'Standardisation and Quality Control - Aid to Marketing', Indian Journal of Marketing, Associated Management Consultants Pvt. Ltd., New Delhi, June 1968.

9

Village Industries: Problems and Prospects

P. C. Thomas

India, the second largest country in the matter of population, has changed from the situation of importing food grains in the fifties and sixties to a position of self- sufficiency and maintains a sizeable buffer stock. The seven five year plans India has completed have brought in welcome changes in the economic scene of the country. Her agricultural sector shows a marked growth. The Industrial sector has also made great achievements. Today India ranks among the first fifteen of the industrially developed countries. Her position till 1947, when she took over her future in her own hands, had been one of dependence on foreign countries for almost every consumer item from safety pins to fountain pens.

Still India considers the fight against poverty and under development as her prime task. She has to accelerate her social and economic development. In order to accelerate growth she cannot depend on foreign assistance as she is already overburdened. Though the governments frequently change, all the governments consider alleviation of poverty as the main task before them. In spite of all the achievements made through the seven five year plans India has the largest number of poor people in the world. India is the poorest among the 125 countries having a population of more than 10 million. More than 50 percent other people are still below the poverty line. In the process of formulation of the eighth five-year plan emphasis is being laid on he removal of poverty, expansion of opportunities for productive employment and meeting the basic needs of the people. For this a new growth centered scheme to accelerate the pace of industrial development in the backward areas is envisaged.

The development of India should mean the increase in the standard of living of the 76.29 per cent of the people living in the 2 lakh villages of India where proper infrastructure for development is not yet available. The advancement of the industrial sector does not reduce the dependence of India on village and small scale industries, it rather looks more up on the village industries for a solution to the teeming problems of increased rural unemployment and increasing demand for consumer goods. Increasing rate of urbanisation is a threat to India's development. When her urban population in 1981 was only 24 per cent of the total population by the year 2000 A.D., it is expected to be 31 per cent. Development of the villages is very essential to restrict the flow of rural folk into the urban centers.

The situation of Kerala also is not different. The density of population in Kerala is one of the highest in the whole world. Her per capita cultivated land holding is the lowest in India. The dependency rate in Kerala is the highest in India. She is deficient in important minerals that are essential for the development of large scale industries. Kerala has always looked upon the village and small scale industries sector for her development. Thus she is rightly called 'a State of Small Scale Industries'. She has no way out but to depend on the village and small scale industrial sector for her development. Nearly 85 per cent of the workers belong to the unorganised industrial sector. But within the unorgainsed sector about two-third wage earning workers are having no ownership means of production. Workers in the unorganised sector face problems of under-employment, low-income, lack of education, organisation and job security.

The number of persons registered with the various employment exchanges in the State has increased from 1.34 lakh in 1959 to 31 lakh in 1989. But the number of placements is only twelve thousand during the year 1987 whereas the number of registrants has been increasing by 1.5 lakh every year. Kerala's urban population is expected to increase from 4.8 million in 1981 to 6.6 million in 1991 and to about 9 million in 2001. The average addition to urban population of 0.2 million per year during the eighth five year plan period. The overall population density of 655 persons per sq. km in 1981 will shoot up to a figure of 875 per sq. km. in 2001.

Statement of the Problem

All governmental efforts have been made from the beginning for the upliftment of the village industries sector. The Government of Kerala constituted a statutory body namely the Kerala Khadi and Village Industries Board (KVIB) in August 1957 to organise, develop and regulate Khadi and Village Industries. In spite of all the organised attempts Khadi and Village Industries could not make any remarkable contribution in raising the income of the rural folk. There is a complaint that KVIC or KVIB has not succeeded in identifying and encouraging potential entrepreneurial talents in the rural sector. Prospective entrepreneurs complain of the lack of sufficient infrastructure and encouragements to make use of their abilities. The existing village industrialists are gripped with the problem of marketing, inadequacy of finance, non-availability of raw materials, lack of managerial and technical knowledge. The mortality rate among the village industries is very high.

Review of Literature

Several studies have been undertaken on the working of village industrial units at the national level. A brief review of such important studies is made here. Even though the post war India has laid due emphasis on the Khadi and Village Industries sector, especially under the leadership of Mahatma Gandhi, the Father of Independent India, enough research has not been done in this field. An organised and systematic attempt in this aspect was initiated by the National Planning Committee appointed in 1938. The Sub-Committee on Rural and Cottage Industries appointed by the National Planning Commission made an elaborate study on the various aspects. It made a survey of the conditions of cottage and village Industries. It also considered the problems of marketing, financing, competition, quality, protection, pricing, taxation etc. In addition, it studied the work and wages in this sector. Another study in this area was done by the United Provinces Cottage Industries Sub-Committee. This Committee studied the influence of Second World War on Cottage and Small Factory Industries in United Provinces. It also attempted to see the extent to which these Industries can be complementary to large-scale industry, and the application possibility of the co-operative principle in this sector. Further, the technical improvement possibilities with particular reference to power were considered. The Planning Commission of the Independent India appointed a Committee in 1955 popularly known as the Karve Committee, to evaluate the village and small scale industries projects of the First Five Year Plan and to prepare an effective programme for the utilisation of the resources for these industries projected in the Second Five Year Plan.

The Village Industries Evaluation Committee, appointed by the Ministry of Commerce and Industry, made an exclusive study of the Village Industries sector. This Committee made a State by State assessment of the progress of the village industries programme under the Khadi and Village Industries Commission, especially during the first three years of the Second Five Year Plan. Though the study laid emphasis on the evaluation of the organisational part with the intention of drafting a more effective Third Five Year Plan, it made a study on all the aspects. The study revealed that the technical research so far undertaken in the area has not been extended to the evolution of tools and implements helpful to raise productivity. The Committee also stressed the need for cheap implements, which the poor village artisan can afford. The Committee also stressed the need for an assured regular supply of raw materials at reasonable prices and fairly secure markets for the product of village industries at prices that will give a fair rate of return. A study was conducted by Basu S.K. on the financial problems of small scale industries that fall within the purview of the Indian Factories Act. This study is an appraisal of the financial problems, especially the role of State Financial Corporations.

The Seminar conducted by the Reserve Bank of India on 'Financing of Small Scale Industries in India' went deep into the problems of small scale industries, the institutional set up, role of government in assisting small industries, the resources of credit institutions and miscellaneous issues. The Seminar identified that: the various information agencies should improve the quality and increase the quantity of information made available; arrangements for regular supply of raw materials needed; not only industrial estates are needed but also marked out industrial areas where adequate electric power is supplied; marketing difficulty is not one of inadequacy of demand, rather delay in payment; need for a change in the attitude of lenders and borrowers; Government assistance should be mainly non-financial, with regard to finance Government's role should be supplementary in nature; more facilities needed in the sphere of management training as well as in matters such as training in the maintenance of accounts and the Government may supply part of the equity if the small entrepreneurs organise themselves into industrial co-operatives.

Dhar P.N. and Lydall H.F. made a notable study of the modern small scale industries. In their book 'The Role of Small Enterprises in Indian Economic Development' they have critically evaluated the various arguments usually advanced in support of small industries. In their assessment of the technical and financial assistance attempted by various institutional agencies, they criticise the policy of creation of smal! units for their own sake. They suggested that the policy should be aimed at the improvement in the efficiency of existing enterprises and the creation of opportunities for enterprising new firms to be successful and to grow. Instead of giving protection, measures to remove disabilities of small firms, and to give them a fair chance to compete in the market, must be pursued. Balakrishnan G. made a study on the financial experiences of small firms under two classifications, that is, with paid-up capital of not more than Rs. 5 lakh, called small companies, and those exceeding Rs. 5 lakh, called large companies, during the period 1950-1952. Another study on the financial aspect of the small scale industrial sector was made by Ramakrishna K. T. This study was limited to the industries coming within the purview of the Small Scale Industries Board. When the governmental and institutional finances were taken for study here the other non- institutional agencies in the sector like the money lenders and indigenous bankers were excluded. The role of the small scale industries in the industrialisation of India and the part played by the Government in assisting and encouraging these industries are evaluated by Umamaheswara Rao in the study small scale industries. He studied not only the policies but also various problems faced by the small-scale industries.

The National Planning Commission in 1962 constituted a high level Rural Industries Planning Committee. The Committee was to review the progress of rural industries. It was also to chalk out programmes for the Intensive development of village and small scale industries in rural areas. The International Perspective Planning Team in their study of the development of small-scale industries found that raw material availability was problem for small scale industries and their under-utilisation of capacity was mainly due to scarcity of labour. The study also enquired into the working of Central and State small-scale industries developmental organisations. The Government of Kerala appointed a Committee to study the organisational and functional aspects of Khadi and Village Industries in Kerala. It enquired into the organisational and technical deficiencies that hindered the targets set for this sector. It also tried to identify the various steps to be taken to overcome these deficiencies and to assess the technical, personnel, finance, workshop, training etc. required for the achievement of targets. The raw material procurement and marketing of finished products were also dealt with. The Committee suggested the exemption of village industries products from the levy of Sales Tax. The Committee went into the details of each industry under the State Khadi and Village Industries Board.

Lakshman T.K. made a study of the cottage and small scale industries in Mysore. It was a case study of the pattern of these industries and their role in the context of a developing economy. It studied 15 cottage and small scale industries in Mysore. Though he had covered 1080 units under these industries he did not attempt a study of all the problems facing these industries. The study was intended to understand the structural pattern, problems and development of cottage and small scale industries and their importance in the future set up of a developing economy. In the study it was found that the non-availability of required quality and quantity of raw material at low prices had considerably affected the quality and size of the output. The study also observed that the crude, obsolete and inferior production technique followed in this sector was due to illiteracy and to the industrialist's attitude to stick on to traditional methods. The low quality and lack of standardisation of products resulted in low prices and limited marketability. The low standard of the product was due to obsolete equipments, inferior technique and low quality of raw material used. Shortage of finance and lack of credit facility were also a problem to the cottage and small scale industralists of Mysore. Ninety per cent of the industralists borrowed both for fixed capital and working capital.

With regard to marketing, the role of middlemen was significant. The demand for the products was seasonal and limited to locality as the products were unstandardised. Competition from within and from organised sector was there. Several prices prevailed in the market. The study also revealed that the labourers in 90 per cent of the units were illiterate and their skill was hereditary. They were ignorant of modern techniques and of operating improved equipments. Seasonal variations in employment were there. No social security measures were there for the workers in the sector.

A symposium held in the name of the late Valkunthbai Metha, the man after Mahatma Gandhl with the idea of the Kliadi and Village Industries discussed in detail the various problems in the small scale sector, especially the Khadi and village Industries sector. The symposium resolved that finance was an important handicap. Both the State-owned and commercial agencies catered inadequately to the requirements of the village industries. Adequate storage facility, both for raw materials and finished products, was to be taken care of. With regard to marketing, wider outlets must be planned which will enable the small scale sector to compete with the large scale sector. It stressed the need for quality control and organised marketing structure. More improved facilities are required in the field of communication, supply and storage. It pointed out the need for the development of potential growth centres, that is, small towns, which will serve as a link between rural areas and metropolitan towns. There is dearth of the right type of personnel in this area. Government should be urged to provide the required technical guidance and training facilities.

The Symposium also suggested that the Government should evolve a Common Production Programme, reserving certain items exclusively for the small scale sector. Nau Nihal Singh made a comparison between the management problems of the Indian small scale industries and those of the various other countries he had visited and studied. The study threw light on the shortcomings in the management of small-scale industries in India and suggested ways for management development. Jain O.P's book Small Scale Industry Exports - A Study into Promotional Techniques made a study of the problems faced by the small scale industries of some countries with regard to export. It also examined areas where these industrial units require institutional assistance for exporting their products. It also brought to light the various measures taken by different countries for the promotion of small industry exports.

A study of the small industry development programme of Kerala was made in 1967 by Oommen M.A. It made an evaluation of the small-scale industry development programmes and examined how far the various objectives of the small-scale industry laid down in the Five Year Plans could be achieved. It went deep into the employment creation and entrepreneurial resources mobilisation aspects. The developmental programmes that were taken up for study were the modernisation of the techniques of production of the major traditional Industries of Kerala, namely, coir and handloom; the industrial estates; the rural industries project; and the special programmes of assistance covering the modern small-scale industries, namely, finance, marketing and services. With regard to modernisation of the traditional techniques, capital-intensive techniques are found more effective from growth perspective. The study also mentions that economically viable techniques generating high rates of surplus may be resorted to and that the resultant unemployment would vanish with the expansion of the industry.

Regarding the industrial estates programme, the failure was attributed to bad planning, lack of assessment of potential resources available, the failure to assess carefully the economic viability and engineering feasibility of estates before they are started. The rural industries project, that had just been started, then had a comparatively lower capital-net income ratio than that of the industrial estates. But the value added per worker was lower than that in the industrial estates. Compared to the industrial estates programme, local resources were utilised to a greater extent in the rural industries. The promotion of skill-based industries was very few and the training programmes, as they were not related to the prospective local demand for skills, did not serve the purpose. With regard to financial assistance, the Government as a financial agency was not very successful. The credit provided was not adequate. There was maldistribution and misdirection of finance. There was no effective supervision of the utilisation of credit. There was not much marketing assistance programme. The need for orientation in favour of goods based on local resources and skills was felt. The agencies to provide knowledge of better techniques and management could not make a major impact. This was due to the lack of adequate technical personnel research facilities and follow-up action. Service extension centers must be located in areas where industries were concentrated. The various training programmes for workers and managers did not help much to improve the productivity. When the industrial estates programme could not make a great headway in fostering latent entrepreneurship, the rural industries projects were successful to a great extent in this regard.

A study was made in 1970 to find out the role of commercial banks in financing small artisans and small scale industries operating in Srinagar. This study, made under the auspices of Banking Commission, was intended to find out the part played by banks and the responsiveness of the small scale units to bank finance. It was also to project the prospects of bank finance in Jammu and Kashmir State in particular and the country in general. The Entrepreneurial Manager in the Small Scale Business, written by William Naumes, is a work aimed at improving the skills of the entrepreneur. Case study method is being resorted to in order to provide practice to potential entrepreneurs in evaluating and solving problems they are likely to face. The management of all the aspects of the small firm is considered. The functional problems like finance, marketing, production and operations are also discussed.

A collective research study, sponsored by the Association of Development Research and Training Institutes of Asia and the Pacific and funded by the International Development Research Centre, Canada, was made to understand the problems of small enterprises in the developing countries. The functioning of the various institutions of these countries, their success and adequacy of these programmes were assessed. When each of the countries evaluates its own performance in this area, each can benefit by learning from the experiences of other countries. The teams assigned to study each country's set-up tried to find out the various sources of entrepreneurial talent and the means to augment it. The functioning of existing supportive organisations, adequacy of existing programmes to stimulate, support and sustain small enterprises, entrepreneurial profile to identify potential entrepreneurs and the comprehensiveness of existing policies. The various teams found that in almost all the countries the policy regarding small industries suffered from lack of integration, organisation and exclusiveness.

Lack of co-ordination among the various organisations to promote small industries was a common feature. Finance was a problem for all these countries. In most of the countries programmes relating to marketing are neglected. Various steps need to be taken by the concerned organisations to ensure quality control of the products, to meet the problems of supply, and create markets etc. The need for collective marketing-cum-input supply centres was recognised. The study also suggested the need for comprehensive industrial potential studies and market surveys to identify the possible products feasibilities, market possibilities etc. This also helps to find out the level of technology required and whether the products are fast moving or slow moving. The need to organise publicity programmes, training programmes and information services was also emphasised. The study observed that there were only very few institutions to provide direct assistance to individual enterprises for technological improvement or to resolve their day-to-day technical problems. The various promotional organisations sponsored by Governments suffered from a culture of bureaucratic life and often had revenue motive. Another point of observation was that it was not necessary for the small scale entrepreneurs to be highly educated.

Mathur S.P. made a study of the entire economic aspect of small scale industries in Agra region. The study critically evaluated the ills which prevented the smooth growth of the small scale sector. The State Policy was analysed and the factors responsible for improper utilisation of raw-materials, man-power and capital resources were brought to light. The promotional aspect of the industry also was considered. The study pointed out the need for a simplified aid pattern, that is, all the assistances under-one-roof. For the growth of small industry, entrepreneurs must be given training in the better-run units. Co-operative sector should be encouraged to take advantage of available facilities. Non-availability of good quality raw-materials inadequate quantities at competitive prices was a problem. False quota holders were the chief cause of raw material scarcity. A single development agency to process all raw material aid to the industry and local depots to stock raw materials would considerably improve the situation. Promotional agencies to provide services at reasonable payments are needed. There is the need to choose suitable product and appropriate technology. Finding adequate fixed and working capital is the greatest problem in the growth of small scale industries. Mathur also considered a powerful marketing organisation to promote sales in the country and abroad necessary Trade Centres are to be established. There should be testing and research laboratory too.

When Papola T.S. examined the non-traditional approach to rural industrialisation he also provided a framework for assessing the role and potential of different industries in the development of rural areas and industrial development of the Country. His study revealed that the modern small scale industries are more effective than traditional ones. The modern-small industries are able to reduce caste- industry bindings. The traditional industries are low-income generating. Papola recommends concentration only on those industries that have a positive income elasticity of demand and the use of appropriate technology is stressed. The household units should have a co-operative basis. Protected markets and increased productivity are also important. Vasant Desai made a study of the problems of small-scale industries, especially, the problems from organisation to management. He throws light on the spreading sickness among small-scale industries. The industrial estates programme, district industries centres and export are also studied in detail. An attempt has been made to find a solution to various problems and to offer a strategy for the eighties.

The study noted that the protection policy followed by the government has only helped to weaken the structure. Modern technology and professional management can make possible a rapid development in the small scale industrial sector. The small scale industries, he suggested, should plan export and diversification. He examined both internal and external problems. Ràm K.Vepa, in his book, Small Industry - The Challenge of the Eighties deals with the important features - credit, technology, marketing and development of backward areas of Indian programmes, and describes similar programmes in other developing countries as well as in the developed countries of the West.

The National Bank for Agriculture and Rural Development (NABARD) appointed a task force in 1983 to suggest ways to improve the role of commercial banks in the Khadi and Village industries sector. It made an assessment of the various types of industries and the best means for credit delivery system, to identify the industries that can be financed by banks, to examine the need for a cover organisation for raw material supplies, marketing, credit and technology and to examine the feasibility of inducing cluster/group approach, establishment of mini rural industries centres etc. The study revealed that the inadequate supply of industrial finance by co-operative banks to the industrial co-operative societies is due to the unsatisfactory working of the co-operative societies. The team suggested that the State Governments should provide the services of paid secretaries, which most of the societies cannot otherwise afford. The study also noted the absence of marketing organisations to link the village industries producers with the markets. For this the need for an organisation at the district level, registered under the State Co-operative Societies Act was suggested. An Apex Marketing Society at the State Level was also recommended. Sales possibility through outlets other than Khadi and village industries outlets is to be explored.

The work on Management of Small Scale Industries by Shashi Bala is a study of the problems, Government policy and assistance and management of small scale industries. The research study was conducted in the Ludhiana district in the Punjab State. The study observed that the smaller the size of the unit, the lesser was its ability to borrow from institutional sources. Traders are an important source among non-institutional sources of credit. In the marketing field, the wholesaler is the main purchaser. This is due to the lack of proper organisation for sales, inability to keep capital locked in unsold products and the greater pressure for liquidity. A seminar was held Jointly by the National Productivity Council (NPC) and the United Nations Children's Fund (UNICEF) in 1985 on the village and small scale industries sector of the Indian economy. The seminar resolved that there is need for market information and technology upgradation. Technology development should not be limited to production process. It should cover packaging, quality, design, transport etc. Production of quality goods with available technology was emphasised. The Seminar brought out the need for an intermediary to provide a link between financial institutions and artisans. The need to improve the artisans' skill and motivational factors was also emphasised. Commercial banks, it was suggested, should reach up to the doorstep of the artisans. There was urgent need for the creation of more infrastructural facilities in the form of godowns, workshop and retail out- let network etc.

A probe into the organisational requirements of village and small scale Industries was made by Mishra S. N. and Kushal Sharma. From which khadi and handloom sectors were excluded. This study was made in the Alwar district of Rajasthan, and it was intended to bring to light the bottlenecks in the existing organisation both in the side of government and entrepreneurs. It also suggested some future strategy in regard to organisational requirements. The study was conducted under the framework of the Integrated Rural Development Programme (IRDP). The study noted the entrepreneurs' lack of technical know-how. Entrepreneurs start business before they get the know-how. Lack of consultancy service, lack of loan and other facilities are problems. It also spelt out the need for organisational linkages. The research made by Bedabati Mohanty in the Cuttack district of Orissa studied the production, cost, investment, employment and marketing aspects of small scale Industries. It also attempted to find out the extent of utilisation of installed capacity by the small industries of the district. The study revealed that capital has the least effect on production. What is lacking in small scale industries is not fixed capital, but working capital to run the industry continuously, resulting in huge excess capacity in the sector. Under-utilisation of capacity was a common feature in the small industries sector.

The study made by Nisar Ahmad with special reference to the State of Jammu and Kashmir was intended to analyse the operational and other problems of the small scale and cottage industries. The problems were analysed both at micro and macro levels and practical measures for the speedy development of small scale and cottage industries in India were suggested. It also examined the entrepreneurial development, quality up-gradation and industrial sickness aspects. Personnel Management in Small Scale Industries is a detailed study made by Apparao P.B. exclusively on the personnel aspect of small scale industries. The study dealt with the aspects, sources of labour, selection methods, skill development, training, wage structure, welfare measures, absenteeism, labour turnover, unionisation, strikes and victimisation of workers. The study was made both from the angle of the management and of labour in the small scale industries.

The Government of India constituted a committee to review the role played by KVIC, its policies and programmes and also its systems and procedures. The Khadi and Village Industries Review Committee (KAVIRC) also intended to recommend ways of giving effective marketing support to village industries. It stressed the need for market research. It suggested the need for a separate Corporation to organise market research, to supply market intelligence, to set up infrastructural facilities for sales outlets, to manage sales outlets at selected important centers, to establish and manage common facilities for processing and finishing wherever necessary to prepare marketing plans, to establish standards of quality and enforce compliance there with and to take all steps necessary for promoting exports of KVIB products.

A study on the Special Employment Programme of the Kerala Khadi and Village Industries Board was made by the Social Services Division of the State Planning Board in 1988. The study was to evaluate the Special Employment Programme which was implemented by the Kerala Khadi and Village Industries Board from April 1, of 1979 with the objective of generating one lakh employment opportunities in three years by organising Khadi and Village Industries activities at the Panchayat level. This study was limited to the Khadi sector. The study revealed that even after six years this programme could not attain even 50 per cent of the target. The various reasons for the failure of this programme were low wages, low productivity, absence of labour welfare schemes and shift from family based approach to centralised management.

The Eighth Five Year Plan Task Force on Traditional Industries of Kerala brought to light the need for an assured supply of raw materials for the village indsutries of Kerala. It also suggested to set up district level raw material depots in all the 14 districts for ready supply to the new units. To overcome the problems of marketing the team suggested the need for marketing complexes to be set up in all semi-rural areas, particularly taluk headquarters. It also stressed the need for adequate provision for publicity and propaganda, training and entrepreneurial development in the Eighth Plan. The study also stated that there should be common brand name, quality testing and attractive packing for the products of KVIB. Proper training should be imparted to salesmen working in the sales depots of KVIB in sales promotion and in courteous behaviour to customers.

Ambili Kumar.V, studied the working of the small-scale industries in Kerala which were registered under the Directorate of Industries and Commerce of the Government of Kerala. He enquired into the financial, capacity utilisation, marketing and managerial aspects of small-scale units in Trivandrum district. In his study he observed that the investment in fixed capital in the small-scale units was declining. In these units fixed capital constituted 60 per cent of the total productive capital. For the small-scale units working capital assistance was more important. The investment in plant and machinery was above 60 per cent. The working capital management of the small scale units was not satisfactory. Stock-in-trade constituted the major share of the gross working capital. Sales were mostly on credit basis. Most of them depended on local sources for major share of their raw material requirement. Trade union movement was comparatively insignificant, 65.2 per cent of the units did not adopt modern techniques of production due to financial difficulties. Percentage of capacity utilisation was decreasing year after year in almost all the categories of industries and the under utilisation of capacity was due to lack of finance. Competition between similar units and lack of demand were the main problems connected with marketing.

It may be noted from the review of literature that the working of the village industrial sector in Kerala has not attracted the attention of the social scientists. A systematic study on the various functional areas of the village industrial units like production, finance and marketing is yet to be undertaken. It was in this background that the present study was undertaken.

Objectives

The present study aimed at the following objectives:

- to assess the problems of the village industries in the procurement of raw materials, labour and other inputs and in the technology adopted for production,
- to ascertain the pattern of investment and the problems related to the utilisation of funds,
- to analyse the strategies in marketing and to ascertain the attitude of the consumers towards the products of village industries.
- to compare and contrast the socio-economic conditions of the workers in the village industrial sector engaged in different types of activities, and
- to make suggestions for the development of the village industrial sector in the State based on the findings of the study.

There were 9451 registered village industrial units in Kerala as on March 31, 1988. This comprised of 6443 individual units, 1270 charitable institutions and 1738 co-operative societies. The study was limited to five districts on the basis of the concentration of units, to the five revenue districts were of Cannannore, Palghat,

Ernakulam, Kottayam and Quilon from the extreme north to the extreme south of the State. The sample of the study covered 90 individual units. 67 charitable societies and 58 co-operative societies, selected on a systematic random sampling from the list obtained from KVIB. The units that came under the sample were engaged in the production and marketing of activities. Apart from this, 285 workers selected at random and interviewed to ascertain in the socio-economic conditions also form part of the sample. The sample of the study also consists of 475 consumers drawn on a random from rural, semi-rural and urban centres.

Primary data for the study were collected from the sample units run by individuals, charitable institutions and co-operative societies. The primary data collection was effected from September 1989 to March 1990. An interview schedule containing questions related to various areas of functioning and the problems thereon were used to collect data from the sample units. Another schedule containing details regarding the socio-economic conditions was used to collect data from the workers selected at random from the units assisted by KVIB (179) and other similar units without KVIB assistance (106). The data collected from these two classes of workers have facilitated comparison. In order to ascertain the attitude of the consumers another schedule was designed and used. Data were collected from 475 consumers residing in rural (125), semi-rural (175) and urban (175) areas selected at random. All the schedules used for the study were pre-tested. Secondary data were also collected from KVIB, State Planning Board, Department of Economics and Statistics of the Government of Kerala and incorporated in the study. The study covers a five-year period from 1984-85 to 1988-89. The study on the socio-economic condition of workers is confined to the financial year 1988-89 though their savings and indebtedness details for the years 1986-87 to 1988-89 are considered. The study of the consumers is also limited to the financial year 1988-89. To analyse and interpret the data collected from different sources stated above, tools and techniques like averages, percentages, ratios, index number, compound growth rate, regression, chi-square test, analysis of variance etc were employed.

The study is intended to probe into the problems of the working village industrial units. No systematic information was available with KVIB about the functioning units especially individuals. In many cases the units selected at random sampling were found to be defunct. Earnest efforts were made to make substitutions in many of such cases. However, in some cases only very few units could be covered. This has forced to limit the sample of the study to 215 units. In some cases systematic records were not maintained by the industrialists, especially individuals, and it created problems in generating data required for the study. In such cases the data collection would be effected through observation method so as to verify the accuracy of the data supplied by the respondents from memory.

Findings

The major findings of the study are summarized below:

Many units covered under the study have been in existence for more than 10 years. Among them individual units were more in number; 51 individual units (56.67 per cent) and 36 societies (28.8 per cent) existed before 1979; 13 individual units (14.4 per cent) and 14 societies (11.2 per cent) existed even before 1969 covering a span of more than 20 years. Individual entrepreneurs considered caste nexus as the prime factor while societies saw marketing facility as the most important factor. Both the Individuals and societies saw the availability of traditional skill as the second important factor. When the availability of KVIB assistance played a great role in the location of societies it had only a minor role in the case of individual units.

Technology: Though the technology followed by the traditional artisans was crude and inferior, some sort of apathy could be noticed among them in giving up the traditional technology. Only 16 individuals and 21 societies admitted that the production technology followed by them was poor. Finance stood as the main hindrance and KVIB norms stood as the second major hindrance in the case of individuals in shifting to better technology, whereas in the case of societies KVIB norms were the main hindrance when finance was the next hindrance.

Capacity utilization: Higher percentage of capacity utilisation was seen among individual units. 71.11 per cent of the individual units and 60.8 per cent of the societies could use 80 to 100 per cent of their production capacity. Individuals as well as societies stated shortage of finance as the main factor responsible for the under-utilisation of production capacity. Shortage of labour was the second factor and competition from within was the third factor that hindered the individuals and societies from making full use of their production capacity.

Raw materials: In both individual units and societies raw material cost shared the major portion of the total cost of production. In the individual units raw material cost share was 50.08 per cent of the total cost of production whereas it was 76.53 per cent in the societies. Village Industries were to make use of raw materials available within the village. A shift from this concept was noticed. Still individuals met 60.65 per cent of their raw material requirement from within the village. Further they gathered 32.85 per cent from nearby areas within the district. The societies met only 33.6 per cent of their raw material requirement from within the village. Many societies and one individual soap unit had to collect a portion of the required raw material from outside the State. Societies collected 12.6 per cent from outside the State. The units were divided into high profit-making units and low profit-making units. Chi-square test of independence of attributes was employed to see whether raw material availability and profit were independent. The chi-square value obtained in the case of individuals was greater than the tabled critical value showing that profit and raw material availability were dependent. The chi-square value obtained in the case of societies was less than the tabled critical value showing that the profit of the societies was independent of the raw material availability.

The individual collected 47.41 per cent of the raw materials directly from the producers in the village. Intermediaries were the second source (38.12 per cent). But they were the main source (50.55 per cent) and producers, the second source (44 per cent) in the case of societies. Both among individuals and societies intermediaries were the main supply source outside the village. Government agencies were the second source in the case of individuals whereas producers were the second source in the case of societies. The individuals as well as societies considered high cost as the main problem they encountered in the procurement of raw materials. Financial constraint was identified as the second important problem both by individuals and societies.

Labour: Labour constituted the major element in the total cost of production of both individual units and societies. In the individual units 39.56 per cent of the total cost of production was the cost of labour and in societies it was 20.65 per cent. Availability of labour was a problem to some village industrialists. Nineteen individuals and 27 societies had the problem of availability of labour but 10 individuals and 23 societies held that labour was available in plenty. Village Industries were no more meant to provide additional income. It had become the main source of income for the workers. The village industry provided, on an average, 224 days of work to the full-time workers and 129 days of work to the part-time workers in the individual sector. Societies provided 235 days of work to the full-time workers and 147 days of work to the part-time workers.

The average daily wages of a full-time worker in an individual unit was Rs. 29.88 and it was Rs. 30.66 in the societies. The average daily wages of a skilled carpenter in the rural construction sector in 1988-89 was Rs. 51.05 and that of a malson Rs. 51.17 and for a rural unskilled male worker it was Rs. 32.92 and for an unskilled female worker it was Rs. 25.32. Wide variation was seen in the wages of various industries and between the individual workers and workers in the societies of certain industries. The working conditions were poor in most of the units. Still 74.86 per cent of the workers considered the working condition satisfactory. 15.08 per cent workers considered their working condition as good. Only 10.06 per cent considered it as poor. Eighty-five individual entrepreneurs and 107 societies found that their workers are co-operative. Five individuals and 13 societies saw them very co-operative. Five societies saw their workers indifferent.

Regarding the satisfaction of work 69.83 per cent of the workers was satisfied with their work. For 19.56 per cent of the workers it was poor. Labour absenteeism was not a problem to village industries. Only 13 individuals and five societies were affected by labour absenteeism. The affected industrialists as well as workers observed that the absented workers preferred other casual employment whenever available. The study also evaluated that more number of non-KVIB workers liked to quit their job for better prospects. Regarding the trade union activities only 23.33 per cent of the workers interviewed had membership in a trade union and 4.44 per cent workers had active involvement in trade union activities.

Other inputs: Other inputs had only an insignificant place in individual units and societies. The cost of other inputs was only 1.34 per cent of the total cost in the individual units and it was only 2.82 per cent in the societies. Fuel availability was not much of problem to both individual units and societies. Twenty-four individual units and 22 societies had some problem in the availability of fuel. When 20 individual entrepreneurs held that the cost of fuel was high, the other four individuals had the problem of irregular supply of electricity. Eleven societies considered the cost of fuel is high. The other 11 societies had the problem of irregular supply of electricity.

Analysis of cost structure: A regression analysis was made to study the effect of cost of raw material, labour and oilier inputs on the individual units and societies over the years 1984-89. In the individual units, significant changes in the cost of raw material over the years were noticed only in carpentry and blacksmithy industries. The carpentry and blacksmithy units incurred an additional amount of Rs. 34,102 towards the cost of raw materials. In the societies, the regression fitted was found significant in match, PCP, soap and carpentry and blacksmithy industries. In the individual units the regression for the cost of labour was found significant in the carpentry and blacksmithy industry. In the societies, the regression was found significant in the match, soap and carpentry and blacksmithy industries. The regression fitted for the cost of other inputs was found significant in the carpentry and blacksmithy individual units. In the societies the regression was found significant in the match, leather and carpentry and blacksmithy industries. As the samples were not sufficient, regression was not fitted for cane and bamboo societies and individual oil, leather and soap units. Cane and bamboo and PCP individual units had not incurred any expense towards the cost of other inputs.

Pattern of investment: The average investment per individual unit was Rs. 51,567 and that of society was Rs. 2,65,654. Wide variation was observed among different industries. The average investment per individual cane and bamboo artisan was Rs. 163 whereas it was Rs. 2,01,280 per individual soap manufacturer. In the societies, the lowest investment was observed in the village oil industry (Rs. 69,399) and the highest investment in the lime industry (Rs. 7,24,298). The average fixed capital investment per individual unit was Rs. 26.669 which was 51.72 per cent of the total investment. The fixed investment per society was Rs. 1,69,813, that is, 63.92 per cent. But the average working capital investment per individual unit was Rs. 24,898 which was 48.28 per cent of the total investment. The working capital investment in the societies was Rs. 95,840 per unit, that is, 36.08 per cent of the total investment.

Composition of fixed assets: The fixed assets constituted land and buildings, plant and machinery, tools and equipments, furniture and fixtures, etc. In the individual units the investment per unit in land and buildings was 49.17 per cent of the total fixed assets. The investment in land and buildings per society was s 68.77 per cent of the total fixed investment. Thus in both individual units and societies land and buildings shared the major portion of the total fixed assets. The investment in plant and machinery was Rs. 10,149 per individual units, that is, 38.06 per cent of the total fixed assets and the investment per society was Rs. 33,490, that is, 19.72 per cent. The average investment per unit in the individual units was Rs. 2,981 (11.17 per cent) and in societies it was Rs. 12,887 (7.58 per cent). The share of investment in furniture and fixtures was 1.6 per cent (Rs. 427) in the individual units and 1.85 per cent (Rs. 3,135) in societies. The other fixed assets like fixed deposits, telephone and electricity deposits, etc. were not seen in individual units. The investment in other fixed assets in the societies was 2.08 per cent of the total fixed assets.

Current assets: Current assets consisted of stock of raw materials, finished and semi-finished goods, cash and bank balance, debtors, other current assets, etc. In the individual units trade debtors stood the major share (54.66 per cent) of the total current assets while in societies stock of finished and semi-finished goods stood high (38.35 per cent). The proportion of raw materials in the individual unit was 18.54 per cent and in the societies it was 30.36 per cent. The share of stock of finished and semi-finished goods in the total current assets was 24.29 per cent in the individual units and 38.35 per cent in the societies. In the individual units, except PCP and soap, the combined stock of raw materials and semi-finished goods was more than 70 per cent of the total current assets. In the societies the combined stock of raw materials, finished and semi- finished goods was above 50 per cent in all industries except lime. The proportion of cash and bank balance in the individual units was 2.51 per cent and it was 9.48 per cent in the societies. Most of the village artisans did not have a bank account. The proportion of sundry debtors in the individual units was 54.66 per cent and in the societies it was 21.11 per cent.

Sources of funds: The Individual units could meet 62.62 per cent of their long-term financial requirements and the societies could meet 41.94 per cent of the requirements with KVIB assistance. The Individual entrepreneurs met 36.58 per cent of their long-term fund requirements from their own pockets and societies met 52.33 per cent from themselves. This was mostly through gold loan and from the friends and relatives. So they started functioning in debt. The insufficiency felt in the working capital was a reflection of the cumulative effect of insufficiency of fixed capital.

Most of the village Industrial units depended fully on KVIB working capital assistance. Hence they found it difficult to tide over any further financial pressure. They were hesitant to borrow from other sources, as their products could not bare the cost of borrowed working capital. Smoothly functioning village industrial units stated that the working capital assistance provided by KVIB was sufficient; the individual units depended on friends and relatives to meet 29.88 per cent of their short-term fund requirements. Their dependence on rural money lenders was only 6.92 per cent. They were able to meet only 16.36 per cent of their requirements through trade creditors. But their trade debtors were very high. The societies met only 10.83 per cent of their short-term fund requirements through KVIB. The societies met their major requirements through friends and relatives (40.09 per cent). They also got only 17.73 per cent from trade creditors. Thus, both the fixed capital and working capital assistance provided by KVIB was insufficient. The industrial units that were not having finance of their own or could not borrow money from their friends and relatives interest-free or at a very low rate of interest found it difficult to survive. Lack of sufficient accounting and management exposure added to the financial problems of the village Industrialists who were not able to make better use of the limited resources they had.

Working capital: The problem of most of the village industrialists was not mainly the shortage of short-term funds but it was the utilisation of available funds. If they were oriented as to the best use of available resources and if proper organised assistance was provided by KVIB most of the units would operate more efficiently. The average working capital requirement of five individual units was Rs. 15.383. It ranged from Rs. 27 to Rs. 93,070. The average annual working capital requirement per society was Rs. 64,723. The average working capital ratio of the individual units was 2.62 whereas it was 3.08 in the societies. All the individual units had a working capital ratio above 2. In the societies only the soap industry showed a ratio below 2. Though the working capital ratio was above 2, liquidity was a problem to most of them.

It was the ratio of cash and bank balance and short-term marketable securities to the current liabilities. The absolute liquidity ratio of the individual units was 0.07 and that of the societies was 0.29. Thus when the stock and debtors were ignored the position of the village industrial units was not satisfactory. Thus, the main problem was not the insufficiency of working capital but its management. Rather than further financial assistance they needed more technical assistance from KVIB to know the market requirements and to plan the production. No form of accounting was seen in individual units except in a soap unit, a village oil unit and some carpentry and blacksmithy units. The investment-turnover ratio of the individual units was 2.55 and that of the societies was 1.26. It is generally considered that sales should be two times the value of the total investment. The individual units showed a slightly higher amount of over-trading. Greater measure of under-utilisation of capacity was there in the societies.

Profit: The profit taken was sales proceeds minus total cost of production, 38.89 per cent of the individual units had a profit between 11 to 15 per cent and 34.44 per cent had a profit of 16 to 20 per cent. The profit of the societies was less, 56.8 per cent of the societies had a profit of 5 to 10 per cent and 20 per cent of the societies had a profit of only less than 5 per cent. The analysis of capital-labour ratio revealed that Rs. 8,362 could provide employment to one person in the individual sector and in the societies; only an investment of Rs. 11,981 could provide employment to one person. The fixed capital required per employee in the individual sector was Rs. 5,744 and in the societies it was Rs. 8,128.

KVIB assistance-sufficiency/insufficiency: The analysis of KVIB assistance to industrial units revealed that 57.78 per cent of the individual artisans got enough assistance from KVIB towards fixed capital and 52.8 per cent of the societies got sufficient fixed capital assistance from KVIB. Fifty per cent of the Individual units and 52.8 per cent of the societies saw the working capital assistance by KVIB as sufficient. Thus the main problem with the village industrialists was not the availability of finance but the inability to make the best use of the available resources. Though the problem was apparently financial, it was really the reflection of weaknesses observed in the other areas.

Nature of profit and capital sufficiency: The individual units and societies were divided into low profit and high profit units, and the chi-square test of independence of attributes was employed. The chi-square value obtained in the case of individual units was 0.04, the table value at 1 d.f. is 3.84. Thus in the case of individual units the nature of profit and fixed capital sufficiency were independent. The chi-square test result obtained in the case of societies was 9.22. Thus in the case of societies profit and fixed capital availability were dependent. In the case of working capital sufficiency chi-square value obtained was 1.34 which was less than the table value. Thus the working capital sufficiency and profit were independent in the case of individuals. The chi-square result in the societies was 5.66. Thus in the societies the working capital sufficiency and profit were dependent. Thus the working capital sufficiency affected the profits of the societies whereas it did not affect the profit of the individual units.

Prospects for expansion: The analysis for prospects for industrial units showed that 4.11 per cent individual units and 36.8 per cent societies wanted to expand their business. KVIB assisted units found it difficult to secure finance for expansion from any other source as the first charge of the assets of these units remained with KVIB. Only societies were given continued assistance by KVIB. Many individual units planned to expand their business with their own finance. Many others expected bank assistance. Eight per cent of the societies could find more than 75 per cent of the required finance from within the society. Twenty per cent of the societies looked upon institutional sources. None of the individuals or societies planned to expand their business with the loans from non-institutional sources. Many village industrialists were hesitant to borrow from commercial banks at the existing interest rate. Out of the 3.7 individual units that planned to expand their business 14 units and 24 out of the 46 societies did not find it a problem to raise the finance needed for their expansion. The Individual units saw the high rate of interest charged by the non-institutional sources as the main hindrance. Societies stated that the expansion assistance provided by KVIB was insufficient. Societies considered the high rate of interest charged by the non-institutional sources as the second hindrance in the expansion of their business.

Sales performance: The compounded growth rate worked out showed a greater increase in the oil individual units (45.55) followed by soap units (41.46). The lesser growth rate was in lime (0.58) followed by leather (0.84). In the societies greater growth rate was observed in cane and bamboo (75.96) and the lesser rate in lime (6.52). None of the individual artisans studied could get the benefit of Khadi Gramodyog Bhavans directly run by KVIB. The marketing share of these Bhavans was only 7.4 per cent in the case of societies. None of the individual units studied sold through G.S. Depots. The societies could carry out 18.32 per cent of their sales through G.S. Depots. Marketing co-operative societies formed with the assistance of KVIB was of much help to the traditional village artisans. Individuals in the pottery, cane and bamboo and oil industries could carry out 10.08 per cent of their sales through these marketing societies. These marketing societies took care of the procurement and timely supply of raw materials, semi-processing of raw materials, storage of finished goods and lending of finance on the basis of the stock of finished goods, collection of loans given and marketing of the finished goods. The middlemen were the major source of purchasing for both the individuals and societies. Individuals depended on other sources for 89.92 per cent of their sales. The societies depended on oilier sources for 67.09 per cent of their sales. Most of the individuals reached the consumers directly by spending a lot of time.

The index number worked out in the present study showed that KVIB was not regular in procurement of finished goods from village industrialists as well as to effect payment. Marketing co-operative societies functioned mainly among individual potters. The societies assisted the traditional artisans in their production, financing and marketing aspects. With the help of KVIC technical experts technical training was given to the potters. This made possible product diversification. The society extended financial assistance to tide over off seasons. The Index number showed some consistency in the sales through these societies. A declining trend was observed in the last two years covered under the study. When the turnover increased, the society allowed the members to sell some portion of their production by themselves. The oilier marketing agencies were mainly the middlemen. A good number of village industrialists reached the consumers directly. Many individual artisans in the pottery, cane and bamboo and PCP industries resorted to door-to-door sales. The steady index number noticed among the individuals in the cane and bamboo industry was because of the regular involvement of the workers, who were not able to move out for other better employment. Not much change in the cane and bamboo production was noticed over years. The societies were gripped more by the problem of credit sales 42.54 per cent of their sales was on credit. The percentage of credit sales among the individual artisans was 33.21. Credit sale proportion in the match societies and individual soap units was high. This was mainly because of the competition from within.

The total sales share of KVIB was very less in the societies. Of the total cash sales of the societies KVIB's share was the lowest, that is, 2.56 per cent. The share of G.S. Depots was only 25.03 per cent. The share of cash sales through others was 72.41 per cent. The individual entrepreneurs were not assisted by KVIB marketing outlets and Depots. Out of the cash sales 88.13 per cent was through other sources including middlemen. Thus the marketing assistance provided by KVIB assisted Depots was meagre and they provided only very little relief to the village industrialists. The total credit sale in the individual units was through other sources. In the case of societies 75.45 per cent of the credit sale was through others. The percentage of credit sales through Depots was less when compared to KVIB depots.

Delay in collection of debt: The credit sales score variance differed significantly in the individual units. In the societies the credit sales score differed significantly among industries. The chi-square test applied to study the interdependence of collection period of sales proceeds and profit in the individuals was insignificant. The period of collection did not directly affect the nature of profit. The chi-square test result in the case of societies was significant showing that the period of collection of credit sales and profit were interdependent. Thus in the societies if the credit sales period prolongs, the profit will be still reduced.

Marketing difficulties: The Individual artisans identified the difficulty in stocking for continuous supply as the main problem confronted by them in the process of marketing. They identified transportation as their next problem in marketing. The societies stated collection of sale proceeds as the main problem encountered by them. Lack of advertisement was the next major problem for them. The societies that sold goods through G.S. Depots considered quick payment as the main factor and regularity in buying as the next factor that made them depend on G.S. Depots. The individual units that depended on co-operative marketing societies stated that they depended on them mainly because of their inability to manage sales on their own. Most of the individual entrepreneurs reached the consumers directly. This was because of their regularity in buying. Societies considered this as the second important factor. Societies depended on middlemen more, and they stated that their inability to manage sales by themselves was the main factor responsible for it.

Benefit/non-benefit of KVIB marketing depots: Many industrial units failed to state how beneficial KVIB marketing depots were. The societies held that the price offered by KVIB was reasonable. This was mainly the opinion of the small match units that could fetch a higher price through Match Federation. Except in match KVIB payments were much delayed. The societies held that KVIB did not advertise their products, and this resulted in slow movement of goods which sometimes caused wastage of goods like soap, leather etc. The societies, especially bigger match units that could sell their products at a higher price in their brand name, viewed that the price offered by KVIB was low. The societies said that the price offered by Depots was reasonable. These depots also helped to avoid exploitation from middlemen. The societies said that the Depots did not give sufficient publicity.

Agency coverage: The correlation study revealed that an increase in the number of sales agencies covered by the individual units increased their level of profit. In the case of societies an increase in the number of sales agencies covered did not end up in an increase in the profit of each unit. With the analysis of variance technique it was seen that in the individual units the agency coverage score differed significantly among various industries. Agency coverage score is the maximum in pottery. In the societies also the agency coverage score differed significantly. The maximum agency coverage score is in match industry.

Sales area: The sales operations of the village industrialist are not confined to the village itself. The Individuals as well as societies market only around 40 per cent of their production within the village. The individual artisans moved out to nearby villages to sell (49.04 per cent) of their production. The tiring loitering of the village artisans not only took away the precious time of an able bodied worker of the village artisan's family it also weakened the bargaining power of the village industrialist, 8.58 per cent of the sales stretched to areas outside the district. Some pottery individuals extended their marketing operations even to areas outside the State. The societies could sell only 39.37 per cent within their home village. They sold the major portion in the nearby villages. Advertisement is very essential to penetrate markets outside the State. The correlation between profit and the coverage of area score in the individual units showed that area had no definite association with profit. In the societies also there is no correlation between area coverage and profit. Thus in both the cases extension of sale was not profitable but it helped to clear off the stock of production. Marketing was a great problem to the village industrialists who had to stretch their marketing operation to areas outside the village with limited resources and transportation facilities. The area coverage score variance studied differed significantly among various industries in the individual sector. In the societies also the area coverage score differed.

Purchase preference: The chi-square test applied to analyse whether the opinion of the consumers that they preferred to buy high quality and branded products differed among the rural, semi-rural and urban consumers. More semi-rural people went for products of high quality and brand names. Difference could be observed in the opinion of the consumers who stated that they preferred only high quality products. More semi-rural consumers were interested in buying products of high quality followed by urban consumers. Twenty-five per cent of the urban consumers preferred to buy products with brand names. There was difference of opinion among the three groups of consumers with regard to low price as the consideration for choosing a product. The semi-rural consumers preferred products of low price. The three groups differed in their answers to the question whether they always preferred village industrial products. Rural people, more than the others, preferred village industrial products. The chi-square test was also applied to study whether the three groups of consumers differed in their opinions. More rural people bought village industrial products because of its low price. More urban people chose village industrial products because of the quality due to its traditional processing. Greater number of semi-rural people purchased village industrial products with an intention to help village industries.

Availability of village industrial products: None of the consumers are contacted knew that lime produced by KVIB assisted units was available in the market. The cane and bamboo, PCP, carpentry and blacksmithy products of KVIB assisted units were known to the consumers of other village industrial products only to a very limited extent. Thus, KVIB took only very little steps to popularize village industrial products. The Kolmogoron - Smirnov test applied to see whether the three groups of consumers differed in their opinion with regard to the availability of village industrial products showed that they differed. The semi-rural and rural groups were identical in their opinion that the village industrial products were available always.

Village industrial products: Chi-square test was done to see whether the three groups of consumers differed in their opinions. More consumers of rural group got introduced to village industrial products accidentally than those in other groups. The local sellers were more instrumental in introducing the products to the rural consumers. Local sellers had no influence with the semi-rural consumers. KVIB exhibitions influenced semi-rural people most. The next influence was on the urban people. KVIB showrooms played a great role in introducing the products among semi-rural groups. Most of the village consumers in the three groups expressed that the price was reasonable. The chi-square test applied to see whether the opinion on the price was independent of the location of the consumers showed that it was independent. Most of the consumers from the three industrial groups stated that the quality was satisfactory. Chi-square test revealed that the opinions of the various groups of consumers on quality and the location of these consumers were interdependent. It was observed that the opinion on quality was related to their area of residence. Large number of consumers from semi-rural and urban groups was satisfied with the quality when compared to the rural consumers.

Lack of standardisation and quality assurance reduced the marketability of village industrial products. Most of the consumers from three groups said that quality assurance from KVIB was needed. Many consumers were of the opinion that the packing must be improved. Chi-square test applied to know whether the consumers differed in their opinion. The rural consumers were large in proportion to the oilier two groups who were satisfied with the quality of village industrial products. Difference could be observed in the opinion regarding packing too. More rural people recommended improvement in packing. With regard to quality specification by KVIB more urban consumers suggested quality specification by KVIB.

Market prospects: All the consumers stated that the village industrial products could thrive. Chi-square test applied to see whether the three groups of consumers differed in their opinion regarding the market prospects of village industrial products revealed that majority of the rural consumers held that there will be a greater market prospect if the products are made available throughout the year and the State. 38 per cent of the semi- rural people also had the same opinion.

Advertisement: The village industrialists as well as the consumers were of the opinion that advertisement can help a lot in increasing the demand for village industrial products. The chi-square test applied showed difference in the opinion of the three groups of consumers regarding the scope of advertisement. Urban people had a higher opinion for advertisement.

Profile of the workers: In KVIB assisted units 20.67 per cent of the workers were in the age group of 31-35 whereas in non-KVIB units 22.64 per cent of the workers were below 20 years. In both KVIB and non-KVIB match units most of the workers were within the age group of 15 to 20 years. Two women workers below 15 worked in a KVIB match unit. The lower age group observed in the match industry is due to low wages. Regarding the marital status not much difference was seen in both the categories of workers. Greater percentage of unmarried part-time workers were seen in KVIB units. Among the full-time workers the percentage of male workers was higher in non-KVIB units. Percentage of women workers in KVIB units was 32.9 while it was 23.08 in non-KVIB units. In the case of part-time workers the percentage of male workers was slightly higher in KVIB units. Twenty one per cent of KVIB workers and 25 per cent of non-KVIB workers are free from unearning family members. Twenty-four per cent of KVIB workers and 25 per cent non-KVIB workers had two unearning family members depending on their income.

Another 25 per cent of non-KVIB workers had three dependent unearning family members when only 17 per cent of the KVIB workers had the same pressure. Seven per cent of KVIB workers were illiterate whereas 21 per cent non-KVIB workers were illiterate. KVIB workers outnumbered both in the case of primary education and secondary education. When the analysis of variance was done no significant difference was observed between the various KVIB village industrial workers and the workers outside KVIB assistance purview. The caste position did not make any considerable difference between KVIB units and outside units. In both categories majority of the workers were from forward communities. The involvement of the scheduled caste/scheduled tribe workers in both the categories was below 20 per cent. More caste nexus was observed in non-KVIB units. No caste nexus was seen in KVIB societies whereas it was evident in some similar individual units which were traditional in nature.

Greater period of involvement was seen among KVIB workers. Fifty one per cent of non-KVIB workers had only 1 to 5 years involvement whereas it was only 42 per cent with KVIB workers. Forty-two KVIB workers and 40 non-KVIB workers had no other source of income than the wages from their working units. The income from other sources was more with KVIB workers. The annual earning was concerned not much difference was seen among the workers in both the categories. The average family of full-time as well as part-time KVIB workers was high compared to non-KVIB workers. The analysis of variance test revealed that the income differed significantly among the workers of the various industries including non-KVIB workers. Most of the workers in both the categories did not have the saving habit. Savings among the full-time workers stood high with KVIB workers whereas with part-time workers it stood high with non-KVIB workers. The analysis of variance test showed no significant difference among the various industry groups in the matter of savings.

The analysis of variance test was also applied to study whether the workers in various groups differed significantly in their spending habit showed that the workers including non-KVB workers, differed significantly in household expenditure, clothing, health and debt repayment. The workers with borrowing habit were very few in both the categories. The comparatively poorly paid workers managed with their meagre income. Higher rate of indebtedness was seen among carpentry and blacksmithy workers in both the categories, who were relatively high-paid. The analysis of variance test showed no significant difference in the indebtedness of the various groups of workers. Most of the-workers in both the categories stated that their work was of help to their families. Not much difference was seen in the extent of benefit derived by the families of both the groups of workers.

Advantage of KVIB workers: Sixty-three per cent KVIB workers stated that they were in an advantageous position over other similar workers while only 37 per cent of the outside workers shared the same view. Four per cent of KVIB workers and 10 per cent of non-KVIB workers stated that their family members were not happy with their work. One hundred and fourteen KVIB workers and 50 non-KVIB workers expressed their opinion. Most of the workers from both the categories who expressed their opinion saw this as a means to earn regular income. Two KVIB workers were motivated to start similar units.

Social factors: When the mass media exposure score of various worker groups was analysed using the analysis of variance test, it was seen that non-KVIB workers stood only eighth in the rank. The maximum mass media exposure score noticed was with KVIB assisted carpentry and blacksmithy workers. The mass media exposure score of KVIB assisted match and cane and bamboo industries stood below non-KVIB workers. Only very few workers in both the categories had the opportunity to meet related government officers and bank officers. KVIB workers in the match and pottery units could meet KVIC technical staff who helped them to improve their skills very much.

Forty-one per cent KVIB workers and 55 per cent non-KVIB workers could provide only financial help to their children or other members of the family but 14 per cent KVIB workers could provide guidance and financial assistance. From the study great difference could be noticed in the aspiration of both the categories of workers. When 41 per cent of KVIB workers wanted to help their younger members/children to reach college level, only 21 per cent non-KVIB workers had such an aspiration. Non-KVIB workers were more content with a secondary school level of education. As many of the workers in both the categories were unmarried they did not express their opinion. Most of the workers in both the categories preferred government job. Many workers had no aspiration.

Forty one per cent KVIB workers and 39 per cent non-KVIB workers had no interest in politics. Workers having political membership were more among non-KVIB workers. Seventy-eight per cent KVIB workers and 65 per cent non-KVIB workers were without any involvement in trade union. Workers with active involvement in union activities were seen only in KVIB units. When the social involvement score of the workers in both the categories was analysed with the analysis of variance test, it was seen that the score differed significantly. The maximum score observed was in KVIB lime industry. Non-KVIB workers ranked ninth. Except for carpentry and blacksmithy the social involvement score of the workers in other KVIB industries stood above non-KVIB workers.

Recommendations

The findings of the study quite obviously stated that the village industries in the State have got a bright future, provided they are well nourished. In order to preserve the traditional skills of the artisans engaged in the village industrial activities. It is imperative that the State and Central Governments should intervene. It is highly rewarding to promote the village industries as they can provide more employment opportunities, help decentralisation, promote socio-economic equality and better utilisation of unutilised or under-utilised local resources. Working individual units and societies were not able to make full use of their production capacity in the absence of sufficient finance.

Assistance in the form of raw materials will help full utilisation of the production capacity. This will ensure that the assistance provided is not diverted for other purposes. KVIB should take more interest to strengthen the existing units. In each Five Year Plan special care is required to strengthen the existing units.

KVIB should take greater interest in the marketing area. The present marketing arrangements are of little help to the village industrialists. A separate marketing department must be started with professionally qualified persons who have aptitude for village industrial development. This marketing department should see to the marketing and marketing research aspects. It should work in close liaison with the technical wing of KVIB. The technical staff must be given orientation through specialised agency like Centre for Management Development in Kerala to equip them with the new product requirements. This knowledge must be imparted to the industrialists through region-wise orientation programmes, training programmes and demonstrations.

Except in very few districts, KVIB showrooms are not making any appeal to the public. The showrooms of Sarvodaya Sangh and many other institutions directly financed by KVIC are making greater appeal to the public through their showroom display and publicity in the festival seasons. KVIB showroom staff must be brought under the Marketing Department and they should be given turnover-linked incentives. The Marketing Department should check the operations of various G.S. Depots. G.S. Depots must be urged to deal in village industrial products of at least three village industrial units. The products of individual entrepreneurs also must be sold through these G.S. Depots, KVIB marketing department should collect and distribute those items which are not within the reach of G.S. Depots. This will help the G.S. Depots with wider coverage of village industrial products. The Marketing Department should concentrate on various publicity programmes like mass media advertisement, exhibition-cum-sale etc. Exhibition-cum-sales need to be conducted in local townships with the active co-operation of local manufacturers and

G.S. Depots, so that the effect of the exhibitions can be followed up through these local units.

The Marketing Department should also evaluate the performance of each marketing outlet so that slow-moving items in each area can be identified and taken to other outlets. This will prevent the goods like soap, leather etc. from going waste by the lapse of time. KVIB marketing department should take care to check the quality of the products. The Marketing Department should maintain proper relation with KVIB departments of oilier states, and explore and utilise the exhibition and marketing possibilities outside the State in co-operation with KVIC. Though the individual entrepreneurs are not given continued financial assistance the marketing department may extend all the privileges to these individuals. KVIB should shift its emphasis from technology to greater employment possibilities. As in carpentry and blacksmithy industries, the industrialist must be given sufficient freedom to choose the technology that he prefers and can afford. The industrialist will take care of the excess financial commitment, if KVIB cannot provide it.

The co-operative inspectors who visit each industrial unit can help them to acquire a working knowledge of accounting or this can be done at different district centers by means of orientation programmes. Orientation programmes should be conducted in different regions of each district centre to give industrialists insight into new technological advancements, management, marketing areas etc. This can be done with the assistance of KVIC staff and experts from outside. The industrialists can also be taken to some units where the technology presented is followed successfully. This will help the village industrialist to experiment and choose for himself the technology of which he is convinced.

KVIB is an entrepreneurial development agency. Much skill is needed in identifying, encouraging and strengthening entrepreneurs. KVIB officers must be given refresher courses which will help to improve their skills in areas such as technology, management, marketing and the like. KVIB should constantly strive to improve the technology in order to increase productivity and improve the quality of the products. To ensure continuous production and better profitability, product diversification is quite essential. This will help to retain the existing businessmen in their business and also expand their business. KV1B/KVIC should train the industrialists for product diversification and make available the necessary technology and resources for it.

The village industrialists in Kerala are inclined to spend more on buildings. The prospective entrepreneurs must be oriented to go for rented premises or semi-permanent buildings or low cost building structures. They should be oriented to spend less on buildings and land initially, thus reducing the initial investment. They should also be taught how best they should use their resources so that they will not meet with the problem of liquidity. Before venturing into a project the prospective entrepreneur should have a clear idea of the extent of KVIB assistance and the additional financial resources they should find to run the business smoothly. The government can give out unused work shed in the mini industrial estates for a few years free of cost. By this time the industrialist can strengthen his working capital position and can find some surplus for investment in land and buildings.

KVIB should take active steps to reduce the role of middlemen both in the procurement of raw materials and marketing of finished goods. This will help to carry out production continuously, to improve quality and standardise production and thereby fetch a fair price for the products. In order to attain this KVIB can encourage marketing societies like the ones seen among traditional potters, screw pine mat weavers, lime and match societies. KVIB should take steps to make payment to the village industrialists as soon as they purchase goods from them. The customer should not suffer for the bad stock in KVIB showrooms, which go bad after expiry.

Co-operative marketing societies must be encouraged in the areas where traditional artisans or some societies like the pottery marketing societies, screw pine marketing societies, the lime societies and the Kerala Cottage Match Federation have concentration. It should be an agency to procure and distribute quality raw materials at the required time and at more or less steady price. Assistance in the form of raw material instead of finance can ensure that they are used for the purpose for which it is intended. The societies can also help to overcome the defect of seasonal availability of raw materials. They can collect market information and do the marketing of the goods produced by the member artisans. They can also help storage of finished goods. The participation of the commercial banks also can be drawn to the village industrial sector through these societies. The banks can identify and reach the genuine artisans through these societies, who in turn, will take care of the collection and remittance of loans or the banks can give loans to the marketing societies as 'key loan' based on the stock of raw materials and finished goods they have.

KVIB, which is not giving continued financial assistance to individual artisans, can extend continued financial assistance to these societies. The societies can collect back the loan from individual artisans without giving much financial burden. This can be a portion of the sale proceeds. The society can take care of quality control and propaganda for the products. Transportation also can be taken care of by these societies. Trained KVIB marketing executives can actively guide and supervise the work of these societies. KVIB can even lend the services of one of its marketing staff to act as the secretary for the society for whose support a portion can be collected from the sale proceeds of the society.

The society can act as a community development centre. It can take care of the well being of the member artisans and their families. Welfare measures, social development projects, literacy programmes, savings programmes etc. for the workers can be carried out through these societies. A G.S. Depot, which will stock other village industrial products, also can be linked with this society, which will help to create a village industry consciousness among the members.

References

Ahmad Nisar, *Problems and Management of Small Scale and Cottage Industries*, New Delhi, Deep & Deep Publications.

Apparao P. B., *Personnel Management in Small Scale Industries*, New Delhi, Deep & Deep Publications.

Bala, Shashi, *Management of Small Scale Industries*, New Delhi, Deep & Deep Publications.

Balakrishna, G., *Financing of Small Scale Industries in India*, Bombay, Asia Publishing House.

Basu, S.K., Place *and Problems of Small Industries*, Calcutta, A. Mukherjee & Co., Private Ltd.

Dagli, Vadllal (Ed.), *Decentralised Development – A Symposium*, Bombay, Vaikunthbai Mehta Smaraka Trust, 1969.

Dhar, P.N., and Lydall, H.F., *The Role of Small Enterprises in Indian Economic Development*, Asia Publishing House.

Department of Economics and Statistics, *Report of the Working of the Special Employment Programme of Khadi and Village Industries Board*, 1987.

Desal Vasant, *Problems and Prospects of Small Scale Industries in India*, Bombay, Himalaya Publishing House.

Deshpande, Manohar U., *Entrepreneurship of Small Scale Industries*, New Delhi, Deep & Deep Publications.

Government of India, Planning Commission, Rural Industries Planning Committee, *Projects for Intensive Development of Small Scale Industries in Rural Areas*, 1962.

Government of India, Planning Commission, *Report of the Village and Small Scale Industries (Second Five Year Plan) Committee*, 1955.

Government of India, Ministry of Industry, *Report of the International Perspective Planning Team*, 1963.

Government of India, Ministry of Industry (Department of Industrial Development), *Report of the Khadi and Village Industries Review Committee (KAVIRC)*, 1987.

Government of Kerala, State Planning Board, Eighth Five Year Plan, *Task Force on Traditional Industries of Kerala*, 1988.

Government of Kerala, Department of Economics & Statistics, *Report on the Sample Survey of Small Scale Industrial Units in Kerala*, 1988.

Government of Kerala, *Report of the Working Group on Khadi and Village Industries in Kerala*, 1964.

Jain. O.P., *Small Scale Industry Exports*, New Delhi, S. Chand & Co. (Pvt.) Ltd.

Khadi and Village Industries Commission, Report *of the Village Industries Evaluation Committee*, 1959.

Kumar Ambili, V., *Working of Small Scale Industries in Kerala with Reference to Trivandrum District*, Ph.D. Thesis (unpublished), Department of Commerce, University of Kerala, November 1989.

Lakshman. T.K., Cottage *and Small Scale Industries in Mysore*, Mysore, Rao and Raghavan.

Mathur, S.P., *Economics of Small Scale Industries*, Delhi, Sundeep Prakashan.

Mishra, S.N., and Sharma, Kushal, *Organisational Requirements of Village and Small Scale Industries*, Delhi, Mittal Publications.

Mohanty, Bedabati, *Economics of Small Scale Industries*, New Delhi, Ashish Publishing House.

National Bank for Agriculture and Rural Development, *Report of the Task Force on Khadi and Village Industries.*

National Planning Committee, Report *of the Sub-Committee Rural Cottage Industries*, Shah K.T.,(Ed.), 1948, Bombay, Vora and Co., Publishers Ltd.

National Productivity Council, New Delhi and United Nations Children's Fund Regional Office for South Central Asia, New Delhi, *Seminar Proceedings Productivity in the Informal Sector*.

Naumes. William, *The Entrepreneurial Manager in the Small Scale Business*. Massachusetts, Addision-Wesley Publishing Company.

Oommen.M.A., *Small Scale Industry in Indian Economic Growth – A Case Study of Kerala*, New Delhi, Research Publications in Social Sciences.

Papola, T.S., *Rural Industrialisation-Approaches and Potential*, Bombay, Himalaya Publishing House.

Ramakrishna K.T., *Finance for Small Scale Industry in India*, Bombay, Asia Publishing House.

Rao. Umamaheswara, *Small Scale Industries*, Bombay, Popular Prakashan.

Reserve Bank of India, *Seminar on Financing of Small Scale Industries in India*, Volume 1, Report of the Proceedings, Bombay, 1959.

Sing, Inderjit and Gupta, N.S., *Financing of Small Scale Industry*, New Delhi, S. Chand & Co. (Pvt.). Ltd.

Sing. Nau Nihal, *Scientific Management of Small-Scale Industries*, Bombay, Lalvani Publishing House.

Sharma, S.V.S., *Small Entrepreneurial Development in Some Asian Countries - A Comparative Study*, New Delhi, Light & Life Publishers.

United Provinces, *Cottage Industries Sub-Committee Report,* 1947.

Vepa. Ram K., *Small Industry - The Challenge of the Eighties*, New Delhi, Vikas Publishing House Pvt. Ltd.

10

Small-Scale Industries and Economic Development

V. Ambili Kumar

Small-scale and cottage industries have been recognised as one of the most important means for providing better economic opportunities for the people of developing countries like India. Indian economy faces numerous basic problems such as disproportionate pressure of population on agriculture owing to lack of rural industrialization, unemployment and unbalanced regional development. The development of the small-scale industrial sector is, certainly, a major formula by which to solve such problems. This is especially true in the case of a State like Kerala, where agriculture occupies the predominant area of economic activity. Growing unemployment among persons, especially those having secondary or higher education, has been one of the most serious socio-economic problems of Kerala since 1960s. Though Kerala has achieved much progress with regard 'to the spread of education, health services, social welfare measures, infrastructure development, etc., the State has not been able to solve the problems of poverty and unemployment to any significant extent. According to the National Sample Survey 38th round (1983) Kerala has the highest rate of unemployment in the country.

The Annual Survey of Industries Report 1980-81, says that Kerala accounts for only 3.4 per cent of the national industrial output from factories, and ranks 10th among Indian States. In terms of industrial employment also, Kerala's position is not better. All indicators, including investment in fixed capital, show that Kerala has a low position compared to its population base in the country. In the industrial sector, the technologically and managerially backward traditional industries have been struggling hard to survive in the face of rising costs.

Statement of the Problem

The role of the small-scale industries in Kerala is crucial, as the primary sector, which has been virtually stagnating during the last decade, is failing to respond to increasing investments, and the large-scale industries, which are mostly in the public sector, are chronically in the red. The importance of small-scale industries lies in the fact that they create immediate and permanent employment on a large-scale at relatively low costs, meet a substantial part of the demand for consumer goods, facilitate mobilisation of resources of capital at various levels, which might otherwise remain unutilised, and bring about integration of the industries with the rural economy on the one hand and the large-scale industrial sector on the other. Besides the large number of village and small-scale industries, the industrial sector of Kerala consists of a few large and medium units, mainly in the public sector. The village and small-scale industrial sector consists of traditional industries like handloom, coir and cashew and modern industries like printing, wood, metal products and chemicals. Considering the growing population and the rising unemployment, it is very essential to develop the industrial sector of Kerala, mainly through the development of small-scale industries. Thus, for greater prosperity, a campaign of wide industrialisation through the popularisation of small-scale industrial units is very essential. However, mere establishment of a number of small-scale units does not ensure efficient economic activity. To achieve this, effective evaluation of the operational influence of government policies and of the working of the small-scale units is essential.

The present study is about the working of the small-scale industrial units in Kerala, with special reference to Trivandrum district. Small-scale industries here mean those units, which are registered under the Directorate of Industries and Commerce, Government of Kerala.

Review of Literature

Many studies have been undertaken to examine the working of small-scale industries in India. An attempt is made here to review such research reports under four major heads, viz., production, finance, marketing and managerial effectiveness. The research reports reviewed here are the contributions of individual researchers, research institutions and study teams and committees appointed by the central and state governments.

Production

Availability of raw materials of the right quality, quantity and price, and at the right time, difficulties relating to labour, use of modern machinery, tools and equipments, using of bye-products and increasing wastage are the major problems relating to production in the SSI units. According to an investigation of machine industries in Lidhiana, Madhav V. Rao observed that small-scale enterprises in India did not function well as suppliers of or ancillaries to larger concerns. The scarcity of materials and equipments was found inducing firms to seek self-sufficiency rather than to complement each other. The National Council of Applied Economic Research (NCAER) study made in 1972 revealed that the major problems regarding production were largely those of shortage of raw materials and inadequate finance.

The Small Industry Extension Training (SIET) Institute, Hyderabad, also, in a survey in the Kozhikode district, Kerala, found that shortage of raw materials formed one of the reasons for sickness. Another report by the same Institute, based on a survey in the Malappuram district in Kerala State, emphasised the need to make use of the available resources within the district itself and to impart training to the uneducated unemployed. Sandesara J.C. suggested the need for a proper assessment of assistance of programmes related to raw materials, machinery on hire purchase, technical assistance and preferential purchase scheme. The small-scale industrial units are generally unable to store large quantities of raw materials. In some cases it would be unnecessary to keep large volumes of raw materials in store, because they mostly depend on advance order from customers. This was clearly brought out by Mohanty Bedabati through a study of small-scale industries in the Cuttack district. She concluded that small-scale industries generally depended on advance order for carrying on production. This dependence had been more in the case of engineering, electrical, chemical and forest-based industries than in the case of others. Since orders were not obtained throughout the year, production by small industries was generally fluctuating in nature. It was also found that except in the case of electrical industry production did not take place continuously throughout the year.

Lakdawala D.T. and Sandesara J.C. reported that 224 or one-fifth of the surveyed small-scale units in Bombay had some difficulties in the supply of raw materials, 146 had problems owing to small purchases and dependence upon retailers and trade credit, 56 on account of import control and similar restrictions and inferior quality of indigenous materials, and 22 from fluctuating prices. A study of small engineering units in Howarh and some units in the Sauga district revealed that middlemen were in predominant source of supplies and that raw material purchases were generally made on credit, extending up to three months. A study in Amaravati district emphasised the non-availability of quality raw materials. The International Labour Organisation pointed out that small firms had seldom been able to obtain the discounts that went with buying in bulk and that small firms could not employ scientists and set up laboratories to test the quality and suitability of different materials. The study by Ramakrishnan. P also pointed out that small units faced problems because they could not make bulk purchases. A study in Hyderabad, Rajkot, Okhla and Ludhiana revealed that almost half of the Hyderabad manufacturers had to resort to the black market to secure raw materials and that the Ludhiana hosiery units suffered a lot more than the cycle and sewing machine parts industries.

Of the remaining ones, 11 complained of procedural difficulties, the time consumed, and financial problems since they would have to buy the quota allotted in one installment and pay for it in lump sum. Ramakrishnan. P and Mahendra. K.L also pointed out the lack of government attention in ensuring the timely availability of quality raw materials under government quota. The views expressed by Krishan Lal Sharma are also of very great relevance at this juncture. In his view, sometimes, quotas were given to those who never manufactured; the capacity of the firms was not taken into account and officials were irresponsible and negligent. On the other hand Jha. L.K was of the opinion that at times the liberal and blanket assistance given to the small-scale sector had resulted in malpractices and that scarce raw materials were sold in the black market. Dhar and Lydall also pointed out that all sorts of personal and political influences was brought to bear in order to obtain raw materials and that some persons who received allocations of raw materials made on easy living by selling them in the open market.

In Rajkot, the pattern of industrial relations was found to be remarkably good. Though the purely temporary workers did not enjoy weekly off-days or holidays with pay, those who had been with the same unit for two years and more were entitled to privilege leave with pay. Problems faced by the trade unions were virtually nil among the small industry workers. Ramakrishnan. P in his study in Delhi found that the industrial atmosphere was peaceful and over 70 per cent of the units had no problems with the workers. Hein Streetfkerk in his study in Bulsar sub-district of South Gujarat pointed out that workers in modern small-scale industry were a largely neglected branch of the Indian industrial system, that there was a complete lack of legal protection for workers in small-scale industry, and that their wages were low. The same point was emphasized by Kalpagam in his study of women workers in the export garments industry of Madras. The unsatisfactory conditions of work were again pinpointed in a study in Bombay. Eugene Staley and Richard Morse were of the opinion that industrial relations should be viewed not only from the angle of social welfare but also from the point of view of attainment of high industrial productivity.

Availability of trained and experienced labour force is a must for the efficient running of small-scale industrial units. The High Level Committee appointed to enquire into the development of electronic industry in Kerala has emphasised the need for the supply of trained technical personnel at different levels of the industry. Labour and productivity are closely related. Moosa Baker is of the opinion that increase in capital per worker is likely to raise the level of productivity of labour and also capital. Without an increase in capital per worker, there may not be a greater increase in the rate of growth of output and employment in the case of small industries in Kerala. The argument for increasing the amount of capital per worker is based on the implicit assumption that output generated per unit of capital invested is a continuously growing function of the capital per worker. This is opposed by the argument for a less capital intensive production, if such technology is available, which is based on the assumption that the relationship between the output per unit of capital (productivity of capital) and capital per worker (method of production) first rises, but falls beyond a certain point. It points out that a more labour-intensive technique would be less efficient than a capital intensive one.

Baker's contention is that all modern industries though small in size but making use of the most efficient methods of production would be having higher capital per worker. He also views that, for a state like Kerala, the approaches like employment creation at the existing wage-level, employment creation at a higher wage-level, and increasing the present wage rates, are equally important owing to its lower rate of current labour absorption in the industrial sector. He suggests that small-scale industries need special consideration in terms of such values of capital intensity and in terms of such criterion. They are useful for determining the role of small-scale industries is identified in terms of their economic characteristics rather than in terms of their size. If industries in Kerala acquire more capital and use more capital per worker, there can be higher improvement in capital yields and labour productivity.

The notion that small industries are less capital-intensive has been disputed by Dhar and Lydall. They argue that modern small enterprises, far from being less capital-intensive than large industries, are in fact more capital-intensive. The apparent contradiction, they say, lies in a failure to see the difference in the characteristics of traditional and modern small industries. In their view, modern small industry workshops are miniature factories having many points in common with their larger counterparts. Both employ more or less the same techniques in production. The authors arrived at the conclusions regarding the capital-intensive character of small industry by calculations of capital cost per worker and correlating it with output per worker on the basis of their case studies. Baljit Singh believes that a more labour-intensive technique, unless it simultaneously reduces capital requirements per unit of output, would fail to serve the very purpose for which it is meant, viz., increased employment and output under conditions of relative scarcity of capital. He is of the view that the respective techniques of small industries for consumption goods and production goods should vary.

Though there is justification for the arguments to follow labour-intensive techniques, it is equally important to consider the need for mechanisation. The advocates of mechanisation argue that productivity and, thus, production can be improved through implementing modernized equipments. This was rightly pointed out by the International Planning Team of the Ford Foundations, stating in its report that stagnation and retrogression of small industry would be bound to occur if the process of modernisation was not introduced. Basu S.K. noted the lack of emphasis on the mechanisation of small industries in the plan programme and expressed his agreement with the West Bengal Government's point of view that the quality and quantity of consumer goods produce by non-mechanised hand industries would not ultimately satisfy the growing demand for a better class of goods in larger volumes by an increasing number of factory workers with rising incomes. The burden of his argument was that due importance should be given to mechanised small industries which could provide both employment and consumer goods.

Subhash J. Rele emphasized that it was often found that a unit had obsolete machinery and equipment or land and buildings which were not actually required. The International Labour organisation also emphasized that small firms had traditional methods of production which had not been adopted by taking advantage of new tools, new materials and new markets and that such adaptation was often a necessary condition for their survival. A study in Bombay revealed that out of the 1960 entrepreneurs interviewed, 634 or 60 per cent saw no way of improving their techniques of production. The difficulties were lack of finance, lack of adequate demand, government restrictions, lack of power supply and inferior quality of products.

The UNESCO Research Centre on Social and Economic Development also found that in many small units the methods of production were traditional; adoption of modern techniques was wither disliked by the entrepreneurs or not feasible. Nanjundan S., Robinson H.E. and Eugene Staley and others were also of the view that an advisory service or extension service to bring the small industrialists into closer touch with modern industrial methods and with new applications of science and technology was one of the most promising devices for small industry development. Pillai. V.R in his report states that, in larger units adopting modern technology, though the average employment per unit of capital is lower, there is a greater prospect of regular and continuous employment, as the entrepreneurs who have sunk their capital cannot afford to let the enterprise fall sick and are compelled to find ways and means of adjusting to changing conditions however adverse. A recent survey report by Rajagopalan also suggests that there can be development only if the small-scale sector adopts modern technology.

But Joshi N.C. opposed high mechanisation of small industry. He strongly felt that, where capital is scarce and unemployment is high, labour-intensive small and village industries, although using relatively crude machinery and having less output per worker, should be encouraged as they offer, employment to more persons and hence increase their earnings and desire for consumer goods. Stades. F.J.N once pointed out that the low productivity in small industry in India could be improved by simple means and without mechanisation, taking into consideration the capital relation between wages and equipment costs in India. As revealed by the technological survey in Japan, the techniques of production selected should be such as to be suitable to the concern, specially in regard to its capacity. The survey reported that the desired technical improvements and development of new techniques would involve problems such as diversity in economic and technical conditions owing to difference in production scale, production system, marketing ability, etc. The need for comprehensive and coordinated studies and research, before mechanising production, was also emphasised.

Using modern techniques of production does not mean that the production problems are solved. This sector was proved facing difficulties to utilise the production capacity fully. In a number of studies it was proved that under-utilisation of capacity and the reasons for it were interrelated. The under-utilisation of production capacity was also proved resulting in increased sickness. National Council of Applied Economic Research (NCAER) arrived at the conclusion that under-utilisation of capacity in most of the enterprises was the result of bottlenecks in both production and marketing. The High Level Committee on Industry, Trade and Power also was of the opinion that under-utilisation of installed capacity forms a major weakness of small-scale sector in the country and in Kerala. The high installed capacity and its minimum utilisation was pointed out as one of the reasons for increasing sickness. Regarding power, only some studies mentioned that small-scale units had some problems owing to power-cuts. The Punjab and Delhi Chambers and Commerce and Industry discussed at a conference some of the problems faced by the small-scale units regarding the sanctioning of power connections, power cuts and power fluctuations.

Finance

Basic and key industries such as capital goods industries form an integral part of the foundation of the economy of industrialisation. These industries, by their very nature, are capital-intensive and, involve a long gestation period. The scope for creating employment opportunities in the large-scale industries is seriously limited by the capital-intensive nature of those projects, on the one hand, and by such factors as lack of labour mobility and inadequate training, on the other. Labour supply being abundant in the countryside, the opportunity cost of labour is almost zero and small-scale industries can utilise labour as a substitute for fresh capital at a nominal cost. Such industries can be set up at a low cost and can provide regular employment opportunities to a large number of people. This fact was emphasised, in 1971, in the report of the Development Commissioner of Small-scale Industries; whereas in India it costs Rs. 60,000 to create direct employment in a large industry, it costs only Rs. 8,000 to provide the same in the small-scale sector and Rs. 3,000 if a small unit runs fully, using the modern managerial and optimization technique. The importance of the SSI sector was highlighted by Rao. R.V also stating that small scale industries are labour employing and are capable of creating more employment and distributing it more widely. Lakdawala and Sandesara observed that in a society, where state provision for any widespread unemployment insurance is ruled out for years to come, the useful function of small scale industries as potential provider of employment with their wide distributional effect cannot be under-rated.

The growth of small-scale industries works as a seedbed for the emergence of organisational talent and entrepreneurship, as pointed out by Robinson. H.E. Another feature associated with small-scale industries is that they are important-light i.e., they use a relatively low proportion of imported equipments and materials in relation to their total capital investment. The sector has also a favourable capital-output ratio in comparison to the large-scale sector. According to an earlier estimation, an investment of Rs.

100 in fixed capital in the organised small-scale sector brought an output of Rs. 528 as against Rs. 110 in the large-scale sector, the value of output produced by the former being approximately 4-8 times that of the latter. Moreover, small industries maintain a community life in as much as there tends to be lesser transfer of personnel. At the national scene a low import intensity in the capital structure of small-scale industries reduces the need for foreign capital or foreign exchange earnings and thus obviates balance of payment difficulties. Besides, in some industries small-scale sector has developed a fairly high level of technical competence. In the light engineering and chemical industries, for example, there exist a degree of technical skill comparable to that of corresponding units in the large-scale sector and the choice between the large-scale and small-scale, in many cases, could now be based solely on economic criteria. This was pointed out by the sub-group on small industries very earlier.

The International Planning Team, which visited India in 1954, observed that there was severe scarcity of capital as well as credit, largely because of low productivity and 'over-population' in many branches of small industry. The Society for Social and Economic Studies emphasised that the dearth of capital resulted from a low income level, a small capacity to save and hence a lack of capacity to invest. Balakrishnan analysed the financial experience of joint stock companies in the small-scale sector and found that they had a low profit-earning capacity owing to higher cost of production and higher rate of interest. Nau Nihal Singh observed that, in the SSI sector, some firms did more business than what they could finance. The SIET Institute, Hyderabad, viewed that lack of finance, avoidable and unavoidable costs diversification of funds to face the overheads, over-ambition to earn more or fear of continuity procurement of funds from external sources at a high rate of interest, diversification of working capital for personal use, etc. were certain major reasons for sickness in the SSI sector.

Bhagwati Prasad and Eresi were of the opinion that most of the SSI units suffered from financial difficulties because they were organised as proprietary concerns and partnership firms with little financial support of their own. According to Tarun, finance was only one aspect of the problem that the small-scale firms faced; the other aspect of the problem was the nature of the policy it was to serve. Mohanty Bedabati observed that investment in fixed capital was not properly utilised or there was under-utilisation of capacity in the small industrial sector. She was of the opinion that what small industries lacked was not fixed capital, but working capital to run the industry continuously, resulting in huge excess capacity in the sector.

Most of the studies revealed the inadequacy of institutional finance and recommended the enhancement of the financial assistance to the small sector. Dhar, in his survey in Delhi found that the only source of external finance consisted of relatives, friends and traders. In the survey of handloom industry in Karnataka and Sholapur, also, it was found that, on the whole, master-weavers and moneylenders constituted the major source of funds in both urban and rural centres. Lakdawala and Sandesara in their survey in Bombay found that 342 firms had 391 cases of borrowing. Baljit Singh in his study in Moradabad found that, of the indebted establishments, 33 per cent were indebted to traders and dealers, 27 per cent to relatives and friends, and 21 per cent to moneylenders. Oomman opined that government as a financial agency to small-scale industries in Kerala had not been very successful, and that the credit given had not been adequate or timely.

Mal-distribution and misdirection of finance were common; and no effective supervision of the utilisation of credit had been made. The Working Group on Small-Scale Industries, set up by the Administrative Reforms Commission, stated, on the basis of a survey conducted by the Central Small Industries Organisation, that on an average only 20 per cent of the credit needs of the small-scale sector were being met by institutional sources. Inderjit Singh and Gupta. N.S also pointed out the inadequacy of institutional credit; it accounted for only 5.1 per cent of the borrowings.

The difficulties to enjoy financial and other assistances were highly stressed by the High Level Committee on Industry, Trade and Power. The committee was of the opinion that though District Industries Centres for all promotional assistance, procedures and formalities, information, project reports, loans, raw materials, etc. the experience of the entrepreneurs was that they had to run from pillar to post for every thing. A study in Saugar district concluded that industrialists preferred a bania (private money-lender) to a co-operative bank to meet their needs because of complicated formalities, cumbersome procedure and undue delay. In a survey, Ramakrishnan found that entrepreneurs were prepared to pay or had paid a much higher rate of interest to non-banking sources to avoid bank formalities. The study by the UNESCO Research Centre on Social and Economic Development in South Asia found that, in Hyderabad, none of the surveyed units had borrowed from the Government or a bank. Pareek also analysed the contribution of institutional sources in financing small-scale industries in Rajasthan. Indiscriminate sponsoring by government agencies to reach the target and difficulties in the availability of bank credit were pointed out as some of the major reasons for sickness in the SSI sector, by Malcolm Adiseshiah.

However, according to Shashi Bala, among institutional sources banks were the most important. Again a study report, by Mohana Kumar, on the role of commercial banks in financing small-scale industries in the Trivandrum district, pointed out that there was severe lack of meaningful commitment towards achievement of the targets on the part of bank officials. They were not, often, equipped to finance the small-scale industries. They financed them as there was compulsion and not as a matter of policy. Thus, there was no serious attempt on their part to achieve the targets.

In obtaining financial assistance, some studies revealed that there existed the problem of competition with large-scale industrial units. Warrior and Vepa found that despite a well-developed institutional framework, it was the urban-based the comparatively bigger entrepreneurs who obtained the bulk of the advances made to the small-scale sector. A survey by the Reserve Bank of India revealed that a substantial proportion of the units which received bank credit was relatively of a big size, in terms of both employment and total assets. The need for financial assistance from the part of government was emphasised in several studies. The Administrative Reforms Commission recommended the establishment of an apex financial institution at the centre to cater exclusively to the needs on the small-scale sector. The High Level Committee on Electronic Industry suggested the formation of an independent and autonomous organisation with the role of an entrepreneur and of a financier.

The survey of small-scale industries in Madurai district recommended that, in granting loans to small-scale industries, the emphasis should be more on the prospects of the industry, the extent of the market for its products, and on the entrepreneur's capacity to run his industries for profit. Jain and Babu also suggested the provision of loan facilities only to genuine entrepreneurs and not to every applicant. The society for Social and Economic Studies and the International Perspective Planning Team were of the view that India had most of the institutional framework for credit the need was for a changed outlook and some improvements in the techniques of making advances.

Marketing

The importance of marketing has been clearly brought out by Paul Hoffman, former Administrator of the United Nations Industrial Organisation, thus: "it is illusory to think that a country can be industrialised by building factories – industrialisation means building markets." The significance of marketing was, once more, emphasized by the National Council of Educational Research and Training (NCERT) by stating that the optimal functioning of an economic system depended upon the even matching of the capability and efficiency levels attained by its productive and distributive systems. The NCERT again reported that marketing was probably the least developed aspects of the

Indian economy and that there had been very little systematic attempt to study its problems in India.

A study by ILO has viewed that the survival of small-scale industrial units depended upon their products on a competitive market in which large industries were also selling. The Small Industries Extension Training (SIET) Institute emphasised the need for greater co-ordination between the various agencies assisting small industries, to ensure production of quality at competitive rates, without which the small industries would continue to face serious marketing problems. Graham Bannock has made the comment that a small firm can't significantly influence its market mainly because of too many competitors. Tambi has emphasized that large-scale units had an edge over small-scale ones in the matter of marketing because of the economies of scale, the financial strength to face set backs and the competence to hire specialised professional managers. Continued production of an obsolete product, and failure to realise that business begins with the customer and not with the product, have been pointed out to be the major reasons for the failure of small industrial units. The International Planning Team, Ramakrishna, Dhar, Baljit Singh, Shetty, the UNESCO Research Centre on Social and Economic Development in Southern Asia and Krishanlal Sharma have given evidences that small manufacturers depended on dealers for marketing their products and, therefore, did not get a fair price. A survey relating to the Rural Small-Scale Industry in the People's Republic of China revealed that most of the small-scale enterprises were producing items for which there was a ready local market. The findings of Mohanty Bedabati also corroborate this conclusion.

A number of studies emphasised the need for market research and information. The seminar, organised by the National Alliance of young entrepreneurs in 1973, on marketing services for small-scale entrepreneurs has stressed the need for an institution of marketing research and feasible studies on product or industry basis so as to enable new entrepreneurs to take up selected lines of manufacture. A study made in Kerala observed that a market study had considerable importance in a State like Kerala where tremendous possibilities for developing markets for a variety of small industry products were available especially because of certain favourable factors such as high density of population, highest rate of literacy, compact markets, well-developed infrastructure and surplus electricity. Jain found that the outstanding problem for most of the exporting firms was lack of information relating to such major areas as export procedures market research and locality agents.

A study by NCAER revealed that inadequate knowledge of foreign markets and insufficient realisation of production problems at home were the basic hindrances to the maximum exploitation of export possibilities. The International Labour Organisation and Ram K. Vepa also emphasised the need for market research and information. The Internal Labour Organisation suggested that co-operative societies or government-aided agencies should undertake market surveys and market research since these would be too expensive for individual small firms. The Working Group on Small-scale Industries for the Third Five-Year Plan also recommended similarly. A survey in Varanasi revealed that the role of government-sponsored institutions in marketing arrangements was not significant. Wholesalers and retailers had an important place in the marketing arrangements of small-scale industries at Varanasi. It was also found that, quality control and standardisation measures were adopted only by a limited number of units. Wanchoo also emphasised the need for quality control.

Managerial Effectiveness

Efficient management is essential for the profitable working of any industrial unit. In very small units among the small-scale units, appointment of management experts may be costly. However, in regard to the importance of efficient management, several studies gave different views. A survey made in 1953 revealed that 89.4 per cent of small business failure was due to inefficient management. At the same time, it was able to note that successful owners had succeeded simply by having greater managerial ability. Stepanek emphasised the need for motivating small entrepreneurs and giving them easy access to the 'how to do's of modern industry. He was of the opinion that capital and equipment would not be sufficient for industrial growth. In U.S.A., about 60 per cent of new business failures were due to lack of management.

Oommen was of the opinion that the poor performance of small-scale industries was due not to any basic weakness in the conception of the various programmes, but to the defects in their design, strategy and implementation. Nau Nihal Singh concluded that all of the bankruptcies stemmed from poor business management; there should be competent management effective covering all the accepted management functions. In his opinion, India could become industrially efficient only by adopting 'management by competence' and not through 'management by inheritance'. Bad management was pointed out as the major reason for sickness of small-scale units, in a survey by the SIET Institute. Singh N.N. has observed that in India over 60 per cent of new business never lasts over 5 years and the reason for the majority of failures is the lack of proper organisation and management know-how.

The majority of the studies have suggested the improvement of the government assistance in different areas of activities. Babu suggested that government assistance should be given only to those who had genuine interest in business, and that the assistance given should be linked with the performance. The survey by the Corporate Studies Group viewed that each type of assistance and protection measures would attract a different group of entrepreneurs. To a majority of the small entrepreneurs the availability of cheap finance, procurement of raw materials and preferential treatment in purchases by the State were likely to be reasonably attractive. On the other hand, for a comparatively larger unit, exceptions from regulatory provisions might be more attractive. While for new and technically qualified persons, a more meaningful form of assistance could be in the form of market guidance, provisions of sheds in the industrial estates, and opportunity to share common infrastructural facilities.

From the conclusions given in the preceding pages it is quite clear that the SSI units have been facing serious problems. The attitude of the small entrepreneurs towards marketing their products is a crucial factor for the success and growth of their units. Besides, it is through the effective management of resources that ultimate objectives of the units are efficiently and economically achieved. Such being the case, it is felt that an in-depth study into the working of the SSI units in Kerala with reference to the Trivandrum district would be very much helpful to the planners, administrators, and the owners of the SSI units of the State and hence the present study.

Objectives of the Study

The study has the following objectives:

- to analyse the financial structure of various categories of small-scale industrial units in Trivandrum district,
- to ascertain whether the small industrial units have been utilising the existing capacity for production in full,
- to know the different methods of marketing and to ascertain the problems in marketing the products and services,
- to analyse the managerial effectiveness in regard to some performance indicators, and
- to suggest measures for improvement based on the findings of the study.

Industrially, Trivandrum district holds the fifth position among all the 14 districts in the State of Kerala. Being the administrative centre of the State, Trivandrum has great importance, and so is its industrial and economic development. Hence, Trivandrum district in Kerala has been chosen for the study. There were 18,954 registered small-scale units in Kerala as on March 31, 1981. Out of this, 2,122 units were registered and located within the sample district.

For a satisfactory sample enquiry, an accurate census of the universe is the most essential requirement. A systematic record of the small-scale industries of Trivandrum district does not exist. As registration of small-scale industries is only optional, many small industrial units are found to be operating without registration. No information could be obtained about the total number of such units and their locations. The study has, therefore, been confined to those small industrial units, which are registered with the Directorate of Industries and Commerce, Government of Kerala. The records maintained by the District Industries Centre (DIC) Trivandrum, were used for preparing a list of small-scale industrial units registered before 31st March 1981. Thus, the study covers those SSI units which were registered with the Directorate of Industries and Commerce before 31st March, 1981, and which were existing at the time of interviews. As per the records of the DIC, Trivandrum, there were 1811, units registered before 31st March 1981, functioning as on March 31, 1986. Of this, 454 units (i.e. 25 per cent) were selected on the basis of stratified random sampling.

The study has covered all the above-mentioned industrial units operating in Trivandrum district. It is observed that while some industries are evenly spread throughout the district, some others like coir and fishnet manufacture are concentrated in particular areas. The study has covered a period of 5 years, from 1981-82 to 1985-86. Information relating to production, marketing, finance and management refers to the yearly data. Such time-series data have been collected to find out the effects of important variables like capital, labour, production capacity utilisation and price increase. In the selection of sample units, a two-stage stratified random sampling technique was adopted. In the first stage, the industries covered under the study were stratified into 29 groups on the basis of the nature of production or services. However, in Trivandrum district, it was noted that, all the 29 groups of industries did not exist. Industries falling only in 19 categories were in operation in the district. It was decided to select 25 per cent of the units from each stratum for intensive study. For each stratum, the ultimate sample units were selected on the basis of simple random sampling. Following this procedure, 454 industrial units were selected from all the strata taken together. A picture of the sample size of different categories of industries is given in Table 10.1.

It was observed during the survey that some industrial units selected from the list, on simple random basis, were either absent or had ceased functioning. Besides, the owners/managers of some industrial units were reluctant to furnish the necessary data for the study. It was observed during interviews that a general feeling of suspicion and hesitation to share the information prevails among the industrialists. In spite of the best efforts to convince the industrialists that the information collected would be represented, classified or tabulated in such a way that the identity of the individual units would not be disclosed, some owners were not very co-operative in supplying information. However, it requires special mention that a considerable number of owners/managers were very co-operative and furnished the real figures and also encouraged the study. Moreover, it was very often difficult to locate the sample units from the addresses recorded with the District Industries Centre (DIC). This necessitated the replacement of such units by suitable units from the reserve list, in order to keep the total sample size undisturbed. Substitutes, however, were provided only for the units which could not be traced out or owners of which could not be contacted in spite of several visits, or in which case the owners/managers refused to give the information, and also for the closed units.

The data for the study were collected from both primary and secondary sources. Primary Data for the purpose of the study were collected directly from the heads of the sample units. For this purpose, an interview schedule was designed carefully in such a way that necessary data on problems relating to production, marketing, finance and management could be obtained. The final interview schedule was designed on the basis of a well-tested interview pattern. The schedule drafted first was tested by conducting a pilot study among 25 selected SSI units in Chirayinkil and Trivandrum Development Blocks. Published and unpublished data were collected from the Trivandrum District

Table 10.1: Classification of Small-Scale Industrial Units of Trivandrum District

Sl. No.	Category of Industry	Number of units in	
		Universe	Sample
1.	Food Products (Part A) - pickles, jams, squash, etc.	10	3
2.	Food products (Part B) - bread, biscuits, etc.	41	10
3.	Beverages, tobacco and tobacco products	-	-
4.	Cotton textiles	19	5
5.	Wool, silk, fiber textiles, etc.	15	4
6.	Jute, hemp and mesta textiles	-	-
7.	Hosiery and garments	94	24
8.	Wood products	228	57
9.	Paper products and printing	280	70
10.	Leather products	19	5
11.	Rubber and plastic products	51	13
12.	Chemicals and chemical products	31	8
13.	Non-metallic mineral products	25	6
14.	Basic metal industries	10	3
15.	Metal products	298	75
16.	Machinery and parts except electrical	7	2
17.	Electrical machinery and apparatus	42	10
18.	Transport equipments and parts	8	2
19.	Miscellaneous manufacturing industries	338	85

20.	Construction	3	-
21.	Activities allied to construction	-	-
22.	Storage and warehousing	-	-
23.	Real estate and business service	4	-
24.	Education, scientific and research services	-	-
25.	Medical and health services	5	-
26.	Recreational and cultural services	-	-
27.	Personal services	107	27
28.	Repairing and servicing	176	45
29.	Services not elsewhere classified	-	-
	Total	1811	454

Industries Centre, the Directorate of Industries and Commerce, the Bureau of Economics and Statistics, the Kerala Financial Corporation, the Small Industries Development Corporation (SIDCO), and the State Planning Board. Published reports of both the Central and State Government institutions were also made use of. Data from research reports, working papers and journals, were also used. Data collected - both primary and secondary - were processed, tabulated and analysed by employing various mathematical tools such as averages, percentages, ratios, etc., and statistical tools such as coefficient of correlation, rank correlation, etc. Data were analysed, keeping the objectives of the study in view. Production in different small-scale industrial units is of different types. Each category of industry produces a variety of items. For a uniform representation the money value of production has been taken into consideration in the process of analysis.

The study suffers from some limitations. Firstly it was attempted to throw light on the general character of the units through the limited sample coverage. Secondly, it was observed during the survey that some respondents showed a cold attitude in furnishing the data, and, to that extent, the analysis suffers from non-sampling error. Lastly, accuracy of data suffers on account of the fact that the owners/managers did not maintain correct records, in many cases. In the absence of any written records, the information supplied by the owner/manager was used. However, all attempts were made to extract correct information through informal discussion.

Findings

The major findings of the study are summarised below:

The age-wise classification of entrepreneurs showed that entrepreneurs falling within the age-group of 21 to 35 formed the largest percentage. 37.89 per cent of the entrepreneurs were below this group. 302 entrepreneurs (66.52 per cent) fell within the age group of 21 to 49. Among the entrepreneurs quite a high percentage of the entrepreneurs belonged to the educated class.

Among the educated, 16.74 per cent were degree holders-graduation, post-graduation, technical or professional. Nearly 80 per cent of the entrepreneurs possessed previous experience in the line of activity they had chosen. 243 entrepreneurs (53.52 per cent) had 10 or more years' experience in the field selected. The study regarding the motivational factors to start SSI units that some entrepreneurs were motivated by more than one factor to start the small-scale units. However, it was found that among all the motivating factors, the wish to find an independent job ranked first. In 173 units, the answer to the question why they selected such type of industrial units was the industrial and business experience they had. No unit was started with the motivation of social standing and prestige.

Investment: Sole trader form of business was the most popular among the small-scale units taken as sample. The average investment per unit was Rs. 3,98,380 in 1981-82, which continuously dwindled to Rs. 3,70,840 in 1985-86. The industry-wise picture indicates variations in investment per unit. For example, when the industrial units manufacturing pickles, jams, squash, etc., rubber and plastic products, machinery and parts other than electrical, as well as miscellaneous manufacturing industries and repairing and service units, showed a continuously reducing trend of investment, the coir industry showed an unsteady trend. Investment per unit in this industry went down to Rs. 5,19,150 during 1982-83, and then increased to Rs. 5,55,830 during 1983-84; it decreased to Rs. 5,34,180 during 1984-85 and once again increased to Rs. 5,62,950 during 1985-86. Such variations were observed in other industries also. It is concluded that a variation in the total investment takes place mainly because of the variation in the total demand for the products. This conclusion is reached mainly on the basis of the fact that, in some industries, investment increased and decreased within a short period of time.

On an average, investment in fixed assets per unit decreased considerably to Rs. 2,01,170 in 1984-85, which stood as Rs. 2,43,420 in 1981-82. Compared to the year 1984-85, additional investments were made during 1985-86, as a result of which investment in fixed capital per unit increased to Rs. 2,04,820 from Rs. 2,01,170. However, it is to be noted that though the amount of investment decreased during the first four years, the rate of decrease was not steady. The rate of decrease was at a diminishing rate and there was a slight increase during the fifth year. The compound growth rate of investment in fixed capital of only four industries - cotton textile, wood, basic metal and personal services - showed positive results. It was in personal services industry that the highest (8.81 per cent) compound growth rate could be observed. The analysis leads to the conclusion that in the small-scale industrial units (other than those mentioned above), investment in fixed capital was declining.

In a large number of the units selected as sample, the capital employed was below Rs. 2,00,000. In 306 units out of 454 (67.40 per cent), the amount of capital employed was less than Rs. 2,00,000. The capital employed for the purpose means the aggregate of the investment in fixed capital plus working capital. The number of units having capital employed above Rs. 2,00,000 was only 148 (32.60 per cent). Out of this, only 78 units had capital employed above Rs. 3,00,000. Many of the units registered as small-scale industries had less than Rs. 2,00,000 as capital employed. The number of units (145 out of 454) having capital employed below Rs. 50,000 points to the shortage of total capital in the SSI sector. The average capital employed per unit amounted to Rs. 3,60,620 in the industries covered under the study. Fixed assets constituted 60 per cent of the total productive capital, and the rest the working capital.

The industry-wise analysis indicated that machinery constituted the most important item of fixed capital in all the industries except industrial units manufacturing pickles, jams, squash, etc., cotton textiles, coir products, leather products, metal products, and miscellaneous manufacturing industries. In these industries, land and buildings formed the most important item of fixed capital. Most of the industrial units spent a considerable portion of the fixed capital investment for plant and machinery.

The percentage of amount spent for plant and machinery differed in different industries from 6.24 per cent in industrial units manufacturing pickles, jams, squash, etc., to 92.20 per cent in units manufacturing transport equipments and parts. In terms of value, the highest amount (Rs. 7,08,090 per unit) was spent for plant and machinery by industrial units manufacturing non-metallic mineral products, and the lowest (Rs. 2,180 per unit) by units engaged in the production of leather products. Most of the units in cotton textile and coir industries had been found using locally assembled machinery and equipments. Investment in plant and machinery formed above 60 per cent of total fixed capital investment, in the case of units manufacturing transport equipments and parts (92.20 per cent), wood products (85.02 per cent), machinery and parts other than electrical (78.76 per cent), non-metallic mineral products (77.95 per cent), repairing and servicing (70.04 per cent), and basic metal products (68.43 per cent).

The compound growth rates of investment in plant and machinery revealed that except in units manufacturing pickles, jams, squash, etc., hosiery and garments, wood products, printing, leather products, chemical products, basic metal and personal services industries, in all other industries, investment in plant and machinery was declining. Compound growth rate was the highest in personal services industry (24.46 per cent). The rate had declined at the highest degree in transport equipments and parts manufacturing industry (10 per cent). The fixed capital investment in plant and machinery per employee for all the units put together for the period of 5 years (1981-82 to 1985-86), worked out at Rs. 9,360. The highest and the lowest investments were found in the non-metallic mineral products and leather products units, amounting to Rs. 24,790 and Rs. 740 respectively.

Working capital: Working capital is generally more important than fixed capital in the manufacturing industries, whereas fixed capital assumes greater importance in industrial units rendering services. But, it was found that in most of the manufacturing industries covered under the sample, the working capital formed only a minor share of the total capital, compared to fixed capital. The working capital requirement was very high in small manufacturing units. The fact is that the working capital requirement would have been very high, had the industrial units worked at full productive capacity. This supports the argument that working capital requirement is more important than the initial investment in fixed assets, in setting up the small industrial units. It means that it is easy to start an industrial unit in the small-scale sector, but difficult to run without interruption in production.

The average amount of working capital required per unit was estimated to be as low as Rs. 16,020 in printing industry because the work of this industry mainly depended on advance order. This might be due to the fact that some units in this category rendered only services, in which case they had not to spend any amount for purchase of paper and ink, which might be supplied by the customers. The working capital requirement in leather industry was the lowest, i.e., Rs. 6,710, because all the units surveyed under this category of industry were very small in size with a small volume of production. In personal services industry, the working capital per unit was calculated as Rs. 46,930, because this industry group also included oil and oilcake manufacturing units where a high amount of working capital was needed. Similarly, in units engaged in repairing and servicing, the working capital would have been lower than the present amount of Rs. 20,370 had the units engaged in tyre-retreading business been excluded. Cash and bank balance constituted the second major share in the gross working capital. Taking all the industries together, it accounted for 29.75 per cent of the gross working capital. The share of cash and bank balance in the gross working capital varied in different industries. It was the industrial units manufacturing pickles, jams, squash, etc., which were found keeping the highest share of gross working capital in the form of cash-either in hand or at bank. The lowest share in this respect was found in basic metal products industry, where only 12.85 per cent of the gross working capital was kept in the form of cash.

The working capital management of the small-scale units, it seems, is not satisfactory. In most of the industrial units, stock-in-trade constituted the major item of the gross working capital. This was followed by cash and bank balances. Though the percentage share of receivables to total current assets was the lowest, there lies the fact that the sales of different industrial units were also diminishing. The major components of current assets have been compared with the net working capital so as to have more detailed information on the working capital management. An analysis of the trend of the percentages of inventory to working capital brings out the fact that it varied in different years. The percentage of inventory to working capital did not show a continuously increasing or decreasing trend except in wood, printing, and machinery and parts other than electrical industries, in which cases it showed a continuously increasing trend. Compared to the period 1981-82, the percentage of inventory to working capital showed a high proportion during 1985-86 in all the industries except cotton textile, coir, electrical machinery and apparatus, and miscellaneous manufacturing industries.

The year-wise percentages indicated that, compared to the year 1981-82, the proportion of receivables to working capital was reduced by 1.83 per cent during 1985-86. But this may not be considered as an indicator of efficiency in collecting the debts from customers, because the volume of average sales per unit was reduced from Rs. 8,25,900 in 1981-82 to Rs. 8,01,640 in 1985-86. In spite of the declining volume of sales, in most of the industries, the percentage of receivables to working capital showed an increasing proportion. This accepts the fact that these industrial units depended on credit sales, heavily, for their survival.

All the industries taken together, the percentage of cash to working capital showed a declining trend during the period of study. When 45.10 per cent of the net working capital was kept in the form of cash in 1981-82, it represented only 36.60 in 1985-86. In all the industries except coir, printing, basic metal and electrical machinery and apparatus industries, the percentage share of cash to working capital declined in 1985-86, compared to the position in the year 1981-82. It is interesting to note that in no industry the percentage share of cash to working capital was increasing continuously over the period of 5 years covered under the study. The analysis of the various sources of working capital finance showed that all the units should earmark an amount for working fund, from their own pockets.

In addition to this, friends and relatives, short-term bank loan, money lenders and advances received from customers, were found the predominant sources of the working finance of the small industrial units. Industry-wise analysis depicted that one unit each in food industry (producing pickles, jams, squash, etc.), cotton textile industry, non-metallic mineral products industry, 3 units in leather industry, and 5 units in printing industry, used production as the only basis for determining the working capital. Similarly, 3 units in hosiery and garments, and 6 units in wood industry, used past experience as the only basis for determining the working capital. Thus, it is clear that the small industrialists in the sample survey realised the need to adopt a scientific system for determining the working capital.

Financing: It was observed that a sizable portion of the funds invested in small-scale industries was contributed by the industrialists themselves. Put together, owned capital, excluding retained earnings and reserves and surplus, constituted nearly 27 per cent of the total capital invested in the sample SSI units. Retained earnings and reserves and surplus together constituted nearly 40 per cent of the total capital investment. Thus, nearly 67 per cent of the total capital was contributed by the owners themselves. Among the different sources of external finance, banks occupied the predominant position. The amount of loans supplied by the banks constituted 21.61 per cent of the total capital.

On an average, the share of bank loan to the total capital was calculated as 21.61 per cent. This formed nearly 65 per cent of the total contribution made by outside parties. The average amount of loan per unit varied widely. It was the industrial units engaged in the production of non-metallic mineral products, which utilised the maximum amount of loans from banks. The amount of such loan due from one unit in the non-metallic mineral products industry was calculated as Rs. 8,26,700. This constituted 54.46 per cent of the total capital. It was in this industry that the share of bank loan to total capital was found the highest (54.46 per cent). On the other hand, the amount of bank loan in industrial units manufacturing transport equipments and parts was found zero. Comparatively higher amounts of bank loans were enjoyed by units in basic metal industry (Rs. 1,65,000 per unit), machinery and parts except electrical (Rs. 1,20,620 per unit), and electrical machinery and-parts manufacturing industry (Rs. 1,19,000 per unit).

Out of the 454 units under the sample, 166 did not enjoy loan facilities from the banks. Of the remaining 283 units which granted loans only after a period of weeks. In the case of 95, out of these 171 units, it took more than 8 weeks to get the loan sanctioned by the concerned banks. But in the case of 54 units, loans were sanctioned within 2 weeks. This quick granting of loan was ascribed mainly to some sort of influence on the bank officials. It was found that, in most of the cases, the repayment of loans from commercial banks and co-operative banks had to be started within a very short period. Out of 288 industrial units which enjoyed bank loans, in 204 (70.83 per cent) cases the repayment of loans in installments began within a period of 6 months. The loans used by 53 units were to be repaid after a period of 2 years. In most of the cases it took more than two months to get the loan sanctioned.

Of the 116 units which applied for loans, only 79 units were granted them. It took a period of more than 2 months in the case of 44 units; 4 to 8 weeks in the case of 28 units, and 2 to 4 weeks in the case of 7 units. It was noted that in no case the loan was sanctioned within a period of 2 weeks. It was also noticed that the Corporation charged comparatively higher rates of interest on loans. This brings out the fact that the small-scale industries had been facing financial problems; in one way or other. What the industries were in need of was real financial assistance to meet the working capital requirements. They were also in need of financial assistance at the time of starting the unit mainly for the purpose of acquiring the necessary fixed assets. In the case of running units, the timely provision of financial assistance to meet the working capital requirements was found very essential. But the serious observation that the amounts of loans obtained used to be diverted for the personal purposes of the industrialist, points to the need for controlling the use of funds granted as loan.

The analysis of the financial structure brings out the importance of borrowed capital in financing the small-scale industries. It was also noted that borrowed capital was heavily used by the small-scale industrial units to meet the running expenses (i.e., working capital requirement). The small industrialists were able to meet the fixed capital requirements with the owned capital, retained earnings and reserves and surpluses. But when the owned capital (excluding reserves and surplus) is compared with the investment in fixed capital, the real inability of the entrepreneurs can be traced out. The owned capital hardly met half of the total fixed capital requirements (owned capital per unit on an average was worked out at Rs. 1,02,090 and the amount of fixed capital at Rs. 2,17,510). The amount of owned capital was insufficient even for plant and machinery (the amount of investment in plant and machinery was calculated as Rs. 1,23,150 per unit and that of owned capital as Rs. 1.02,090 per unit). The fixed capital requirements were found being met satisfactorily from internal sources, only in the long run. It means that at the time of starting the unit the industrialists faced severe problems of finance. In the case of rented premises, it was found that the industrialists had to pay large amounts as refundable advance.

Final Production: There was wide variation between one category of industry and another, in respect of production. Variation was observed in respect of the quantum of production and the trends in production. The contribution from different categories of industries to total production in the small-scale industrial sector had been varying. The highest contribution was made by the units falling under wool, silk, and fiber textile industry. The sample units under this category were mainly those manufacturing coir products.

Average production by all the industries amounted to Rs. 1,39,86,030 in 1981-82, which increased to Rs. 1,45,22,520 in 1983-84, and decreased to Rs. 1,34,98,160 in 1985-86. There existed wide differences among the industries in respect of their average size of production. The average annual production per unit in 1981-82 varied between Rs. 28,27,950 and Rs. 27,010 in coir industry, and hosiery and garment-making industry, respectively. During the years covered under the study, the average production per unit was found to be the highest in coir industry and the lowest in the hosiery and garment-making industry. The compound growth rate of production showed a negative trend in the small industry sector in the majority of the units. In most of the industries, the compound growth rates were found negative. It was the highest (15.78 per cent) in electrical machinery and apparatus industry, closely followed by machinery and parts other than electrical industry (14.22 per cent). On the other hand, the highest positive growth rate was observed in cotton textile industry (17.31 per cent). There existed great inter-industry variation in the small-scale industrial sector in respect of production. The idle capacity was found to be the higher in the case of transport equipments and parts (60.40 per cent), electrical machinery and apparatus (60.24 per cent), and repairing and servicing (51.62 per cent). It was also observed that the percentage of capacity utilisation had been decreasing year after year in almost all categories of industries. The ranking of different reasons for under utilisation of production capacity revealed that it was lack of finance which played the predominant role in the under-utilisation of production capacity.

Raw material: Increase in the price of raw materials was a noticeable fact. Prices of raw materials showed an increasing trend at different rates during the period covered under the study. The percentage of raw materials to total cost increased by 14.47 over the five years in the case of rubber and plastic products, which was closely followed by units producing bread, biscuits, etc., with 13.98 per cent, metal products with 12.63 per cent, leather products and chemical products with 11.46 per cent each, and printing industry with 11.17 per cent. Out of the 454 units, 210 units (46.26 per cent) made local purchase of raw materials, 127 units (27.97 per cent) purchased from near-by areas, and 115 units (25.33 per cent) from outside the district in addition to local purchases. Only 10.35 per cent (47 units) of the total units procured raw materials from outside the State. The industry-wise analysis showed that, among the manufacturing industries, dependence on middlemen was found to be high in chemical products and non-metallic mineral products, in which 50 per cent of the units depended on middlemen for raw materials. On the other hand, it was only 5.33 per cent in the case of metal products. A large number of units considered carrying cost of inventory to fix inventory level and only 5.95 per cent considered price fluctuations. 14.10 per cent of the units surveyed kept inventory on the basis of the supply conditions of materials.

Labour: The information collected from the units covered under the study revealed that a vast majority of the small-scale units provided employment to less than 10 workers. The existence of trade unions in the units covered in the sample was found to be comparatively insignificant. It was seen that out of 3,650 workers employed during 1985-86, by all the units covered under the study, 2,996 workers were not members of any trade union. It means that only 17.92 per cent of the workers were members of trade unions. The study also revealed that out of the units covered under the study in 386 industrial units there were no trade unions, in 337 units (87.31 per cent) the labour-management relation was reported to be very good or good. It was stated to be very good in 93 units, good in 244 units and satisfactory in 49 units. Not even a single entrepreneur in the sample units under this category reported that it was poor.

An analysis of the related fibres showed that only in 26.42 per cent units, the owners viewed that the level of workers' satisfaction fell above 80 per cent. In 32.12 per cent of the units under the sample, the level of workers- satisfaction was below 60 per cent. A comparison of the levels of satisfaction of workers in units having and units not having trade unions brought to light the fact that, in the case of industrial units having trade unions, the level of workers' satisfaction was higher than 70 per cent, only in 23.53 per cent units. In the case of units having no trade union, in 54.66 per cent of the total units, workers' satisfaction was higher than 70 per cent. It was noted that 65.20 per cent of the total units did not adopt modern techniques of production mainly owing to financial difficulties. In addition, in 55.29 per cent of the total units, it was, the lack of demand which prevented the improvisation of production techniques. When 17 entrepreneurs faced opposition from labour force, only 8 were unable to modernise the production techniques on account of the non-availability of improved machines and tools in the domestic market. On an average, Rs. 28,902 was found to be invested in total assets to provide employment to one individual, in the small-scale industrial sector. The total investment per worker was the lowest in hosiery and garments industry which required only Rs. 5,422 to provide employment to one individual. It was the highest in industrial units manufacturing pickles, jams, squash, etc., where an amount of Rs. 57,197 was to be invested to create employment to one person.

It is also noted that all the units in wood industry faced the problem of abnormal wastage mainly owing to poor quality of raw materials. Inferior techniques, obsolete machinery, lack of storage and preservation facilities, and poor quality of raw materials, were the equally important factors leading to abnormal wastage. In cotton textile industry inefficiency of labour was found to be the major reason for abnormal wastage.

Marketing: A major portion of the goods and services produced in the small industry sector was distributed to consumers directly by the manufacturers. However, exceptions were noted for cotton textile, coir, chemicals, rubber and plastics, non-metallic mineral products, electrical machinery and apparatus and transport equipments manufacturing industries. The analysis of the area-wise distribution of sales of various industrial units revealed that most of the small-scale industries had been oriented to local market. Excluding categories of industries, mainly engaged in rendering services, it was found that 59.20 per cent of the total sales of all manufacturing industries were effected within the district. It was observed that the majority of these units had been forced to sell within the district, because they did not have the means to go very far, involving increased cost of advertisement, transportation and other expenses. It was described by some entrepreneurs that they found it difficult to expand their markets owing to the wide advertisement and publicity done by the large-scale competitors.

It was observed during the survey that not even a unit exported its products directly. The products of coir industry were exported but indirectly. The industrialists sold the products to sole selling agencies at Alleppey who exported them subsequently under their own brand names. The reasons for the bad position in the field of export sales were many - first, the financial constraints faced by the small industrial units; secondly, the lack of market information and guidance relating to export; thirdly, the poor quality of products, and lastly, the very small size of the units. Generally, there was a declining trend in the volume of sales. The industry-wise figures of sales showed that there was a wide variation in the volume of sales per unit as well as in the trend of sales. The average sales per unit varied from Rs. 45,000 in 1985-86 in leather industry to Rs. 43,36,020 in 1983-84 in coir industry. It was noted that the average sales per unit was the highest in coir industry, and the lowest in leather industry. The compound growth rate of sales calculated in the case of cotton textile industry was the highest (19.28 per cent). A positive trend of growth rate was found in the case of cotton textile industry, coir industry, hosiery and garments, rubber and plastic products, chemicals and chemical products, non-metallic mineral products and transport equipments and parts manufacturing industries. The negative growth rate was the highest (-15.48 per cent) for the electrical machinery and apparatus making industry.

All the units covered under the study faced some difficulty in relation to marketing. A large number of the units in the sample faced more than one problem. The analysis revealed that though one unit faced various difficulties for marketing the products, competition between similar units and lack of demand were predominant. The data collected from the small-scale industrial units in relation to the ISI mark, showed that the number of small industrial units using the ISI mark was very low (out of the 454 units surveyed, only 11 manufacturing units used the ISI mark). The survey revealed that all the manufacturing units in the sample used brand names for their products. No unit conducted marketing research in the required manner. However 8 units out of 454, conducted small surveys with a view to collecting opinions from consumers. It was found that most of the units in the small sector did not, or were unable to spend huge sums for advertising. An analysis of the factors responsible for the unhealthy competition, prevailing at present, led to the conclusion that it was the result of improper planning in the SSI sector. Information related to the existing capacity and the present and future demands for the products was not available with any government or trade association.

Financial Analysis: It was noted that most of the units (79.52 per cent) followed the commonly accepted practice of selling on both cash and credit bases. Most of the industrial units in the small sector sold goods on credit and had to wait for more than 3 weeks to collect the sums from the customers. This contributed a lot to their prevailing financial difficulties. The figures of average annual sales and net profit revealed that net profit showed varying percentages of sales in different industries, ranging from 2.82 per cent industrial units manufacturing electrical machinery and apparatus to 20.18 per cent in cotton textile industry.

The average annual production per worker, in the small-scale sector as a whole, was Rs. 56,130. It ranged between Rs. 1,840 in hosiery and garments industry and Rs. 2,21,400 in coir industry. Annual production per worker was estimated to be above Rs. 1,00,000 in the case of coir industry, units manufacturing electrical machinery and apparatus, transport equipments and parts, and oil manufacturing units. Production per worker was found to be comparatively lower in tailoring units, cotton textile industry, units manufacturing pickles, jams, squash, etc., leather industry, units manufacturing bread, biscuits, etc., printing industry and wood industry. Productivity of capital varied from one industry to another, in the survey. The amount of capital required per unit of output was found to be the lowest (0.15) in coir industry, and the highest (4.63) in units manufacturing pickles, jams, squash, etc. In other industries the range of variation in capital-output ratio was from 0.23 to 4.25.

The capital-output ratio was 4.63 in industrial units manufacturing pickles, jams, squash, etc., because of heavy investment in land and buildings and relatively low volume of production. On an average, when an amount of Rs. 2,92,810 was invested in fixed assets, the output per unit was estimated to be Rs. 67,040 only. Out of the amount invested in fixed assets, Rs. 2,73,000 was invested in land and buildings only. The capital-output ratios varied with different levels of investment. It was found that in the size of investment up to Rs. 50,000, the efficiency of capital was the highest in cotton textile industry, as only 0.33 unit of capital was necessary to produce one unit of output. The analysis of capital-output ratio in different industries and in different ranges of investment indicated that the nature of industry as well as the size of investment has considerable influence on the ratio of capital to output. The industry-wise ratios indicated wide differences in investment-output ratio. It varied from 0.03 in coir industry to 1.08 in cotton textile industry. A comparison of the ratio of fixed capital to output, with that of investment in plant and machinery to output, brought out some hidden facts. It was revealed that in some cases a major part of the total investment was spent for land and buildings or similar fixed assets.

The comparison of the rate of net profit to sales, for the five years covered under the study, revealed that there was a declining trend in operating results in the small industry sector. The rate of this decline was the highest in basic metal industry where the percentage of net profit to sales declined from 13.63 in 1981-82 to 4 in 1985-86. The sample small-scale industrial units offered a return of 14.15 per cent on total investment. Return on investment was observed to be the highest in coir industry, closely followed by leather industry. The rate of return on investment varied from 2.28 per cent in industrial units manufacturing pickles, jams, squash, etc., to 42.59 per cent in coir industry. The coefficient of correlation between investment and net profit was found to be significant in all the industries except food, cotton textile and transport equipments and parts making industries. The significance of correlation was measured by 't' test. A negative correlation coefficient was observed in food industry which implied that any additional investment in the industry probably would reduce the net profit. However, though correlation coefficient was positive (0.75) in cotton textile industry, the 't' test revealed that there was an insignificant relationship between total investment and net profit.

A classification of the return on investment according to the size of investment revealed that the highest (38.50 per cent) return on investment was achieved by industrial units having investment up to Rs. 50,000 in the small industry sector. This was closely followed by units having the investment size of Rs. 2,50,001 to Rs. 3,00,000. The coefficient of correlation between owners' funds and net profit revealed an insignificant relationship in food industry, cotton textile industry and basic metal industry, which meant that investment of additional fund by the owners might not result in increased net profit. The 't' test proved that the correlation coefficient was significant at 5 per cent level in leather industry, rubber and plastic industry and non-metallic mineral products industry. In the small-scale industrial sector as a whole, the correlation coefficient was found to be significant at 5 per cent level.

There existed significant correlation between sales and net profit in all industries except industrial units manufacturing pickles, jams, squash, etc. and cotton textiles. In leather and non-metallic mineral products industries, correlation between sales and net profit was found to be significant at 5 per cent level, which meant that a comparatively larger volume of sales would make a change in net profit. In leather industry and non-metallic mineral products industry, the correlation coefficient was calculated at 0.90 and 0.85 respectively. It was higher in coir industry (1), basic metal products (1), units manufacturing machinery and parts other than electrical (1) and units manufacturing electrical machinery and (1). The coefficient of correlation between sales and net profit for the small-scale industrial sector taken together was calculated at 0.95. The 't' test showed that the correlation between sales and net profit was significant at 1 per cent level.

Recommendations

On the basis of the findings of the present study, the following recommendations are being made, for improvement of the small-scale sector in Kerala.

The State Government should initiate steps to establish an agency with autonomous status to supply plant and machinery to the small-scale industrial lease. In case there are problems in establishing such a new agency, this type of service can be extended by the existing government agency, the Kerala State Small Industries Development Corporation (SIDCO) by properly restructuring its activities and areas of functioning in an efficient manner. It was noted in the case of a large number of SSI units that the lion share of the available funds was utilised for the acquisition of land and buildings. This has caused inadequacy of funds for acquiring plant and machinery and meeting working capital requirements. To overcome this difficulty, it is suggested that the District Industries Centres and other responsible government agencies take initiative to provide the required land and buildings on rent to the SSI units. Such a support would act as an inducement to the new entrepreneurs with managerial skill, also, to start SSI units.

The existing arrangements, for loans granted to the SSI units for acquiring plant and machinery, adopted by the financial institutions, are found to be not satisfactory in the sense that the units are compelled to buy certain specified brands of plant and machinery under the instructions of the financial institution. This leads to the acquisition of poor quality plant and machinery and, in some cases, even items which may not be the desired ones. To overcome this, the SSI units should be given the freedom for the selection of the plant and machinery in accordance with their needs. Commercial banks and similar financial institutions should be given directives by the government to sanction loans for the working capital requirements of the SSI units at a subsidised rate, by giving top priority. The cumbersome formalities, followed at present should also be made easier especially with regard to the timely disbursement of the loan. The financial institutions and commercial banks which extend financial support to the SSI units should ensure themselves that the money borrowed from them is utilised by the owners of the SSI units for the purpose for which it is taken. Periodical on the spot inspection by the staff of the financial institutions/banks is recommended. It is suggested that an application received for financial support in the form of a loan, from SSI units should be disposed of by the financial institutions and banks, within one month. It requires special mention that the Kerala Financial Corporation which is mainly responsible, for the development of the SSI sector in the State as a government agency should take particular care in this regard. The genuineness of the applications should also be thoroughly verified so as to ensure that the assistance is not misutilised.

It is high time that the activities of the Directorate of Industries and Commerce, Government of Kerala, and that of the Kerala Financial Corporation are coordinated in such a way that the activities of one become complementary to those of the other. The Labour Department of the Government of Kerala should be more vigilant for the prompt settlement of the disputes between management and workers. The setting up of industrial tribunals at Taluk level is suggested for this purpose.

In order to avoid the problem of non-availability of raw materials in time, the intervention of the government becomes most inevitable. It is suggested that the allotment of raw materials under government quota be enhanced. In addition, the availability of such quota of raw materials in time and of the required quality should also be ensured. Some co-operative societies with the membership of industrialists in the small-scale sector can be established to solve the crisis of the non-availability of raw materials in the required quantity and at the right time. The societies can pool the requirements of the members in a particular area directly from the manufacturers or large wholesalers and can take advantage of the economy in bulk purchasing. This arrangement facilitates the elimination of middlemen who take advantage of the situation and exploit the SSI units. The co-operative societies can also undertake functions allied to purchases like quality testing, storage, transportation, etc. The financial and other supports extended by the government for the promotion of the co-operative sector can also be availed of by SSI units under this arrangement.

It was noted that many of the SSI units had to wait long to secure power connection. The government should instruct the Kerala State Electricity Board to give priority to the applications of the SSI units, in granting power connection. It is also recommended, in connection with the power supply, that the Electricity Board should ensure an uninterrupted supply of power for at least 10 hours a day to the SSI units. The Board should also ensure that the SSI units are charged only for the actual consumption of electricity. The SSI units should make arrangements either by establishing their own testing laboratories in the units or by registering with the Bureau of Indian standards to ensure the quality of their products, which has great significance in the market. In this the government can help the SSI units by opening Quality Testing Centres at least at Taluk head quarters for the benefit of SSI units.

Stringent measures should be taken at the government level for the strict execution of the price preference scheme for government purchases and reservation of items for the production specified for the SSI sector. The Government can think of exempting the SSI units from sales tax at least for some items, so as to encourage them to face the competition from large units. In order to avoid the competition from within the SSI sector the government can consider the imposition of restrictions on the number of units for a specified item of products in a particular area, say, block or taluk.

The Centre for Management Development (CMD), the autonomous body established by the Industries Department, Government of Kerala can work out effective schemes to impart training to the managers of SSI units. Such a training should enlighten the trainees on the various scientific principles and techniques which can be adopted for the efficient management of SSI units. The Kerala Industrial and Technical Consultancy Organisation Ltd. (KITCO) and the Small Industries Service Institute (SISI) can also take the initiative for conducting training on these lines. The Economics and Statistics Department of the Government of Kerala should take particular care to establish management information system in all the District Industries Centres (DICs). This system should facilitate information regarding the number of registered and unregistered SSI units in the district, and about the nature and quantity of products manufactured, the level of investment, the nature and quantity of raw materials used, the number of persons employed, machinery used, techniques of production, market conditions, capacity utilisation, etc. of each unit.

References

Adiseshiah, Malcolm S., *Mid-Year Review of the Economy: 1986-87*, Working Paper No. 76, August 1986.

Administrative Reforms Commission, *Report of the Working Group on Small-Scale Sector*, Simla: The Government of India Press, 1969.

Administrative Reforms Commission, *Report of the Working Group on the Small-Scale Sector*, Delhi: Manager of Publications, Government of India, 1968.

Annual Survey of Industries, Central Statistical Organisation, 1968.

Anon, *Working Class in the Small Sector*, Economic and Political Weekly (Vol. XII, No. 12, March 19, 1977).

Asian Productivity Organisation, *Technological Survey of Small Industry in Japan: 1969*, Asian Productivity Organisation, 1971.

Babu P., *A Study of the Sociological Characteristics of Small-Scale Industries*, Ph.D. Thesis, University of Kerala, 1978.

Baker Moosa A., *Role of Small-Scale Industries in the Economic Development of Kerala*, Ph.D. Thesis, University of Calicut.

Balakrishnan G., *Financing Small Industries in India: 1950-52*, Bombay: Asia Publishing House, 1961.

Bannock, Graham, *The Economies of Small Firms*, Oxford: Basil Black Well, 1981.

Basu S. K., *Place and Problems of Small Industries*, Calcutta: A Mukherjee (P) Ltd., 1957.

Bedabati Mohanty, *Economies of Small-Scale Industries*, New Delhi: Ashish Publishing House, 1986.

Bhattasali, Birendra Nath, *The Specific Advantages of Small-Scale Industries*, Development Commissioner, Small-Scale Industries, Government of India, 1971.

Dewett, Singh and Verman, *Indian Economics*, New Delhi: S. Chand & Co., 1972.

Dhar P. N. and Lydall H. F., *The Role of Small Enterprises in Indian Economic Development*, Bombay: Asia Publishing House, 1961.

Dhar, P. N., *Small-Scale Industries in Delhi: A Study in Investment Output and Employment Aspect*, Bombay: Asia Publishing House, 1958.

Donham P., *Wither Small Business*, Harvard Business Review, 1957.

Government of India, Ministry of Commerce and Industry, *Report on Small Industries in India by the International Planning Team*, the Ford Foundation, 1954.

Government of India, *Report of the sub-group on Small-Scale Industries*, 1965.

Government of Kerala, *Report of the High Level Committee on Industry*, Trade and power, *op.cit.*

Goyal S. K., Rao K. S., et al., *Small-Scale Sector and Big Business*, New Delhi: The Indian Institute of Public Administration, 1984.

International Labour Organisation, *Services for Small-Scale Industry*, Geneva: La Tribune De Geneva, 1961.

International Labour Organisation, *Small-Scale Engineering Industries in the Punjab: Economic and Labour Conditions*, New Delhi: International Labour Office, India Branch, 1961.

International Perspective Planning Team, the Ford Foundation, *Development of Small-Scale Industries in India: Prospects, Problems and Policies*, Ministry of Industry, Government of India, 1963.

Jain O. P., *Export Prospects of Small Industries in India*, Export Horizons, New Delhi: Publication Bureau, Government of India, 1975.

Jain O. P., *Small Industry Exports*, New Delhi: S. Chand & Co. (Pvt.) Ltd., 1971.

Jha L. K., *Shortages and High Price: The Way out*, Delhi: Indian Book Company, 1976.

Joshi N. C., *Cottage and Small-Scale Industries in India*, New Delhi: Sumeja Book Centre, 1956.

Kalpagam U., *Labour in Small Industry: Case of Export Garments Industry in Madras*, Economic and Political Weekly (Vol. XVI, No. 48, November 28, 1981).

Kumar C. S. Mohana, *Role of Commercial Banks in Financing Small-Scale Industries in Trivandrum District (with special reference to the State Bank of Travancore)*, M.Phil. Dissertation, Calicut, 1984.

Lakdawala D. T. and Sandesara J. C., *Small Industry in a Big City: A Survey in Bombay*, Bombay: Bombay University Press, 1960.

Lasser T. K., *How to Run a Small Business?*, New York: McGraw Hill, 1955.

Mahendra K. L., *Small-Scale Industries and the Public Sector* (in; Role of State Sector in Developing Countries Ed.), New Delhi: People's Publishing House, 1977.

Mishra, J. N., *Small-Scale and Cottage Industry in Saugor District*, Jabalpur: Singhai Mojilal and Sons.

Morgan, Arthur E., *Industry for Small Committees*, Community Service Incorporated, Ohio: Yellow Springs.

Nanjundan S., Robinson H. E., et al., *Economic Research for Small Industry Development: Illustrated by India's Experience*, Bombay: Asia Publishing House, 1962.

National Council of Applied Economic Research (NCAER), *Study of Selected Small Industrial Units*, New Delhi: NCAER, 1972.

National Council of Applied Economic Research (NCAER), *Study of Selected Small Industrial Units*, New Delhi: NCAER, 1972.

National Council of Applied Economic Research, *Small-Scale Industries of Mysore*, Calcutta: Sree Saraswathy Press Ltd., 1963.

National Council of Applied Economic Research, *Survey of the Handloom Industry in Karnataka and Sholapur*, Bombay: Asia Publishing House, 1959.

National Council of Educational Research and Training, *New Perspectives in Marketing*, Delhi: Cambridge Printing Works, 1972.

Oomman M. A., *Small-Scale Industries in Kerala: A Case Study of the Role of Small Industries in Economic Growth*, Ph.D. Thesis, University of Kerala, 1967.

Padolecchia, Siro P., *Marketing in the Developing World*, New Delhi: Vikas Publishing House Pvt. Ltd., 1979.

Pareek H. S., *Financing of Small-Scale Industries in a Developing Economy*, Delhi: National Publishing House, 1978.

Prasad, Bhagwati and Eresi K., *Equity Base: A Study of Small Units*, The Indian Journal of Commerce, Vol. XXXIX, Part 2, No. 147, April-June, 1986.

Rajagopalan D., *Small-Scale Soap-making Units in Pondicherry State*, M.Phil Dissertation, University of Madras, 1979.

Ramakrishna K. T., *Finances for Small-Scale Industry in India*, Bombay: Asia Publishing House, 1962.

Ramakrishnan P., *New Entrepreneurship in Small-Scale Industry in Delhi*, Delhi: Economic and Scientific Research Foundation, 1975.

Rao, Madhav, V., *Problems of Development of Small Scale Enterprises as Ancillary to Large Concerns*, Delhi: Mimeo, Institute of Economic Growth, 1962.

Rao R. V., *Cottage and Small-Scale Industries and Planned Economy*, N.P.: Sterling Publishers, 1967.

Rele Subhash J., *Small-Scale Sector: Modernisation Crucial for Progress*, Eastern Economist, Vol. 75, No. 21, 1980.

Report of the High Level Committee on Development of Electronic Industry in Kerala, 1972.

Report of the Working Group, *Small-Scale Industries-Programmes of Work for the Third Five Year Plan*, Ministry of Commerce and Industry, Government of India, 1959.

Report on Punjab Industrial Power Conference: August 18th and 19th (Chandigarh: Punjab and Delhi Chamber of Commerce and Industry, 1965.

Reserve Bank of India, *Report on the Survey of Small-Scale Industrial Units and Small Artisans: All India*, RBI, 1972.

Robinson, Hanery Edwin, *Productivity and Small-Scale Industries*, Productivity, National Productivity Council, 1962.

Sandesara, J. C., *Incentives and their impact: Some Studies on Small Industry*, Economic and Political Weekly, Vol. XVIII, No. 48, November 27, 1982.

Seminar Report, *Fostering Small Industries*, Eastern Economist, August 24, 1973, Vol. 61, No. 8.

Sharma Krishanlal, *Entrepreneurial performance in Role Perspective*, Delhi: Abhinav Publications, 1975.

Shashi Bala, *Management of Small Scale Industries*, New Delhi: Deep & Deep Publications, 1984.

Shetty M. C., *Small-Scale and Cottage Industry in a Developing Economy: A Study of Their Rationale, Structure and Operative Conditions*, Bombay: Asia Publishing House, 1963.

SIET Institute, *Identification of Product Opportunities in Kerala: A Market Study*, Hyderabad: SIET Institute, 1979.

SIET Institute, *New Industrial Possibilities in Malappuram (Kerala)*, Hyderabad: SIET Institute, 1978.

Singh Baljit, *The Economies of Small Scale Industries: A Case Study of Small Scale Industrial Establishments of Moradabad*, Bombay: Asia Publishing House, 1961.

Singh N. N., *Successful Management in Developing Countries: Organising Small-Scale Industries*, Bombay: Orient Longman Ltd., 1977.

Singh, Inderjit and Gupta N. S., *Financing of Small Industry*, New Delhi: S. Chand & Company Ltd., 1971.

Singh, Nau Nihal, *Scientific Management of Small Scale Industries*, Bombay: Lalvani Publishing House, 1970.

Small Industry Extension Training (SIET) Institute, *Industrial Possibilities in Kozhikode District*, Hyderabad: SIET Institute, 1978.

Society for Social and Economic Studies, *Capital for Medium and Small-Scale Industries*, Bombay: Asia Publishing House, 1959.

Stades F.J.N., Netherlands Technical Consultancy Services, The Hague, *Report on Small Industry in India*, Ministry of Commerce and Industry, Government of India, New York.

Staley, Eugene and Morse, Richard, *Modern Small Industry for Developing Countries*, New York: McGraw Hill Book Company, 1965.

State Bank of India, *Economic and Statistical Research Department*, Survey of Potential for Financing Small-Scale Industries- Varanasi Centre (Part 1), Bombay: State Bank of India, 1968.

Stepanek, Joseph E., *Small Industry Advisory Services: An International Study*, Glencoe III: The Free Press, 1960.

Streefkerk, Hein, *Too Little to Live on Too much to Die on*, Employment in Small-Scale Industries in Rural South Gujarat, Economic and Political Weekly (April 11, 1981).

Subramanian R., Shivakumar K., et. al., *Entrepreneurship in Small-Scale Industries in Madurai City and its Environs*, Madras: Sangam Publishers, 1975.

Tambi J.M.L., *Marketing Strategy for Small-Scale Industries*, (in: Marketing Management and the Indian Economy Ed. By S. Neelamegham), Delhi: Prominent Printers, 1978.

Tarun, Tara Nand Singh, *Small-Scale Industries and India's Economic Development*, N.P.: Deep & Deep Publications, 1986.

The American Rural Small-Scale Industry, *Rural Small-Scale Industry in the People's Republic of China*, University of California Press, 1977.

U. S. Small Business Administrative News Release, 1959: Cited in Joseph E. Stepanek, *Managers for Small Industry: An International Study*, Illinois: The Free Press.

UNESCO Research Centre on Social and Economic Development in South Asia, *Social Aspects of Small Industries in India*, Delhi: United India Press, 1962.

UNESCO Research Centre on Social and Economic Development in Southern Asia, *Small Industries and Social Change*, Delhi: United India Press, 1966.

Vepa Ram K., *Small Industry in the Seventies*, Delhi: Vikas Publications, 1971.

Wanchoo N. N., *Standardisation and Quality Control-Aid to Marketing*, Indian Journal of Marketing, Vol. 1, No. 2, June 1968.

Warrior K. K., *Small-Scale Industries in Sivakasi and Sattur*, New Delhi: Planning Commission, Government of India, 1957.

11

Traditional Industries in Kerala

M. Sarngadharan and G. Raju

Since July 1991, a series of reforms in industrial policy, the external sector, financial and fiscal areas have been executed in the economy. These reforms have ushered in a new phase in the industrial development of the country. However, there have been sharp differences of opinion on the rationale for the reforms and more importantly, their impact on the productivity of the industrial economy. While the supporters of the reforms expect greater growth, competitiveness and productivity, the critics are skeptical both about the possibilities of growth as well as nature of growth it would lead to. In particular, it is pointed out that the enjoying liberalization is without regard to the needs of the traditional sector industries in terms of long-term objectives. Earlier, because of industrial licensing and other promotional and regulatory policies and because of the greater role accorded to the public sector it was possible for the government to direct substantial investment to backward sectors and areas. But as a result of liberalisation which resulted in the de-licensing of industries and removal of subsidies, government is unable to direct investment to specific sectors or areas where it feels it is most efficient. This will further aggravate the fate of traditional industries, which are already at their weakest point.

This situation raises an important question, whether the traditional industries have the capacity to survive and grow in an increasingly competitive market. This also opens up various issues for more detailed enquiry into: the strength and weaknesses of the traditional industries; the alterative strategies for strengthening their capabilities; and the induced changes in institutions and policies.

Major Traditional Industries in Kerala

Traditional industries, in terms of employment and production play a vital role in the economy of Kerala. However, criticism is also raised that the dominance of these industries of low-value added products results in low over-all productivity of the industrial sector. The most important traditional industries in the state of Kerala are Coir, Handloom, Cashew and Beedi industries. These four industries together provide employment for about one million persons.

A common feature shared by all these traditional industries is the regional concentration on account of geographical, historical and sociological factors as well as resource endowment. For instance, Coir industry had flourished throughout the Coastal belt of the state, with concentration in Chirayinkil (Thiruvananthapuram district), Kundara and Karunagappally (both in Kollam district), Ambalapuzha and Cherthala (in Alapuzha district). Manufacture of Coir products was concentrated in Alapuzha district. Similarly, most of the Cashew processing units were confined to in and around Kollam district. Again, beedi industry is located predominantly in Kannur district and Handloom industry is concentrated in Kannur and Thiruvananthapuram districts. One striking feature common to all these industries is that their production technology remained stagnant at the level of handicraft. Another feature was that all these industries were heavily dependent on external market, especially in the earlier decades. Above all, the wages in traditional industries were below the subsistence level and the work places lacked even the basic amenities. Moreover, employment in the traditional industries was often seasonal in nature and highly susceptible to the fluctuations in the external demand. And it is this low wage rate that prevailed in the traditional industries and the despicable working conditions were the major reasons attributed to the emergence of a strong trade union movement in this sector.

Kerala with its high social development indicators with poor industrial growth (the ranking in terms of industrialisation being tenth among the other Indian states) presents an interesting case study. In attempting to understand the problem and potential of traditional industries in Kerala the initial step is to take an inventory of research studies already done. A close look at these studies would enable the researchers to identify the gaps in the literature and the new issues that need to be taken up for more detailed analysis with a view to developing suitable growth strategies for the traditional industries and to enriching the reform packages to address the sector in terms of long term objectives.

The present study was undertaken with the objective of making a thorough review of the existing literature in the area of traditional industries in Kerala such as Coir, Handloom, Cashew and Beedi industries. The study deals with the research work carried out in the area in various research departments of Universities of Kerala, Thiruvananthapuram; Center for Development Studies, Ulloor; Cochin University of Science and Technology, Kochi; Calicut University, Kozhikode and other state government institutions/bodies. Besides these, researches carried out by individual researchers were reviewed and incorporated in the study.

Coir Industry

Except a few coir manufacturing units in the factory sector, the coir industry is essentially a cottage industry, concentrated in the coastal strip of Kerala, mainly because of the special facility for retting of coconut husks along the coastal regions. The industry broadly consists of four activities, viz., fiber extraction, spinning, manufacturing and export. Coir products are manufactured mostly for export market. The first two activities mentioned here are mostly organised as cottage/household industry. It is the factory sector engaged in manufacturing activities that converts the coir yarn into final products like coir mats and mattings, rugs, carpets, etc.

In Kerala alone, nearly 3.5 lakh people were directly involved in the coir sector out of about 5 lakh dependents of the industry. During the period April 2000 to March 2001, 1053.98 MT of coir fiber valued at Rs. 148.17 lakh was exported from India which is 30 per cent higher in terms of quantity and 26 per cent higher in value than export of coir fiber during 1999-2000 the same period of the previous year. During the period April 2000 to March 2001, 14607.30 metric tones of coir yarns valued at Rs. 3738.39 lakh were exported. There is an increase of 12 per cent in terms of quantity and value compared to the export of the same period of the previous year. The Coir Industry Act of 1953 and the establishment of the Coir Board in 1954 were hallmarks in the development history of Coir industry in Kerala. As an important foreign exchange earner, and as one providing employment for a large number of people, particularly of the Coastal area, the Coir industry has always been given priority by the Government of Kerala in the development plans of the State.

The main thrust of the coir development scheme in the Third Five Year Plan was reorganisation of production and marketing of coir under Co-operative Societies. As on 31-3-1999, there existed 829 coir co-operatives consisting of 525 primary societies, 56 manufacturing societies, 11 small scale produces societies, 2 husk procurement and distribution societies and 73 fiber societies. Besides the Kerala State Coir Co-operative Marketing Federation (COIRFED) operates in this sector as Apex Co-operatives Society.

The Co-operative coir sector however, finds it difficult to compete with the private processors and a major problem facing these Coir industry as a whole is the non-availability of adequate quantities of husk at reasonable prices. Another main problem confronting the industry is the severe competition it has to face from less costly synthetic substitutes in international markets. The volume of exports of coir and coir product has been on the decline since 1960-61 from 64,782 tonnes to 61,031 tonnes in 1999-2000, though in value forms, there has been remarkable increase from Rs. 8.55 crore to Rs. 303.05 crore during this period. The scarcity of adequate coconut husk at reasonable price to sustain the workers throughout the year has been a growing problem in recent years. The growing trend of mechanisation, the development of brown fiber industry in the neighbouring states have posed serious threat to the future of coir industry in the state. Above all, the coir sector was facing a number of new challenges because of the liberalised scenario and deregulations being the order of the day. The industry should be more realistic to compete in the global market.

Scholars have undertaken a number of studies that went into the details of various aspects of coir industry. Their studies fall under the categories of dissertations and theses, working papers, published articles and books. A belief review of the existing literature in the field of Coir industry in Kerala is presented below. Janardhana Pillai M. L. (1922) in the Economic Development Board of Travancore, opined that the foreign competition and tariff responsible for the decline in the profits and failures of the Indian Coir firm. He suggested for increasing the export duty on Coir yarn and by raising the tariff value for Coir yarn. Venketaraman J. K. (1940) in his study identified various factors that contributed to the migration of the industry to the town of Alleppey. The first and most important reason was arrangement for the adequate supply of wearing yarn at Alleppy. The beach yarn and vycome yarn, the coarser varieties of yarn, widely used for pile fabrics, were produced in the vicinity of Alleppy. Alleppy was also well connected to the hand twist wheel spin yarn producing areas in the Southern Travancore by an elaborate system of inland water transport. On the other hand, the manufacturers outside Travancore was dependent on the import of Coir yarn from Travancore. Export duty on Coir yarn and fibre at 5 per cent on the tariff value, imposed by the Travancore Government, gave a decisive competitive advantage for the manufacturers in Travancore.

George K. (1953) in his presidential address at the General Body Meeting of Alleppy Chamber of Commerce criticised that the Indians were accused of bringing disrepute to the industry by shipping substandard products in their efforts to lower the prices. To the bitter resentment of the Indians, the European firms began to undertake advertisement campaigns in trade journals about the genuine coir products manufactured in European factories. Bhaskaran Unnithan (1956) argued that the stability and expansion of the industry on the economic basis depend almost entirely on the cost of production and the provision for efficient marketing and the creation of conditions for a contented labour working harmoniously with the employer in the increased production of quality goods intended for export. The foreign and home markets must be developed by a more efficiently organised system of publicity, propaganda and trading agreements with other countries. He was of the view that the reconstruction of the industry could be useful only if it is based on co-operation.

A study conducted by the State Planning Board (1973) estimated that 90 per cent of weavers would be displaced in case of full scale mechanisation of the weaving sector. Similarly mechanisation of Creel mat production will displace 1424 man years employment out of the present 1750 man years of employments. Pylee M. V. (1975) in his study of problems and prospects of Coir industry in India found that the rapid escalation of the Coir yarn prices in the year 1974 due to chaotic conditions in the Coir yarn spinning section created a serious crisis for the small-scale sector. Prakash A. B. (1977) found that the Coir goods for the Indian market were mostly of lower quality and rejects from the export goods, which ultimately reduced the price of Coir product in internal market also. The rejected goods have to be sold at far lower prices. The small producers were at the mercy of the trader's judgment with respect to quality of grade and prices of products.

Meera V. (1983) opined that the Coir working of women formed the back bone of the democratic women movement in Ambalapuzha and Shertallai taluks. The growing militancy of the working woman was reflected in their increased participation in struggles and union activities. Women participated in large numbers in the food campaign and anti-Japanese propaganda. Working women were mainly rallied under the demands for equal wages for equal work and maternity benefits. The FAO (1983) in their study concluded that the trend of price escalation reduced the competitors of the Coir products in the international market and contributed to a market shift to floor coverings made of their hard fiber such as sisal. Though available information hinted possibility of such a substitution in market demand, it was unlikely that relative prices had played any significant role in the process. The price movement of important hard fibers did not reveal any consistent trend. Thomas Issac (1983) made an attempt to document and analyse the evolution of industrial organisation with respect to traditional industries in Kerala. He traced the evolution of the organisation of weaving Coir fabrics from large-scale manufactory to progressively smaller and smaller weaving units until the production structure came to be characterised by the predominance of domestic units.

It was noted that the Coir weaving industry was passing through an even more momentous transformation. Efforts were being made to reorganise production in large-scale units on the basis of machine technology. He attempted to analyse the condition that accounted for the extra ordinary perseverance of the lower firms of production and the condition that made their dissolution inevitable. He considered class struggle between the employers and the worker to be the primary determinant of industrial organisation within the choices made possible by the material basis of production. Thus the decentralisation of production in Coir weaving was considered to be a response to the rising trade union movement, which increasingly eroded the possibilities of absolute exploitation. The domestic industry outside the protection of labour laws and trade unions was the ultimate stage of this process. The spread of trade union movement as well as small producers movement in the domestic sector hindered the possibilities of increasing the surplus on the basis of technology. This was argued to be the background of the latest phase of evolution of the coir weaving industry, that is, introduction of the power loom. The spinning of Coir, which exhibited a very wide spectrum of pre-manufactory form of industrial organisation also received his attention. Even here there was a tendency towards structural retrogression. Reorganisation of the industry on the basis of co-operatives of workers was put forward as a solution to the decentralisation and the consequent deterioration of the condition of labour. However, the experience of the co-operative sector in Coir spinning was not successful.

Pyarlal Raghavan (1995) concluded that despite the large mobilisation of workers in support of co-operatives, the performance showed a deteriorating trend over time in terms of employment generation as well as financial viability. The demand for Coir products had declined over time and the raw-material scarcity became actuate. The co-operatives, which paid the minimum wages, were handicapped in competing with private sector in the input market. The attempt of the Government to intervene in the husk market in favour of the former could only worsen the raw material crises. The prolonged stalemate had undermined the morale of the work force and contributed to the bureaucratisation of the co-operative structures through increasing Government intervention.

The survey of literature narrated above, warrants serious studies on Coir industry in Kerala from social, economic and political dimensions.

Handloom Industry

Among the traditional industries in Kerala, handloom industry has a significant place as one providing employment for about 1.5 lakh persons. More than 80 per cent of the looms are concentrated in Kannur, Kozhikode and Thiruvananthapuram. The industry is widely scattered and still remains largely unorganised. As on 31-3-2001, there were 43,756 handloom units in the state, of which 41,256 units were in the Co-operative sector. The remaining 2500 units were functioning as household units, except a few in the corporate sector. Of the total estimated 1,34,753 workers, 1,28,861 in the Co-operative sector and 5872 workers in other establishments.

The production in the handloom sector was reported to be 67.47 mm valuing Rs. 303.3 crore as on 31-3-2001. Of this, the production in the co-operative sector was estimated at 65.6 mm, valuing Rs. 295.2 crore and the production in the household sector (including private corporate sector) to be 1.87 mm, amounting to Rs. 60.75 crore. Between 1976 and 2001, there was significant expansion in the co-operative sector, the number of units under it registered an increase from 22,548 to 41,256 an 83 per cent increase in 25 years. The natural consequences of this are a corresponding decline in the number of units in the private sector. There was an absolute decline in the total number of units from 9,00,300 in 1976 to 44,756 units in 2001 and the decline in the private sector was from 67,482 to 2,500 a decline to less than one twentieth units in 1976.

The organisation of handloom units within the co-operative fold was started in Kerala with the Second Five Year Plan. Kerala's Second Five Year Plan provided an outlay of Rs. 16 crore for the organisation of co-operatives in the industry. The actual plan expenditure during the First and Second plan together on this account was Rs. 2.66 crore. By the end of the Second Plan, there were only 391 co-operative societies, which increased to 755 as on 31-3-2001, showing an increase about 50 per cent. The Kerala State Handloom Weavers Apex Co-operative Society (Hantex) was established in 1976, for developing the co-operative sector. Again in 1977, the Kerala State Handloom Development Corporation (Handveev) was established for assisting the handloom weavers outside the co-operative fold.

Despite various measures and concentrated efforts, the handloom industry in the state is still under several stress and stains, due to problems like scarcity of yarn and its soaring prices, accumulation of stock due to poor marketing openings, competition from the mill sector and outside the state obsolete technology and so on. In short, the handloom industry is in the doldrums. All the production units in the organised sector, viz., co-operative societies and the Handloom Development Corporation are working on a loss. A review of the major studies in the form of dissertation, working papers, published articles and books is attempted here in the remaining part of this section.

Venkataraman's study (1935) titled 'The handloom industry in south India', explored the nature of the relationship between production and marketing. He was of the view that the system of production determined the method of distribution. Thus the individual weaver producing for himself marketed his products by hawking. But when the production was more organised, as in handloom factories, marketing was done through a plethora of agencies like commission agent mail order houses and showrooms. The Fact Finding Committee (Handloom & Mills) (1942) attributed the crisis in handloom industry to the cumulative effect of a number of factors. These included changes in the tariff policy, shift in consumer taste and competition from the mill sector. There was also a general lack of dynamism in the industry due to the fact that the majority of weavers were enmeshed in a strong dependency relationship with middlemen. The growing competition of the power loom sector, which emerged around the Second World War period, was also clearly mentioned by the committee. Ghosh (1947) while discussing the problems of handloom weavers, streamed its locational importance. Weavers living in close proximity to market, enjoyed a decided advantage, as otherwise weavers had to walk 20 to 25 miles losing two to two-and-half days a week to dispose off their products. However, he was of the view that locations need not be over emphasized. The problem of handloom industry in general was discussed by Kothari (1958). The problem of financing and its implications on uneconomic production got added emphasize.

While examining the question of the implementation of minimum wages for handloom weavers in Kerala, the committee of the government of Kerala (1960) documented the problems of weavers and its capital lightness. NCAER's (1960) enquiry into the economics of handloom industry in selected centers of Karnataka and Maharashtra was comprehensive. The organisational deficiency and the resultant dependence of units and its undesirable consequences were focused by the study. Commending the measures taken and to mitigate the woes of the industry, a word of caution was: "neither the legislative restriction of manufacturer by mills, nor the system of subsidy and rebate on handloom products can be a long term solution. A systematic reorganisation of the industry through the formation of co-operatives which will cover production, marketing and finance is necessary if handloom industry is to survive the world of technological advances". Ichalkarananji Kulkarni (1961), while examining the problems and prospects of weavers, stressed the need for the conversion of handloom into power loom. Shetty (1963) while studying the small industries of Delhi referred to handloom. He observed the problems of the industry of the area as scarcity of finance and low capacity utilisation. He found that although being a perennial occupation, peak season employment in handloom was confined to 4.5 months in a year. The working group (1965), a High power study team (1974) and the committee of Loksobha (1978) had also gone in-depth into the problems of the industry.

Lakshman (1966) covered cottage and small industries of Mysore. He emphasized the need for strengthening the organisational base of cottage industries. Other problems cited were low level of skill formation, the supreme role of middlemen, poor standards of raw materials and low quality products imperfect sales organisation and keen competition form mills. The focus of PEOs study (1967) was on marketing, employment, technological and co-operativisation programmes of handloom industry in selected centers. The study noted the hereditary nature of handloom industries. Adoption of modern tools was low due to unawareness, lack of skill and at times due to unsuitability. The handloom development programmes were more beneficial to co-operatives members. But in the organisational set up of co-operatives, there was weak link between upper society and primary society which led to inadequate marketing arrangements resulting in unstable employment of co-operative sector weavers.

Riazuddin's (1968) enquiry was on the economies of cottage industries of Gangpur, Allahabad. The study covered handloom industry. The methodological difficulties associated with the study of rural industries were narrated in detail by him. The disorganised nature of handloom, according to him, led to marketing problems. The other problems were procedural delay, lack of skill and lack of governmental assistance to desired extent especially for sectors like handlooms. Oommen (1972) in his study of small industries in Kerala compared handlooms with power looms. The study reveled that surplus generation although was high in handlooms compared to power loom, reinvestable surplus turned out to be considerably low due to high propensity to consume. However, he held the view that as there is considerable underutilisation in power loom, if given a proper deal, chances of generating surplus was more.

Upadhaya (1973) examined certain economic aspects of handicrafts, with reference to Aurangabad including handlooms. As against the general problems of marketing faced by small and cottage industries. He concluded that the more pressing problem was lack of finance. The High Powered Study Team (1973) committee in 1973 inquired into all aspects of the handloom industry, organisational, technical and functional and observed that increased co-operativisation of the industry would be an effective means where by many of the problem of the handloom industry could be solved. Analysing the functioning of the reservation system and the availability of the necessary inputs to the handloom industry, the committee noted that in practice very little protection was in fact being given. This was due to the poor enforcement of the various policy measures undertaken.

Sivaraman B. (1974) was of the view that given the experience of the entry of power loom in the cotton textile industry, it was inevitable that this scale of mechanisation would almost drive the handloom out of the industrial scene. Chaudhari K. N. (1974) pointed out that there was a qualitative difference between production for the local market and production for export. In case of former, few considerations, apart from prices were really vital. However for the export trade, a host of commercial considerations like quality, price, bulk orders and delivery time were all equally important. Consequently and also due to the greater risk involved, a center catering to the export trade would exhibit greater responsiveness to market conditions. Mohanan (1977) discussed the issue of widespread unemployment among weavers of Kannur and identified the related problem as lack of innovation, the role of intermediaries, unplanned production and the failure of Government in building a firm base for the industry. Nedungadi (1977) lack of internal demand appeared as more important and to him unless internal demand was created there could be no durable solution to the problem of handloom industry.

Ramakrishnan (1978) highlighted the problems resulting from the dependence on middle men and the competition from power loom. The export performance of the industry, its markets and the related problems were explained by the Economic Times Review Bureau (1978). The protection policies and lack of innovation were particularly mentioned as the problem of the industry. The nature of co-operative unity and the exploitative practices of master weavers were the subject of discussion in Yagaiah's (1979) paper. The study undertaken by the Centre for Studies in Decentralised Industries (1980) covered organisational aspects, operations, marketing resource utilisation, structure of cost, wage and raw-material availability with reference to selected handloom centres of Tamilnadu and Maharastra. The study underlined the need for building up market intelligence, especially in the co-operative sectors as the poor feedback of market information led to low off take of products of the societies. The system of subsidy largely benefited the traders. According to the study, the master weaver, as integral part of the system, evolved new pattern and on whom large weavers depended. Therefore, the felt need was to extent institutional facilities to them and disciplining them to pay a fair wage to the weavers.

Identifying the marked links and intermediaries formed the focuses of another study of Centre for Studies in Decentralised Industries (1981) in Eastern Uttar Pradesh. The linkage involved in moving the products out of the region was traced and it found 2/3 intermediaries operating in the area catering to far off markets. Conventional system of producers themselves selling to the consumers was rarely observed. It was also found that a good part of the margin was enjoyed by the middlemen. Ray Chaudheri (1982) discussed the state of the industry in the Mughal period, characterised by an incredible richness both in quality and variety of fabrics. But the technology stagnation, endemic in the industry was on ominous portent for the future. However, Punjab, the Bengal region, and the Coromandel coast exhibited greater signs of utility and dynamism. Geetha Devi (1982) studied the cost structure of the industry in the two centres of Kannur and Thiruvananthapuram districts. She found that due to a variety of reasons the cost structure was higher in Kannur than in Thiruvananthapuram. The problem of finance, the institutional facilities and their scheme found focus in SBI Bulletin (1982). Chandersekhar (1982) attempted a critical review of government programmes and policies since independence and found that the policies largely benefited the power looms. Narayanan (1982) and Ramunny (1983) emphasised the problems of raw material, its price, lack of research and development, the facility of the rebate system, lack of contacts with overseas markets, wage policy, quota policy and competition.

Jain (1983) on a similar exercise arrived at the same conclusion. He went to the extent of questioning the official estimate of annual production of handlooms. Bhat (1983) discussion centered around the problem of women workers in handloom industry and he emphasized the need for the diversification of their operation to retain their employment status. Bharathan (1983) studied the handloom industry in Tamilnadu. He observed a number of changes in the industry during the period 1961-71. Thus the industry was becoming more urban and non-household in character. Further, while production for the domestic market declined, export went up. Consequently, changes occurred both in product mix and in organisation of production. The State Planning Board (1983) reviewed the programmes of the export promotion projects and intensive handloom development projects. The study pointed to the low pace of progress of the programmes and persistence of actual problem of unemployment among weavers covered by the programme. The inefficiency of the implementing agency, the Kerala Handloom Development Corporation, was the main focus of the study.

A brief discussion of the problems of the industry was made by Moulic and Parushotham (1984). According to them the inefficiency originated from their poor resource base and limited earning capacity. A special feature published by Malayala Manorama Daily (1984) discussed similar issues in detail with the same observations. Kutty Krishnan A. (1985) in his study concluded that the industry in Kannur as else where was unorganised, its capital structure was highly lopsided, production methods were antiquated and traditional and labour was not formerly trained. The technology of production was age old with no attempts to upgrade it. The entrepreneurship was lacking and only the middle men got the best out of the game. The poor illiterate labour, particularly family labour is exploited. Quality, the hallmark for marketing, was in doubt and in the long run the industry would be loosing its hold in traditional, national and international market. The unorganised nature of the industry was also identified as another weakness. The traditional sectors were encouraged to produce Polyvastra as it results in increased productivity and earnings of labour. The study conducted by Sharma (1985) revealed that the programme did not succeed due to the absence of forward and backward linkages and marketing problems. Examining the same issue Gondhia (1985) suggested for excise duty exemptions to encourage the production of Polyvastra. Its importance in reducing the problem of unemployment was particularly given stress.

Jain L. C. (1985) observed that the phenomenal growth of the power loom sector at the handloom sector was due at best to the apathy and at worst, to the active connivance of Government officials. Decrying the move to entrust the handloom sector with the production of controlled cloth in the 1985 Textile Policy, he concluded that this was the best way of enhancing technological stagnation in the industry, and eventually making it a sick industry. It was also stated that since the production controlled cloth was not remunerative, the earnings of weavers would come down. The study undertaken by Sarngadharan M. (1985) revealed that the handloom co-operatives in Kerala did not succeed in improving the member weavers compared to non-members. However, it was found that the co-operative getting together helped the member weavers to improve their social status.

Rajagopalan V. (1986) in his study of Handloom industry in north and south of Kerala revealed that the industry, reflecting the varied historical experiences of the two regions had developed on quite distinct lines. Thiruvananthapuram and Kannur exhibited wide variations in type of industry and loomage, composition of workforce and degree of co-operative coverage. This was turn led to a divergence in the organisation of production and marketing channels. The industry was relatively more organised in Kannur and catered to distant market in contrast in Thiruvananthapuram, it was highly decentralised in nature and dependent on the local domestic market. The increasing co-operativisation of the industry in Kannur was a reflector too of the crises in the late 1970s. The study also pointed out that both Hantex and Hanveev, were increasingly concentrating on the domestic market. It was also observed that the industry in Kannur was in severe crisis. The exclusive reliance of the Kannur industry or the unpredictable export markets, contributed a great deal to the uncertainly in the industry. The growing tendency of many manufacturers in Kannur to sub-contract part of their orders to weavers based in Tamil Nadu, was detrimental to the long term interests of the industry. The exclusive reliance by Hantex and Hanveev on remote parts of the state was also cause for concern. The flow of cheap handloom goods from neighbouring states in large quantities, the changing consumer tastes and the aggressive marketing strategies of Co-optex were the serious threats faced by Hantex and Hanveev. Thus the entire traditional handloom industry in Kerala was facing a number of challenges, especially in production and marketing fields. Rajagopalan (1986) in his another study attempted to document the inter-regional differences in the handloom industry of Kerala.

Roy T. (1989) in his historical review of the handloom industry deserved emphasis: there was an essential continuity between pre and post independence periods in respect of the dominant form of dependence (contract with large producers) and dominant form of capital (producers as against traders); still, the distinctions of producers as a class had been diffused as availability of liquid funds encouraged speculation and Factories Act of restricted direct production on a large scale; and despite reservation, handloom market was constrained by product-specialisation and preference shifts, but those tendencies were not operative in short run. Another study by Mridual Eapen (1991) in the handloom co-operatives examined the financial aspect of the Hantex, the apex body of handloom co-operatives, by evaluating its overall growth performance – the organisation of handloom industry into a commercially viable entity, its marketing strategy and financial performance. The study found that the Hantex had not only a poor financial trade record despite active funding by the government, but also failed to discharge the primary functions of assisting primary weaver's co-operatives satisfactorily. The study also highlighted the improper marketing strategy of the society and the organisational failures, which led to the failure of the industry to re-orient the productive pattern according to the changes in the demand pattern and also to a sharp increase in the prices of handloom clothes. Pyarlal Raghavan's study (1995) examined the general crisis of the industry and its impact on the performance of co-operatives in the handloom industry. The study revealed that though the co-operatives facilitated a significant increase in the wage rates, the number of days of employment declined. The major hurdle was failure of the central co-operatives to enhance sales to fully utilise the production capacity of the industry. The relatively high prices of handloom goods as well as the failure of the industry to diversify into new products were also highlighted in the study.

The above mentioned information leads to the conclusion that the handloom industry in Kerala requires immediate attention of the social scientists for an indepth study into the various issues in the light of liberalization, privatization and globalization policies adopted in the economy.

Cashew Industry

The three major cashew growing states in India are Kerala, Tamil Nadu and Karnataka, though it is grown in small areas in other states like Andhra Pradesh, Orissa, West Bengal, Assam and Maharashtra. More than one fourth of the total area and about 60 per cent of the total production in India are accounted by Kerala. Cashew industry is an important foreign exchange earner for the state.

The factory sector of the cashew industry used to have a counterpart in cottage sector, where a large number of women and child labourers did the processing, called Kudivarappu, at a wage rate less than that in the organised sector. With the establishment of Cashew Development Authority (CDA) in 1970 for stabilising the industry and to free the workers in the cottage processing sector from the unlawful exploitation by the exporters and private factory owners, the cottage processing sector gradually dwindled in size. The KSCDA in 1990-91 had 70 factories under its control, with 50722 workers. In addition to the corporation, the Cashew workers Apex Industrial Co-operative Society Ltd. (CAPEX) was established in 1984 for taking up and converting the closed cashew factories as primary societies with cashew workers as members. The CAPEX had, during 1990-91, 10 cashew factories, employing 6028 workers. As per the Kerala Raw Cashew nuts Procurement and Distribution Act 1981, the CAPEX is the sole agent of the Government for the monopoly procurement of raw cashew nuts in the state, which was started with the objective of ensuring fair prices for the cashew growers and equitable distribution of raw cashew among the cashew processors.

The industry is passing through serious difficulties now. The major problem faced in this industry is non-availability of adequate quantities of raw materials. The domestic production of raw nuts is not enough to provide employment to workers even for three months in a year. About 65 per cent of requirements of raw nuts were earlier imported from East African countries. But these countries themselves started cashew processing units and thus imports from these countries started declining. Added to this is the large-scale migration of the cashew processing units to be adjoining states of Karnataka and Tamil Nadu due to lower cost of processing there. Despite of the problems faced by the industry, export earning from this industry in the state has been increasing over the years. The total value of exports of Rs. 107.07 crore in 1976-77 went up to Rs. 1387.04 crore in 1999-2000 showing 1295 per cent increase over a period of 23 years. Several studies on this sector highlighted the socio economic condition of cashew workers in Kerala. In order to have a better understanding an attempt is made here to review the existing literature.

The study of John Thomas Chirayat (1965) highlighted the salient features of the cashew industry, its relevance to foreign trade, and the growth of trade unionism in the industry. It also threw light on the methods of processing, employment, productivity and welfare activities in the industry in the early 1960s. A study conducted by the State Planning Board (1969) discussed the problems faced by the industry in 1960s. The RBI study group (1973) on financing cashew industry reviewed the practice and procedures followed by Commercial banks in respect of monetary advances to the industry, made recommendation regarding the procedures and methods to be followed and the credit limits and financial discipline to be enforced by commercial banks. They found that the capital base of the industry was low and suggested that a portion of the profits should be ploughed back to augment the capital base. Krishnaswamy (1976) has attempted to throw light on such aspects of the industry on its allocation, trends in area under cultivation, production, export and kernel prices. Eman Beevi (1978) reviewed the effect of stable legislation on wages and working condition in the cashew industry in Kerala. She found that the average daily earnings of workers increased as a result of the fixation of minimum wages, but the annual average earnings decreased owing to the diversion of processing activity to Tamilnadu as well as to the resultant reduction in the employment days in Kerala.

The Proceedings of the National Seminar on Cashew Industry (1981) which covered 19 research papers, gave a detailed discussion of the problems and development in the industry. The seminar discussed the need to increase production of raw-nuts, to use improved processing machinery, to keep down the cost to production, and to establish ancillary industry to ensure the commercial use of the by-products of cashew. The seminar noted the low equity base of the industry and suggested that the industry be reorganised in the form of limited companies so that the profits could be ploughed back to strengthen the equity base. Regarding exports, the seminar noted the wide fluctuations in the price of kernels, and suggested that India, Brazil and Mazambique, the three major producing countries, should make a joint effort to bring about some measures of stability in the prices. Kannan (1983) analysed the major issues involved in the cultivation, distribution, processing and marketing of cashew, and examined the prospects of development of cashew industry in India. A major finding of the study was that the government policy of promoting exports was without adequate appreciation of the linkage with the processing sector and the cultivation of crop in the agricultural sector. The study also found that despite the high level of profitability in the industry, the level of wages had been very low. The worker also had experienced an erosion of quantum of employment owing to the diversion of processing activity to Tamilnadu. Dharmarajan P. G. (1984) made a comparative study of the cost structure of the industry in Kerala, Karnataka and Tamilnadu. He found that due to a variety of reasons the cost structure was higher in Kerala than in other two states.

Balan Pillai (1986) examined the extent to which collective bargaining in cashew industry in Kerala could be held responsible for its decline. It was found in the study that both market forces and industrial relations forces was relevant in explaining the decline of the industry, but the role of the latter as evidenced by collective bargaining was only a minor one. Studies by Thomas

Mathew (1986) and Rema (1986) and Balasubramanium (1987) dealt with the marketing and pricing trends of both raw-nuts and kernel. A high level committee (1989) formed to suggest strategies for the development of industries observed that the social purpose of setting up of the K.S.C.D.C. had not been achieved in a substantial manner, as it provided employment only to 32,000 workers for 100 day a year and that at a high cost. The committee came to the conclusion that the maladies of the industry stemmed from the reluctance of the government and the unions to face the fact that there were practically no advantages in organising the industry on a factory scale since the cashew processing industry did not involve high technology. The committee suggested that organising the industry in the household sector was more logical and advantageous to both manufacturers and workers.

A study conducted by Deyanandan M. N. (1991) reported that owing to the shortage of raw-nuts the KSCDC could not work for more than 100 days a year. The raw-nut cost of the corporation showed an increasing trend. Another area of concern was the increasing processing cost. Labour cost and factory expenses were the major components of processing cost. The sales revenues of the corporation are not commensurate with the raw-nut cost. The corporation has no definite policy as to the fixation of export sales price of kernels of various grades.

Sudha J. (1997) attempted to look into the way welfare policies had been administered in the state of Kerala with special reference of cashew processing industry. The study found that government intervention meant to protect labour interest was not an independent phenomenon. It was the result of a number of struggles wagered by the organised labour. On the whole, workers were satisfied with the performance of the Welfare Fund Board. But majority of the workers were not satisfied with the ESI services. Moreover, the workers had strong reservation on the changed methods of working of trade unions. The leaders were not attending properly to the problems of the labourers. Moreover the workers felt that considerable number of middle level and lower level trade union leaders were in the payroll of private processors. The study also revealed that the monopoly procurement policy of the government totally failed to achieve the twin objective of earning remunerative prices for cashew growth and to have a equitable distribution of nuts among the procession based on number role strength. At the same time private processors would provide to their workers maximum number of days of work during the period when there exited no monopoly procurement. The study found that the government intervention, direct and indirect, helped the cashew worker to improve their working and living condition, considerably when compared with thirties, forties, fifties and sixties.

A more detailed study covering all the variables mentioned in the above mentioned studies would be able to bring out new information to streamline the working of Cashew industry in the state to cope with the needs of the present day set up.

Beedi Industry

There are around 20 to 25 crore beedi workers in the country who light up to 10 lakh fresh beedis per minute. Of the 700 gram of tobacco consumed by an average Indian adult in a year 300 gram is beedi tobacco while cigarettes account for only 200 grams. Beedi smokers outnumber cigarette smokers in rural areas as well as in urban areas. The turnover of the beedi industry is estimated to be rupees four to rupees five crore per day. According to the report of the Council for Scientific and Industrial Research in 1973 there were around thirty six lakh people working full and part time in the beedi industry in India. Thus beedi industry constitutes one of the most important sources of non-agricultural employment in India. According to 1971 census, there were 10 lakh beedi workers employed in the beedi industry. The eight districts of Maharashtra, Madhyapradesh, Andhrapradesh, West Bengal, Tamil Nadu, Kerala and Bihar accounted for 90 per cent of this employment. When the overall employment in this industry increased by 10 per cent during 1961-71, Kerala registered an increase of 40 per cent. A significant increase of women employment was also noted in this industry. During the period, in Kerala the proportion of women workers increased from 2 per cent to 12 per cent. Another significant feature noticed was that around 60 per cent of the beedi workers were employed in the household sector.

An interesting characteristics of the beedi industry, whether it is a non-household establishment or households of workers, is that no machinery whatsoever is used in the production process. It is a highly labour intensive industry, the only equipment needed for beedi production being a bamboo tray and scissors. The division of labour is limited due to the relatively simple process of beedi manufacturing. The organisation of production in the beedi industry showed significant interregional variation. In some centers the employment of household workers is only 10 per cent while in other centers, household sector accounted for more that 70 per cent of the employment. Kannur district in Kerala was the solitary center where beedi workers were engaged in production through co-operative societies, accounting for 41 per cent of the total employment at that center. The beedi industry may be organised either in workers co-operatives or in the private sector. Then are hardly ten to fifteen beedi co-operatives in the country and most of them are small in size. In some places the beedi co-operatives manufacture beedi for private firms which market them. The private sector predominates the industry. The beedi firm may directly employ the workers or utilise middlemen or contractors to employ the workers. The actual workplaces may be divided into large establishments, small establishments and households. Large establishments may be defined as those which come under various regulations and pay the statutory benefits to the workers. The production in the households may be either under the trade system or commission system. In the former system, the raw materials are sold and the finished products purchased from the worker. The commission system is more akin to a piece wage rate. The household worker is paid a commission on the basis of their outturn.

In Kerala, the beedi industry came to be firmly established in Kannur after the First World War when the Muslim tobacco entrepreneurs utilised their trade connection and started exporting beedi to Ceylon and later to Burma. The export trade encouraged the growth of a large number of small petty establishments grew into concerns employing 20 to 30 workers. The growth of demand for beedi in the export market was accompanied by the expansion of local beedi consumption. The growth in the local beedi consumption was boosted by the attractive advertisement techniques resorted to by the beedi entrepreneurs. The nature of beedi operation did not require any fixed capital equipment except for bamboo tray and scissors which was owned by the workers. The concentration of work process at on work place was also not required. The supply of labour was relatively scarce in the beedi industry till the 1930s. The work force in the beedi industry was mostly male workers. Moreover, children in large number were used to be employed in the manufacture of tobacco production.

The labour condition of the beedi workers deteriorated considerably with the expansion of the industry and the increase in the supply of labourers. There were no fixed uniform hours of work or intervals in the beedi establishments. The whole week was working period with no holidays whatsoever. There was no guarantee for regular employment throughout the year. The emergence of trade unions movement in the beedi industry was a response to the deplorable labour condition in the industry. The absence of minimum wage legislation in the beedi industry till the late 1960s was partly responsible for the lower wage rates in the industry. In the decentralisation phase of the industry, the production of beedi was shifted from the small scale establishments owned by middlemen to the worker's own households. The final factor which forced the decentralisation to household production was the notification of the Government of Kerala in August 1968 which sought to implement the Beedi and Cigar Workers (Conditions of Employment) Act 1966. In addition to the aim of eliminating middlemen in the industry, the Act also sought to improve the working conditions in the beedi industry.

The most significant development in the beedi industry in the recent period has been the emergence of the Co-operative sector. The first Beedi Co-operative Society was registered in 1934. In the initial years, the working of most of these co-operatives was not successful. Accordingly in December 1968, the Government of Kerala declared to launch the Kerala Denesh Beedi Workers Central Co-operative Society (KDBWCCS). The KDBWCCS has a two tier structure with one Central Society and 22 Primary Societies. The role of primary societies is confined to the production of beedi and the maintaining of accounts. The central society adds a mark up of 3 per cent to the value of the raw materials it supplies to the primary societies to cover up the incidental expenses. Unlike the co-operatives in other traditional industries of Kerala the beedi co-operatives in Kannur district proved to be highly successful. The co-operatives were able to provide employment to a large section of the beedi workers of Kannur district. It was a pace setter for higher wages and improved labour condition in the industry, at the same time maintaining its financial viability. The KDBWCCS Ltd. provided employment to 24249 persons as on March 31, 2000. During 1999-2000, 481.29 crore beedi worth Rs. 81.79 crore were produced. The net profit of the society was 39.15 lakh, that is, 48 per cent greater than that of the previous year. State government allotted a sum of Rs. 10 millions for the development of the society during 2000-01.

Several studies on the socio-economic condition of the beedi workers in different parts of the country reveled their continuing struggle for survival while sustaining in this occupation despite low wages, irregular employment and different forms of exploitation by the middlemen and agents, lack of credit, education and medical facilities and negligence in government policies. Their condition has not improved remarkably, despite a number of legislations and the struggles of trade union. Several studies depicted that although the government had fixed the minimum wages for the beedi workers, they never realised it and continued to be exploited by their employers. Though the

Minimum Wages Act provided for payment for weekly holidays, annual leave, materiality leave for women workers, sick leave and medical benefits, the workers were yet to be provided with these benefits. A brief review of research studies are attempted here. Ravi. K. (1979) gives a broad profile of the industrial structure as well as the prospects of the beedi industry in Kerala. According to Mohan (1983) the co-operative experiment in the beedi industry has directed considerable journalists intact but a proper academic evaluation is yet to be made. Oommen M. A. (1984) as a part of the effort to study the problem of locational shift of industries from Kerala to the adjacent states also looked into the problems of beedi industry in Kannur. However he makes no attempt to study the evolution of the industry historically. Mohandas (1986) in his paper beedi workers in Kerala has brightly surveyed the labour condition in the beedi industry with the help of a field study.

The study of Pyarlal Raghwan (1986) on the beedi co-operatives revealed that it was more successful compared to the other industrial co-operatives. It has shown a steady expansion of employment and earnings for its members without compromising on its financial viability. In theses co-operatives, Government intervention was restricted to that of a facilitator. The initiative from below ensured that co-operative organisation came to be identified with the struggle to protect workers interest. This resulted in the active mass participation and it contributed to the enhancement of efficiency and productivity. The success of beedi co-operatives was to a large extent due to buoyant market conditions of tobacco products. The production of beedi was decentralised from large establishment to the household workers. But unlike the other traditional industries, the beedi co-operatives emerged as viable unit of production. The study documented the various phases of the evolution of the beedi industry in Kannur district. The change in the industrial organisation of the beedi industry can be broadly divided into four phases. The growth of large scale beedi establishment from 1930-37 period of the first phase. The second phase was the decentralisation of product to smaller establishment under the brand system during the period of 1937-51.

Under these two phases, the beedi entrepreneurs directly recruited and employed the workers to manufacture beedi. The emergence of the indirect system of production through middlemen in the beedi industry was a significant transformation of industrial organisation during the post independence period. Middle men recruited and employed the workers to manufacture beedi in small-scale establishment at that stage. These systems of indirect production in small-scale establishments dominated the indirect structure during the period 1951-61. The latest phase of evolution in the Kannur beedi industries started in 1968 and has three characteristics. First, production of beedi was shifted from small-scale establishment to the household workers. Secondly, a number of leading beedi shifted their product to Karnataka and the adjoining taluks of Kasargod and Hosdarg in Kannur district, where workers were relatively less organised and wages were lower. Thirdly, the phase also witnessed the emergence of co-operative sector in the beedi industry in which beedi produced was centralised in large work centers. These changes in the organisation of production enabled the beedi firms to evade the various legislation, which regulated the functioning of the beedi industry, and conferred various statutory benefits to the workers. It also enabled the beedi firms to employ relatively unorganised workers in low wage rates area and thereby to expedite and sharp the efforts of the beedi firms to minimize the cost of production. The shift of production to low wage areas allowed the beedi firm to increase the employment and unorganized women workers.

The emergence of the co-operative sector was an important development during the fourth phase. Unlike the co-operatives in other traditional industries of Kerala, the beedi co-operatives in Kannur district proved to be a successful venture. The co-operatives were able to provide employment to a large section of the beedi workers in Kannur district. It was a pace setter for higher wages and improved labour condition in the industry, and at the same time maintaining its financial viability. The success of the co-operatives can be attributed to the commitment and motivation of the workers and trade unions and the efficient management.

References

Balan Pillai, K. (1986), *Economic Impact of Collective Bargaining on Cashew Industry in Kerala*, Ph.D. Thesis (Unpublished), University of Kerala, Thiruvananthapuram.

Balasubramanion, P.P. (1987), Prospects of Utilisation on Cashew Apples in India, *Indian Cashew Journal*, 1(2), April-June.

Beevi Emam, A.J. (1978), *Impact of Minimum Wages Legislation on Cashew Industry*, M.Phil Dissertation (Unpublished), CDS, Thiruvananthapuram.

Bharathan, K. (1983), *The Cotton Handloom Industry in Tamilnadu – Some Characteristics and Aspects of Change from the Post Independence Census Data*, Madras Institute of Development Studies, Working Paper No. 4.

Bhaskaran Unnithan (1956), *Coir Industry in Travancore-Cochin Department of Economics*, Ph.D Thesis, University of Travancore, Travancore.

Bhatt Ramesh, M. (1983), Women should be Partners in Handloom Sector, *Yojana*, 27 (5), March 31.

Center for Studies in Decentralized Industries (1980), *A Case Study of Handloom Industry – Tamilnadu and Maharastra*, Bombay: Mebta Trust.

Center for Studies in Decentralized Industries (1981), *A Case Study of Wholesale Market for Handloom Cloth in U.P.*, Bombay: Mebta Trust.

Chandersekhar, C.P. (1982), Textile Industry, Growth of the Decentralised Sector, The Economic Times (A national daily in English), August 9.

Chaudhari, K.N. (1974), The Structure of Indian Textile Industry in the 17th and 18th Centuries, *Indian Economics and Social History Review*, June-September.

Chaudhari Ray (1982), Industry and Economy Reforms, Bombay.

Deyanandan, M.N. (1991), *The Kerala State Cashew Development Corporation – An Evaluation Study*, Ph.D. Thesis (Unpublished), University of Kerala, Thiruvananthapuram.

Dharmarajan, P.G. (1984), *A Study of the Cost Structure of the Cashew Industry in Kerala, Karnataka and Tamilnadu*, Ph.D. Thesis (Unpublished), University of Cochin, Cochin.

Food and Agricultural Organisation (FAO) (1983), *Coir, Economic Characteristics, Trends and Problems*, Commodity Bulletin Series (44).

Geetha Devi, S. (1982), *Handloom Production in Kerala – A Case Study of Thiruvananthapuram and Kannur Centers*, M.Phil Thesis, University of Kerala, Thiruvananthapuram.

George, K. (1953), *Proceeding of the General Body Meeting of Alleppy Chamber of Commerce*, 15 April.

Ghosh, N.N. (1947), *Small Industries: Their Plan in Port Ware Industrialization*, Ahamadabad; General Printing & Publication Ltd.

Gondhia Ratibahi (1985), Polyvastra and Job Creation, *Commerce*, 150 (3844), Jan. 26.

Government of India, High Level Committee (1989), *Report on Coir Industry*, New Delhi.

Government of India, Ministry of Commerce, Working Group (1965), *Report on Handlooms*, New Delhi.

Government of India, Ministry of Commerce (1973), Report of the High Powered Study Team on the Problems of Handloom industry, New Delhi.

Government of India, Ministry of Industry, Committee of Loksobha (1978), *13th Report on Handloom and Powerloom Industries, Part – I Handloom Industries Estimation Committee*, New Delhi.

Government of India, Ministry of Industry (1974), Report on Handloom Industry, New Delhi.

Government of India, Planning Commission (1967), *Study of Handloom Development Programme*, New Delhi.

Government of Kerala (1960), *Report of the Minimum Wages Committee on Employment in Handloom Industry*, Thiruvananthapuram.

Government of Kerala, State Planning Board (1969), *Cashew Industry in Kerala* (mimeo), Thiruvananthapuram.

Government of Kerala, State Planning Board (1973), *Report of the Study Group on Mechanisation of Coir Industry in Kerala*, Thiruvananthapuram.

Government of Kerala, State Planning Board (1984), *Report of High Level Committee on Industry Trade and Power*, Thiruvananthapuram.

Ichalkarananji Kulkarni (1961), The Weaving Industries, *Artha Vijanana*, 13 (1-9).

Indian Bank (Ed.) (1981), Proceeding of National Seminar on Cashew Industry, December, Kollam.

Jain, L.C. (1983), Handloom Face Liquidation, *Yojana*, 18(35), March 31.

Jain, L.C. (1985), The New Textile Policy and of Handloom, *Economic and Political Weekly*, July 6.

Janardhana Pillai, M.L. (1922), *Economic Development*, Government of Travancore, Travancore.

John Thomas (1965), *A Study on the Cashew Industry in Kerala*, Industry study series, Report No. 1, Thiruvananthapuram: Labour and Industrial Bureau.

Kannan, K.P. (1983), *Cashew Development in India: Potentialities and Constraints*, New Delhi: Agricole Publishing Academy.

Kothari (Ed.) (1958), *Why Khadi and Village Industries*, Ahamadabad: Nav Jivan Publications.

Krishnaswamy (1976), Marketing and Pricing Policy of Cashew Nut, *Cashew Bulletin*, 13 (8), Cochin, August.

Kuttykrishnan, A. (1985), *Economics of the Handloom Industry in Cannor District*, Ph.D. Thesis, University of Mysore, Banglore.

Lakshman, T.K. (1966), *Cottage and Small Scale Industries in Mysore – A Case study of their Patter and Role in the Context of Developing Economy*, Mysore.

Malayala Manorama (1984), *Strengthening Handloom*, A Manorama feature, September 21.

Mathew Thomas, M. (1986), Cashew in India: Yesterday, Today and Tomorrow, *Indian Cashew Journal*, Cochin, 16(1).

Meera, V. (1983), *Women Work and Class Struggle – A Study of Coir Industry in Kerala (Mimeo)*, New Delhi, Centre for Women Development Studies, New Delhi.

Mohanan, K.P. (1977), Unemployment Widespread in Handloom, *Mathrubhumi* (A national daily in Malayalam), April 14.

Mohan, N. (1983), Federal Co-operatives: An Overview and a Case Study, *Lok Udyog*, July 17, (4).

Moulik, T. K. and Purushotham, P. (1984), What Ails Silk Industry, *Commerce*, 148, (3798) March 10.

Mridual Eapen (1991), *Hantex: A Economic Appraisal*, Working Paper, 242, CDS, Thiruvananthapuram.

Narayanan, C. (1982), Crisis in Handloom Sector, *Mathrubhumi* (A national daily in Malayalam), March 25.

National Council of Applied Economic Research (1960), *Survey of Handloom Industry in Karnataka and Aholapur*, New Delhi: Asia Publication.

Nedungadi, P.V.K. (1977), Basic Problems of Handlooms in Internal Markets, *Mathrubhumi* (A national daily in Malayalam), April 19.

Oommen, M.A. (1972), *Small Industry in Indian Economic Growth – A Case Study of Kerala*, Delhi: Research Publication Society.

Prakash, A.B. (1977), Coir Industry in Doldrum, *Social Scientist Journal of Indian School of Social Science*, 6(1) August.

Pyarlal Raghavan (1995), *Dynamics of Indian Co-operation : A Study of Traditional Industries in Kerala*, Ph.D. Thesis, CDS, Thiruvananthapuram.

Pylee, M.V. (1975), *A Study of Coir Industry – Problems and Prospects*, Cochin Coir Board, Cochin.

Rajagopalan, V. (1986), *Handloom Industry in North and South Kerala – A Study of Production and Marketing Structures*, M.Phil Thesis (Unpublished), CDS, Thiruvananthapuram.

Rajagopalan, V. (1986), *Inter Regional Differences in Handloom Industry*, Working paper 135, CDS, Thiruvananthapuram.

Ramakrishnan Nair, P.K. (1978), Need to Set up Handloom International, *Mathrubhumi* (A national daily in Malayalam), April 27.

Ramunny Murkoth (1983), Problem of Handloom Industry in Kerala, *Indian Express*, Dec. 9.

Ravi, K. (1979), *Economics of Beedi Industry in Kerala*, M.A. Project Report (Unpublished), University of Calicut, Calicut.

Rema, M. (1986), Problems of Cashew Industry, *Indian Cashew Journal*, Cochin, 17(3).

Reserve Bank of India (1973), Report of the Study Group on Financing of Cashew Industry, *RBI Bulletin*, Bombay, May.

Riazuddin, A. (1968), *Cottage Industries in Gangapur*, Allahabad: Literacy and Cultural association.

Roy, T. (1989), *Transition in Handloom Weaving 1900 to 1939*, Ph.D. Thesis (Unpublished), CDS, Thiruvananthapuram.

Sarngadharan, M. (1985), *Impact of the Working of Handloom Weavers Co-operative Societies in Kerala*, Ph.D. Thesis (Unpublished), Calicut University, Calicut.

Sharma, Y.C. (1985), Potential of Polyvastra, *Commerce*, 150(3844), Jan. 26.

Shetty, M.C. (1963), *Small Scale and Household Industries in Developing Economy*, New Delhi: Asia Publishing House.

Sivaraman, B. (1974), Report on Handloom Industry, New Delhi.

State Bank of India (1982), Handloom Industry, *SBI Monthly Review*, 21(8) August.

Sudha, J. (1997), *Welfare Policies in Traditional Industries – A Case Study of Cashew Industry*, Ph.D. Thesis (Unpublished), University of Kerala, Thiruvananthapuram.

The Economic Times Review Bureau (1978), Growth of the Decentralised Sector, *Economic Times* (A National daily), August 9.

The Fact Finding Committee (1942), *Report on Handloom Mills*, New Delhi.

Thomas Issac, T.M. (1983), Clan Struggle and Transition to Specifically Capitalist form of Production: Some Conclusion of a Study of Coir Industry in Kerala, *Social Scientist*, 2(127), December.

Upadhaya, M.N. (1973), *Economics of Handicrafts Industries*, New Delhi: S. Chand and Co.

Venketaraman, K.J. (1940), Coir Industry and Trade on Malabar Coast, *Journal of University of Bombay*, 8(4), January.

Venketaraman, K.S. (1935), *Report on Handloom Industry in South India*, Madras.

Yahaiah, T. (1979), Handloom Industry in India, *Yojana*, December 16.

12

Marketing of Banking Services

K. K. Muraleedharan

The product range or range of services available from banking industry in India was limited till the end of the 1980s. However, the situation has changed drastically since the introduction of reforms in the banking sector in the 1990s. The banks in India now offer a wide range of services such as merchant banking, factoring, forfeiting, leasing, hire purchasing, securitisation, portfolio management, custodian services and so on. The marketing operations of the banks have also been streamlined in such a way as to get adjusted with the technological upswing in innovations, namely total branch automation, automated teller machine, electronic fund transfer, anywhere banking, anytime banking, home banking and plastic cards.

Kerala is one of the highly banked states in India. The high literacy rate, remittance from abroad and comparatively higher standard of living have helped the people of Kerala to make use of the banking system as an integral part of their day to day life. A noteworthy feature of the banking development in the state was the spread of bank branches into the interiors even prior to nationalisation in 1969. About 75 percentage of the total bank branches in Kerala were functioning in rural areas at that time. The nationalisation of banks has brought about unprecedented development in respect of bank branch expansion and banking business. Even in remote areas of villages, branches of commercial banks, co-operative banks and regional rural banks are competing each other in providing banking services. This high level of competition indicates that application of bank marketing is inevitable to banks in Kerala.

Statement of the Problem

As the society moves through the beginning of the 21st century the marketing concepts are fast changing. The traditional marketing concepts were focusing on satisfying consumer needs and wants. But the changing marketing concepts are now focusing on a third consideration, that is, welfare of society. Emphasis is now being placed on how marketing affects the society as a whole in an age of scarce resources, environmental degradation and worldwide competition. This social orientation, questions whether satisfying customer needs serves the long term interest of society. Thus the new concepts referred to, as the social marketing concept has become a management philosophy that blends the welfare of society as well as the interest of the firm and its customers. Marketing touches the lives of all members of society. Through the cost of purchase, large or small, a significant amount of the earnings was for purchase. It is to be noted that exchange of goods and services is not happening automatically but it stresses that exchange is to be created. This entails that it is not enough if a producer creates a product but should also see to create market too for his product. Thus, marketing is a sophisticated and a complicated activity to be performed by a trading as well as service organisations.

To get success in the field of marketing, various policies must be adopted by the producer. Marketing mix is one of the important policies to be adopted by the producer for the same. In marketing, the producer first analyses the nature of the consumers' need and then plans his product to give satisfaction to the consumers'. That is all marketing efforts to be taken by the producer focus attention around the consumers' need. The managerial activity, therefore governed with the market and market behaviors to identify target groups of consumers through market information. Thus the management plans to meet the consumers, needs and to face competitions. All these programmes involve a number of functions, which are to be planned carefully. This includes market analysis, predictions and forecasting the needs of the public. Thus, identification of demand and supply involves various functions of marketing to attain success in the market and the combination of these functions is known as marketing mix.

It is a fact that no two classes of customers are alike. Every customer, who approaches a bank, has entirely different expectations and intentions. A middle-income man on the verge of retirement needs an additional source of income to supplement his pension. So his focus will be on a monthly income deposit scheme. The investor cannot be wooed with anything less than the best market rate for his funds, for him the reinvestment scheme earning interest has to be designed and delivered. This is equally true for loaning and subsidiary services as well. Since it would not be flexible to expand business to cover all segments under a branch, some segments should be single out for special coverage. These segments and their potential value would constantly undergo changes and the banker must ensure that no viable worthwhile business slips through his hands due to his indifference.

Review of Literature

Literature on marketing bank services is abundant. But these works are general in nature indicating mostly the governmental policies and their commitment towards the operation of banks only. However, few of the studies are reviewed here, as they would facilitate a clear backing for carrying out the present study.

An exhaustive study was conducted by Rajeev K. Seth in 'Marketing of Banking Services'. A major aspect of his study was the concept of psychological ownership and its relevance in bank marketing and an approach for developing customer satisfaction, product packages and need for local touch. Saxena K.K. in his study 'Bank Marketing' emphasised marketing wise and product development in banking. In his study he stressed the importance of market segmentation which co-related to product development. Murugesan D. in his paper, 'Role of Marketing in Banking Services' has examined about the banking services of post-liberalisation period. He emphasised how effectively banks could provide diversified service without complaining on profitability. Asthana A.K. conducted a case study on 'Marketing of Banking Services' in the Mehsana Urban Co-operative Bank Ltd, Mehsana (Gujarat). The study was to identify the proper combination of marketing mix in banking services. Mousmi Ghosh in a case study highlighted the helplessness of a customer for availing service from nationalised bank. Bishwambhar Shah conducted a study on 'Product Strategy for Banking Sector Post Liberalization Period'. In the study he analyses the various aspects of products strategy in relation to banking sector in India encompassing the performance of banking sector after liberalization, need for product strategy and constituents of product strategy. Negu Reddy K. and Ratnakumari S. conducted a study on the attitudes of borrowers towards credit lending system of Regional Rural Banks. The study was based on Rayalaseema Grameena Bank, Andhra Pradesh and it was found that Socio-economic status had significant association with all categories of borrowers without exception.

Though there are a few studies in Kerala with regard to marketing of banking services, no attempt has so far been made to analyse the marketing of banking services by the banks in Kerala. It is against this background the present study was conducted.

Objectives of the Study

Objectives of the present study are:

- to assess the new products and services available from the banks to the customers in Kerala.
- to ascertain the impact of information technology on the bank deals in Kerala.
- to ascertain the marketing strategies adopted by the bank branches in Kerala for marketing their products and services.
- to examine the extent of acceptance of the banking products and services by customers in Kerala, and
- to evaluate the attitude of the bank personnel vis-à-vis customers towards marketing of new products and services of banks.

The entire study was completed on the basis of mainly primary data collected from customers and bank personnel. For all practical purposes unlike other states in India it is a unique phenomenon of the state of Kerala that for a study in banking, co-operative banks and commercial banks are not separated for the reason that a customer has equal chances to opt for the commercial banks and co-operative banks. The type of accounts inclusive of loan account in any branch of a co-operative bank and a commercial bank are of similar nature. As the bank is service oriented industry, customer assumes greater focus and such being the case, data were collected from 900 bank customers. Taking into consideration the fact that the bank personnel are directly dealing with the customers on behalf of the bank, primary data were collected from 270 bank personnel also. In addition to primary data, secondary data were collected from reports of government departments and government agencies.

The socio-economic conditions of the people in Kerala are uniform throughout the state and as such it was felt appropriate to select 3 districts of Kerala giving due consideration to the geographical location and the availability of the rural, urban and semi-urban population. Accordingly, Kozhikode district was selected from north, Ernakulam district from the centre and Trivandrum district from the south. Multi stage sampling was adopted to choose bank customers. In the first phase, districts were selected to represent urban, semi-urban and rural population. In the second phase, equal number of bank customers was selected from urban, semi-urban and rural areas of each district. In the third phase, bank branches were selected to ensure equal representation for commercial and co-operative banks. Thus 300 bank customers, each from all the three districts were selected to make the total sample for the study of bank customers 900. Of these, 300 bank customers were selected from rural areas, 300 from urban areas and 300 from semi-urban areas. Apart from 900 customers, 270 bank personnel were selected giving equal representation for all three districts and the rural, urban and semi-urban areas.

Data were collected in two separate interview schedules designed for the study after a pre-test. The schedule initially developed for the study with a view to collect data from bank customers were pre-tested among 30 bank customers selected from rural, urban and semi-urban centers. Similarly the schedule used for bank personnel was also pre-tested among 15 bank personnel chosen from rural, urban and semi urban bank branches. The data collected were statistically tested by employing tools like weighted average and chi-square test

It was noted during the period of collection of data that in a state like Kerala with high literacy, banking industry was not able to attain popularity for the new products and services introduced for marketing. Bank personnel were also not an exception to the general nature of low awareness of the features and feasibility of the new products. Such being the case, on many occasions there arose the need for explaining the terms used in the banking industry and used in the interview schedule, to the customers as well as bank personnel. In addition to these, there were initially, efforts from the part of bank personnel and the bank customers to evade from providing answers to some of the questions raised. However, earnest and sincere efforts have been taken to convince them about the importance and relevance of the study and by providing necessary clarifications to their queries at the time data collection.

Findings

The major findings of the present study are summarised here.

Majority of bank personnel covered in the present study are from the clerical category (66 per cent. In southern region, clerks constituted 74 per cent of the total respondents from bank personnel which formed the highest group. As far as the total service of the bank personnel were concerned more than 54 per cent of the respondents from bank personnel having the experience of 20 years and above. Regarding the educational qualification of respondents from bank personnel, 67 per cent possessed bachelors' degree in one subject or other and 25 per cent had post graduate degree also. Regarding technical education, 95 per cent did not have any such qualification at all. Regarding the respondents from bank customers, 82 per cent were male respondents. As far as occupations of the customers covered under the study were concerned 43 percent was from business and 35 per cent from private service. Agriculture conducted only insignificantly.

For the convenience of the present study, products and services of banks were divided into different categories. They were deposits, international banking, consultancy, advances, other products and miscellaneous. The commercial and co-operative banks in Kerala have same types of deposits except NRI deposit. Because RBI has not yet permitted Co-operative banks to deal with NRI deposits. Under the category of international banking two products were identified for analysis. They were letter of credit and foreign currency. Fourteen per cent of bank personnel covered under the study responded that they dealt with letter of credit. In location-wise there was wide variation in the business of letter of credit. Business of letter of credit was highest in urban areas and was only one per cent in rural bank branches. In region wise, central region came first in the business of letter of credit. Fifty three percent of the bank personnel covered under the study revealed that they dealt with foreign currency. In region-wise analysis also it was found that in the business of letter of credit and foreign currency, central region made substantial dealings.

Important products and services analysed under the category of advances were term loan, bill discounting, advances for import and export, secured loan and unsecured loan. The study revealed that among the advances term loan was the most acceptable product to customers in Kerala. Location-wise analysis of advances for import and export trade, bank personnel covered under the study revealed that highest dealings of this product was in semi-urban area. In region-wise it was in the central region where maximum transaction of this product occurred. In the case of secured loan, location wise analysis revealed that it was in urban area that maximum transactions occurred. Region wise analysis disclosed that Southern region came first in dealings of this product.

In location-wise and region-wise, bank personnel covered under the study responded that products and services covered under the category of 'consultancy' got very poor response from customers in Kerala. Products studied under the category of 'other products' were factoring, loan syndication, higher purchase and leasing. The study revealed that these products have not yet created a ripple in Kerala. Important products studied under the heading 'miscellaneous' were lockers, credit card, debit card, collection and standing instructions. Location wise analysis revealed that it was in urban area the maximum use of these products occurred. In region-wise analysis it was found that lockers, collection and standing instruction were the products which were in high demand and among the regions, southern region came first in its use. In the case of debit card and credit card these transactions have not yet created a serious impact on banking business in Kerala.

Training is an act of increasing the knowledge and skill of employees for doing a job. Study has been conducted to see how far training has been provided to bank personnel, which disclosed that among the three categories of the bank personnel and their training in bank marketing, there were statistically significant differences. Even though majority of bank managers had undergone training in marketing service, bottom level employees, i.e. clerks of the bank who are directly interacting with customers, received only nominal training.

The study conducted to see the market potentiality of bank services pointed out that there was no highly potential area for marketing bank services. It was mainly due to the fact that Kerala is one of the highly banked states in India. Among the new products introduced by the banks, on the basis of weighted average score, high acceptance was to credit card both in location wise and region wise. Marketing depend heavily on effective communication which flew between the producer and consumer. Chi-square test revealed that statistically significant relation existed in both location-wise and region-wise with mode of communication. Majority of bank personnel covered under the study disclosed that personal contact was the best method of communication in both location wise and region wise. Similarly majority of the bank customers covered under the study revealed that combined application of personal contact with bit notice was the best method of communication.

Regarding computerisation in banks i.e. electronic data recording in bank branches, the present study revealed that no bank was wholly depending on computers for maintaining records. Bank personnel who came under the study revealed that among the locations, urban area came first in using computers along with manual records (93 per cent). In region wise analysis also, the study revealed that application of both manual records and computers was the order. Among the regions, northern region came first in this regard. Further analysis was also conducted regarding the quality of information system maintained in the banks. The present study revealed that the quality of information system was 'good' and there was no wide variation between locations. In region wise analysis also the quality of information system came under the category of 'good' and among the regions central region came first (82 per cent) in this regarded. The quality of information system came under the category of 'good' as far as the bank as a whole was concerned. A great percentage of bank personnel (92 per cent) revealed that branch wise information system was better than that of bank as a whole.

As far as the strategies adopted by the bank were concerned, statistically significant relation existed between location and strategies set apart for exploring profitable opportunities. Among the locations, semi-urban area stands first (76 per cent) in this regard. In region wise analysis also there was statistically significant relation between region and strategies adopted by the bank for exploring profitable opportunities. Among the regions central region came first in this regard. As far as the effectiveness of marketing strategies, which were helpful to policy, makers were concerned; there was no statistically significant relation with location. Further more, the effectiveness of strategies helpful to policy makers was the same in all locations. In region wise analysis, statistically significant relation existed between region and strategies adopted by banks, which was helpful to policy makers. In the case of effectiveness of strategy for attaining target, the study revealed that there was no statistically significant relation with locations. It was also found that the effectiveness of strategy for attaining target was somewhat equal both in urban area and semi-urban area. In region wise analysis, statistically significant relation did between region and the effectiveness of strategy for attaining target. It was identified that among the regions, southern region came first

Marketing strategies adopted by the banks were also analysed to see that whether it was effective for better management of bank both in location wise and region wise. Location wise analysis showed that statistically significant relation existed between location and strategies adopted by the bank for better management, and among the locations semi-urban area came first in this regard. It was also disclosed that for better management the same type of strategies were not sufficient in all locations. In region wise analysis, there was no statistically significant relation between region and the strategies adopted by bank for better management. As far as the effectiveness of the strategies was concerned, southern region came first in this regard.

Analysis was conducted to see the opinion about benefits of bank marketing on the point of view of bank personnel. For that, weighted average scores were calculated in category wise, location wise and region wise. All categories of bank personnel had unanimous opinion about the benefits of bank marketing. Weighted average score disclosed that the first important gain was satisfying customers, second benefit was excelling competition and third benefit was understanding customers. In location wise, the first and foremost intention of bank marketing was satisfying customers indiscriminately whether the bank was located in urban, semi-urban or rural areas. Region wise weighted average score revealed that satisfying the customer was an important object of bank marketing except in central region. In central region maximum importance was given to excelling competition. By going through all these analysis, it was clear that satisfying the customer was of utmost importance by application of marketing principles in banks in Kerala.

Attempt was also made to assess the attitude of bank customers regarding the application of marketing principles in banks. Regarding the necessity of application of marketing principles in bank, 99 percent of the customers in occupations wise, location wise and region wise were of the view that application of marketing principles was either essential or highly essential in banks. In order to assess the benefits of the bank marketing, weighted average scores were calculated in location wise, region wise and occupation wise, which revealed that satisfying customers was the first and most important benefit of marketing of bank services.

For identifying area or areas required for financial support of the banks for development, analysis has been conducted in location wise and region wise. In both cases, statistically significant relation did not exist. Majority of the bank personnel covered under the study (33 per cent) disclosed that combined group of agriculture, business/industry and service occupied first for the development with support of bank in northern region. But in central region it was business/industry that occupied first and in southern region all areas occupied equal importance. Similar attempt was also made to assess bank customers point of view regarding the area found potential for development with the support of bank. The study revealed that statistically significant relation existed in occupation wise, location wise and region wise with the area that required financial support for development. Majority of the bank customers covered under the study (82 per cent) were of the view that the potential area which required financial support was business/industry. Occupation wise analysis revealed that except from agriculture, majority of bank customers from all other occupations opined that the area that required financial support was industry /business. In location wise and region wise analysis, industry/business group was identified as the potential area, which required financial support for development from banks. The study also disclosed that bank customers were least interest in financial support for agricultural sector.

It was found that more than 92 per cent of the bank personnel responded that their branches did not conduct any survey with regard to market potential. The result of the chi-square test brought out the fact that there was no statistical significant relation between location or region and reason for not conducting survey for assessing market potential. Location wise and region wise analysis further revealed that the dominating reason for not conducting surveys for assessing market potential was lack of instruction from top and the feeling that no such attempt was needed. Of these two important reasons, lack of instruction from top was the prime reason for not conducting surveys.

As for the methods adopted by banks for deposit mobilisation, it was found that there was statistically significant relation between location and views on methods of deposit mobilisation. Majority of the respondents from bank personnel opined that meeting customers personally was the best method for mobilisation of deposits by banks. Interaction with bank personnel revealed that most of the customers were not interested in making public, the matters connected with their deposits. In region wise also, meeting customers personally was the most favored method for deposit mobilisation. Among the regions central region came first in this regard.

Attempt was also made to assess the response of bank customers towards different methods adopted by bank for deposit mobilisation. The analysis revealed that statistically significant relation existed between location and different methods of deposit mobilization. Location wise analysis revealed that majority of bank customers (93 per cent) were of the view that meeting customers personally or meeting customers personally and advertisement jointly were best methods for deposit mobilisations, semi-urban area came first in this regard. In region wise analysis also, statistically significant relation existed between region and methods of deposit mobilisation. The study further revealed that meeting customers personally or combination of personal meeting with advertising were the best methods for deposit mobilisation. It was also found that among these two methods personal meeting was the highly favored method among the bank customers. In case of meeting customers personally, southern region came first (58 per cent). But in the case of meeting customers personally and advertising, which was identified as the next preferred method, northern region came first.

The acceptance of available products of banks by the customers, the study showed that in urban area fixed deposit and savings bank deposit were most highly acceptable products to customers. Further more they enjoy the same degree of preferred one but in the rural area savings bank deposit was the most acceptable one. From the region wise analysis, it was learned that in northern and southern regions fixed deposit was the most acceptable one but the central region showed preference for savings bank deposit. Thus, the most acceptable product of banks by customers was savings deposit both in location wise and region wise.

Analysis was conducted about the position of NRI deposit in location wise and region wise. Majority of the bank personnel that came under the category of respondents (81 per cent) opined that NRI deposit in banks was either high or moderate. Region wise analysis was also conducted which reveled that NRI deposit in southern region came first. But majority of bank personnel from urban area and rural area stated that, NRI deposit was moderate. As far as the trend of NRI deposit was concerned, statistically significant relation existed between location and trend of NRI deposit. In region wise also the relation was statistically significant. The study further showed that the bank personnel who came under the category of respondents opined that the trend of NRI deposit was stalemate. But in southern region, majority of them stated that NRI deposit was increasing. From the point of view of the bank customers the study observed that there was no statistically significant relation between location and trend of NRI deposit. In region wise it was such that there was statistically significant relation. In occupation wise analysis also it was found that the relation was statistically significant.

It was found that there is statistically significant relation between the marital status of the customers in dealings with the bank and location or region. The bank customers opined that influence of marital status was 'medium' in region wise and location wise. But in region wise, influence of marital status on the behavior of customers in relation to banking was high in central region and medium in northern and southern region. It was generally found that many of them started dealings with the bank after marriage.

The social factor taken for study was age. Bank personnel's response revealed that statistically significant relation existed between location of the bank and the age of bank customers in dealings with the bank. It was also found that influence of age was medium in dealing with bank in location wise and region wise. Another important fact was that both bank personnel and customers opined in the same way. Another social factor, status of the family and its influence in dealing with the bank was also analysed in location wise and region wise. It was found that the relation is statistically significant. Majority of bank personnel who came under the study disclosed that the influence of the status of the family in dealing with the bank was medium but the customers opined that the status of the family was 'low' in dealing with the bank. Opinion leaders and intermediaries was the next social factor taken for study. Majority of bank personnel who came under the study (75 per cent) revealed that the influence of opinion leaders and intermediaries was 'low' in locations. In region wise also bank personnel responded that the influence was 'low'.

Among the economic factors the level of income was the first factor taken for the study. The study revealed that there was no statistically significant relation between location and level of income on the behavior of the customer in dealing with the bank. In region wise analysis also there was no statistically significant relation. Another economic factor taken for study was savings. The chi-square test revealed that there was statistically significant relation between savings and attitude of customers towards bank. By close verification it was clear that among the three locations influence of savings was maximum in rural area. In region wise analysis, the study disclosed that influence of savings on customer behavior was maximum (80 per cent) and less (51 per cent) in northern region. Expenditure was the next important factor taken for study. There was no statistically significant relation between expenditure and customer behavior in dealing with the bank in location wise and region wise. Among the locations, the response of bank personnel was somewhat equal, that is there was no wide variation between different locations. But in region wise analysis central region came first (52 per cent) and in both northern and southern region the bank personnel's attitude was the same. The same question was asked to the customers also to obtain their attitude towards economic factors. It was found that statistically significant relation was discerned between the level of income and location in dealing with the bank. By close observation the attitude of the customer was found to be the same as that of bank personnel. Customers' attitude is more or less equal in all locations. In region wise analysis it was found that there was no statistically significant relation between level of income and customers dealing with the bank. Majority of customers coming under the study, more than 95 per cent opined that the influence of the level of income was high.

Psychological factors were also an important element, which influence customers dealing with the bank. Important factors taken for study were awareness of the product, motivation, and conditioning. As far as the awareness of the product is concerned, the study reveals that there was no statistically significant relation between awareness of the product by the customers and customers' behaviour towards bank. The study also disclosed that influence of the awareness of the product had 'medium' impact in customers' behaviour on banks. Bank personnel also opined that among the locations, urban area came first in the category of medium. In region wise analysis, statistically significant relation existed between awareness of the product and behaviour of customers towards bank in region wise. It was also found that influence of customers' behaviour due to awareness of the products was medium and among the regions, southern region came first in this regard. In the case of the second psychological factor, motivation, customers' behaviour in location wise was statistically significant. Among the locations, rural area came first (60 per cent) in this regard.

In region wise analysis, the study disclosed that there was statistically significant relation between motivation and customers' behaviour. In region wise analysis the study further revealed the influence of motivation on customer behaviour was low and among the regions southern region came first in this regard. Conditioning was another psychological factor taken for the study. The study revealed that statistically significant relation existed between locations and conditioning. Further, bank personnel opined that conditioning of a product of a bank had low influence in the behaviour of the customer. In region wise analysis also there was statistically significant relation between conditioning bank product and customers' behaviour. Further more, southern region came in this regard.

Similar questions were asked to top customers also and it was found that statistically significant relation existed between the awareness of the product and customers' attitude towards bank. Among the locations, urban area came first in this regard. In the case of motivation, bank customers disclosed that the influence of motivation on customer behaviour is medium and among the locations, rural area comes first (63 per cent) in this regard. In region wise also, statistically significant relation was exposed at 5 per cent level of significance. Furthermore influence of motivation on customers dealing with the bank was medium and among the regions, southern region came first in this regard. Regarding conditioning, the final psychological factor taken for study both location wise and region wise analysis by applying chi-square test revealed that there existed statistically significant relation between conditioning and bank product and customers behaviour. More than 75 per cent of customers were of the view that the influence of conditioning on customers' behaviour was low. In region wise also more than 83 per cent of the customers opined that influence of conditioning on customer behaviour was low and among the regions, southern region came in this regard.

In the present study an attempt was also made to analyse the influence of promotional factors of bank marketing. Of this, the first factor was advertising. The study revealed that 70 per cent of the bank personnel were of the view that the influence of advertising in bank marketing was 'moderate' in location wise and region wise. Among the location urban area came first in this regard. In region wise analysis it was found that central region came first in influence (78 per cent) and northern region showed the lowest. The second factor taken was development of new products. Many of the products introduced by banks were readymade and they were not in the right from of the requirements. In addition to that, there were a lot of changes in the outlook of customers due to external and internal environment towards the attitude to deposits and financial requirements. The bank personnel opined that influence of public relation in the promotion of bank marketing was high both in location wise and region wise. Further the study revealed that rural folk did not voluntarily approach the bank due to their inability to interact with bank personnel for presenting their requirements. In region wise analysis, it was not only high but the influence of public relation was somewhat equal in all regions. Majority of the bank personnel coming under the category of respondents opined that the influence of personal relation was very high in promotion of bank marketing both in location wise and region wise.

The other two factors taken with regard to promotion of bank marketing were price mixing and place mixing. Majority of the bank personnel responded that the influence of these factors in promoting bank marketing was very low both location wise and region wise. The bank customers responded that the influence of these factors was moderate in location wise and region wise.

Another factor taken for study with regard to promotion of bank marketing was physical attraction. Majority of bank personnel (77 per cent) opined that influence of physical attraction was moderate in bank marketing in location wise and region wise. It was also identified that among the regions, southern region came first. Through interaction with bank personnel, it was learned that physical expression, behavior and manner of bank personnel are important factors in connection with bank marketing. The views of the bank customers were also similar.

The study revealed that the influence of ATM in promotion of bank marketing was very low in location wise and region wise. In location wise it was a weak factor for promoting bank marketing in rural areas. But the same opinion was not shared by the urban and semi-urban areas. In region wise analysis, the influence was very low in southern region. Telemarketing is also a promotional factor; the study revealed that the influence of telemarketing was very low in bank marketing both in location wise and region wise. Bank personnel opined that among the locations, it was the rural area and among the regions, it was the central region that recorded the least influence. One more factor taken for study in connection with bank marketing was the influence of professionalism. The study revealed that the influence of professionalism in bank marketing was high. Among the locations, the greatest influence was in semi-urban area (74 per cent) and lowest was in rural area. In region wise analysis, it was found that the greatest influence is in northern region.

The same factors were taken for study to assess customers' attitude. Majority of customers (61 per cent) opined that influence of advertisement was moderate in bank marketing both location wise and region wise. Among the locations, urban area came first in respect to staining that the influence of advertising was moderate. In region wise analysis central region came first. The attitude of the customer was similar to the bank personnel regarding the influence of advertising in bank marketing. The information furnished by the customers revealed that developing new products had high influence in marketing. The bank customers coming under the category of respondents disclosed that influence of public relation in bank marketing was very high both in location wise and region wise. In location wise analysis, it was found that among the locations, rural area came and in region wise analysis the southern region came first.

The customers responded in the same way in which the bank personnel responded regarding the influence of personal relation in bank marketing and the customers gave the highest preference for personal relation for bank marketing. Customers' accessibility to bank personnel to express their requirements and to get the right direction was considered the prime aspect of bank marketing. The information disclosed in the study showed that more than 88 per cent of the customers both in location wise and region wise opined that telemarketing as a factor for influencing bank marketing had low or very low effect in bank marketing.

It was also not attempted to know the attitude of bank personnel on nationalisation. It was found that there was no statistically significant relation between location and views on nationalisation. Majority of bank personnel coming under the category of respondent disclosed that they supported nationalisation of banks (78 per cent) and among the locations urban area came first in this regard. In region wise analysis, the study showed that there was statistically significant relation between region and views on nationalisation. The study further showed that the bank personnel favoured nationalisation in all regions. And among the regions, southern region came first (90 per cent) in this regard. In the case of reason for supporting nationalisation, it was found that there was no statistically significant relation between location and reason for supporting nationalization. The study also showed that support for nationalisation was highest in the rural area and low in urban area. In region wise analysis, the study revealed that there was statistically significant relation between region and reason for supporting nationalisation. It was also clear from the study that, bank personnel supported nationalisation mainly because of social control. The study revealed that the basic reason why bank personnel did not support nationalisation was that it would lead to lack of competitiveness.

Similar attempt was also made to study the attitude of the customers towards nationalization. The study disclosed that there was no statistically significant relation between location or region and views on nationalisation. In both cases, bank customers responded that social control was the major reason for supporting nationalization. In region wise analysis southern region came first in this regard. The reason for not supporting nationalisation was verified with bank customers and it was revealed that as was the case with bank personnel they did not favour nationalisation because it dampened competitiveness. In location wise analysis semi-urban area, and in region wise analysis central region came in this regard.

Suggestions

On the basis of the finding of the study, following suggestions have been made to improve the marketing of bank services.

Because of the special features of Kerala in social and economic front, the common frame of the bank products and services, is not sufficient for the requirements of banking industry in Kerala. Socially better standard of living and economically limited development of industries created flux situation in bank marketing. Products and services required by Kerala are different from other parts of the country. Therefore, there is utmost need for identifying and designing right products to suit the requirements of Kerala market.

Any product designed must have two core elements. First it must be according to the need of the customer and second, products must be slivered according to the expectation of the customer. As far as delivery of products or services is concerned it has location and behavioural aspects involved in it. Delivery of the products must be so efficient that both the customers and bank personnel understand the essence. However, the problems of delivery should be settled through localised solutions. Technology 'iould aim at eliminating work related block due to crowding. For this it is required to ensure delivery of products and services at the place and time of convenience of customer. The very essence of introduction of technology must satisfy customer needs and expectation and it should not be for the convenience of the employees of the banks.

During the post nationalisation, there has been wide spread of bureaucratisation, which has resulted unto erosion of managerial ability and destruction of motivation. Nationalisation has resulted into wide spread of bank branches throughout the country particularly in Kerala. However, the type of products and services are limited and predetermined by the RBI and Finance Ministry. In practical sense, bank personnel now become only an intermediary in between the upper financial authority and the needy (customer) simply to transmit the products and services without value addition. No talent is required for these services, but simply verify whether conditions predetermined by authority is fulfilled or not, which resulted into erosion of quality. Hence for bank marketing in the present liberalised and competitive financial market, bank personnel should be remotivated in terms of knowledge, skill and attitude. Bank managers should create work culture that encourages initiative and maximize employee motivation.

Quality rating system is not available for products and services of the bank except a kind of time norms, which is generally violated. So generally even the right products cannot be giving customer satisfaction. So, for overcoming this situation 'bench mark' at two points, that is one at bank as a whole and another at branch level must be implemented. Introduction of a system to assess the customers' satisfaction is the need of the hour. This will help to evaluate quality of the bank marketing from the customers' point of view. This will assist to implement remedial measures.

At present, for delivery of bank products and services, the existing systems and procedure is creating lot of hurdles. As a result people get hooked to rules. The general features of internal environment of the bank are more inward driven than outward looking. Therefore it is essential to revise system and procedure to make it customer oriented. For this, the system and procedures should be revised in such a way that it must cope with new challenges and opportunities. Awareness of both the customers and front line personnel of non-conventional products is inadequate. In practice, bank personnel in the bottom level are unable to present right product and services to right customers even though they are available, so effective method is required to avoid such a situation. Attitude of bank personnel is very important in bank marketing. Even in computerised branches accuracy and speed have improved, but reorientation to focus on customer needs and aspiration is needed. It is also needed to identify options through which their needs and priorities can be met in the best possible way. In other words a system that start with customer feedback and end with redefined products and services needs to be implemented.

Even though amenities to bank personnel are available to a certain extend in banks, the amenities available to customers are not upto the expectation. Hence all possible steps are required to be taken in this regard. In bank branches, 'Help counter' must be provided with bank personnel having positive approach or provide 'book let' on promoting banking habit among customers. Flexible timing, anywhere banking, extension of business hours and single window services must be introduced. In Kerala NRI accounts are available in branches of commercial banks. But now co-operative banks are not yet permitted to do this. Therefore co-operative banks are also be permitted to carry business on NRI products

References

Asthana, A. K. *Marketing of Banking Services by the Mahasana Urban Co-operative Bank Limited*, Mehasana (Gujarat). The Banker, January 1998.

Bishwanbhar Jha, *Product Strategy for Banking Sector Post Liberalszation Effect*, The Management Accountant, July 2000.

Mousumi Ghosh, *Customer Service in Nationalised Bank*, The Management Accountant, July 2000.

Murugesan, D. 'Shreyas', February - March 98.

Nagi Reddy, K. and Ratnakumar, *Indian Journal to Applied Psychology* Vol. 26(1), 1992.

Rajeev K. Seth, *Marketing of Banking Services*, Macmillan India Ltd, Delhi, 1998.

Saxena, K.K. *Bank Marketing,* Skylark, Publications, 1988.

13

Consumer Behaviour in Retail Marketing of Textiles

Jacob Thomas

The global reputation of Indian textiles might be one of the contributory factors that had enabled the Indian merchants to establish trade links with the Jews and the Arabs. The Cacca Muslin, the Cashmere Shawl, the Gujarat Patola and the Bandthanies, the Benarese and the Surat Brocade are some of the textiles products of the ancient India with exemplary appearance and super-fine quality, which had always been great attractions for global merchants. The economic history of India unveils that production and marketing of textiles has been the provider of livelihood for Indians. The textile industry has been occupying a significant position in the economy of India, by virtue of its contribution to the industrial output, employment generation, and foreign exchange earnings. Textile and clothing sector contributes four per cent of the GDP, one-third of the total exports of the country, and 14 per cent of the industrial outputs (Lal A. R., 2002). And being the largest sector next to agriculture, the textile industry is employing about 21 million people (Reddy, V. P., 2003). The textile industry braces the Indian economy by acting as an inexhaustible source of revenue. It contributes substantially to excise duty and customs duty as well.

Indian textile industry is the confluence of five different sectors such as mill, powerloom, handloom, apparel and hosiery. All these sectors are complementary to one another in relation to raw materials or finished products. The mill sector consists of spinning and composite mills. The spinning mill holds the apex position in the Indian textile industry, as it is the sole source for producing yarn from raw cotton. The composite mills carry out both spinning and weaving, and they are the major source of supplying cloth for domestic and overseas market. The powerloom and handloom sectors go hand in hand because the latter depends on the former to a great extent. Installation of powerloom has significantly lightened the workload of weaving units and hence increased their productivity.

The structural pattern of the Indian textile industry takes a deviation, with the emergence of the Readymade Garment (RMG) sector. The RMG sector produces tailored clothing or apparel by incorporating fashion/style of high value. An important feature of the RMG sector is that the lion's share of RMG units is floated as small scale industrial units. This sector produces 'knitted textiles' both for general and industrial purposes, like 'occupational garments', 'medical textiles', 'pan belt-runners', 'packaging materials' and upholstery items'. This sector also represents textile handicrafts consisting of 'carpet' 'mat' 'furnishing items' and inputs for 'interior decoration'.

Although there has been a commendable growth in the export of textiles, the exporters are confronted with many hurdles such as low productivity of cotton cultivation has resulted in inadequate supply of raw cotton in the domestic market, which has affected the potential of yarn export; since ginning is not carried out properly, the long-staple filament gets mixed with short-staple filament resulting in poor quality, thus exported yarn is characterised by poor quality, particularly in the case of long-staple filament; most of the textile manufacturing units in India (medium and small size) are operating with outdated machinery, which has adversely affected quality and cost competitiveness; the textile industry of India comprises several sectors, which are mutually competing in character and the growth of one sector has an implied negation of the growth of the other sector; owing to strong passion for branded textile products in the international market, the Indian manufacturers have to establish tie-up with the manufacturers of internationally reputed brands, this causes extra load on selling cost, which has ultimately affected price competitiveness; and in tune with the WTO agreement, India has agreed to reduce tariff on various items of textiles, it indicates that Indian textile industry has to withstand competition from countries producing cheap textiles with good quality in both foreign and domestic markets.

It is explicit from the present scenario of export market of textiles that the Indian textile industry has to march ahead in terms of quality, price competitiveness and value addition. This reveals that unless a deliberate attempt is made by the Government, the cotton growers, the raw material suppliers, the producers, the Indian exporters will not be able to cope with the quota free world. Any inertia in ushering with strategic schemes would result in the dwindling of India's present position among the textile exporters in the global market during the post Multi Fibre Agreement period.

The 'Uruguay' round of multilateral trade organisation came out with a WTO agreement on textiles, called the Agreement on Textile and Clothing (ATC) to substitute the Multi-Fibre-Agreement (MFA) of 1973. The MFA has been providing several advantages to textile exporting countries under the umbrella of Quantitative Restriction (QR). With the dawn of 2005, the Indian textile industry would be exposed to a strange environment with regard to international trade on textiles. Because, the stage-wise phasing out of MFA, as per the WTO agreement, will be completed by 2004 and there will be no more covenant of Quantitative Restriction for global trade on textiles. The major impacts of the phasing out of MFA on the Indian textile industry can be identified as: unrestricted, unlimited access for the Indian textile products to the global market, particularly to the WTO member countries, which account for half of the global textile trade; the restructured tariff provides equal advantages to all exporting sectors such as mill, powerloom and handloom; the lowered tariff enables the Indian textile industry to get integrated with the global textile market and the global trade will be monitored and governed by multilateral agreement' (Nair R., 2003). From this perspective, it seems reasonable to analyse whether the present setup of Indian textile industry is potential enough to cope with the changing scenario of international trade. Accordingly, the scope of the textile industry in the post-MFA period is assessed with certain parameters like technology, quality, value addition, cost and fiscal support.

If the Indian textile industry has to survive in the post-MFA period, technological upgradation must be done in both spinning and weaving sectors. 'A study conducted by the South Indian Textile Research Association (SITRA) has revealed that in 25 per cent of the mills, the average of the ring frames is more than 25 years and only 20 per cent of cone winders are automatic'. The slow momentum of technological upgradation is mainly due to the poor performance of the textile engineering industry in India. Now the textile mills of India depend on foreign countries for the supply of sophisticated machines and accessories. The foreign market seems to be inaccessible for small and medium size units. This has a far-reaching consequence on the apparel sector, as most of the apparel manufacturing units are floated as SSI units.

The government of India has launched several schemes, and one of the schemes is characterised by financial assistance, which is named Technology Upgradation Fund (TUF). This scheme has achieved only a little momentum in the textile sector, for instance, in Tamil Nadu only 18 per cent of the powerloom units have availed the scheme even after three years of its launching (Mital R., 2003). However, certain encouraging trends have been witnessed in the sphere of technological upgradation of the textile industry. As an example Bombay Dyeing has invested Rs. 115 crore in modernization and Raymonds has made textiles its core business in preference to steel and cement (Colourage, 2003). At this juncture it can be suggested that for improving the technological competitiveness, emphasis must be given to strengthening and promoting textile engineering industry. As an immediate step, the Government should extend adequate support to textile manufacturing units, to import machines and accessories. Concession on import duties and financial assistance at subsidized rates of interest may be suggested as the viable measures in this regard.

Quality competitiveness is another thrust area of the Indian textile industry to be reviewed for the purpose of assessing its capability to exist in the global market during the post-MFA period. Quality does mean fitness for use, conformance to specification and fulfilling the consumer requirements (Srinivasan A.K. and Gaur R. K., 1999). The quality requirements are factors that ensure satisfactory or expected performance of textile articles during their use by the consumers (Singh A. and Aswati M., 2003). As far as the texture quality of cotton textiles is concerned, India maintains a unique position in the global market because of the adequate home production of 'long staple cotton'. The supply of high quality cotton can be improved further, if the cotton growers can shift from conventional method of cultivation to modern methods by using high yielding variety of cotton plants. 'American hybrid cotton cultivation in new areas and increase in productivity can contribute significantly to increased cotton production' (Jain K.S. and Naik G., 1999). Synthetic textile manufactures in India seem to be very keen on adding new generation garments/clothing/to meet the competition in a quota-free market. 'Flame resistant synthetic fibre have been developed which are required for end use such as defence application, industrial use, space and civil use' (Gokarnan N., 2000).

Potentiality in value addition may be pointed out as another avenue where the Indian textile industry has to concentrate its attention, to occupy a legitimate place in the international market of textiles during the post-MFA period. This has a special relevance, as there is a change of trend in customers' taste and preference in the direction of readymade garments. Value addition can be materialised by inducting new features of fabric, colour, design/prints, style/fashion and retail brands. Since a sizeable number of garment manufacturing units have been floated as SSI units, value addition in the garment sector appears to be a utopian idea. The new textile policy of 2000 has announced the 'dereservation of garment sector' to facilitate the entry of large manufacturing units. 'With the dereservation, the garment industry will be able to grow unhindered to face competition, particularly from Bangldadesh, Sri Lanka and Pakistan' (The Indian Textile Journal, 2000). With a view to inducting innovative garments, the Clothing Manufacturers' Association of India has launched a Garment Training Institute at Pune. Targeting a wider exposure of fashion, the National Institute of Fashion Technology (NIFT) organised an international conference on technological innovation in fashion industry on October 12, 2000. Resorting to Computer Aided Designing (CAD), the garment sector has come to the verge of attaining proficiency in developing ultra-modern designs. These strategic measures may enable the Indian textile industry to achieve new horizons of value addition.

At present the Indian textile industry is characterised by high 'financial cost' and comparatively reasonable 'weaving cost'. 'The financial cost is the combined cost of depreciation and investment, in India, which amounts to 71 per cent of the total spinning cost, whereas the lowest financial cost in Italy and Japan is 38 per cent and in USA it is 50 per cent; the capital interests rate of India is also the highest at 18 per cent whereas that of USA is 7.5 per cent, Japan 5.5 per cent, Brazil, Taiwan, Korea at 10 per cent which are comparatively lower' (Katti V., 1997). If the Indian textile industry has to retain its share in the international market in the years to come, it has to achieve price competitiveness by slackening cost of production, particularly the financial cost. The Government of India has been providing fiscal support for the development of textile industry since independence. '8 per cent of the excise duty is retained in respect of cotton yarn while that of non-cotton fabrics has been reduced from 12 per cent to 10 per cent and a similar reduction of 2 per cent is earned in the case of garments' (Handloom Export Promotion Council, 2003).

Reduction of excise duty on clothing and apparel catalyses the domestic consumption as it has a direct impact on the end consumer. It has become vivid that the Indian textile industry has reached the crossroads of development. Nevertheless, much effort is required for achieving global competitiveness to keep its market share unaffected in a quota-free world. In order to achieve global competitiveness, a three dimensional strategy by blending product innovation, foreign direct investment and value addition has become the need of the hour. A result-oriented approach in these directions is to be initiated, as Indian textile industry will have to face fierce competition from countries like China, Pakistan, Bangladesh, Sri Lanka, Indonesia and Vietnam.

Textiles of any kind can be marketed throughout the country; however, its production is confined mainly to the region in and around the *Coromandel Coast* and the *Deccan Plateu* in the Indian penisula. 'In terms of the textile mills, Tamil Nadu occupies the apex position with a total number of 860 mills, followed by Maharashtra and Gujarat with strength of 205 and 149 mills respectively. In the powerloom sector, Maharashtra is the forerunner with a strength of 6,92,603 looms, Tamil Nadu is the second largest state with 3,16,994 looms and Gujarat ranks the third with 3,08,609 looms. Regarding handloom, Assam ranks first with 14,09,000 looms, Tamil Nadu and West Bengal share the second and third positions with 4,29,000 and 3,38,000 looms respectively (Compendium of Textile Statistics, 2002). Cotton weaving was the only textile industry prevailing in Kerala during the ancient period and was carried on by hereditary weavers. The *Chaliyans, Kaikolans and Chettians* were active in weaving cloth (Menon, Achyutha C., 1969). The weavers of Thiruvananthapuram and Kannur districts still possess the heritage of excellent hand-woven clothing.

The mill sector came into existence in the state during the colonialist domination of the Europeans. It occupies less significance in the industrial economy of Kerala and ranks far below, as compared to the neighbouring state of Tamil Nadu. Kerala accounts for 36 textile mills, 2672 powerlooms and 52,000 handlooms (compendium of Textile Statistics, 2002). Kerala does not have a climate conducive to cultivating cotton and hence the state has to depend on other states for the supply of yarn. Besides, labour unrests and unfavourable physical and environmental factors have resulted in the stagnant growth of textile industry in Kerala. However, the state extends support to the Indian textile industry by setting up a vast and dense market for its products. In Kerala the urban market annually consumes an average of 13.90 meters of cloth with a value of Rs. 1,333.58, the annual average consumption rate of the semi-urban market is 11.15 meters of cloth having a worth of Rs. 704.79, and the rural market accounts for an annual average consumption of 5.99 meters of cloth with an estimated value of Rs. 389.33 (Textiles Committee, 2002).

The uniqueness of Keralites which distinguishes them from the rest of the inhabitants of India is their personal hygiene and eloquence for esteem appearance by way of dressing up. Unlike the other states in India, the retail network of textiles in Kerala is widely distributed, that 'itinerant cloth vendors' are seen in every nook and corner of the state. Typologically, the textile retaining units in Kerala can be broadly classified into two, namely, the government and the private. The former includes those units which are either owned or supported by National Textile Corporation (NTC), Kerala State Handloom Weavers Co-operative Society (Hantex), Kerala State Handloom Development Corporation (Handveev), Tamil Nadu Handloom Weavers Co-operative Society (Co-optex), and Khadi and Village Industries Board (KVIB). On the basis of the nature of the organisation, the private selling outlets can again be classified as organized and unorganised. The organised selling outlets include general textile shops, exclusive showrooms, franchise, and chain stores and the unorganised retailing units comprise mainly itinerant/door-to-door vendors. Thus, it is apt to point out that Kerala is well covered by a network of textile retailing outlets targeting the end consumers.

Statement of the Problem

The history of man's transition from primitive life to civilised life throws light on three facets of phenomenal changes in his attitude, such as consciousness about nutritious food, desire for convenient dwelling place, and passion for comfortable clothing. All human activities are driven by these facets of attitude and hence food, shelter and clothing have been universally accepted as the Basic Human Necessities (BHN). Though clothing is ranked the third factor in BHN, in Kerala, it often appears as the 'prime factor' taking priority among the needs to be satisfied. It may be observed that Keralites are overwhelmingly interested in dressing up impressively. And they may willingly go in for a compromise regarding food and shelter.

The tradition of Keralites in observing personal hygiene and dressing up with situational ethnicity may be pointed out as the cardinal factors that mark a difference between Keralites and the rest of Indians. One might stress that Keralites are always dress conscious in character. The inhabitants of Kerala have been using an exclusive pattern of clothing as the semiotic expression of their membership in a particular religion or caste. Traditionally, each religion or caste has its own 'dress code' to be observed on auspicious as well as normal occasions. Thus, each pattern of clothing seems to be unique. The uniqueness is apparent in the style, fabric, colour, design and mode of dressing.

The dressing habit of Keralites and their preference for the style of clothing witnessed drastic changes during the colonial period. It is worth mentioning that the induction of the 'mill made textiles of Manchester' in the Kerala market had paved the way for developing a trend among the consumers to prefer coloured clothing. Till that time, Keralites mainly used clothing of white or off-white colours. Besides, the colonial movement became instrumental to petering out some of the traditional wear from the Kerala market by persuading Keralites to switch over to clothing of the western style. The dislodging of dhotis by trousers, known as pants in users' parlance, can be cited as a typical example of this trend. The clothing style and habit of the Keralites went on changing even after independence. Certain identifiable changes in the characteristic features of the consumers in Kerala, like increase in income, educational advancement, information exposure through the mass media, new occupational avenues, occupational migration, awareness of the global trend of modernity, urbanisation and westernisation, have brought about spectacular changes in dressing habits and the consumption of clothing as well. 'It has to be accepted that radical changes have taken place in clothing style even among the conservative Keralites' (Lalithambika J., 2003). In brief, with the march of time, the dressing habit and the style of clothing of Keralites have been subject to several changes. This has made the textile market of Kerala dynamic. So long as the market for a product is dynamic, it signalises the gravity of marketing risk.

Understanding the consumers more closely and precisely is the 'panacea' for the problem of the dynamic behaviour of the market. This is seen to be result-fetching, as the purchase decision of the consumers determines the fate of a product in the market. A behavioural approach in designing marketing strategies seems to be indispensable to fortify the existing market share applicable to each retailer. Such an approach must be in the line of a meaningful analysis of the purchase behaviour of the prospective consumers, because 'profit is made from people not product' (Keth W.C., 1986). The study was undertaken against this backdrop.

Review of Literature

Only a few important studies have been made on the various aspects of the textile industry in Kerala. Regarding the marketing of textiles in the state, with special reference to the behavioural aspects of the consumers, no systematic studies have been initiated in the field of marketing research other than the one by the Textile Committee appointed by the Government of India, which conducted the National Household Survey on Market for Textiles and Clothing, in 2001. Nevertheless, a few researchers have come forward with the goal of analysing the different aspects of the textile industry. A brief review of the available literature is attempted below.

Padmanabhan (1974) examined the sickness of the cotton textile mills in the organised sector on a national level. He assessed the composition of assets, liabilities, and net working capital. He has observed that the current ratio is instrumental to predicting the short-term solvency of a firm. He has also pointed out that equity/debt ratio is effective in testing long-term solvency. The various sectors of the textile industry, such as mill, powerlooms, handlooms, the knitting industry and khadi, and their relationship have been studied by Sreenivasan (1984). He has analyzed the position of certain industries, which are closely integrated to the textile industry, such as the silk industry, the wool industry, the man-made fibre industry and the textile machinery industry. He has also listed out the problems and prospects of the Indian textile industry.

The high variations in profit among mills of the same size have been the focal point of the study initiated by Dhulasi Brindha (1985). She has made an effort to diagnose the causes for the low profitability of mills in Madurai city, taking into account for factors; size of the firm in terms of total financial asset, technology adopted in terms of capital intensity modernization in terms of additional investment in machines and capacity utilization of spindles and looms. She has come out with the conclusion that technology and modernization are the factors having a greater impact on the profitability of the mills. The study also throws light on the fact that there is positive correlation between profit and growth of the mills.

Kevin (1988) has made a comparative analysis in his study on the textile industry in Kerala and Tamil Nadu. He has studied the profitability of the textile industry and the individual mills as well. In the study, the cost structure, machine productivity, machine utilisation, and labour productivity of the mills have been analysed. In order to locate the factors responsible for inter-mill variation in profitability, he has made an effort to analyse the financial structure of the industry, so as to assess its long-term solvency. He has also evaluated the working capital management of the industry by employing fund-flow statement. The study revealed that the industry had witnessed a decline in profitability during the period under study. He has established that there is considerable inter-mill variation in profitability, and has identified certain factors responsible for the variation, such as labour cost, interest payments and gross value added. Machine productivity, machine utilisation and labour productivity have been traced as the three factors, which determine the value of outputs of a mill, which in turn, influences the gross value added. The study has further revealed that the features of the industry are low profitability, low ownership contribution, high debt financing, excessive reliance on short-term fund, scarce initial resource generation, poor debt servicing capacity, negative working capital, insufficient liquidity, and overstocking of raw material.

In 1990, the Government of Kerala constituted an advisory committee to study the problems and prospects of the textile industry in the state. The committee has come out with the finding that the textile mills in the public sector had not been well managed. The outstanding comment of the committee was that efficiency and professionalised management are the core factors for the success of any industry in the state, which is a land of high wage payment as compared to the neighbouring states. The committee has suggested modernisation of the textile units in the state and the slackening of the work force to the norms recommended by the Textile Research Association. The South Indian Textiles Research Association (SITRA) conducted a study on cost control and costing in spinning mills, in 1992. The study has assessed the causes for sickness and identified the symptoms that portend the sickness in spinning mills. It has emphasised that in the textile industry, the sickness is mainly caused by the incapacity to induct cost control measures in time. The study has also identified certain conditions to be complied with by the sick mills, in order to get into the list of revived units.

Balakrishnan (1994) conducted a survey on labour absenteeism among the member mills of SITRA. The survey has become an eye-opener to the member mills so as to evaluate and compare their performance and absenteeism with others, in order to judge the extent of forward and backward movement contributed by absenteeism over a given period of time. The study has highlighted that there was wide disparity in the rate of absenteeism among the member mills of SITRA. The magnitude of unjustifiable variation itself amplifies the need for slashing the rate of absenteeism in the mills, which was of a high degree. The study has further pointed out that unauthorised absenteeism was the most detrimental of the different types of absenteeism. It was found that in 1993 the member mills of SITRA had lost 2.5 per cent of their capacity utilisation because of absenteeism.

Ratnam (1996) compiled the publication of SITRA relating to a period of four decades, on productivity measurement. The compiled work incorporates various concepts, coining of appropriate terminology, carrying out of surveys, application of procedures developed, formulating norms to judge the top ten productivity level winners at various times in the industry, and periodic review. It has also formulated guidelines for the industrial units in the textile sector to adopt the best possible alternatives open to them so as to achieve improvement in future. The relative performance of spinning mills under different sectors in Kerala was analysed by Mohan Kumar (1997). The focal point of his study was to identify the factors responsible for productive as well as financial performance. The study has revealed that productivity of labour, capital, spindle and raw materials has an impact on the amount of the gross value added per unit of each sector. It also highlighted that a high index is the indication of the increase in the gross value added, economies in sales, increase in efficiency, etc. The major factors, which influence the technical efficiency, have been evolved from the study and listed as capacity utilisation, wage rate and maintaining a well-equipped research and development wing.

The Government of Kerala set up a committee for studying the problems of the textile units under the Industries Department in 1999. The committee has identified the sick units in the public and private sectors in the textile industry. It was brought out by the committee that the cotton yarn industry was characterised by certain pitfalls like high cost, demand-supply misfit, low market price, and accumulation of loss, which needed urgent remedial measures. According to the committee, the situation had become worse by low momentum of sales in the South East Asian countries and the gravity of the problem had been intensified by the surging of exchange rate. The committee formulated performance parameters of the profitable mills in the industry. Modernisation of machinery, imparting training on new lines of operation, and financial restructuring with appropriate capital leverage were the important recommendations of the committee. In 1999, the Government of Kerala constituted yet another committee to study the problems of the private sector textile mills in the state. The committee identified several problems like need for modernisation, low profit, high interest on borrowings, high cost of labour and power. The committee mainly suggested rehabilitation measures in the direction of raising seed capital fund, designing productivity norm, sales tax deferral and exit policy.

Manilal (2000) studied the organisational set up, the performance and the constraints of the Kerala State Textile Corporation (KSTC). He has pointed out that the financial risk of KSTC has increased on account of the enhancement of total liabilities over assets, and that increase in the volume of sales has not become conducive to improving working result due to high operating cost. The study further highlighted that wastage in the production process of the mills under KSTC is higher than the standard set by SITRA. The study brought out that the low demand for the yarn produced by KSTC has resulted in aggravating the financial weakness of the mills. Certain recommendations such as increasing capacity utilisation, modernisation of machinery, quality control on procurement of raw cotton, increase in the sale of yarn, rationalisation of manpower, financial restructuring, and installation of effective management information system, have been suggested by the study.

The National Household Survey on Markets for Textiles and Clothing was initiated by the Textile Committee of the Government of India, in 2001, and its report was published in December 2002. The survey focused on the task of collecting and analyzing the information about the current purchase of textiles by the households in the country. It also intended to assess the effect of various factors like income, price, area, gender, fabric, etc. on the consumer demand and to ascertain the shift in demand on account of change in consumer preference. The survey revealed that the textile industry has three sectors of market, namely the household sector, the non-household sector (including institutional, medical and technical textiles) and the export sector. It has been brought out by the survey that the proportionate share of consumption of these sectors is 60 per cent, 21 per cent and 19 per cent respectively, of the total production of cloth in the country. And it has been put forward by the survey that among the various textiles products, the blended ones enjoy a high demand in the domestic market. The survey further reveals that the per capita purchase of textiles by the household sector had increased to 18.65 meters in 2001. The effort made by the Textile Committee to undertake the National Survey is the pioneer attempt to analyse and study the textile industry from the perspective of the end-user or the ultimate consumer. Though the survey has explored factors like market share, demand and consumption of textiles, it is silent in respect of many factors that affect consumer decision-making process. Formulating marketing strategies without understanding the consumers and the factors that affect their decision-making process is a leap in the dark. The study was undertaken in this background.

Objectives of the Study

The study was initiated with the specific objectives of assessing the extent of influence of the following factors on the purchase decision of consumers in the textile market of Kerala.

- Product specification in relation to brand preference, quality, colour, fabric, fashion, readymade garments, domestic textiles, foreign textiles and price.
- Preference for source of buying in relation to shop attributes, location, sales force, provision for replacement and suggestion of family members.
- Advertisement in relation to television, radio, newspaper, magazine, poster and bill board/banner.

- Sales promotion in relation to discount, gift, packaging, incentives and credit scheme.
- Socio-economic factors in relation to social status, economic status, residential status, occupational status, casual income, foreign contact, educational status, government policy, and festivals.

Being a pioneer work, the study was designed to be exploratory. Data were collected from consumers, sales forces, dealers and secondary sources. More dependence was on primary sources like consumers, sales forces, and dealers in textiles. Multi-stage sampling was adopted for designing the sample frame for the study, consisting of consumers and sales forces/dealers. The first stage was the distribution of the sample on the basis of their geographical location, dividing the state into three regions – Northern, Central and Southern. In the second stage, with a view to segregating the respondents on the basis of social changes like urbanization and modernisation, the geographical location was sub-divided into villages, towns and cities. In the third state, the respondents were selected on a random basis from one panchayat, one municipality and one city corporation from each of the three regions of Kerala – the Northern, Central and Southern. In order to ensure due representation of the three categories of population, Kozhikode district from the North, Ernakulam district from the Centre and Thiruvananthapuram district from the South were selected. Accordingly, Perambra panchayat, Vadakara municipality and Kozhikode Corporation were identified from Kozhikode district; Mulamthuruthi panchayat, Moovatupuzha municipality and Kochi Corporation from Ernakulam district, Vamanapuram panchayat, Neyyatinkara municipality and Thiruvananthapuram Corporation were chosen from Thiruvananthapuram district, to carry out the field survey.

The sample population of the consumers covered under the study was 900, selecting 50 respondents each from the three panchayats, 100 respondents each from the three municipalities, 150 respondents each from the three city corporations. A pilot study was carried out to ascertain the distribution of consumers in factors like gender, religion, age, education, occupation and income. The final selection of the respondents was made by giving due representation to each stratum so as to make the sample frame under the stratified random sampling. The size of the shop was the criterion for selecting the textile shops from where the sales forces/dealers were chosen to be contacted for collecting the relevant data. Accordingly, the textile shops were grouped into small, medium and large, from each panchayat, municipality and city corporation covered under the sample for the study. Textile shops with a total investment below Rs. 1,00,000 were categorized as the small size, shops having a total investment of Rs. 1,00,000 – 5,00,000 were identified as the medium size, and shops with a total investment of more than Rs. 5,00,000 were grouped as the large size shops. The strength of the sales force covered under the sample was 426, consisting of 26 from the small, 113 from the medium and 287 from the large textile shops.

Separate interview schedules were developed for the collection of primary data from consumers, sales force/dealers. The interview schedules were finalized by conducting a pilot study among 60 consumers and 40 sales forces of different categories. Discussions were also held with experts in the field before finalizing the interview schedules. It was found appropriate to hold formal and informal discussions with various categories of people involved in the operations of the textile market, like – wholesalers and other intermediaries. The data collected through observation were also used for analysis and interpretation. Secondary data were collected from research reports and publications like Compendium of Textile Statistics 2002, Report on National Household Survey on Market for Textiles and Clothing 2002, The Indian Textile Journal, and The Indian Textile Magazine. The data related mainly to a period of 10 year, commencing from 1991-92, were collected and made use for the study. Primary data were collected from the respondents during the year 2001-2002. The data were analysed by using statistical tools like Time Series, Weighted Score, Z test and Exponential Trend.

The present study was carried out by designing an exploratory method. It being a pioneer work in the area, excessive dependence was required on primary data collected from consumers of varied socio-economic backgrounds. There was no alternative available but relying upon their responses. There is a possibility for bias in such responses. The dealers and the sales forces were initially non co-operative in providing the data required for the study. However, when convinced of the importance as well as the relevance of the study, they extended support, and efforts were made to collect reliable data to the maximum extent possible. Despite such earnest efforts, the chances of bias in the responses cannot be fully ignored. Thus, the study suffers from the limitations of dependence on primary data collected from two broad categories of respondents hailing from different socio-economic groups. However, maximum care was taken to eliminate the bias in the responses through counter-checking and observation, so as to make the result of the study fruitful, scientific, rational and logical.

Findings

The major findings of the present study are summarised under five broad categories. Product specification: In the regional markets, the consumers had different perceptions about the influence of brand preference on the purchase of textiles. But it was found that the difference in the perceptions of the consumers was not significant in the regional markets. The consumers in the urban, semi-urban and rural markets had different perceptions about the influence of brand preference. The difference in the perceptions of consumers in the urban, semi-urban and rural markets was also not found significant. The sales forces had different opinions about the influence of brand preference of consumers on their purchase decision. However, the difference in their opinion was not found significant.

Quality was perceived as a factor having a very high degree of influence on the consumers in the regional markets. Significant difference was noted in perception between consumers in the Northern and Central, Southern and Central regions, but no significant difference was observed in the perceptions of consumers between the Southern and Northern regions. Consumers in the urban, semi-urban and rural markets perceived that quality exercised a very high degree of influence on their purchase of textiles. It was also found in the study that significant difference existed in perception between consumers in the urban and semi-urban, urban and rural markets. But no significant difference was observed between consumers in the semi-urban and rural markets. The sales forces had the opinion that quality exerted a very high degree of influence on the decision-making process of consumers. It was noted that significant difference existed between the opinions of the sales forces of large and small selling outlets, but no significant difference was found in opinions between the sales forces of medium and small selling outlets.

In the regional markets, the consumers perceived that their colour preference exercised a very high degree of influence on their purchase of textiles. It was also observed that there was significant difference in perception between consumers in the Northern and Central, and Southern and Central regions, but no significant difference was noted between consumers in the Northern and Southern regions. The urban, semi-urban and rural consumers perceived that colour preference had a very high degree of influence. It was also observed that there was significant difference in perception between consumers in the urban and semi-urban, urban and rural markets, and no significant difference was found between consumers in the semi-urban and rural markets. The sales forces had the opinion that colour preference of consumers exercised a very high degree of influence on their purchase of textiles. The study brought out that there was significant difference in opinions between sales forces of large and medium selling outlets, but no significant difference was noted between the sales forces of large and small, medium and small selling outlets.

The consumers in the regional markets perceived that the nature of fabric exercised a very high degree of influence on their purchase decisions. Significant difference was noted in perceptions between consumers in the Northern and Central, Central and Southern and Southern regions, but no significant difference was found between consumers in the Northern and Southern regions. In the urban, semi-urban and rural markets, consumers had the perception that nature of fabric exercised a very high degree of influence. Significant difference was found in perception between consumers in the urban and semi-urban markets, but no significant difference was observed between consumers in the urban and rural, semi-urban and rural markets. The sales forces had the opinions that consumers' preference for the nature of fabric had a very high degree of influence on their purchase decision. It was observed that significant difference exists in opinion between the sales forces of large and medium selling outlets. However, no significant difference was noted between the sales forces of large and medium, medium and small selling outlets.

In the regional markets, consumers perceived that fashion exercised a very high degree of influence on their purchase of textiles. Significant difference in perception was found between consumers in the Northern and Central, Central and Southern regions; however, no significant difference was noted between consumers in the Northern and Southern regions. The consumers in the urban, semi-urban and rural markets had also the view that fashion exercised a very high degree of influence. However, it was found that there was significant difference in perceptions between consumers in the urban and semi-urban, urban and rural markets. Yet no significant difference was observed between semi-urban and rural markets. The sales forces had difference in their opinions about the influence of fashion on the purchase of textiles. It was found that the difference in opinions between the sales forces of large and medium, large and small selling outlets was significant, and that between the sales forces of medium and small selling outlets was not significant.

The consumers in the regional markets had different perceptions about the influence of preference for readymade garments on their purchase of textiles. It was observed that the difference in the perceptions between consumers in the Northern and Central, Central and Southern regions was significant, but no significant difference was noted between consumers in the Northern and Southern regions. But the urban, semi-urban and rural consumers perceived that preference for readymade garments exercised a very high degree of influence. Significant difference was observed in perceptions between consumers in the urban and semi-urban, and urban and rural markets, but no significant difference was found between consumers in the semi-urban and rural markets. The sales forces differ in their opinions about the influence of consumers, preference for readymade garments on purchase of textiles. The study revealed that the difference in opinions between the sales forces of large and medium, large and small selling outlets was significant, and that between medium and small selling outlets was not significant.

In the regional markets, the consumers perceived that preference for domestic textiles exerted a very high degree of influence on their purchase decision. It was also found that there was significant difference in perceptions between consumers in the Northern and Central, Central and Southern regions, but no significant difference was noted between consumers in the Northern and Southern regions. The urban, semi-urban and rural consumers had the view that preference for domestic textiles had a very high degree of influence. However, it was observed that there was significant difference in perceptions between consumers in urban and semi-urban, rural markets, but no significant difference was noted between consumers in semi-urban and rural markets. The sales forces had the opinions that consumers' preference for domestic textiles had very high degree of influence. However, significant difference was observed between the sales forces of large and medium, and large and small selling outlets, but no significant difference was found between the sales forces of medium and small outlets.

The consumers in the regional markets had different perceptions about the influence of their preference for foreign textiles on their decision making process. The difference in the perception of consumers was also found significant in the regional market. It was noted that the difference in perceptions between consumers in the urban and semi-urban, semi-urban and rural markets was significant, whereas no significant difference was found between consumers in urban and rural markets. The sales forces showed difference in opinions about the influence of consumers' preference for foreign textiles on their purchase of textiles. The difference in opinion was also found significant between the sales forces of large and medium, medium and small selling outlets, but no significant difference was observed between the sales forces of large and small selling outlets.

In the regional markets, the consumers had the opinion that the price of textiles exerted a very high degree of influence on purchase of textiles. The study also revealed that significant difference in the perception of consumers in the regional markets was in existence. Consumers in the urban, semi-urban and rural markets held the view that price had a very high degree of influence. Significant difference was also noted in perceptions of consumers between urban and rural, semi-urban and rural markets, whereas no significant difference was seen between consumers in semi-urban and rural markets. The sales forces had the opinion that the influence of price on consumers was very high. But no significant difference was found in the opinions of the sales forces.

Preference for source of buying: The consumers in the regional markets perceived that attributes of textile shops exercised a very high degree of influence on their selection of shops. However, it was found that there was significant difference in the perceptions of consumers in the regional markets. Consumers in the urban, semi-urban and rural markets held the view that attributes of textile shops exerted a very high degree of influence on their choice of shops. But it was observed that there was significant difference in the perceptions of consumers in the urban, semi-urban and rural markets. The sales forces had the opinion that attributes of their shops exercised a very high degree of influence on consumers. Significant difference was also found in the opinions of the sales forces of large, medium and small selling outlets.

In the regional markets, consumers had different perceptions about the influence of location of shops. It was found that there existed significant difference in the perceptions of consumers in the regional markets. The urban, semi-urban and rural consumers had different perceptions about the influence of the location of shops. The difference in the perceptions of consumers in the urban, semi-urban and rural markets was also found significant. The sales forces showed difference in opinion about the influence of the location of their shops on consumers. The difference in opinion of the sales forces between large and medium, between medium and small selling outlets was significant, while the difference between the sales forces of large and small selling outlets was not significant.

In all regional markets, the consumers perceived that interaction with the sales personnel exercised a very high degree of influence on their selection of textile shops. It was found in the study that there existed significant difference in the perception of consumers in the regional markets. The urban, semi-urban and rural consumers had the view that interaction with the sales forces exerted a very high degree of influence. Significant difference in the perceptions of consumers in the urban, semi-urban and rural markets was also found in the study.

Consumers in the regional markets perceived that provision for replacement had a very high degree of influence on their choice of textile shops. It was observed in the study that there was significant difference in the perceptions of consumers between the Northern and Central, between Southern and Central regions, but no significant difference was noted between the consumers in the Northern and Southern regions. The consumers in the urban, semi-urban and rural markets had the perception that provision for replacement exercised a very high degree of influence. The study also revealed significant difference in the perceptions of consumers among urban, semi-urban, and rural markets. The sales forces in large, medium and small selling outlets had the opinion that provision for replacement had a very high degree of influence and the study brought out significant difference in the opinion of the sales forces also.

In the regional markets, consumers had different perception about the influence of suggestions of family members on shop selection. The consumers in the urban, semi-urban and rural markets perceived that suggestions of family members had only a medium degree of influence. Yet it was found that there was significant difference in perception between consumers in urban and semi-urban, semi-urban and rural markets and no significant difference was seen between consumers in urban and rural markets. The sales forces showed difference in opinion about the influence of suggestions of family members of consumers on selection of shop. The difference in opinion of the sales forces between large and small, large and medium selling outlets was found significant, while such difference was not found between the sales forces of medium and small selling outlets.

Influence of advertisement and sales promotion: In the regional markets, television advertisement exercised a very high degree of influence on consumers. Significant difference in the perceptions of consumers between the Northern and Central, Central and Southern regions was observed in the study. But no significant difference in perception between consumers in the Northern and Southern region was found. The urban, semi-urban and rural consumers believed that television advertisement exercised a very high degree of influence. The study brought out significant difference in the perceptions of consumers in the urban and semi-urban, semi-urban and rural markets. Yet no significant difference was observed between consumers in the urban and rural markets. The sales forces had also the opinion that television advertisement influenced consumers to a very high degree.

Significant difference was found in the opinions of the sales forces between large and medium, large and small selling outlets. However, the difference in the perceptions of the sales forces between medium and small selling outlets was not found significant.

The degree of influence of radio advertisement was perceived by the consumers in the regional markets as medium. The study revealed significant difference in the perceptions of consumers in the regional markets. The perception of consumers in the urban, semi-urban and rural markets indicated that radio advertisement had only a medium degree of influence. Yet significant difference was observed in perception between consumers in the urban and semi-urban and rural markets, but no significant difference was noted between consumers in the urban and rural markets.

In the regional markets, consumers perceived that newspaper advertisement exerted a very high degree of influence. It was also observed in the study that there was significant difference in the perceptions of consumers in the regional markets. The urban, semi-urban and rural consumers held the view that newspaper advertisement had a very high degree of influence. Significant difference in the perceptions of consumers between the urban and semi-urban, urban and rural markets was found in the study while the difference between consumers in the semi-urban and rural markets was not found significant. The opinions of the sales forces revealed that newspaper advertisement had a very high degree of influence on consumers. The study brought out significant difference in opinion between the sales forces of large and medium, large and small selling outlets, while no significant difference was noted between the sales forces of medium and small selling outlets.

The consumers in the regional markets had different perceptions about the influence of magazine advertisement. It was observed in the study that the difference in the perceptions of consumers in the regional markets was significant. The difference in the perceptions of consumers in the urban, semi-urban and rural markets about the influence of magazine advertisement was found significant. The sales forces had the opinion that magazine advertisement exercised a very high degree of influence on consumers. No significant difference in the opinions of the sales forces was observed

Consumers in the regional markets had different perceptions about the influence of poster advertisement. Significant difference in the perceptions of consumers in the regional markets was found in the study. The perceptions of urban, semi-urban and rural consumers about the influence of poster advertisement were different. The difference in perceptions of urban, semi-urban and rural consumers about the influence of poster advertisement was different. The sales forces had the view that poster advertisement exercised a very high degree of influence. Significant difference between the opinions of the sales forces of large and medium, large and small selling outlets was noted in the study. But no significant difference was found between the sales forces of medium and small selling outlets.

Consumers in the regional markets had different perceptions about the influence of billboard/banner advertisement. It was found that the difference in the perceptions was significant. In the urban, semi-urban and rural markets, consumers had different perceptions about the influence of billboard/banner advertisement. The difference in perceptions between consumers in the urban and semi-urban, urban and rural markets was found significant, while that between consumers in semi-urban and rural markets was not found significant. The sales forces held the opinion that billboard/banner advertisement had a very high degree of influence on consumers. No significant difference was found in their opinions.

The perceptions of consumers in the regional markets revealed that discount had a high degree of influence on their purchase decision. Significant difference in the perceptions of consumers in the regional markets was noted in the study. The urban, semi-urban and rural consumers perceived that discount exercised a high degree of influence on their purchase decisions. It was observed that there was significant difference in perception between the consumers in the urban and semi-urban and urban and rural markets. But no significant difference was noted in perception between consumers in semi-urban and rural markets. The sales forces had the opinion that discount exercised a high degree of influence on consumers. No significant difference was observed in their opinions

It was perceived by the consumers in the regional markets that gift schemes exert only a medium degree of influence. The study revealed significant difference in the perceptions of consumers among the regional markets. The consumers in the urban, semi-urban and rural markets had the view that gift schemes had only a medium degree of influence. It was observed in the study that there existed significant difference between the perceptions of consumers in urban and semi-urban, urban and rural markets. Yet no significant difference was found in perception between consumers in the semi-urban and rural markets. The sales forces had the opinion that gift schemes had only a medium degree of influence on consumers. Significant difference was noted between the opinions of the sales forces of large and medium, large and small selling outlets, but no significant difference was observed in the study between the opinions of sales forces of medium and small selling outlets.

The consumers in the regional markets perceived that packaging had only a low degree of influence. Significant difference was noted between the perceptions of consumers in the Northern and Central, Central and Southern regions. However, no significant difference was observed between the Northern and Southern regions. The urban, semi-urban and rural consumers had different perceptions about the influence of packaging. The difference in perception between consumers in the urban and rural markets was found significant and that between consumers in the semi-urban and rural markets was not found significant. The sales forces had the opinion that packaging had a very low degree of influence on consumers. It was observed in the study that there was significant difference between the opinions of the sales forces of large and medium, large and small selling outlets, but no significant difference was found between the sales forces of medium and small selling outlets.

In the regional markets, the consumers had different perceptions about the influence of incentives. It was found in the study that the difference in their perceptions was significant. In the urban, semi-urban and rural markets, the consumers had the view that incentives exerted a medium degree of influence. However, it was found that there was significant difference in the perceptions of consumers in the urban, semi-urban and rural markets. The sales forces had the opinion that incentives had only a medium degree of influence on consumers. It was found in the study that there was significant difference in opinions between the sales forces of large and medium, and large and small selling outlets, but no significant difference was observed in the study between the sales forces of medium and small selling outlets. The analysis made it explicit that the sales promotion devices had low potential to attract the consumers in the textile market.

Socio-economic factors of buyers: Consumers in all the regions perceived that their social status had a high degree of influence on their purchase of textiles. Significant difference in the perceptions of consumers among the regional markets was noted in the study. Consumers in the urban, semi-urban and rural markets viewed that their social status exercised high degree of influence. It was found that there was significant difference in the perception of consumers in semi-urban and rural markets. The sales forces had different opinions about the influence of consumers' social status on purchase of textiles. The difference in the opinion was significant.

Consumers in the regional markets perceived that their economic status had a very high degree of influence on their purchase of textiles. However, it was found that there was significant difference in the perceptions of consumers in the markets. The urban, semi-urban and rural consumers had the opinion that their economic status exercised a very high degree of influence. It was found in the study that there was significant difference between the perceptions of consumers in urban and semi-urban, urban and rural and semi-urban and rural markets. The sales forces had the opinion that the economic status of consumers exercised a very high degree of influence on the purchase of textiles. No significant difference in their opinions was brought out by the study.

The consumers in the regional markets had different perceptions about the influence of their residential status on their purchase of textiles. The difference in the perceptions was found significant. The urban, semi urban and rural consumers had different perceptions about the influence of residential status. The difference in perception between consumers in the urban and rural, semi-urban and rural markets was found significant. No significant difference was observed between the perception of consumers in the semi-urban and rural markets. The sales forces showed difference in opinion about the influence of residential status on the purchase decision of consumers. There existed significant difference between the opinions of the sales forces of large and medium, large and small selling outlets. But the difference between the sales forces of medium and small selling out lets was not found significant.

In the regional markets, consumers perceived that their occupational status had a very high degree of influence on their purchase of textiles. It was observed in the study that there was significant difference in perception of consumers between the Northern and Central, Central and Southern regions. However, no significant difference was found between consumers in the Southern and Northern regions. In the urban, semi-urban and rural markets, consumers had the view that their occupational status had a very high degree of influence. Significant difference was noted in the perceptions of consumers between the urban the urban and rural, and urban and semi-urban markets. No significant difference was found between consumers in semi-urban and rural markets. The sales forces had the opinion that the occupational status of consumers had a very high degree of influence on purchase of textiles. Significant difference was observed in the opinion of the sales forces of large and small and large and medium selling outlets. Yet no significant difference was noted between the sales forces of medium and small selling outlets.

The consumers in the regional markets perceived their casual income exercised only a medium degree of influence on them while they purchase textiles. It was found in the study that there was significant difference in the perceptions of consumers in the regional markets. The urban, semi-urban and rural consumers had the view that their casual income had only a medium degree of influence. Significant difference in the perceptions of consumers in the urban, semi-urban and rural markets was found in the study. The sales forces had difference in opinion about the influence of the casual income of consumers on purchase decision. The difference between their opinions was found significant.

Consumers in the regional markets had different perceptions about the influence of their foreign contact on decision-making regarding textile consumption. Significant difference was found in their perceptions. The consumers in the urban, semi-urban and rural markets had different viewpoints about the influence of their foreign contact. It was found that difference in the perceptions was significant. The sales forces had different opinions regarding the influence of the foreign contact of consumers on purchase decisions regarding textiles. It was found in the study that the difference in opinion of the sales forces between large and small, medium and small selling outlets was significant. But between the sales forces of large and medium selling outlets was not found significant.

The consumers in the regional markets perceived that the influence of Government Policy on the purchase of textiles was very low. Significant difference was found in perceptions between consumers in the Southern and Central, Central and Northern regions. However, no significant difference was noted between consumers in the Northern and Southern regions. The urban, semi-urban and rural consumers had the opinion that the Government Policy exercised only a very low degree of influence. No significant difference was noted in the perceptions of consumers in the urban, semi-urban and rural markets.

In the regional markets, consumers had different perceptions about the influence of their educational status on their purchase decision relating to textiles. The difference in the perceptions was found significant. There was difference in the perceptions of consumers in the urban, semi-urban and rural markets about the influence of their educational status. It was found in the study that the difference in the perceptions between consumers in urban and rural markets, semi-urban and rural markets was significant, but no significant difference was noted between consumers in urban and semi-urban markets. The sales forces had the opinion that the educational status of consumers had a high degree of influence in purchase of textiles. No significant difference was observed between the opinions of the sales forces of large, medium and small selling outlets.

Consumers in the regional markets have different perceptions about the influence of festivals on purchase of textiles. The difference in the perceptions between consumers in the Central and Northern, Central and Southern is significant while it is not significant between consumers in Southern and Northern regions. Consumers in the urban, semi-urban and rural markets had different perceptions about the influence of festivals while purchasing textiles. The difference in perceptions between consumers in the urban and semi-urban markets, semi-urban and rural markets are significant, but that between urban and rural markets is not significant. The sales forces had different opinions about the influence of festivals on textiles consumption. The difference in the opinions between the sales forces of large and medium, large and small outlets is significant while that between medium and small selling outlets is not significant.

Recommendations

Market Monitoring Cell (MMC): Since the dynamism of market is a challenge for the textile marketers, the market must be constantly reviewed. This embosses the need for setting up an agency like 'Market Monitoring Cell' (MMC). The prime objective of the proposed MMC is collection and dissemination of information about consumers. The MMC must be designed with a two- tier structure comprising of Executive body at the top level and Field Assistants at the bottom level. Executive body as the controlling authority of the MMC can be constituted in collaboration with the Textile Dealers' Association (TDA) of Kerala. Field Assistants are to be employed for undertaking surveys. The MMC can seek financial support from the TDA and managerial as well as technical assistance from the Textile Committee, Kannur, which is a Government of India organisation exclusively, meant for uplifting the textile sector. The MMC has to initiate consumer survey at least once in a year by giving emphasis on the changing needs of consumers and purchase pattern. The documentation of the information gathered must be done by designing an annual bulletin, which can be published under the label of the MMC/TDA. This ensures an uninterrupted flow of market information, which facilitates the marketers to launch customer-based strategies.

Revival of the handloom sector: In the textile market of Kerala, the consumers have a zeal for domestic products. Cotton handloom fabrics constitute the major share of the domestic textiles. This highlights the desirability of a multi-dimensional revival of the handloom sector so as to cater to the requirements of the modem market environment. Both the production and marketing operations have to be revived for achieving this goal. A Non Government Organization (NGO) is to be promoted for supervising and monitoring the revival programmes and the NGO must be linked with The Handloom Development Corporation/The Handloom Weavers' Co-operate Society Khadi and Village Industries. Development of new products, blending of modernity with the traditional designs, induction of new generation colours, training programmes to the weaving community, modernisation of looms etc. are some of the viable schemes for the revival and modernisation of the production aspects of the handloom sector. A new horizon of marketing can be achieved by promoting the sale of handloom products in association with The Kerala Tourism Development Corporation

(KTDC) by carving out a new branch of tourism titled 'Handicraft Tourism'. The NGO which is focusing on the monitoring of the revival of production activities can coordinate participation of other handicraft industries to promote the handicraft tourism and thereby promoting the sale of handloom products. The effective implementation of the new schemes of production and marketing with the intervention of the NGO will be resulting in the overall development of the handloom sector to survive in the midst of competition during the post – MFA period.

Product enrichment: The textile market of Kerala has already witnessed a drastic change in several aspects of consumer behaviour. Now a day, the consumers have a strong passion for quality, brand and madeups. In order to cope with the change in the attitude of consumers, the textile marketers have to go in for a comprehensive approach ensuring the potential for satisfying the consumers. This evinces need for product enrichment characterized by quality and brand. Research and development for introducing new generation of textiles, induction of new fashion/style, colour etc are some of the features, which enrich the quality of a product in the textile market. In the post- MFA period, the consumers will be exposed to numerous brands at affordable price and there will be a tendency to patronize such products. The upcoming trend of using ready-to-wear is also a notable deviation in the attitudinal path of the consumers in Kerala market. Perfectly made ready-to-wear from foreign countries are waiting at the doorstep of the Kerala market for the day on which the phasing out of MFA is going to be completed. The marketers have to give suggestions to the manufactures for launching products by giving emphasis on quality and brand. The readymade sector should also be strengthened enough to meet the challenges in the years yet to come. The proposed MMC can provide the relevant information so as to avoid the threat of mismatching the demand and supply of textiles in the Kerala market.

Training programmes for the sales forces: The sales forces are the key factor of the successful functioning of textile retailing units. Since the activities of the sales forces have several dimensions, they have to be educated properly to carry out their operations effectively. This ventilates the need for organising training programmes for the sales forces. The TDA can act as a facilitator to sponsor the training programmes. It can make use of technical assistance from academic institutions, organisations like Textile Committee, and Industries Department for designing the curriculum of the training programmes. Communication skill, customer attention, counter service, cordial interaction with consumers etc. must be the thrust areas of the curriculum. A Quality Circle (QC)- consisting of experienced sales forces must be formed for giving exposure to the realistic situations in the selling outlets. In order to provide an opportunity for interaction between the sales forces and consumers, the TDA must organise periodical seminar /workshop on the topics related to practical aspects of in store sales. This would equip the sales forces of the textile retailing outlets of Kerala to interact with their prospective consumers effectively, which is conducive to reinforcing customer loyalty.

Cost competitiveness: Most of the large and medium selling outlets are being promoted through the television advertisement. However, the study reveals that the consumers have positive perceptions about the influence of the press media. Since the television advertisement is contributory to escalating the cost, it is better to launch and economic package of advertising programme' by way of harmonious blending of both the electronic and press media. This is possible by limiting the television advertisement to a scale of 'information generation' and it must be supplemented by press advertisement; because press advertisement has the added advantage of reinforcing the message. Kerala, being a state of high literacy rate, the press advertisement has a strong potential to penetrate through the decision making process of the masses. An approach of striking a balance between television and press advertisement, the marketers can significantly reduce cost of sales, which paves the way for achieving cost competitiveness. With the entry of foreign countries in the domestic market by virtue of ATC, cost competitiveness is the only means to meet the competition from countries like China, South Korea, Taiwan and Indonesia.

Redesigning of packaging: At present, almost all the textile retailers' resort to polythene covers as packaging material. Owing to ecological and environmental problems, consumers are found to be reluctant toward accepting polythene covers. This calls for redesigning the packaging materials to cope with the attitude of consumers. An easy way out of this hurdle is to roll back to the age-old concept of paper covers. It is worth noting that the present day consumers are novelty seeking in character and they are longing for a harmless packaging other than the traditional one. Inducting packaging by using jute or coir products is a viable suggestion to cater to the requirements of the consumers. Retailers who maintain large selling outlets can adopt the new texture of packaging on customer retention.

Regional marketing: The difference in the socio-economic environment of consumers in Kerala is explicit in their propensity to consume, attitude, information search and processing, interaction with the reference group, decision making process etc. Such being the situation, the marketers have to launch a strategy, which is matching with the prevailing environment of every market segment. This spells out the need for a 'regional marketing' approach. Regional marketing denotes developing marketing mix applicable to the relevant segment. This can be manifested through specialties in product procurement, formulating appropriate pricing policy, organisation of selling outlets, devising the most suitable tool of promotion etc. In order to launch the strategy of regional marketing effectively, the marketers are to be provided with the needful information regarding the changing dimensions of the behavioural aspects of consumers. The proposed MMC can act as a provider as well as facilitator of the infrastructure for designing regional marketing by collection and dissemination of the relevant information. This enables the marketers to translate the needs of their prospective consumers into products.

The textile market is going to be exposed to a strange environment by 2005. The phasing out of MFA will be completing and the country has to open the domestic market as per the provisions of the ATC. Several member countries of WTO have already attained competitiveness to launch their textile products at a lower price in the Indian market. Understanding the consumers very closely and identifying their needs very specifically seem to be the panacea for meeting the fierce competition in the domestic market. The timely implementation of the above suggestions in the retailing scenario of textiles in Kerala is mediatory to making the textile industry of India as a "money spinning" industry.

References

Arndt John, *Role of Product Related Conversations in the Diffusion of a New Product*, Journal of Marketing Research, August 1964.

Balarishnan, M.S., *An Interfirm Comparison of Absenteeism,* SITRA, Coimbatore, 1994.

Caroline E.W., *The Clothe You Buy and Make*, Mc Graw Hill Book Company Ltd., New York, 1960.

Dhulasi Birundha, *An Economic Study of Profits in Spinning and Weaving Mills in Madurai City*, Ph. D. Thesis (unpublished), Madurai Kamaraj University, madurai, 1985.

Dorfman, Robert, *The Price System*, The Prentice Hall of India Ltd., New Delhi, 1979.

Eaassy. Mike, *Fashion Marketing*, Blackwell Science Ltd., Oxford, 1995.

Gokarnan, N., *New Generation Polyester*, textile Magazine, June 2000.

Gupta, Puja, *Evaluation of Design – Solutions in the Textile Apparel Industry*, Clothesline, July 2001.

Hampstead, Laurance, *Colour and Line in Dress*, Prentice Hall Inc., New York, 1997.

Jain Kumar S. and Naik Gopal, *Econometric Modelling of the Indian Cotton Industry for Forecasting and Policy Simulations*, Indian Journal of Agricultural Economics, Indian Society of Agricultural Economics, Mumbai, April – June 1999.

Katti, Vijaya, *Textile Industry Vision 2010*, Yojana, December 1997.

Kevin S.K., *A Study of the Textile Industry in Kerala with Comparative Reference to Tamil Nadu*, Ph.D. Thesis (unpublished), Cochin University of Science and Technology, Cochin, 1988.

Mohan Kumar, P.S., *Cotton Textile Industry – A comparative Analysis of Different Sectors*, Reliance Publishing House, New Delhi, 1997.

Padmanabhan, M., *The Silk Mill Problems - The Indian Cotton Textile Industry*, Ph.D. Thesis (unpublished), University of Bombay, Bombay, 1974.

Sreenivasan K., *Indian Textile Industry*, SITRA, Coimbatore, 1984.